Copyright 2000 D Armour

First printed July 1997
Reprinted December 1997
Second edition 1998
Third edition 2000

A catalogue record of this book is available from the
British Library.

ISBN 0-9530444-2-4

All rights reserved. No part of this publication may be reproduced, stored in a retrieval system or transmitted in any form without prior permission of the publisher

Published by Small Plane Publishing
2 Mundens Lane, Alweston, Sherborne, Dorset DT9 5HU

Typeset by SMALL PLANE

Printed by Creeds, Broad Oak, Bridport, Dorset

THE
LIGHT AIRCRAFT
DATA BOOK

Third edition

Des Armour and Edwin Shackleton

SMALL PLANE PUBLISHING
Alweston, Dorset.

ABOUT THIS BOOK

I wanted a book on small, private aeroplanes - there were plenty of books on air liners, military and business jets but nothing much on my sort of aeroplane; the sort you find around the small airfields and strips - and at the various air shows and rallies. So, by dint of a lot of drawing, rooting out information and photographs, this book came about.

I am much indebted to my co-author, Edwin Shackleton, who is not only a mine of aeronautical information but has a place in the Guinness Book of Records as having flown in the greatest number of aircraft types - 700+ at the latest count!

Also, in the small section on rotorcraft, I must thank Paul Kelsey who talked me into doing it, supplying the photos and checking the work.

Others I must mention are, my Burmese cat, Shan, who, by frequently pouncing on the keyboard, is responsible for all typographical errors and my wife Elizabeth whose efforts to turn me into a gardener, instead of an aeronautical scribbler, failed gloriously!

Des Armour

PREFACE TO THIRD EDITION

Many more light aircraft types, both old and new, have been added for this edition and previous entries updated. I have kept to the original aims of including only types that still exist and may be seen in the UK - flying mainly, others static and some waiting to appear from long periods of storage and restoration.

The type classification gets *more* complicated, with VLAs, SLAs and 450kg microlights. As even the *experts* are still haggling over which type belongs in which category I have largely stuck to my old classifications - see note below.

ERRORS, OMISSIONS AND ECCENTRICITIES

In the case of de Haviland Gipsy engines my computer argued with me - and wanted to spell it *Gypsy* - sometimes I gave in to it!

I have been economical with engine type numbers (on the grounds of space mainly) and have generally referred only to the maker and horse power,

My system of aircraft size/weight/power categorisation is the old one ie. Microlights: 859 lb.(390 kg.) AUW, 5 lb/sq. ft.(25 kg/sq. m.) wing loading, Ultralights: 1200 lb.(545 kg.) AUW, 75 hp. max. - all others are Light Planes.

In the tables, where no 'official' figure was available I have calculated it and it is shown in *italics*

'Climb' in the performance figures refers to 'initial climb'..

THE PHOTOGRAPHS

Edwin Shackleton, Rod Simpson, Paul Kelsey and myself have supplied most of the photographs. Here and there I have slipped in my drawings.

I am indebted to *all* the following, who have helped me with photographs:

PHOTO CREDITS (Shown, after type entry, in index)

a	Air Britain	m	Les Millen
ae	Aeroprakt	ma	Mainair
ama	Alastair Malcolm Aviation	mc	Miles Collection
bn	Britten-Norman	n	Newtonair
bs	Barbara Schlussler	p	Piper
c	Chichester-Miles	ph	Peter Huggett
ce	Cessna	pk	Paul Kelsey
d	Des Armour	s	Rod Simpson
dm	David McIntyre/Ed Hicks	sp	SPP Collection
dn	David Nunn	sw	Seawind Amphibians
e	Edwin Shackleton	tcd	TCD
gp	George Pereira	tt	Terry Taylor
I	Ikarus	u	Urban
ib	Ian Bellamy	ftp	FTP Aviation Photos

COVER PHOTOS

Front top.   Cessna F172 E   (DA)
Front lower. Christen Eagle 2   (ES)
Back top   Phillips Speedtwin (DA)
Back lower   SE5 replica   (DA)

Join the
POPULAR *flying* ASSOCIATION

The representative body in the United Kingdom for amateur aircraft construction, recreational and sport flying.

Contact us at:
THE POPULAR FLYING ASSOCIATION
TERMINAL BUILDING, SHOREHAM AIRPORT
SHOREHAM-BY-SEA, WEST SUSSEX BN43 5FF
Tel. 01273 461616   Fax. 01273 463390

Access our web site
http://www.pfa.org.uk

The objectives of the Popular Flying Association

To promote and extend the sport of recreational flying by minimising its cost through the advice and services provided by the Association for:

- the encouragement of amateur design, construction and operation of light and ultra-light aircraft
- the formation and administration of co-ownership groups and clubs
- the preservation and operation of vintage aircraft
- the discharge of regulatory responsibilities assigned by statutory bodies and government departments
- the co-operation and negotiation with government departments and other interested organisations to ensure that members' best interests are protected
- generally to carry out such acts as may be conducive to the encouragement and development of recreational flying.

Why join the PFA?

If you have bought this book, then almost certainly, you are a person who thrills to the sight and sound of small aeroplanes. You, no doubt, visit your local airfield to enjoy this heady activity – but a lot of people want to stop all this going on! Small airfields and strips are being closed down every year.

The PFA not only oppose airfield closures, they regulate and oversee the design and construction of home built aircraft, and issue the all-important Permit to Fly. You will note that, throughout the book, many homebuilt types are deemed PFA acceptable; this means that the design meets rigid safety criteria and that its construction will be monitored by a PFA Engineering Inspector giving advice and encouragement at every stage.

Benefits of Membership

- Discounted admission to the PFA Annual Rally – Europe's greatest Fly-In event – up to 2,000 aircraft attending from all over the world.
- Your personal copy of the Association's magazine *Popular Flying*, packed with information including building tips, venues and air show reports.
- PFA Struts – groups of PFA members who meet to talk about flying and building light aircraft – your sort of people. Contact PFA HQ for your nearest.
- Access to a range of services provided by PFA Engineering.
- PFA Pilot Coaching Scheme access.
- PFA Member's Credit Card.

Support the PFA – join today!

CONTENTS

HIGH WING, FIXED TAIL WHEEL UNDERCARRIAGE	Page 5 - 30
HIGH WING, FIED NOSE WHEEL UNDERCARRIAGE	32 - 44
HIGH WING, RETRACTABLE UNDERCARRIAGE	45
MID WING, FIXED TAIL WHEEL UNDERCARRIAGE	46 - 53
LOW WING, RETRACTABLE TAIL WHEEL UNDERCARRIAGE	54 - 58
LOW WING, MONO WHEEL	59 - 60
LOW WING FIXED TAIL WHEEL UNDERCARRIAGE	61 - 91
LOW WING, RETRACTABLE NOSE WHEEL UNDERCARRIAGE	92 - 99
LOW WING, FIXED NOSE WHEEL UNDERCARRIAGE	100 - 120
FLEX WINGS	120
BIPLANES	121 - 141
TWIN ENGINES	142 - 150
PUSHERS	151 - 160
TANDEM WING, CANARD	160 - 164
AMPHIBIANS	165 - 168
ROTORCRAFT	169 - 175
INDEX	176 - 181

Note

Within type sections above, the aircraft are in approximate age order

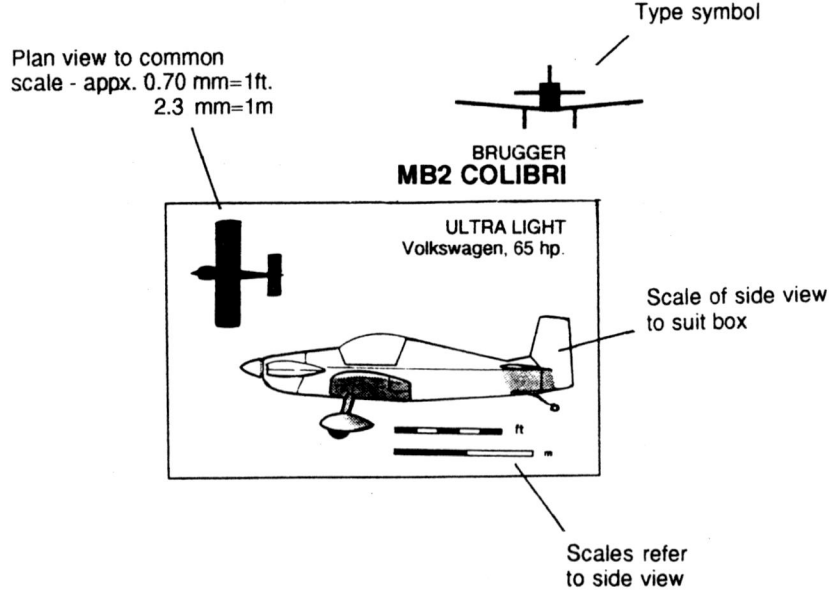

The Aeronca two seat C3 - affectionately known as the 'flying bathtub' - was produced before WW2 by the Aeronautical Corporation of America Inc in Cincinnati. Production was briefly undertaken in the UK at Peterborough as the Aeronca 100 and 19 were made, 11, of both types survived wartime storage to fly again after hostilities ceased, and 3 were still flying in 1993.

Of steel tube, wood and fabric construction, the Aeronca has been fitted with many engines in the past, the classic being the Company's own Aeronca E113 which developed 40 hp and ,in the British version ,was made by J A Prestwich as the JAP J-99.

Maybe not the most beautiful aeroplane ever designed, the C3 is nonetheless an enduring eye-catcher at fly-ins and in spite of its 'draggy' wire-braced wing still gives very economical flying - 3 gal/hr.

7 on UK Reg. (3 flying) and 12 in world museums.

AERONCA C3

ULTRALIGHT
Aeronca JAP, 40 hp.
Continental, 65 hp.

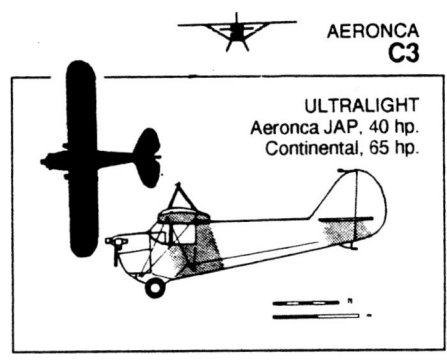

DATA	IMPERIAL		METRIC	
Span	36	ft	11	m
Wing area	142	ft^2	13.3	m^2
Aspect ratio	9.1		9.1	
Empty weight	569	lb	258	kg
Loaded weight	1150	lb	522	kgz
Wing loading	7.4	lb/ft^2	36	kg/m^2
Max speed	107	mph	171	kmh
Cruise speed	87	mph	139	kmh
Stalling speed	48	mph	76	kmh
Climb rate	450	ft/min	138	m/min
Range	200	mls	320	km

CIVILIAN COUPE

LIGHT PLANE
AS Genet Major, 100hp.

The two seat Coupe was the sole product of the Civilian Aircraft Company of Burton-on-Trent, the ABC Hornet powered prototype flying in 1929.

Five of the boxy Coupes were built between '29 and '31 at the firm's plant at Hedon, the municipal airport of Hull. Apart from the prototype all subsequent models had AS Genet Major five cylinder engines and were typed as Coupe Mk2.

The Coupe was of mixed wood and metal construction, skinned all over with plywood and was, in its time, considered pretty 'state of the art' in an era of mainly wire braced bi-planes. All controls were push rod operated and, unique for its day, the main wheels were fitted with brakes. They regularly took part in the inter-city air races of the period.

One aircraft, G-ABNT, kept going until 1939 when it was stored for the duration of WW2. Restored to airworthy condition by Shipping and Airlines Ltd at Biggin Hill, this venerable machine may be seen again on the vintage air show circuit.

Parts of other Coupes, of unknown history, are also in store at Biggin Hill.

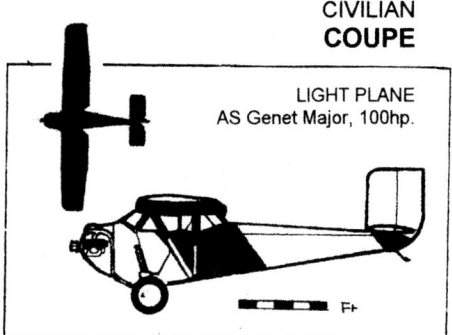

DATA	IMPERIAL		METRIC	
Span	35.5	ft	11	m
Wing area	168	sq.ft	15.7	sq.m
Aspect ratio	7.5			
Empty wt	985	lb.	447	kg.
Loaded wt	1500	lb.	681	kg.
Wing loading	8.9	lb/sq.ft	43	kg/sq.m
Max speed	105	mph	168	kmph
Cruising speed	96	mph	154	kmph
Stall speed	50	mph	80	kmph
Climb	810	fpm	250	mpm
Range	360	mls	576	km

DESSOUTER MONOPLANE

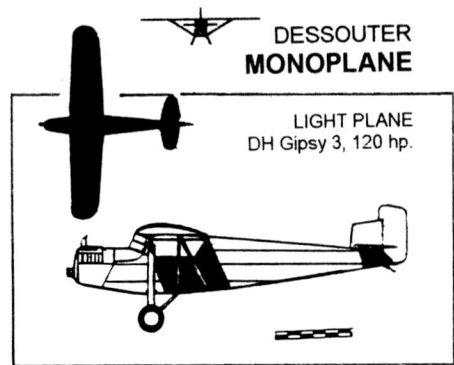

LIGHT PLANE
DH Gipsy 3, 120 hp.

The Dessouter Aircraft Company of Croydon modified the Cirrus powered Dutch Koolhoven FK41 in 1929 and called it the Dolphin. Later, re-engined with a Hermes 1, it was known simply as the Dessouter Monoplane. A Mk2 with a Gipsy III engine and a re-designed tail appeared in 1930.

41 Dessouters (inc. 13 Mk2s) were built up to 1931, ten of which went abroad.

Of all wood construction with ply covered fuselage and cantilever wing the 'Monoplane was the first three seat cabin monoplane built in the UK.

They were operated by National Flying Services, National Aviation Day displays and the Red Cross – as an air ambulance.

In 1933 G-AAPZ led the Kings Cup air race but was beaten into fourth place in the last mile or so.

Eight existed up to WW2; five were impressed and did not survive. G-AAPZ, originally owned by R.O. Shuttleworth and kept at Old Warden is now airworthy.

An Australian Dessouter was airworthy up 1951 where another non-flying one exists.

DATA Mk2	IMPERIAL		METRIC	
Span	35.7	ft	11.3	m
Wing area	183	sq.ft	17.2	sq.m
Aspect ratio	7			
Empty wt	1180	lb.	535	kg.
Loaded wt	1900	lb.	862	kg.
Wing loading	10.4	lb/sq.ft	50.7	kg/sq.m
Max speed	125	mph	200	kmph
Cruising speed	100	mph	160	kmph
Stall speed	55	mph	88	kmph
Climb	1000	fpm	308	mpm
Range	500	mls	800	km

COMPER CLA-7 SWIFT

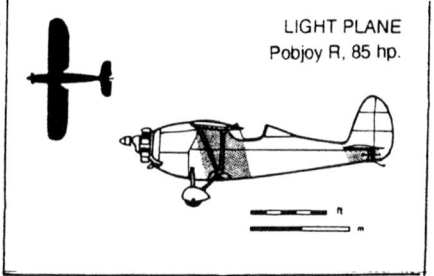

LIGHT PLANE
Pobjoy R, 85 hp.

Nick Comper founded the Comper Aircraft Co. at Hooton in 1930 and designed the CLA-7 Swift. Its type number refers to the Cranwell Light Aeroplane Club where Comper worked on his earlier designs.

A small sporty high winger with an open cockpit the Swift was initially powered by an ABC Scorpion and eight were produced in its first year. The 85 hp. Pobjoy geared radial engine became the favoured power unit for the thirty Swifts finally produced.(Gypsy Majors were also fitted - giving a V max. of 165 mph).

Swifts were great little racers, always performing well in the Kings Cup air races and in 1931, with C A Butler at the controls, G-ABRE broke the England - Australia record in 105 hours.

Four are still on the British Register including one new home-built from original drawings. Three are in museums abroad

DATA	IMPERIAL		METRIC	
Span	24	ft	7.4	m
Wing area	90	ft²	18.46	m²
Aspect ratio	6.4		6.4	
Empty weight	540	lb	245	kg
Loaded weight	985	lb	447	kg
Wing loading	10.9	lb/ft²	53.4	kg/m²
Max speed	140	mph	224	kmh
Cruise speed	120	mph	192	kmh
Stalling speed	40	mph	64	kmh
Climb rate	1000	ft/min	308	m/min
Range	360	mls	576	km

A pioneering US kit-plane from the late '20s designed by 'Ace' Corben and, initially, powered by motor cycle and Ford Model A car engines. The Baby Ace is a single seater with wooden wings attached to the welded tube fuselage by triangulated struts and a pair of parallel lift struts; powered, these days, by a Continental A65 (65 hp).
Corben had excellent build plans published in *Mechanix Illustrated* and was one of the first people to supply proper kits of parts
Close relatives of the Baby Ace are the Junior Ace, side by side two seater (model E) and the latest - first flown in 1956 - a refined single seater, of almost identical appearance apart from 'V' lift struts in place of the parallel pair, this is the Ace Aircraft Company of Chesapeake's Model D Baby Ace; available as a kit or plans.
Only two are on the UK Register (and one Model E); the Model D is PFA approved.
The data below is for the Ace Aircraft Model D.

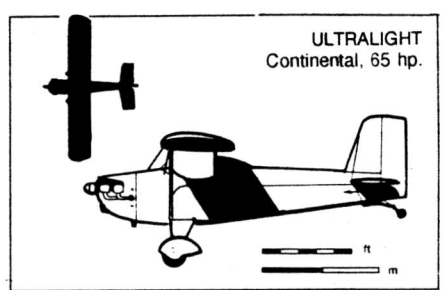

CORBEN
BABY ACE

ULTRALIGHT
Continental, 65 hp.

DATA	IMPERIAL		METRIC	
Span	26.5	ft	8.05	m
Wing area	112	ft²	10.5	m²
Aspect ratio	6.3		6.3	
Empty weight	575	lb	261	kg
Loaded weight	950	lb	431	kg
Wing loading	8.5	lb/ft²	41.4	kg/m²
Max speed	110	mph	177	kmh
Cruise speed	100	mph	161	kmh
Stalling speed	34	mph	55	kmh
Climb rate	1200	ft/min	366	m/min
Range	350	mls	563	km

The Aircamper was designed by Bernie Pietenpol in 1932 one of the pioneers of the American light plane movement.
Of extremely simple construction, the plans and instructions on how to build it were serialised in a pre-war flying magazine and many hundreds were made and are still being built!
Suitable aero engines were not available in 1932 so Pietenpol designed the Aircamper around a Model 'A Ford car engine and the first Aircampers flew with this heavy, 40 hp. unit. The most common motor became the 85 hp. Continental - and the performance figures below refer to this type.
It is an all wood aeroplane with fabric covered wings and tail unit; all the 'struttery' is metal and the large wheels are usually motor cycle wheels!
One example in the USA has just been retired to a museum after 60 years flying!
29 on the 'Register and others being built.

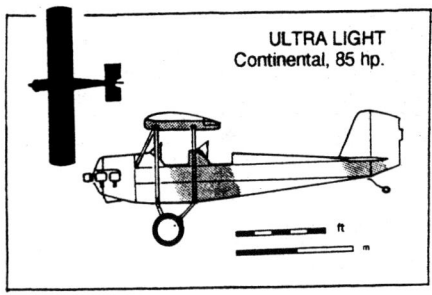

PIETENPOL
AIRCAMPER

ULTRA LIGHT
Continental, 85 hp.

DATA	IMPERIAL		METRIC	
Span	29.5	ft	9.1	m
Wing area	140	ft²	13.3	m²
Aspect ratio	6.2		6.2	
Empty weight	620	lb	287	kg
Loaded weight	1020	lb	463	kg
Wing loading	7.3	lb/ft²	35.6	kg/m²
Max speed	85	mph	136	kmh
Cruise speed	75	mph	120	kmh
Stalling speed	40	mph	64	kmh
Climb rate	500	ft/min	154	m/min
Range	200	mls	320	km

A 1933 aeroplane that was in production at Fairchild's in Maryland, USA, until 1947 when around 1000 had been made. The first models, powered by a 145 hp. Warner Scarab radial engine, were three seaters, and in 1938 the four seat version with the Super Scarab and 'in line' Ranger engines of 165 and 175 hp. went into production.

The fuselage is of welded steel tube with fabric covering over wooden framing and the wing, all wood with fabric aft of the ply' covered leading edge.

The sturdy wide track undercarriage is a noteworthy feature.

During WW2 several hundred were delivered to the RAF and ATA under the Lease Lend deal, serving in many war theatres. With peace many were bought for 'civilianisation' and were sold all over Europe - 9 still remaining on the UK Register - 4 of which are flying. 25 in world museums.

FAIRCHILD
F24 ARGUS

LIGHT PLANE
Warner Scarab, 165 hp.

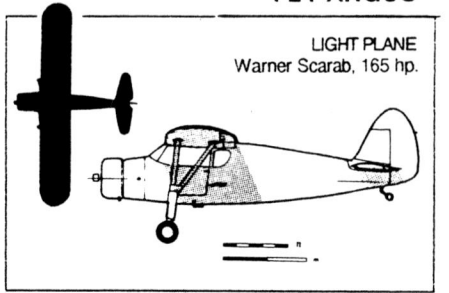

DATA	IMPERIAL		METRIC	
Span	36.3	ft	11.2	m
Wing area	173.6	ft²	16.3	m²
Aspect ratio	7.6		7.6	
Empty weight	1482	lb	672	kg
Loaded weight	2562	lb	1163	kg
Wing loading	14.8	lb/ft²	72	kg/m²
Max speed	124	mph	198	kmh
Cruise speed	112	mph	179	kmh
Stalling speed	58	mph	93	kmh
Climb rate	500	ft/min	154	m/min
Range	720	mls	1152	km

First flown in 1933, the three seat DH 85 Leopard Moth was designed as a replacement for the earlier DH 80 Puss Moth - of similar configuration, but with a welded steel tube fuselage. In both these Moths the pilot sat centrally in front and the two passengers side by side in the rear.

The construction is all wood with fabric covered wing and fuselage (over a stressed skin plywood box); the tailplane is wire braced and the 'V' bracing struts are arranged to allow the wings to fold alongside the fuselage.

A total of 132 Leopards were built, pre war, some going into storage but most into communications work with the armed forces during hostilities. Forty four survived the conflict, many flying again in the immediate post war years and up to the present day. 7 on the UK UK Reg. 4 flying. 3 in world museums.

DE HAVILAND
LEOPARD MOTH

LIGHT PLANE
Gipsy Major, 130 hp.

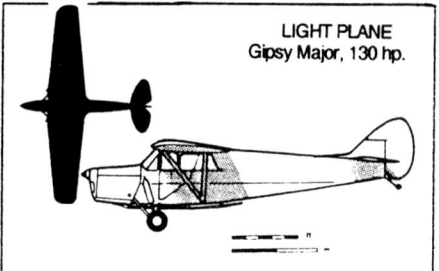

DATA	IMPERIAL		METRIC	
Span	37.5	ft	11.55	m
Wing area	206	ft²	19.4	m²
Aspect ratio	6.8		6.8	
Empty weight	1405	lb	638	kg
Loaded weight	2225	lb	1010	kg
Wing loading	10.8	lb/ft²	52.7	kg/m²
Max speed	137	mph	219	kmh
Cruise speed	119	mph	190	kmh
Stalling speed	50	mph	80	kmh
Climb rate	625	ft/min	192	m/min
Range	715	mls	1144	km

G N Wikner, an Australian cousin of Edgar Percival, set out to design and build a very cheap cabin two seater. In 1936, with the help of V Foster, the first Wicko was built in London at a furniture factory.

Wikner's cost cutting aims lead him to install a 3.5 litre Ford V8 car engine and it was so powered for its first flight. The 450 lb of this non-aero engine was an inevitable power/weight penalty and was shortly replaced by a Cirrus Minor of 90 hp.

The structure was all wood with ply-covered fuselage and wings, dual control and split trailing edge flaps were standard.

Nine production aircraft were built at Eastleigh fitted now with Gipsy Major engines of 130 hp.

All the private Wickos were impressed at the start of WW2 – only one survived. (With the official name of Warferry!).

Wikner's prototype, stored during the war, was resurrected and flew again briefly – but is no more.

The surviving Wicko, G-AFJB, is under restoration and is expected to fly in the year 2000.

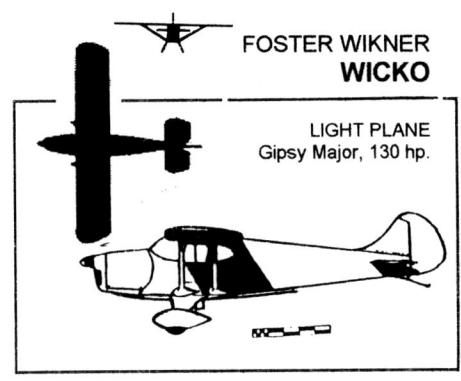

FOSTER WIKNER WICKO

LIGHT PLANE
Gipsy Major, 130 hp.

DATA	IMPERIAL		METRIC	
Span	34.5	ft	10.6	m
Wing area	153	sq.ft	14.4	sq.m
Aspect ratio	7.8			
Empty wt	1255	lb.	570	kg.
Loaded wt	2000	lb.	908	kg.
Wing loading	13	lb/sq.ft	63	kg/sq.m
Max speed	140	mph	224	kmph
Cruising speed	103	mph	165	kmph
Stall speed	55	mph	88	kmph
Climb	800	fpm	246	mpm
Range	480	mls	768	km

The Minor first flew in 1936 when it was manufactured by Luton Aircraft Ltd in Bedfordshire to the designs of C.H.Latimer-Needham who had adapted it from the earlier tandem wing experimental aircraft the LA-2. Several were built by home constructors prior to WW2 and in 1960 the design was overhauled and restressed to the latest British Airworthiness Requirements and plans marketed for homebuilders.

Plans of this single seater have been sold world-wide and the straightforward construction of this docile aeroplane has attracted many builders with over 30 currently on the British Register.

Various engines have been fitted, the data below is for the Aeronca JAP J99 37 hp model.

The PFA approved design is all wood with ply and fabric covering.

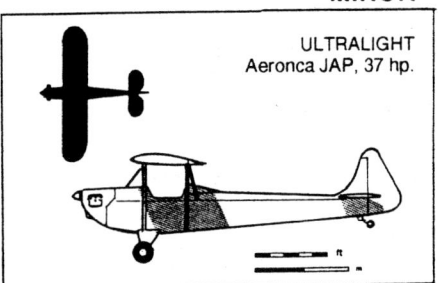

LUTON MINOR

ULTRALIGHT
Aeronca JAP, 37 hp.

DATA	IMPERIAL		METRIC	
Span	25	ft	7.6	m
Wing area	125	ft^2	11.6	m^2
Aspect ratio	5		5	
Empty weight	390	lb	177	kg
Loaded weight	750	lb	340	kg
Wing loading	6	lb/ft^2	29.3	kg/m^2
Max speed	69	mph	111	kmh
Cruise speed	63	mph	102	kmh
Stalling speed	28	mph	45	kmh
Climb rate	250	ft/min	76	m/min
Range	180	mls	290	km

LUSCOMBE
SILVAIRE 8E

LIGHT PLANE
Continental, 75 hp.

The two seat Silvaire first flew in 1937, a product of the New Jersey company, Luscombe, pioneers in the production techniques of small metal aircraft.

The components were accurately die cut and jigged for true fit and interchangeability. Over a 1000 were built pre war (up to 1942) and when production was resumed a further 4660 were made - after various company changes.

The fuselage is an all metal monocoque with side by side seating and cantilever main legs, operating on under floor oleos. Early models had fabric covered wings over metal spars and ribs with 'V' strut bracing; the later models had metal skinned wings and single strut brace. All control surfaces are covered in a fluted light alloy skin and final variants had a squaredoff fin and rudder.

A pretty aeroplane still, its metal structure aiding its longevity. There are an impressive 80 on the British Register.

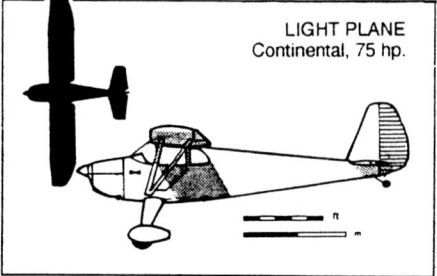

DATA	IMPERIAL		METRIC	
Span	35	ft	10.7	m
Wing area	140	ft^2	13	m^2
Aspect ratio	8.75		8.75	
Empty weight	710	lb	322	kg
Loaded weight	1310	lb	594	kg
Wing loading	9.4	lb/ft^2	45.6	kg/m^2
Max speed	115	mph	185	kmh
Cruise speed	110	mph	176	kmh
Stalling speed	42	mph	67	kmh
Climb rate	900	ft/min	274	m/min
Range	500	mls	800	km

PIPER
J3 CUB

LIGHT PLANE
Continental, 65 hp.

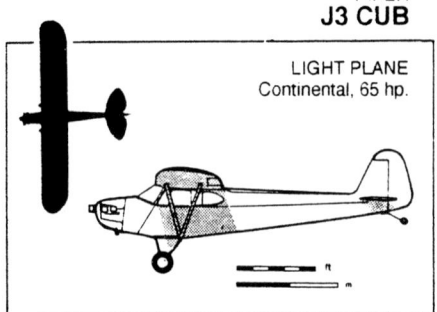

The Piper Cub range is extensive, all stemming from the E2 Cub of 1931 - manufactured by Taylor Aircraft up to 1937 - moving up to the re-designed J2 and J3, which first flew in 1937. All of which had two seats in tandem, Continental and Lycoming engines of 40 to 60 hp., good economy and small field performance. (80% of J3s were fitted with 65 hp Continentals

The construction of the J3 comprised a welded steel tube fuselage, two wooden (later metal) sparred wings with metal ribs and fabric covering aft of the sheet metal nose, 'V' struts to the lower longerons, and a bungee sprung undercarriage.

20,000 J3 Cubs were made up to 1947, many of them being for the US forces, (as the L-4).

100 are on the UK Register – most imported since the war.

Production was resumed after the war and the J3 became the PA 11 Cub Special with wing tankage and fully enclosed engine.

DATA	IMPERIAL		METRIC	
Span	35.2	ft	10.8	m
Wing area	178.5	ft^2	16.8	m^2
Aspect ratio	7		7	
Empty weight	750	lb	340	kg
Loaded weight	1220	lb	554	kg
Wing loading	6.8	lb/ft^2	33.3	kg/m^2
Max speed	100	mph	160	kmh
Cruise speed	87	mph	140	kmh
Stalling speed	40	mph	64	kmh
Climb rate	514	ft/min	158	m/min
Range	300	mls	480	km

Introduced in 1938, the two seat Piper J4 was the first in the Piper range to have side by side seating.

Initially powered by a 50 hp. Continental with the cylinder heads exposed, and later 65 and 75 hp. Continentasl which were fully cowled.

Other refinements over its predecessor, the famous J3 Cub, were, hydraulic brakes, navigation lights and improved instrumentation - trailing edge flaps were still a model or two away.

Production continued up to WW2 and 20, then in the UK, were impressed into the RAF, only five survived the war. Production was resumed with peace.

The structure, like the J3, comprises a welded steel tube fuselage, wooden sparred wings with built up light alloy ribs under a fabric covering. Lycoming engines from 50 to 75 hp. are fitted.

Many are still flying in the USA, and though less numerous than the legendary J3, there are a handful on our Register.

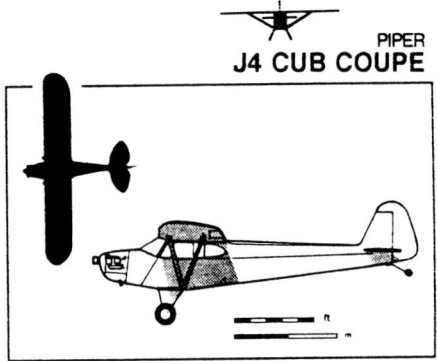

PIPER
J4 CUB COUPE

DATA	IMPERIAL		METRIC	
Span	36.15	ft	11.1	m
Wing area	183.75	ft^2	17.3	m^2
Aspect ratio	7.1		7.1	
Empty weight	865	lb	393	kg
Loaded weight	1400	lb	636	kg
Wing loading	7.6	lb/ft^2	37.2	kg/m^2
Max speed	100	mph	160	kmh
Cruise speed	96	mph	154	kmh
Stalling speed	42	mph	67	kmh
Climb rate	450	ft/min	139	m/min
Range	455	mls	728	km

In 1938 a British firm, Taylorcraft Aeroplanes (England) Ltd., was formed to manufacture, under licence, the successful two seat, side by side, high winger designed and built in the USA by the Taylor Young Airplane Corp. of Ohio.

The Taylorcraft company produced 22 before the outbreak of WW2, when, after Air Ministry trials, a 100 were ordered for communication duties. About half of this batch survived the war to become civil registered again.

In 1946 the company name was changed to Auster Aircraft Ltd. under who's initiative over 400 different Taylorcraft/Auster variants were produced in the immediate post war years.

Taylorcraft in the USA resumed production after the war and, after many management changes are still in business.

There are eleven of the Plus Ds on the UK Reg.

TAYLORCRAFT
PLUS D

LIGHT PLANE
Blackburn Cirrus, 90 hp.

DATA	IMPERIAL		METRIC	
Span	36	ft	11.1	m
Wing area	167	ft^2	15.7	m^2
Aspect ratio	7.7		7.7	
Empty weight	890	lb	404	kg
Loaded weight	1450	lb	658	kg
Wing loading	8.7	lb/ft^2	42.4	kg/m^2
Max speed	120	mph	192	kmh
Cruise speed	102	mph	163	kmh
Stalling speed	45	mph	72	kmh
Climb rate	1000	ft/min	308	m/min
Range	325	mls	520	km

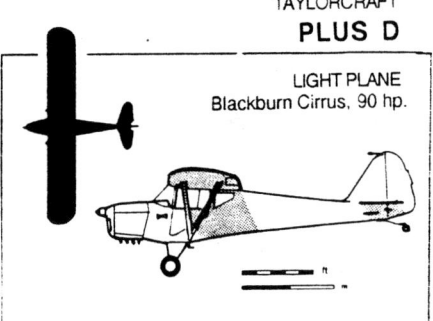

90 hp. Continental version

See page opposite for linked Auster history.

The American Taylorcraft company had been making small aeroplanes since 1936 with welded tube fuselages, wooden spar wings, all fabric covered. They came in Models A,B,C and D.

In 1939 a Model B was used as the basis for Taylorcraft (England) Ltd' first product, typed Model C but soon altered to Plus C. These were built on American jigs but with beefed up tubing to meet British ARB requirements. Initially powered by a 55 hp. Lycoming, they were re-engined with Cirrus Minors of 90 hp. for Army use and re-styled Plus C/2 and then Plus D.

The Lycoming models were clearly under-powered after the British mods. had increased the weight.

The blurring of C to Plus C to Plus C/2 and thence D make history tracing dependent on contract number identification rather than registration or engine type.

TAYLORCRAFT PLUS C
LIGHT PLANE
Lycoming, 55 hp.

DATA	IMPERIAL		METRIC	
Span	36	ft	11.1	m
Wing area	185	ft^2	17.4	m^2
Aspect ratio	7		7	
Empty weight	812	lb	368	kg
Loaded weight	1218	lb	553	kg
Wing loading	6.6	lb/ft^2	32	kg/m^2
Max speed	85	mph	136	kmh
Cruise speed	74	mph	118	kmh
Stalling speed	30	mph	48	kmh
Climb rate	350	ft/min	108	m/min
Range	210	mls	336	km

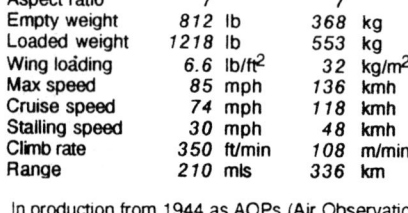

In production from 1944 as AOPs (Air Observation Post), over 1000 were built and many are still flying today in civilian guise.

The Auster 4 (or Model G) was powered by a Lycoming engine of 125 hp. which gave it a cruising speed of 110 mph. Improvements over it's predecessor (the Mk 3) included, a third seat, improved cabin glazing - involving lowering the top longeron for better rear view, a tail wheel in place of a skid and a 'proper' fuel gauge in place of the float and vertical wire poking up from the tank in front of the windscreen.

The Auster 5 (Model J) was a Mk 4 with a blind flying panel and an elevator mounted trim tab replacing the trimming 'paddle' beneath the tailplane.

When civilianised models were re-engined with Gipsy Major 1s (130 hp) they became Mk 5 Ds.

Of standard Auster construction, welded tube fuselage, wooden wing spars with metal ribs all fabric covered, they had split trailing edge flaps and navigation lights - but no engine starter.

The soundness of the basic Taylorcraft/Auster design and its enduring airworthiness have ensured that these veterans still grace our skies half a century after leaving the factory. There are approx. 50 still on the 'Reg.

Details below are for the Mark 5.

AUSTER MARK 4, 5, 5D
LIGHT PLANE
Lycoming, 125 hp.

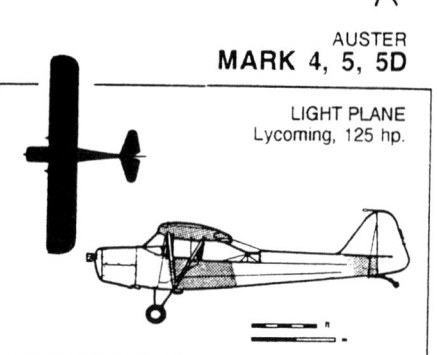

DATA	IMPERIAL		METRIC	
Span	36	ft	11	m
Wing area	185	ft^2	17.4	m^2
Aspect ratio	7		7	
Empty weight	1160	lb	526	kg
Loaded weight	1850	lb	840	kg
Wing loading	10	lb/ft^2	48.8	kg/m^2
Max speed	130	mph	208	kmh
Cruise speed	110	mph	176	kmh
Stalling speed	30	mph	48	kmh
Climb rate	720	ft/min	222	m/min
Range	250	mls	400	km

A pre WW2 design that first flew in 1939, the two seat Major was derived from the single seat Minor and used many of the latter's components.

Both aircraft were creations of C.H.Latimer-Needham the prolific pre war British light plane designer.

The pre war and immediate post war aircraft were powered by 62 hp. Walter Microns while later versions used 65/85 hp. Continentals.

The design rights were acquired by Phoenix Aircraft in 1958 and, after some 'Airworthiness hikes, marketed as a 'plan only' homebuilt.

Construction is all wood, the strut braced wings having two spars and fabric covering aft of the main spar, the nose being ply wood covered. The fuselage is wooden with ply wood covering and the tail surfaces are fabric covered.

A PFA approved design, with 4 on the Register, one is flying in Ireland and others are being restored.

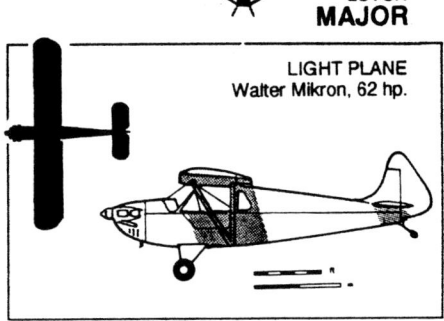

LUTON
MAJOR

LIGHT PLANE
Walter Mikron, 62 hp.

DATA

	IMPERIAL		METRIC	
Span	35.15	ft	10.72	m
Wing area	163	ft²	15.3	m²
Aspect ratio	7.6		7.6	
Empty weight	600	lb	272	kg
Loaded weight	1100	lb	500	kg
Wing loading	6.7	lb/ft²	33	kg/m²
Max speed	105	mph	169	kmh
Cruise speed	95	mph	153	kmh
Stalling speed	35	mph	56	kmh
Climb rate	700	ft/min	213	m/min
Range	300	mls	483	km

AUSTER - AN OUTLINE

The roots of Auster are American. The North American firm The Taylorcraft Aviation Company was formed in 1936 and built side by side, two seat, high wingers with welded tube fuselages and wooden spar wings with metal ribs, all fabric covered. They came in Models A,B,C and D and just before WW2 a few were imported into the UK - six Model As with a 40 hp. Continental and one Model B.

The type proved popular and British Taylorcraft was formed at Thurmaston to build the American Model A under licence - strengthened to British airworthiness standards and re-engined with a 55hp. Lycoming - as the Model C, soon re-named Plus C.

Twenty three Plus Cs were built along with nine Plus Ds (90 hp. Cirrus Minor 1) before the war began in 1939.

Practically all these early British Taylorcrafts were impressed into Army Co-operation work after all the American engines had been replaced with the Cirrus. An order for 100 was placed, initially, and the name Auster was coined - a gentle wind. Over 1600 followed that initial order, Marks 1, 3, 4 and 5 doing sterling work in the battlefields of Europe and North Africa. Mark 5s - a Mark 4 with a Blind Flying Panel - were the most numerous with approx. 800 produced.

NOTE: Strictly classifying the war-time Austers one should use Roman numerals for the Mark numbers - but I have stuck to Arabic throughout.

After the war the firm, renamed Auster Aircraft Ltd., entered the civilian market with the J1 Autocrat and became the only post war British firm to manufacture and export light aircraft in quantity.

Many WW2 4s and 5s are still flying along with the numerous later models, all enthusiastically watched over by The International Auster Pilots Club.

Investment and foresight in aviation were sadly lacking in the early sixties and Auster began to break up, becoming, briefly Beagle-Auster and in 1962 the name Auster disappeared.

Early Auster history is appended to the Auster 5 page.
The AOP 6 is also designated Auster 6 and Auster Model K.

Powered by a Gipsy Major of 145 hp, the AOP 6 followed the Auster 5 in to military service, 379 being made during the years 1946 to 1953 - a fair number of these retiring into civilian roles (15 on the UK Reg.) g.).

The AOP 6 was the first production Auster to have the one piece moulded windscreen in place of the multi panelled type.

Operated as a two seater with the rear space taken up by a bulky service radio the AOP 6 had Mk 5 type rear glazing and metal auxiliary aerofoil flaps (permanently extended).

The type saw service in most of the post war hot spots including Palestine, Korea and Malaya.

A two seat dual trainer version was typed as the Mk 7 (or Mk 10) and 87 were made between 1949 and 1952.

Mk 6s and 7s were fitted with floats, skis and long range tanks for Antarctic exploration in the '50s. (The float planes have a ventral fin to counter the forward float area)

16 Mk 6s were produced as glider tugs and called Tugmasters.

AUSTER AOP 6

LIGHT PLANE
Gipsy Major 7, 145 hp.

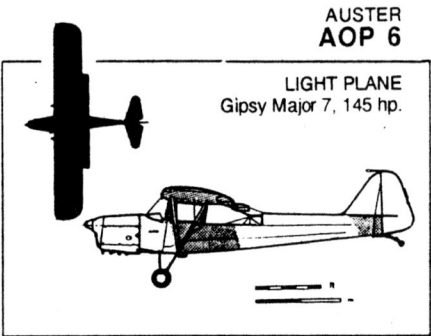

DATA	IMPERIAL		METRIC	
Span	36	ft	11.1	m
Wing area	185	ft^2	17.4	m^2
Aspect ratio	7		7	
Empty weight	1423	lb	641	kg
Loaded weight	2147	lb	975	kg
Wing loading	11.6	lb/ft^2	56.6	kg/m^2
Max speed	124	mph	199	kmh
Cruise speed	107	mph	171	kmh
Stalling speed	37	mph	59	kmh
Climb rate	737	ft/min	227	m/min
Range	345	mls	552	km

Early Auster history is given on the Auster 5 page.

Virtually a J2 with a Cirrus Minor 1 engine of 90 hp, it was a two seater with a straight topped rear fuselage and no flaps.

Only 26 were built over a period of twelve years (1946 - 1958) most going overseas. (Referred to as the J4 Archer, the J4 was, in fact, never *officially* dubbed with that name).

J4s followed the standard Auster construction practice ie. welded tube fuselage twin wooden sparred wings with fabricated metal ribs, all fabric covered and a bungee sprung undercarriage.

In 1951 a J4 made the headlines by taking off pilotless, whist being started, and flying for two hours reaching 8000 feet and only crashing when it ran out of fuel! A tribute to its inherent stability. (A similar incident happened in Australia in 1955 - also a J4!)

There are 5 on the UK Register – not all airworthy.

AUSTER J4 'ARCHER'

LIGHT PLANE
Cirrus Minor 1, 90 hp.

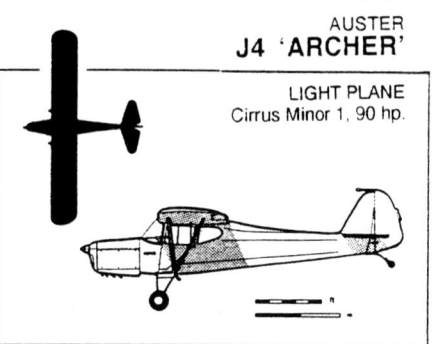

DATA	IMPERIAL		METRIC	
Span	36	ft	11.1	m
Wing area	185	ft^2	17.4	m^2
Aspect ratio	7		7	
Empty weight	957	lb	434	kg
Loaded weight	1600	lb	726	kg
Wing loading	8.6	lb/ft^2	42	kg/m^2
Max speed	110	mph	176	kmh
Cruise speed	95	mph	152	kmh
Stalling speed	37	mph	59	kmh
Climb rate	700	ft/min	215	m/min
Range	320	mls	512	km

Early Auster history is appended to the Auster 5 page.

After the hundreds of camouflaged spotter planes - Auster 3s, 4s and 5s - rolled out at Rearsby and Thurmaston during WW2, the peace came - and with it the first civilian Auster - the J1 Autocrat.

Developed from the Auster 5, the Autocrat had a one piece moulded windscreen, split trailing edge flaps, three seats and was powered by the economical Cirrus Minor 2 of 100 hp.

It was in production from 1946 to 1953, during which period 414 were made, many going for export.

An Autocrat that blazed the Auster name in the world of aviation was G-AERO; owned by the magazine *The Aeroplane*, it was seldom out of the news - like landing on HMS Illustrious! - and must have been a great salesman.

The J1A version had a bench type rear seat - making it the first four seat Auster and re-engined with 130 hp. Gipsy Majors or Lycomings it became the J-1N Alpha.

There are approx. 100 on the UK Reg. - and the details below are for the J1.

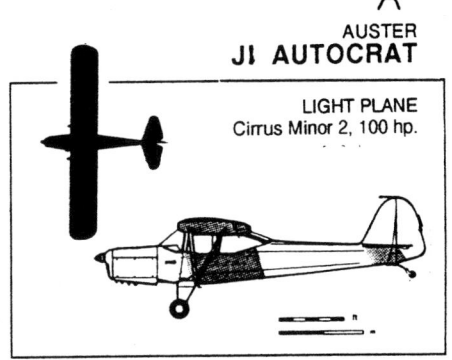

AUSTER
J1 AUTOCRAT
LIGHT PLANE
Cirrus Minor 2, 100 hp.

DATA	IMPERIAL		METRIC	
Span	36	ft	11	m
Wing area	185	ft^2	17.1	m^2
Aspect ratio	7		7	
Empty weight	1052	lb	476	kg
Loaded weight	1850	lb	840	kg
Wing loading	10	lb/ft^2	49	kg/m^2
Max speed	120	mph	193	kmh
Cruise speed	100	mph	160	*kmh*
Stalling speed	30	mph	48	kmh
Climb rate	560	ft/min	180	m/min
Range	220	mls	354	km

The charming little NORD 858 always makes me smile. A shoulder wing two seater from SNCAC whose design originated in a 1946 design competition as the NC 850. Though not the winner, an order for 100 was placed for the '853 variant which had twin fins and a Minie engine of 80 hp.

Taken over by SNCAN in 1949, in mid production the '853 continued with the addition of an 'S' to its type number (NC 858S) and 95 were finally completed. Various models followed with seating and engine changes but of generally the same configuration. The NC 858, shown in the drawing and photo, is the model with the Continental C90 of 90 hp. - the earlier '854 had a 65 hp. Continental and many Minie powered '853s were re-engined with Continentals.

A single strut braces the round tipped wing to the steel tube, fabric covered, fuselage and the main identification feature, the twin finned tailplane, is also braced with a single strut. Other features are the well glazed cabin and the external u/c shock strut.

There are nine '858s and variants on the UK Register.

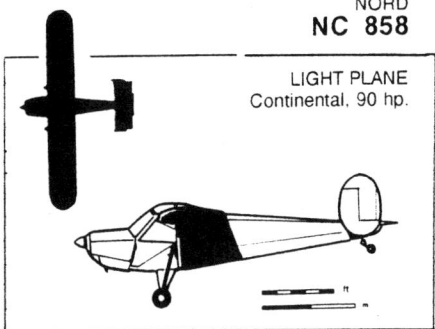

NORD
NC 858
LIGHT PLANE
Continental, 90 hp.

DATA	IMPERIAL		METRIC	
Span	37	ft	11.3	m
Wing area	166	ft^2	15.6	m^2
Aspect ratio	8.2		8.2	
Empty weight	863	lb	392	kg
Loaded weight	1480	lb	672	kg
Wing loading	8.9	lb/ft^2	43.5	kg/m^2
Max speed	114	mph	182	kmh
Cruise speed	97	mph	155	kmh
Stalling speed	45	mph	72	kmh
Climb rate	850	ft/min	261	m/min
Range	280	mls	448	km

Early Auster history is appended to the Auster 5 page.
In production from 1946 to 1952 the J2 Arrow was a two seater with a fuselage that reverted to the straight top longeron (ie. no fuselage 'tadpoling') and was powered by a 75 hp. Continental engine.

Designed down as a less expensive club and private owner aeroplane, the Arrow had no flaps and had a production run of 44, the majority going abroad.

A pretty aeroplane that harked back to the pre war Taylorcrafts.

A 65hp Continental engined version, named the J2 Atom was under-powered, only one was flown and that destroyed in a gale at Rearsby in 1947.

Some later Austers had belly fuel tanks for increased range - the Arrow had available a cylindrical tank in the cabin roof.

Three J2s are on the UK Reg. Two are airworthy – and one won Best Classic Aircraft at the 1999 PFA Rally.

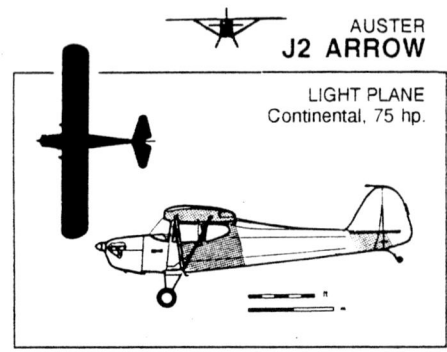

AUSTER
J2 ARROW

LIGHT PLANE
Continental, 75 hp.

DATA	IMPERIAL		METRIC	
Span	36	ft	11.1	m
Wing area	185	ft^2	17.4	m^2
Aspect ratio	7		7	
Empty weight	872	lb	396	kg
Loaded weight	1450	lb	658	kg
Wing loading	7.8	lb/ft^2	38	kg/m^2
Max speed	98	mph	257	kmh
Cruise speed	87	mph	139	kmh
Stalling speed	35	mph	56	kmh
Climb rate	510	ft/min	157	m/min
Range	320	mls	512	km

A post WW2 development of the 1940 J5 Cub Cruiser with increased tankage, cowled cylinders and tidier interior. As in the J5 the pilot sat in front and the two passengers, side by side, behind him/her.

The PA 12 was in production from 1946 to 1948, during which time over 3500 were made - in spite of the recession of '47. The fuselages were welded steel tube and the wings had metal ribs threaded over wooden spars, the whole being fabric covered.

The PA 12 was the first Cub to have the less draggy 'gear with internal bungees rather than the external leather/bungee strut bags.

The PA 14, a close relative, had seating for four and a 115 hp. Lycoming engine.

Around about 1700 are flying in the USA and eight are still on the UK/Eire Register. All the early Pipers have 'fan clubs' and many books have been written about the company, founded by Bill Piper in 1930 when he took over Taylor Brothers Aircraft Corp.

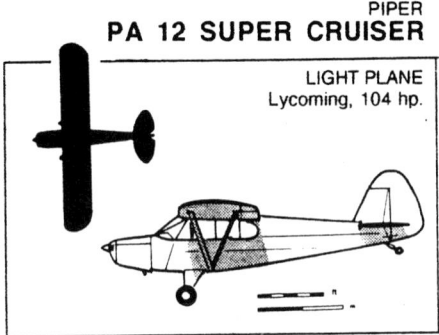

PIPER
PA 12 SUPER CRUISER

LIGHT PLANE
Lycoming, 104 hp.

DATA	IMPERIAL		METRIC	
Span	35.5	ft	11	m
Wing area	179.3	ft^2	16.8	m^2
Aspect ratio	7		7	
Empty weight	950	lb	431	kg
Loaded weight	1750	lb	794	kg
Wing loading	9.8	lb/ft^2	46.6	kg/m^2
Max speed	115	mph	184	kmh
Cruise speed	105	mph	168	kmh
Stalling speed	50	mph	80	kmh
Climb rate	510	ft/min	157	m/min
Range	600	mls	960	km

DE HAVILAND CANADA
BEAVER

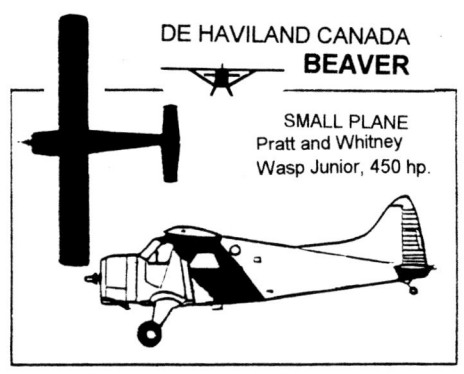

SMALL PLANE
Pratt and Whitney
Wasp Junior, 450 hp.

The all-metal Beaver produced by De Haviland of Canada carries a pilot and six passengers and is powered by a 450 hp. Pratt and Whitney Wasp Junior.

A rugged bush aircraft capable of operating on floats, skis – and wheels: the Beaver first flew in 1947 and was snapped up by the US Air Force who ordered 970 of them. Beavers were supplied to many other air forces and operators and 1,692 were built before production ceased in 1968. (This includes the later Turbo Beaver, eleven seater).

Five acquired UK civil registrations, DH's own, G-ALOW and the others, ex military, included G-BUVF, currently based and flying in the Netherlands.

Four are static in UK collections.

The sole Beaver 2, manufactured in 1953, (G-ANAR), which has an Alvis Leonides of 550 hp. returned to Canada in 1971.

A big success, the Beaver led to demand for a 'Super Beaver – this was the DHC 3 Otter of which 465 were built.'

DATA	IMPERIAL		METRIC	
Span	48	ft	15	m
Wing area	250	sq.ft	23.5	sq.m
Aspect ratio	9.2			
Empty wt	2810	lb.	1275	kg.
Loaded wt	4820	lb.	2188	kg.
Wing loading	19.3	lb/sq.ft	94.2	kg/sq.m
Max speed	179	mph	286	kmph
Cruising speed	137	mph	219	kmph
Stall speed	60	mph	96	kmph
Climb	1020	fpm	314	mpm
Range	455	mls	728	km

CESSNA
MODEL 170

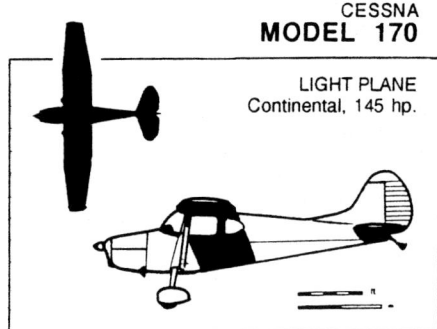

LIGHT PLANE
Continental, 145 hp.

One of the first of the long line of Cessna monocoque high-wingers, the 170 was a four seat development of the two seater 120/140 and it first flew in 1947 with a Continental C145 engine of 145 hp.

Early 170s had fabric covered, 'V' strutted, parallel chord wings and no dorsal fin extension; from '48 the 170As had all metal, single strut braced half span tapered wings and a fin dorsal extension.

With the 170B came bigger flaps and the 0-300 series Continental - still 145 hp. and from '55 amongst other refinements, larger rear windows.

Over 5000 170s were built between 1949 and '56 and were to lead to the famous trike geared Cessna 172.

It is interesting to note that a new 170 cost $ 8000 and today a forty year old one would set you back $20000. Bob Grimstead flew a 170 for *Pilot* and wrote, '...this is a pilots aeroplane, handling in the air is 'classic' as befits its generation .. on the ground ... in a cross wind, it is 'stimulating'.

There are four on the 'Register, 3 airworthy.

DATA	IMPERIAL		METRIC	
Span	36	ft	11.1	m
Wing area	174	ft^2	16.3	m^2
Aspect ratio	7.4		7.4	
Empty weight	1425	lb	646	kg
Loaded weight	2200	lb	999	kg
Wing loading	12.6	lb/ft^2	61.5	kg/m^2
Max speed	135	mph	216	kmh
Cruise speed	120	mph	192	kmh
Stalling speed	52	mph	83	kmh
Climb rate	660	ft/min	203	m/min
Range	495	mls	792	km

Reminiscent of the big radial engined high wingers of the '30s - the Stinsons, the Howard DGA 'Mr Mulligan' - the Cessna 190/195 was 'throw back'. It first appeared in 1947, an all metal cantilevered wing, five seater that was in production for six years during which time about 1000 were made.

Powered by Continental or Jacobs radials in the 240 - 300 hp band, the C195 was, in its day, no sluggard, cruising at 170 mph and climbing at over 1000 fpm. The view from the cockpit is notoriously bad and the big radials are thirsty and take some looking after - but they sound fabulous!

Although 1000 were made, this was a poor take up by Cessna standards and those that did sell went to commercial bush and survey operators - plus a batch of twenty to the US Air Force - it was too clunky and thirsty for the private market.

There are two on the UK Register.

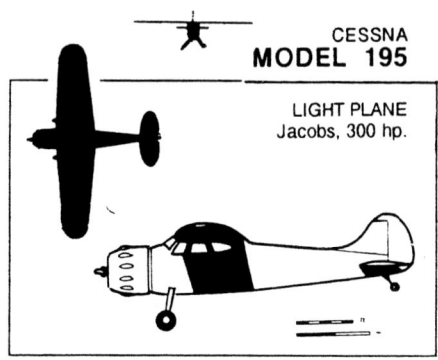

CESSNA
MODEL 195

LIGHT PLANE
Jacobs, 300 hp.

DATA	IMPERIAL		METRIC	
Span	36.2	ft	11.1	m
Wing area	218	ft²	20.5	m²
Aspect ratio	6		6	
Empty weight	2100	lb	953	kg
Loaded weight	3350	lb	1521	kg
Wing loading	15.4	lb/ft²	75	kg/m²
Max speed	200	mph	320	kmh
Cruise speed	174	mph	278	kmh
Stalling speed	62	mph	99	kmh
Climb rate	1135	ft/min	350	m/min
Range	805	mls	1288	km

The Aeronautical Corporation of America - or Aeronca. was founded in 1929 and its most famous pre war design was the C3 'Flying Bathtub" (many still flying!). During the war they produced a tandem two seater, strut braced high wing monoplane, the L3B, for the American forces.

With the peace, they came up with three models, the Champion, with tandem seats, the side by side Chief and the four seat Sedan. Over 7000 of these types were made before Aeronca ceased production in 1951. The Chief has a fabric covered welded steel tube fuselage, and wings with pressed aluminium ribs threaded over two wooden spars - fabric covered. ; the undercarriage, in an era of Bungee springing, had the luxury of Oleo sprung legs. The cockpit has the air of a '40s car with dual wheels - and a glove pocket. A fifty year old gem!

20 are on the UK Register.

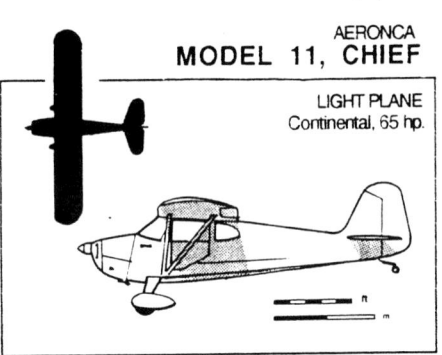

AERONCA
MODEL 11, CHIEF

LIGHT PLANE
Continental, 65 hp.

DATA	IMPERIAL		METRIC	
Span	36	ft	11.1	m
Wing area	175	ft²	16.4	m²
Aspect ratio	7.4		7.4	
Empty weight	770	lb	350	kg
Loaded weight	1250	lb	567	kg
Wing loading	7.14	lb/ft²	34.8	kg/m²
Max speed	95	mph	152	kmh
Cruise speed	85	mph	136	kmh
Stalling speed	42	mph	67	kmh
Climb rate	400	ft/min	123·	m/min
Range	260	mls	416	km

After WW2, Cessna, allegedly, after taking a long look at the Luscombe, came up with two new models, the 120 and the 140, two seaters with stressed skin monocoque fuselages and fabric covered wings braced with 'v' struts. Both models had the, then unique, spring steel cantilever undercarriage legs (a Steve Wittman patent) and 85 hp. Continental engines. The 140 was an up market version of the 120 and had additional windows, flaps and electric starter.
The all metal wing, tapered from half span, and braced by a single strut came in 1948 with the 140A and were to become a Cessna 'trade mark'.
Over 7000 Cessna 120/140s were built plus 500 140As.
The Cessna 170, a four seat version of the 140A, went on to become the '172 one of the all time world best sellers.
There are 40 Cessna 120/140s on the UK Register and five of the, much prized 170s

CESSNA
MODEL 120/140

LIGHT PLANE
Continental, 85 hp.

DATA	IMPERIAL		METRIC	
Span	32.8	ft	10.1	m
Wing area	160	ft²	15	m²
Aspect ratio	6.5		6.5	
Empty weight	800	lb	363	kg
Loaded weight	1450	lb	658	kg
Wing loading	9	lb/ft²	4.4	kg/m²
Max speed	120	mph	192	kmh
Cruise speed	105	mph	168	kmh
Stalling speed	50	mph	80	kmh
Climb rate	550	ft/min	880	m/min
Range	450	mls	720	km

The T29 Motor Tutor first flew in 1948 and was intended for ATC use - though as a single seater this must have limited its training role.
The all wood wings and tail were those of Slingsby's T8 glider and the fuselage design and construction was carried out by Martin Heath Ltd. who built Slingsby gliders under licence. The glider skid was replaced by a conventional undercarriage.
Two prototypes were built and an order placed by the ULAA (the PFA predecessor) for six more. These were only partially completed when the order was cancelled. The fuselages of these incomplete aircraft were taken up by various other builders and appeared as complete aeroplanes in later years.
These hybrids were made without Slingsby drawings and embody many variations.
With the release of ex ATC T31 Tandem Tutor gliders, several rebuilds to single seat Motor Tutor are current with others still under conversion mainly powered by VW 1834 cc engines.
There are 17 Motor Tutor variants on the 'Register only four of which appear to be airworthy.

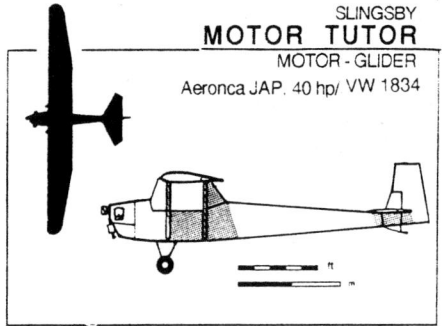

SLINGSBY
MOTOR TUTOR

MOTOR - GLIDER
Aeronca JAP. 40 hp/ VW 1834

DATA	IMPERIAL		METRIC	
Span	43.3	ft	13.3	m
Wing area	200	ft²	18.8	m²
Aspect ratio	9.4		9.4	
Empty weight	555	lb	252	kg
Loaded weight	800	lb	363	kg
Wing loading	4	lb/ft²	19.5	kg/m²
Max speed	75	mph	120	kmh
Cruise speed	65	mph	104	kmh
Stalling speed	28	mph	45	kmh
Climb rate	250	ft/min	77	m/min
Range	200	mls	320	km

Using 'war surplus' Cub wings, shortened by six feet, the PA 15 Vagabond was Piper's first post war product. A utility design, powered by the economic Lycoming O-145-B engine of a nominal 65 hp., the Vagabond (original Piper name - Cub Vagabond) was only in production for two years in which time 387 were sold.

The PA 17 Vagabond Trainer - or Vagabond de Luxe - followed, having dual controls, improved instrumentation and comfort plus a Cub type bungee sprung undercarriage (the PA15 relied on low pressure tyres) and a Continental A65 engine of 65 hp.

Many original PA 15s were upgraded to PA 17 standard.

Construction comprises fabric covered welded tube fuselage, wooden or metal spar wings with pressed alloy ribs fabric covered aft of the metal nosing. The tailplane is wire braced.

There are 29 PA 15/17s on the UK Register and the data below is for the PA 17.

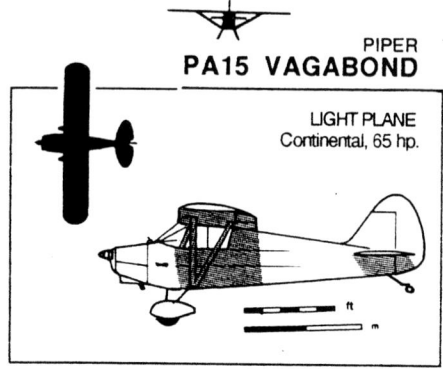

PIPER
PA15 VAGABOND

LIGHT PLANE
Continental, 65 hp.

DATA	IMPERIAL		METRIC	
Span	29.3	ft	9.0	m
Wing area	147.5	ft^2	13.8	m^2
Aspect ratio	5.8		5.8	
Empty weight	695	lb	315	kg
Loaded weight	1150	lb	522	kg
Wing loading	7.8	lb/ft^2	38	kg/m^2
Max speed	100	mph	160	kmh
Cruise speed	90	mph	144	kmh
Stalling speed	48	mph	77	kmh
Climb rate	500	ft/min	154	m/min
Range	247	mls	395	km

The family of Cubs, Super Cubs Super Cruisers etc. is legion and goes right back to 1931 when it was the Taylor E2 Cub and in '38 the everlasting, exposed cylinders, J3 Cub. Over the years 40,000 Cubs of all types have been produced and are flying all over the world.

The PA18 Cub was the first post WW2 design to roll out of the Piper factory in Pennsylvania in 1949 and went on to clock up some 20,000 aircraft produced.

The Super Cub is a tandem two seater (like the pre war Cubs) and is built on standard American lines, welded tube fuselage, two wooden wing spars threaded with light alloy girder ribs, the whole being fabric covered. Trailing edge flaps were fitted on some models and the landing gear is a bungee sprung split axle with steerable tail-wheel.

An easy and forgiving aeroplane to fly with a well proven airframe requiring the minimum of maintenance.

There are 131 on the UK Register.

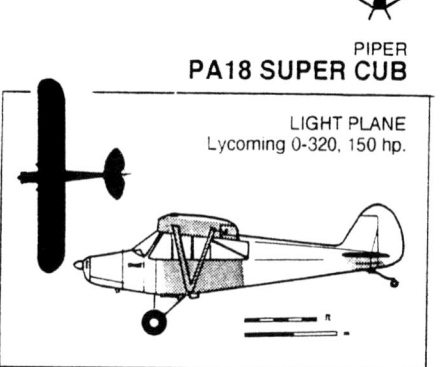

PIPER
PA18 SUPER CUB

LIGHT PLANE
Lycoming O-320, 150 hp.

DATA	IMPERIAL		METRIC	
Span	35.2	ft	10.8	m
Wing area	178.5	ft^2	16.8	m^2
Aspect ratio	7		7	
Empty weight	930	lb	422	kg
Loaded weight	1750	lb	794	kg
Wing loading	9.8	lb/ft^2	47.8	kg/m^2
Max speed	130	mph	208	kmh
Cruise speed	104	mph	166	kmh
Stalling speed	45	mph	72	kmh
Climb rate	960	ft/min	296	m/min
Range	460	mls	736	km

The military Bird Dog used the civil Cessna 170s wings, tail unit and undercarriage, it was a tandem two seater as opposed to a 2x2 four seater. The engine was a 213 hp. Continental in place of the 170s 145 hp unit and it had a 'joy-stick' instead of a control wheel. The airframe was all metal with big flaps and good STOL performance with AOP style extensive cabin glazing to give 360° vision, and, in ground attack style, four under-wing rocket pylons.

First flown as Model 305A in 1950 its military designations were variations on 0-1 and L19 including turbo versions (XL19B and XL19C) and trainer (TO-1D).

Built under licence in Japan and used by many foreign air forces, the Bird Dog saw service in Korea and when production ceased in 1958 over 3000 had been made. De-mobbed in 1967 this rugged, but thirsty, little leaper was snapped up by civilian buyers -about 150 still flying, but only one in the UK. (One is static at Middle Wallop).

CESSNA
BIRD DOG

LIGHT PLANE
Continental, 213 hp.

DATA	IMPERIAL		METRIC	
Span	36	ft	11.1	m
Wing area	174	ft^2	16.3	m^2
Aspect ratio	7.4		7.4	
Empty weight	1614	lb	732	kg
Loaded weight	2430	lb	1103	kg
Wing loading	13.9	lb/ft^2	68	kg/m^2
Max speed	115	mph	184	kmh
Cruise speed	104	mph	166	kmh
Stalling speed	35	mph	56	kmh
Climb rate	1150	ft/min	354	m/min
Range	530	mls	848	km

The two seat, 65 hp. Vagabond, the first of the 'short winged' Pipers, was joined by a four seat version, initialy named PA 16 Clipper - Pan Am objected, and the type was re-designed and re-named the PA 20 Pacer.

The Pacer, as well as four seats, had flaps, a larger tailplane with horn balanced elevator, increased tankage and dual control wheels in place of sticks.

In production from 1950 to 1954, over 1000 Pacers were built; initially with the 125 hp. Lycoming, a few later models had a 115 hp. Lycomings.

The PA 20-135 had a 135 hp. Lycoming engine and a two position Aeromatic prop.

The tricycle gear version, the PA 22 Pacer, in production from '51 to '63 - is often regressed to 'tail wheel' configuration, such is the lure of the 'tail dragger'!

The Pacer airframe follows standard Piper practice, welded steel tube fuselage frame, wooden spar wings with metal ribs, all fabric covered - the wings braced with 'V' struts.

There are 15 on the UK Register and many hundreds in the USA.

PIPER
PA 20 PACER

LIGHT PLANE
Lycoming, 115 hp.

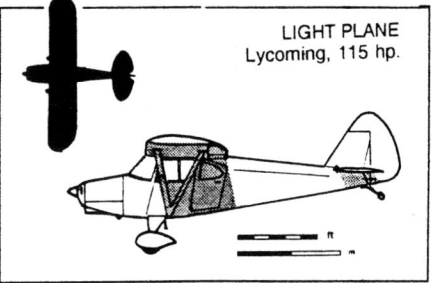

DATA	IMPERIAL		METRIC	
Span	29.3	ft	9.02	m
Wing area	147.5	ft^2	13.8	m^2
Aspect ratio	5.8		5.8	
Empty weight	900	lb	408	kg
Loaded weight	1650	lb	749	kg
Wing loading	11.2	lb/ft^2	54.8	kg/m^2
Max speed	141	mph	225	kmh
Cruise speed	134	mph	214	kmh
Stalling speed	50	mph	80	kmh
Climb rate	800	ft/min	246	m/min
Range	536	mls	856	km

See Auster Mark 5 for early Auster history.

A four seater, in production from 1952 to 1958, the J5B Autocar had a 'new look' fuselage - the rear decking was humped to follow the curve of the domed perspex cabin roof. It also sported a horn balanced rudder of increased area, fuel tanks in both wing roots, landing flaps and a sloping engine bulkhead that permitted the luxury of an electric 'self starter'.

Powered by a Gipsy Major 1 of 130 hp. the Autocar fulfilled many roles and was fitted with both floats and skis; and with a large tank in the passenger space it performed as a crop sprayer.

When fitted with the more powerful Cirrus Major 3 of 155 hp. the designation became the J5G and 92 of this model were made.(The Gipsy engined J5B had a production run of 82)

It is staggering to note that these Autocrats sold for £1500 new! - you could only buy a good prop' for that today!

Many were sold abroad including a batch for the Australian Navy and others for 'dusting and pest control in developing countries.

Eleven are on the UK Register, most are airworthy. Details below for J5G.

AUSTER J5G AUTOCAR
LIGHT PLANE
Cirrus Major 3, 155 hp.

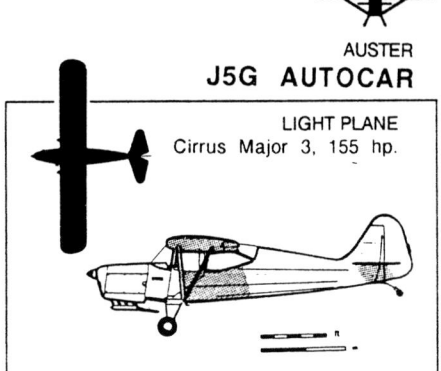

DATA	IMPERIAL		METRIC	
Span	36	ft	11.1	m
Wing area	185	ft²	17.4	m²
Aspect ratio	7		7	
Empty weight	1367	lb	620	kg
Loaded weight	2450	lb	1112	kg
Wing loading	13.2	lb/ft²	84	kg/m²
Max speed	127	mph	203	kmh
Cruise speed	110	mph	176	kmh
Stalling speed	35	mph	56	kmh
Climb rate	710	ft/min	218	m/min
Range	485	mls	776	km

The Aiglet Trainer had the standard Auster wing reduced in span by four feet and improved ailerons to bring it into the semi aerobatic category (-3 to +4.5).

The windscreen was of the one piece moulded type, the cabin was four inches (10 cm) wider and the seat backs were raised to facilitate four point harness'.

The fuselage was a basic J5 up-stressed for aerobatics - not to be confused with the J1B Aiglet a non aerobatic crop sprayer with a J1 fuselage.

Ninety two were made during the period 1952 - 1956 many going overseas.

One J5F, G-AMOS, set up no less than 28 point to point world records for its category in the early fifties and G-AMLR flew to Australia and back.

When fitted with a 36 ft. span (Autocar) wing the name changed to J5R Alpine.

A famous Alpine was G-APAA owned and operated by the AA and used for traffic reconnaissance.

There are 13 on the UK Register, mostly airworthy.

AUSTER J5F AIGLET TRAINER
LIGHT PLANE
Gipsy Major 1, 130 hp.

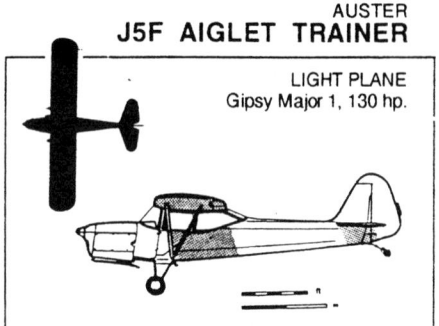

DATA	IMPERIAL		METRIC	
Span	32	ft	9.8	m
Wing area	164	ft²	15.4	m²
Aspect ratio	6.24		6.24	
Empty weight	1324	lb	601	kg
Loaded weight	2200	lb	999	kg
Wing loading	13.4	lb/ft²	65.4	kg/m²
Max speed	125	mph	200	kmh
Cruise speed	107	mph	171	kmh
Stalling speed	33	mph	53	kmh
Climb rate	670	ft/min	206	m/min
Range	270	mls	432	km

The AOP 9 was the last aeroplane produced in quantity by Auster, 150 being supplied to the AOP squadrons and 35 going to the Indian Air Force.

The AOP 9 has an all metal airframe but retains fabric covering, it has hydraulically operated flaps combined with drooping ailerons and a 180 hp. Cirrus Bombardier fuel injection engine. The semi cantilever undercarriage legs have hydraulic shock absorbers and the tailplane, abandoning the traditional Auster flat plate section became a proper aerofoil. The wing strut bracing is by single strut instead of 'V' struts.

A dorsal fin extension and fuselage strakes were additions that appeared after some hair raising spinning trials.

AOP 9s saw service in the trying conditions of the Malayan jungle, where they served with credit.

An AOP 11 was made - an AOP 9 with a 260 hp. Lycoming for military trials - but by 1962 helicopters were taking over the AOP role.

There are 17 AOP9s on the UK Reg. most airworthy.

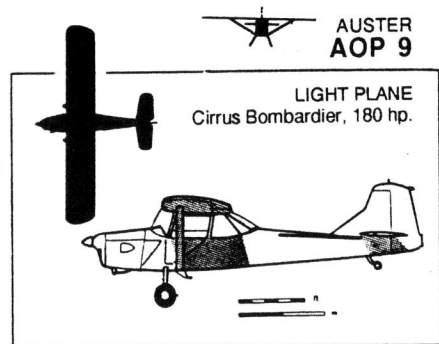

AUSTER
AOP 9
LIGHT PLANE
Cirrus Bombardier, 180 hp.

DATA	IMPERIAL		METRIC	
Span	36.5	ft	11.2	m
Wing area	198	ft^2	18.6	m^2
Aspect ratio	6.7		6.7	
Empty weight	1558	lb	707	kg
Loaded weight	2350	lb	1064	kg
Wing loading	11.8	lb/ft^2	58	kg/m^2
Max speed	118	mph	189	kmh
Cruise speed	100	mph	160	kmh
Stalling speed	44	mph	70	kmh
Climb rate	920	ft/min	283	m/min
Range	242	mls	387	km

Designed by air race pilot and pioneer of the post war North American home-building movement Steve Wittman, the Tailwind first flew in 1953 - and still looks 'trendy' after 42 years!

The Tailwind's construction is along what was 'standard American' for its day, i.e. welded steel tube fuselage with fabric covering, a single strut braced wooden wing, part fabric covered.

The single raked back cantilever undercarriage leg is a distinguishing feature - and at the time, fairly unique.

Seating two, side by side, the Tailwind is a small aeroplane (22 ft. span) that looks and flies like a bigger one.

Over the years a range of motors from 85 to 140 hp. have been fitted and earlier models did not have the raked fin and rudder.

A PFA approved type, with 14 on the 'Register and several being built.

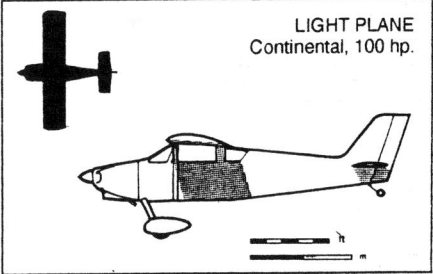

WITTMAN
TAILWIND
LIGHT PLANE
Continental, 100 hp.

DATA	IMPERIAL		METRIC	
Span	22.6	ft	7	m
Wing area	90	ft^2	8.46	m^2
Aspect ratio	5.7		5.7	
Empty weight	750	lb	340	kg
Loaded weight	1300	lb	590	kg
Wing loading	14.4	lb/ft^2	70.3	kg/m^2
Max speed	170	mph	272	kmh
Cruise speed	155	mph	248	kmh
Stalling speed	55	mph	88	kmh
Climb rate	900	ft/min	277	m/min
Range	450	mls	720	km

BEAGLE HUSKY

Derived from the Auster J1/N Alpha, the Husky was the last in the range, finally being produced by Beagle Aircraft Ltd. in 1960 - the year of its first flight.

The Austers are all based on the, pre WW2, American Taylorcraft and have welded steel tube fuselages, covered in fabric, and two wooden sparred strut braced wings with metal ribs under a fabric skin.

The Husky is powered by a 160 hp. Lycoming engine, is a full four seater and out-performs its stable mates the Alpha, Arrow, Alpine etc.

The large dorsal fin is a distinguishing feature of the Husky as is the Lycoming engine - *most* other Beagle/Austers having Gypsy, Cirrus or Blackburn inverted, in line engines.

The Auster family is numerous and ageless - though Huskiies are fairly rare; seven on the 'Reg. (six flying).

LIGHT PLANE
Lycoming, 160 hp.

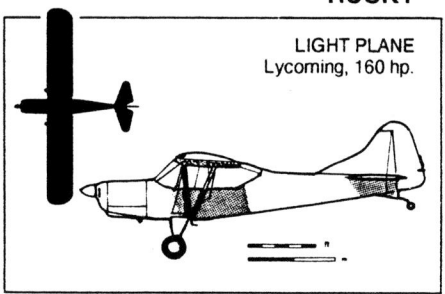

DATA	IMPERIAL		METRIC	
Span	36	ft	11	m
Wing area	185	ft^2	17.2	m^2
Aspect ratio	7		7	
Empty weight	1450	lb	658	kg
Loaded weight	2450	lb	1111	kg
Wing loading	13.2	lb/ft^2	64.6	kg/m^2
Max speed	124	mph	198	kmh
Cruise speed	108	mph	174	kmh
Stalling speed	55	mph	88	kmh
Climb rate	640	ft/min	197	m/min
Range	460	mls	740	km

Taylorcraft Aeroplanes (England) Ltd. became Auster Aircraft, which became Beagle - Auster, and finally, Beagle Aircraft - the family resemblance is plain to see!

The Terrier, which first flew in 1961, was a civilian version of the Auster AOP 6, a British Army air observation post of 1945 vintage which was a Gipsy engined version of the AOP 5 with a Lycoming. 300 AOP 6s were made including the T7 trainer.

The Terrier, of which only 65 were produced, is still well represented in the lists with thirty currently shown on the UK Register.

Differing from its military predecessor in having larger tail surfaces, three seats, luxurious seating and trim, and a long exhaust pie and silencer below the fuselage (this is deleted on some aircraft).

Construction is standard Auster - welded steel tube fuselage, metal wing ribs and wooden spars, fabric covering.

A glider tug version was also produced called the Tugmaster.

BEAGLE A 61 TERRIER

LIGHT PLANE
Gipsy Major. 145 hp.

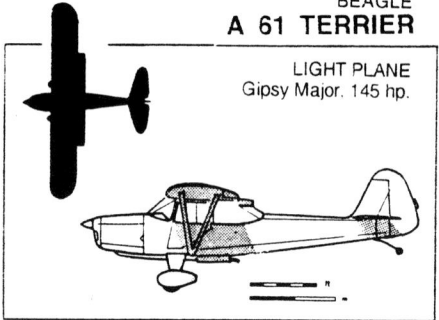

DATA	IMPERIAL		METRIC	
Span	36	ft	11.1	m
Wing area	184	ft^2	17.3	m^2
Aspect ratio	7		7	
Empty weight	1490	lb	676	kg
Loaded weight	2400	lb	1089	kg
Wing loading	13	lb/ft^2	63.6	kg/m^2
Max speed	124	mph	198	kmh
Cruise speed	108	mph	173	kmh
Stalling speed	50	mph	80	kmh
Climb rate	600	ft/min	185	m/min
Range	300	mls	480	km

The Polish Wilga - or Thrush, in English - is a versatile aircraft with a STOL performance being equally at home as a sports tourer, or in an agricultural role, a parachutists hack, towing gliders or an air ambulance.

Though fairly rare in this country - 4 on the UK Register - 900+ have been built and sold all over the world in many variants and is still in production

First flown in 1962 the all metal Wilga has a distinctly insect like look about it, the trailing link mounted main wheels definitely owe something to the praying mantis!

The main plane, rather surprisingly for a low speed utility aircraft is cantilevered - though the tail plane is strut braced.

The fuselage makes much use of external fluting as do the flying control surfaces.

In its day the Wilga held the world altitude record for its class with 33,428 ft (6836 m).

A special 'export' version, the Wilga 2000, has a 300 hp Lycoming, large leg fairings and an extended dorsal fin.

Data below for Ivchenko Wilga.

PZL WILGA

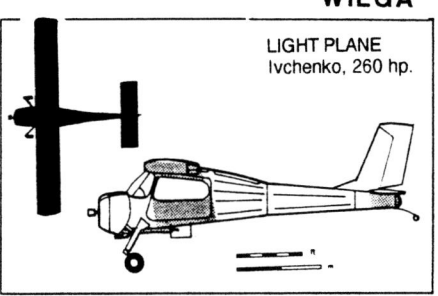

LIGHT PLANE
Ivchenko, 260 hp.

DATA	IMPERIAL		METRIC	
Span	36.5	ft	11.14	m
Wing area	170	ft²	16	m²
Aspect ratio	7.8		7.8	
Empty weight	1874	lb	850	kg
Loaded weight	2755	lb	1250	kg
Wing loading	16.2	lb/ft²	79	kg/m²
Max speed	120	mph	192	kmh
Cruise speed	104	mph	166	kmh
Stalling speed	50	mph	80	kmh
Climb rate	1245	ft/min	380	m/min
Range	370	mls	592	km

First flown in 1963 the Maule M4 Rocket, designed by Belford Maule and Manufactured at Moultrie, Georgia, has been the basic airframe for all the subsequent variants - mainly engine size changes. (A seaplane and turboprop version are available)

The M5 Lunar Rocket has a 210 hp. Continental engine, four seats and a genuine STOL performance - the M6 has 235 hp. and the M7 is the first Maule to have a tricycle undercarriage.

The fuselage is of welded steel tube with fabric covering and a large integral fin; the wings are all metal and braced with 'V' struts - as is the tailplane.

Maules are distributed in the UK by Aeromarine and the Moultrie plant has made 1700 of them.

Popular with South American bush operators thanks to its tough capacious fuselage and STOL feature. 32 are on the UK Register - including M4, M5, M6 and M7s.

MAULE M5 LUNAR ROCKET

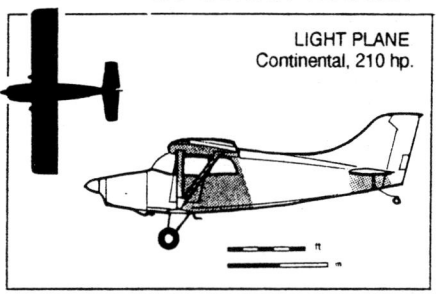

LIGHT PLANE
Continental, 210 hp.

DATA	IMPERIAL		METRIC	
Span	30.8	ft	9.5	m
Wing area	138	ft²	12.9	m²
Aspect ratio	6.9		6.9	
Empty weight	1300	lb	590	kg
Loaded weight	2400	lb	1089	kg
Wing loading	17.4	lb/ft²	85	kg/m²
Max speed	170	mph	272	kmh
Cruise speed	160	mph	256	kmh
Stalling speed	40	mph	64	kmh
Climb rate	1500	ft/min	462	m/min
Range	700	mls	1120	km

British designed and built by E. Clutton and E. Sherry, the FRED - standing for, Flying Runabout Experimental Design - first flew in 1963 powered by a 500 cc. Triumph motor cycle engine. A variety of engines have been fitted since; mainly 1500 cc. VW, though some flew with the American Lawrence radial.

Plans have been available since 1970 and have proved very popular with the home builder.

The structure is all wood with ply and fabric covering and the thick wing is wire braced. The tail unit consists of a cantilever tail plane with push rod operated elevator and an aerodynamically balanced, finless, rudder.(Ed. A fixed fin mod is recommended). The long undercarriage legs, attached to the top longerons, have coil springs at the top and scooter wheels at the bottom.

The wings fold easily along side the fuselage for ease of storage or towing - which can be done with a motor cycle!

There are 32 FRED's on the 'Register and they are PFA approved.

CLUTTON FRED

ULTRALIGHT
Volkswagen, 1500 cc.

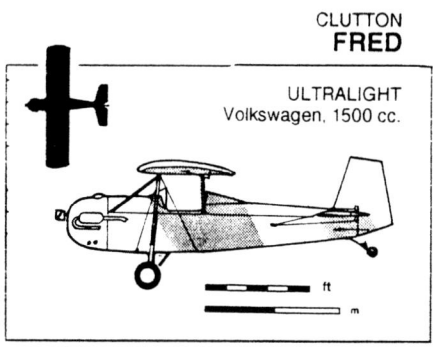

DATA	IMPERIAL		METRIC	
Span	22.5	ft	7	m
Wing area	110	ft²	10.3	m²
Aspect ratio	4.6		4.6	
Empty weight	533	lb	252	kg
Loaded weight	773	lb	351	kg
Wing loading	7	lb/ft²	34	kg/m²
Max speed	75	mph	120	kmh
Cruise speed	55	mph	88	kmh
Stalling speed	40	mph	64	kmh
Climb rate	400	ft/min	122	m/min
Range	200	mls	360	km

FLAGLOR SKY SCOOTER

ULTRALIGHT
VW 1500. 40 hp.

The charming single seat Sky Scooter is an American design by Ken Flaglor, which first flew in 1967. It is designed for home building and plans are available from Headberg Aviation Inc of Longwood, Florida.

Construction is all wood with Ceconite covered wings, rear fuselage and control surfaces. The wing centre section and engine mount are steel tube and the wing leading edge is light alloy sheet.

The wings are wire braced to the lower longerons and to a steel pylon above the centre section. The tailplane is strut braced and the rudder is fin-less.

A short spring leg carries the main wheels and a sprung and steerable tail wheel brings up the rear.

The design power unit is a Volkswagen 1500 cc flat four developing about 40 hp.

The design is PFA approved, though none are currently under construction.

The one Sky Scooter currently on the UK Register (G-BOWE) turned many a head when it flew in to the big PFA Rally at Cranfield in 1999.

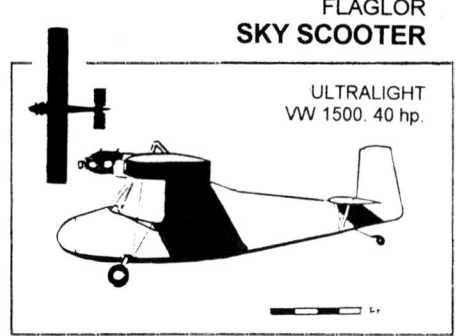

DATA	IMPERIAL		METRIC	
Span	27.9	ft	8.5	m
Wing area	115	sq.ft	10.7	sq.m
Aspect ratio	6.7			
Empty wt	390	lb.	177	kg.
Loaded wt	625	lb.	283	kg.
Wing loading	5.4	lb/sq.ft	26.5	kg/sq.m
Max speed	80	mph	129	kmph
Cruising speed	65	mph	105	kmph
Stall speed	34	mph	55	kmph
Climb	325	fpm	100	mpm
Range	175	mls	282	km

AERONCA/BELLANCA
CHAMPION - CITABRIA

The two seat, in tandem, Aeronca 7 Champion first flew in 1944 and was produced in considerable numbers, 7,200 of the 7AC Champion and 509 of the military variant the L-16A.

In 1954 Champion Aircraft got the rights from Aertonca and made 773 model 7s as the 7EC Traveller and the Nose wheeled Tri Traveller (472 made) also the aerobatic Citabria. Bellanca bought Champion in 1970 and re-engined the 7AC with a 60 hp. Franklin; they also produced variants of the Citabria culminating in the fully aerobatic Model 8 Decathlon. American Champion Aircraft took over when Bellanca closed down in 1980 and are producing Decathlons and Citabria's.

A few tricycle gear converted Champions are to be seen rejoicing in the name of Tri- Champion.

There are 33 Champion/Bellanca/Citabria on the UK Register.

LIGHT PLANE
Lycoming, 150 hp.

DATA	IMPERIAL		METRIC	
Span	33.5	ft	10.2	m
Wing area	165	ft^2	15.5	m^2
Aspect ratio	6.8		6.8	
Empty weight	1067	lb	484	kg
Loaded weight	1650	lb	749	kg
Wing loading	16	lb/ft^2	78	kg/m^2
Max speed	125	mph	200	kmh
Cruise speed	117	mph	187	kmh
Stalling speed	51	mph	130	kmh
Climb rate	725	ft/min	223	m/min
Range	509	mls	814	km

BEDE
BD-4

Designed by Jim Bede, the *enfant terrible* of the American kit plane scene, the BD-4 is an eye-catching, angular, two or four seater with, unusual for a high winger, a cantilever wing.

The fuselage, of all metal construction, is of extremely simple geometry for ease of construction, and the wings have tubular spars that double as fuel tanks, with composites forming the wing section profile.

BD-4s may be seen with either nose wheel tricycle or taildragger undercarriages.

A variety of engines are fitted ranging from 100 to 200 hp. - the data below is for the 180 hp. Lycoming model which has a very useful cruising speed and range.

Four are on the 'Register, and the type is approved by the PFA. - in the two seat version.

LIGHT PLANE
Lycoming, 180 hp.

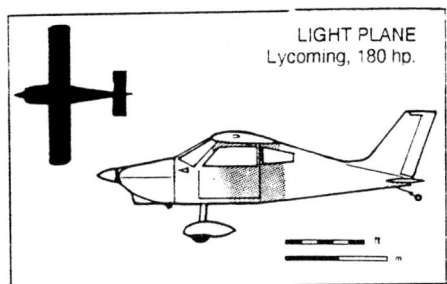

DATA	IMPERIAL		METRIC	
Span	25.5	ft	7.85	m
Wing area	102	ft^2	9.6	m^2
Aspect ratio	6.4		6.4	
Empty weight	1080	lb	490	kg
Loaded weight	2000	lb	908	kg
Wing loading	19	lb/ft^2	92.7	kg/m^2
Max speed	183	mph	293	kmh
Cruise speed	174	mph	278	kmh
Stalling speed	63	mph	101	kmh
Climb rate	1400	ft/min	431	m/min
Range	750	mls	1200	km

An Australian design the Thruster is a two seat side by side microlight with good flying characteristics that has caught on well in this country with over 100 on the British Register.

The Thruster is currently back in production after a lapse of some years and is marketed by Thruster Air Services of Ginge, Oxon.who say that a '450kg rules' Thruster is imminent.

Popular as a club trainer with its side by side seating, though differing from most microlights in this category in having 'tail dragger' gear. (Ed. Nose wheel versions are also now available).

The main airframe components are of light alloy tubing, stressed for +7-4g - a very sturdy design - with the crew seated in a GRP pod behind a generous windscreen. The main wheels are mounted on spring steel legs and are un-braked. Later models have wheel spats.

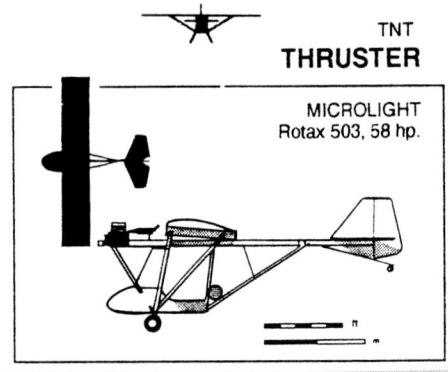

TNT
THRUSTER
MICROLIGHT
Rotax 503, 58 hp.

DATA	IMPERIAL		METRIC	
Span	31.5	ft	9.7	m
Wing area	161.5	ft^2	15.2	m^2
Aspect ratio	6.14		6.14	
Empty weight	330	lb	150	kg
Loaded weight	816	lb	370	kg
Wing loading	5.0	lb/ft^2	24.4	kg/m^2
Max speed	92	mph	147	kmh
Cruise speed	69	mph	110	kmh
Stalling speed	37	mph	59	kmh
Climb rate	500	ft/min	154	m/min
Range	172	mls	276	km

The Avid Flyer, a side by side two seater, comes in many variants, STOL, Heavy Hauler, Speedwing, Aerobatic and Commuter.

All versions have tail wheel or nose wheel options. Of fabricated tube with Dacron covering, the kit containing all aluminium and foam items and can be built - it is claimed - in 800 man hours.

First flown in it's country of origin, the USA, in 1983 where ten years of development and build experience have produced a reliable and popular aeroplane with a 1000 built in the USA and 40 in the UK at the time of writing.

The original design team included Dan Denney who went on to design the Kitfox – some parts of which are, indeed, interchangeable.

A special Jabiru engined version has been built and is flying in the UK.

LIGHT AERO
AVID FLYER
ULTRALIGHT
Rotax 582, 65 hp.

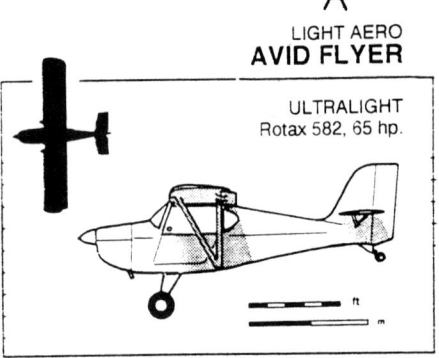

DATA	IMPERIAL		METRIC	
Span	29.8	ft	9.2	m
Wing area	122	ft^2	11.5	m^2
Aspect ratio	7.3		7.3	
Empty weight	400	lb	181	kg
Loaded weight	911	lb	413	kg
Wing loading	7.44	lb/ft^2	36	kg/m^2
Max speed	95	mph	152	kmh
Cruise speed	85	mph	136	kmh
Stalling speed	32	mph	51	kmh
Climb rate	1400	ft/min	422	m/min
Range	350	mls	560	km

Probably the most popular kit plane yet marketed. with over 1500 sold since it was introduced in 1984 - and is still being produced at the rate of 20 - 30 a month by Denney Aircraft Co. at their works in Idaho.

Designed by Dan Denney, the Kitfox has a welded steel tube fuselage (supplied complete in kit) and a wing based on two dural tube spars with ply ribs and fabric covering as on the fuselage.

The wings fold easily for towing or 'garaging', and the landing gear options available include floats, skis and amphibian floats. Push rods operate the full span flaperons and elevators whilst the rudder relies on cables for its motion.

At the time of writing there are 100 on the UK Register – plus others being built.

The Kitfox 3 is identical in appearance to the '2' but is stronger to accommodate the Rotax 912. (the data below is for the Rotax 582 ,64 hp version *ES*

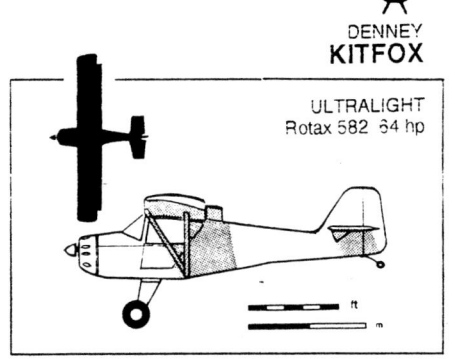

DENNEY
KITFOX

ULTRALIGHT
Rotax 582 64 hp

DATA	IMPERIAL		METRIC	
Span	31.5	ft	9.7	m
Wing area	130	ft^2	12.2	m^2
Aspect ratio	7.6		7.6	
Empty weight	440	lb	200	kg
Loaded weight	950	lb	431	kg
Wing loading	7.6	lb/ft^2	35.6	kg/m^2
Max speed	114	mph	182	kmh
Cruise speed	105	mph	168	kmh
Stalling speed	25	mph	40	kmh
Climb rate (solo)	1300	ft/min	400	m/min
Range	230	mls	368	km

Fisher Flying Products of Edgeley, North Dakota have produced a range of aeroplanes including the Koala, Skybaby, Classic, Dakota Hawk and, recently, the R80 80% Tiger Moth replica. In 1984 the two seat version of the Koala, the Super Koala, made its first flight; since then, over 1000 kits have been sold.

A Mike Fisher design, the side by side Super Koala first flew in the UK in 1996P with a Rotax 532 of 64 hp. and at an all up weight of 830 lb. comes within the 'Ultralight' category.

The Kit, which comes in Standard or Quick build form, is all wood, with a geodetic type structure on the wings and fuselage sides. In the Quick Build version the spars, ribs, fuselage sides and empennage are ready assembled. Electric engine start, wheel brakes and spats are optional extras.

The Super Koala's performance is noteworthy; with two up, it will cruise at 85 mph, stall at 32 mph and climb at 1100 fpm - all on a modest 64 hp.(Late News :- An 80 hp Jabiru 2200 is being fitted)

Available from Alastair Malcolm Aviation Ltd. Park Farm, Throwley, Faversham, Kent, the Super Koala is PFA approved. There are three on the UK Register.

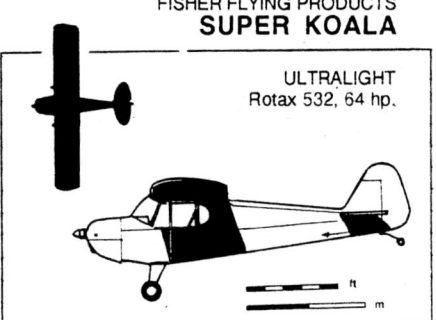

FISHER FLYING PRODUCTS
SUPER KOALA

ULTRALIGHT
Rotax 532, 64 hp.

DATA	IMPERIAL		METRIC	
Span	31	ft	9.5	m
Wing area	140	ft^2	13.2	m^2
Aspect ratio	6.9		6.9	
Empty weight	400	lb	181	kg
Loaded weight	830	lb	377	kg
Wing loading	6	lb/ft^2	29	kg/m^2
Max speed	95	mph	152	kmh
Cruise speed	85	mph	136	kmh
Stalling speed	32	mph	51	kmh
Climb rate	1100	ft/min	339	m/min
Range	150	mls	291	km

A Canadian light plane (UK group A) from the drawing board of Daryl Murphy (with a little help from Dick Hiscocks who designed the DH Beaver - the Rebel looks a bit like a little Beaver!).

The Rebel first flew in 1990 and the manufacturers of this smart all metal kit plane claim that 400 kits have already been delivered. There is an ultralight version sold as the Maverick.

The wing has three spars, stamped L.A. ribs and is braced by a single strut to a fuselage strongpoint. Wings and semi monocoque fuselage are covered in aluminium sheet and they are stressed for +9,-6g. Three engine options are available, Rotax 582, Rotax 912 and Lycoming 0-235 - which is the version the data below refers to.

With detachable wings and an upward folding tailplane the Rebel can have a narrow storage profile.

The Rebel is PFA approved; there are nine on the 'Register plus others being built.

MURPHY REBEL

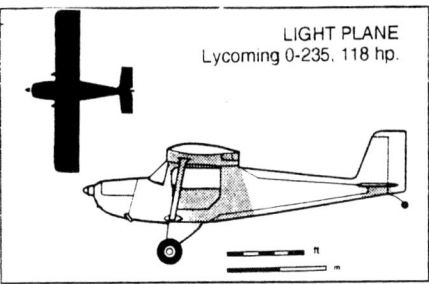

LIGHT PLANE
Lycoming 0-235, 118 hp.

DATA	IMPERIAL		METRIC	
Span	30	ft	9.24	m
Wing area	150	ft²	14.1	m²
Aspect ratio	6.1		6.1	
Empty weight	850	lb	386	kg
Loaded weight	1650	lb	749	kg
Wing loading	11	lb/ft²	53.7	kg/m²
Max speed	120	mph	192	kmh
Cruise speed	110	mph	176	kmh
Stalling speed	32	mph	51	kmh
Climb rate	800	ft/min	304	m/min
Range	400	mls	640	km

Another light 'plane from the Mike Whittaker stable - this one being aerobatic. First flown in 1987 the MW 7, the smallest of the MW range, follows the well proven configuration of the earlier MW 5 and 6, and continues the use of large diameter light alloy tubes to carry the main loads.

A good looking single seater which may be seen with various cabin configurations, dependent on the constructor and on later models, a larger fin and rudder. (This is now standard)

As with all previous MW models the motor is mounted at the front end of the 'tail boom' and the rudder and all moving elevator at the other, but unlike earlier models the '7' is a 'taildragger with a well sprung tailwheel mounted below the fin.

Ten are on the 'Register – PFA approved.

WHITTAKER MW 7

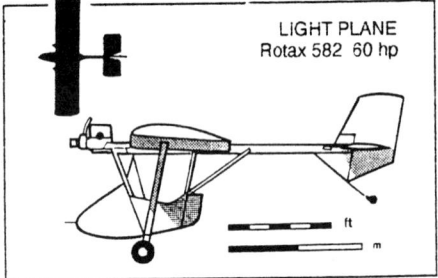

LIGHT PLANE
Rotax 582 60 hp

DATA	IMPERIAL		METRIC	
Span	22	ft	6.8	m
Wing area	88	ft²	8.3	m²
Aspect ratio	5.5		5.5	
Empty weight	300	lb	136	kg
Loaded weight	600	lb	272	kg
Wing loading	6.8	lb/ft²	33.2	kg/m²
Max speed	92	mph	147	kmh
Cruise speed	74	mph	118	kmh
Stalling speed	40	mph	64	kmh
Climb rate	1000	ft/min	308	m/min
Range	100	mls	160	km

MW 7

GENERAL AIRCRAFT OWLET - A reminiscence.........

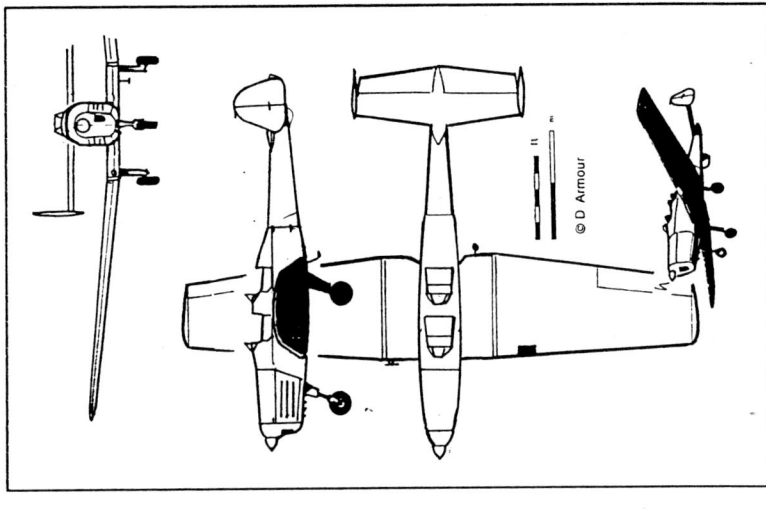
© D Armour

General Aircraft, having produced a range of Monospar aircraft and the more advanced, all metal, Cygnet side by side two seater, and before getting involved in big time glider production, produced a tandem cockpit 'Cygnet' in the early years of the war and named it the Owlet.

The Owlet first flew in 1940 and was a tandem, two seat trainer using many Cygnet components; the wing tips were squared off, and a new open cockpit module slotted in place of the glazed side by side cabin.

Reputedly aimed at training RAF pilots in the art of tricycle gear operations (Douglas Bostons were then reaching RAF squadrons) its sister, the Cygnet, would appear to have been better qualified for this role, having side by side seating and an enclosed cockpit - I think the Owlet was aimed at the general RAF *ab initio* role which was based on tandem seating - right up to Advanced (Master, Harvard).

One aircraft was built, G-AGBK, shortly camouflaged and given a service number, its career was short. The record states that it was damaged beyond repair in a heavy landing at White Waltham in 1942.

I have another story. I had a chance to examine the Owlet when it flew in to Woodley and later when enquiring about its subsequent fate was told that it had been strafed by a German fighter and that the crew had baled out, the aircraft crashing to the ground but not burning. On examining the wreckage, only one bullet hole was found in it - and that right through the RAF roundel!. The story is almost certainly apocryphal - but I like it.

⊳A.

Span	32.4ft(10 m)	
Length	24.6ft(7.6 m)	
Wing area	173ft^2/(16.3 m^2)	
Aspect ratio	6.1	
Empty wt	1563 lb(709kg)	
Loaded wt	2300lb(1044 kg)	
Wing loading	13.3lb/ft^2 (65 kg/m^2)	
V max	125 mph/(200 kph)	
V cruise	110 mph/(176 kph)	
V min	55 mph/(88 kph)	
Climb	770 ft/min(237 m/min)	
Range	450 m(720 k)	

The Chrislea CH3 Ace first flew at Heston in 1946. It was powered by a 130 hp. Lycoming and had a single fin and rudder (soon changed to twins), the fuselage was a welded tube structure and the wings had steel spars and aluminium ribs, all fabric covered.
Chrislea's 'big idea' was to simplify the flying controls by doing away with the rudder bar and moving the rudder with a sideways movement of the 'steering wheel'.
The Super Ace (Gipsy Major 10) was produced at the re-located Chrislea works at Exeter and first flew in 1948 - initially with the 'all purpose' steering wheel, but later models reverted to orthodoxy. A tail-dragger version the Skyjeep followed in 1949 with a Blackburn Cirrus Major (155 hp) and an upward hinged rear decking for awkward loads (ie. a stretcher).
Lack of orders caused the firm to fold in 1952 when 23 Super Aces and 3 Skyjeeps had been built. Most of the Super aces finished up in foreign lands, one survivor is in Japan and another in Australia. One is airworthy; three are on the UK Register.

CHRISLEA SUPER ACE

LIGHT PLANE
Gipsy Major 10, 145 hp.

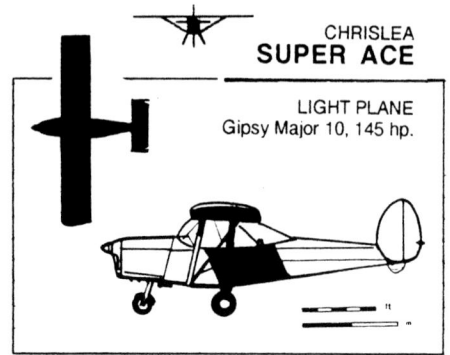

DATA	IMPERIAL		METRIC	
Span	36	ft	11	m
Wing area	177	ft²	16.6	m²
Aspect ratio	7.3		7.3	
Empty weight	1350	lb	613	kg
Loaded weight	2400	lb	1090	kg
Wing loading	13.2	lb/ft²	64	kg/m²
Max speed	126	mph	202	kmh
Cruise speed	112	mph	179	kmh
Stalling speed	43	mph	69	kmh
Climb rate	750	ft/min	231	m/min
Range	400	mls	640	km

First flown in 1950 the four seat Tri Pacer is the tricycle gear version of the PA20 Pacer and is the only Piper high wing trike.
Of traditional Piper construction, welded tube fuselage, two spar wing, fabric covered and fitted with a variety of Lycoming engines ranging from 125 to 160 hp.
The main variants are the 1958 PA22-150 Caribbean - not so fully equipped as the original model - and the two seat, 108 hp. Colt of 1961, two seat trainer. Float plane and ski versions also appear.
Production of all PA22's ended in 1963 when over 9000 had been made, many hundreds of which are still flying world-wide, including 60 plus on the British Register.
Details below are for the 160 hp. PA22 Tri Pacer

PIPER PA 22 TRI PACER

LIGHT PLANE
Lycoming, 160 hp.

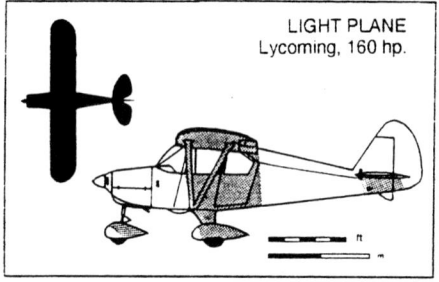

DATA	IMPERIAL		METRIC	
Span	29.2	ft	8.9	m
Wing area	147.5	ft²	13.7	m²
Aspect ratio	5.8		5.8	
Empty weight	1110	lb	504	kg
Loaded weight	2000	lb	908	kg
Wing loading	13.6	lb/ft²	66.3	kg/m²
Max speed	141	mph	226	kmh
Cruise speed	134	mph	214	kmh
Stalling speed	55	mph	88	kmh
Climb rate	800	ft/min	246	m/min
Range	655	mls	1055	km

Alfons Putzer KG, the German company, began building sailplanes in 1953 and in 1958 a motor glider – from this the two seat Elster (Magpie) was developed.

First flown in 1959, 21 of the all wood Elsters were purchased by the German government for flying club use.

The prototype was powered by a Porsche 678/3 engine but production aircraft had 95 hp. Continental C90-12F and were designated Elster B. A glider towing version the Elster C was powered by a 150 hp. Lycoming O-320.

About 30 Elsters in all were built and in the mid sixties Putzer became Sportavia – Putzer GmbH.

The fuselage is an all wood ply' skinned monocoque and the high, semi elliptical wing has a single wooden spar braced by a metal strut. The tricycle undercarriage is rubber block sprung, the nose wheel is steerable and the main wheels have mechanical brakes. The side-by-side seats are reached via upwards hinged doors.

Three Elsters are on the UK Register, all ex-German registered, only one of which is currently airworthy.

An interesting 'Super Motor Glider'!
An interesting 'Super Motor Glider'!

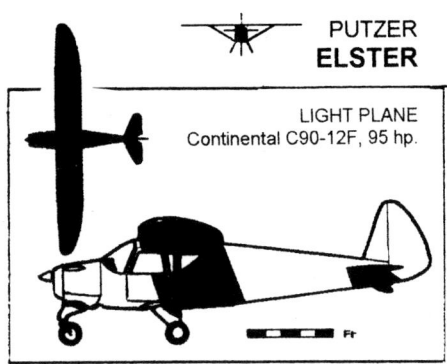

PUTZER ELSTER

LIGHT PLANE
Continental C90-12F, 95 hp.

DATA	IMPERIAL		METRIC	
Span	43.3	ft	13.2	m
Wing area	188	sq.ft	17.7	sq.m
Aspect ratio	10			
Empty wt	1014	lb.	460	kg.
Loaded wt	1543	lb.	700	kg.
Wing loading	8.0	lb/sq.ft	39	kg/sq.m
Max speed	104	mph	180	kmph
Cruising speed	93	mph	150	kmph
Stall speed	46	mph	74	kmph
Climb	'720	fpm	220	mpm
Range (appx)	280	mls	450	km

Thirty five thousand Cessna 172 buyers can't be wrong! One of the most successful 'planes ever built, the 172 first flew in 1955 and was a tricycle gear version of the model 170 of 1945 - so the basic design is 47 years old! The 170 differed from the 172 in having an unswept fin and rounded profile rudder and elevator.

Two thousand of the total production have been built in France by Reims Aircraft - the French built Cessnas are prefixed with an 'F'.

It is also supplied to the US armed forces, fitted with a 210 hp. Continental, as the T-41 Mescalero trainer and to various South American air forces for a range of duties.

The wing with its tapered outer panels and single strut brace, low set tailplane, all round view cabin and swept fin with dorsal extension are all distinctive features.

About **350** are on the UK register.

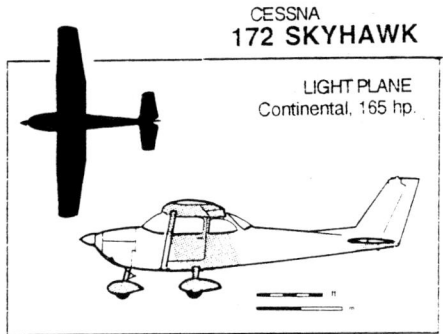

CESSNA 172 SKYHAWK

LIGHT PLANE
Continental, 165 hp.

DATA	IMPERIAL		METRIC	
Span	36.16	ft	11.1	m
Wing area	174	ft^2	16.3	m^2
Aspect ratio	7.5		7.5	
Empty weight	1260	lb	572	kg
Loaded weight	2300	lb	1044	kg
Wing loading	13.2	lb/ft^2	64.4	kg/m^2
Max speed	138	mph	220	kmh
Cruise speed	130	mph	208	kmh
Stalling speed	57	mph	91	kmh
Climb rate	645	ft/min	198	m/min
Range	720	mls	1152	km

Developed from the Cessna 180 tail dragger the 182, with nose wheel undercarriage, initially retained the 180's unswept fin and rudder and first flew in 1955. An period of development resulted in the swept fin version of 1960, and in 1962, the stepped rear fuselage with the 'Omnivision' rear window.
The aircraft is all metal and has the typical Cessna wing braced by a single strut.
In appearance, the '182 is almost identical to the '172 but has a more swept fin and rudder and is a foot (0.3 m) longer than the '172 - which, strangely, came after the '182, chronologically.
The '182 has a more powerful engine, a six cylinder Continental of 230 hp., and can seat up to six people. Built in France by Reims Aviation as the Skyrocket this version is, in fact, a six cylindered '172. Reims have, quite recently, considered re-starting '182 production. Around 100 '182s are on the UK Register - including the 182 R which is the retractable gear version.
Some 18,000 were built.

CESSNA MODEL 182 SKYLANE

LIGHT PLANE
Continental. 230 hp.

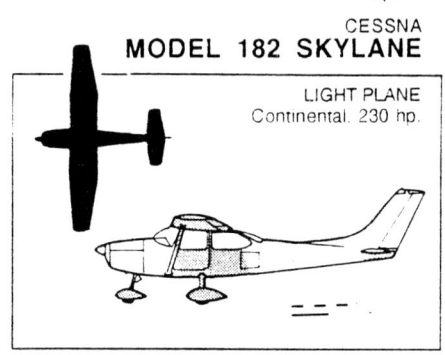

DATA	IMPERIAL		METRIC	
Span	36	ft	11.1	m
Wing area	174	ft²	16.3	m²
Aspect ratio	7.4		7.4	
Empty weight	1550	lb	703	kg
Loaded weight	2800	lb	1271	kg
Wing loading	16.1	lb/ft²	78.6	kg/m²
Max speed	167	mph	267	kmh
Cruise speed	155	mph	248	kmh
Stalling speed	59	mph	94	kmh
Climb rate	905	ft/min	1448	m/min
Range		mls		km

When first flown in 1957 the '150 had a vertical fin and rudder and a full depth rear fuselage, by the time the 150F arrived the fin was swept and the rear fuselage slimmed to allow for the wrap around rear window. A two seat side by side all metal two seater, a reliable Continental engine, tricycle landing gear and electrically operated flaps make the '150 & 152 the all time most popular trainer, with a total production of 24,000.
The Reims Aviation built aircraft are prefixed with an 'F' (i.e. F150).
The 152 has a 110 hp Lycoming, 28 volt electrics, new fuel tanks and a 30 degree flap setting.
Both 150 and 152 are produced as Aerobats.
The derisory 'Spam Can' tag is ill deserved for one of the worlds most successful aeroplanes.

CESSNA MODEL 150 / 152

LIGHT PLANE
Continental 0-200, 100 hp.

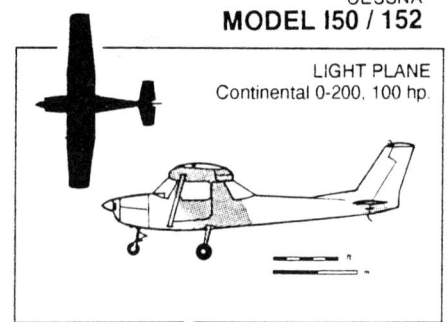

DATA	IMPERIAL		METRIC	
Span	32.6	ft	10	m
Wing area	157	ft²	14.7	m²
Aspect ratio	6.8		6.8	
Empty weight	975	lb	442	kg
Loaded weight	1600	lb	726	kg
Wing loading	10.2	lb/ft²	50	kg/m²
Max speed	123	mph	197	kmh
Cruise speed	98	mph	157	kmh
Stalling speed	50	mph	80	kmh
Climb rate	670	ft/min	200	m/min
Range	300	mls	480	km

BEAGLE
A109 AIREDALE

LIGHT PLANE
Lycoming, 180 hp.

When Beagle took on the Auster concern they designed the four seat Airedale as a competitor to the prolific Cessnas then beginning to flood the country. Though considerably improved, the Airedale was essentially an old 'low tech' Auster and was not enough to check the American invasion.

The improvements embodied in the new aeroplane included, a swept back fin and rudder, an all metal wing structure - though still partly fabric covered, improved interior (to 'car standards'), front and rear doors, slotted flaps, disc brakes and stearable nose wheel undercarriage and improved instrumentation.

The prototype first flew in 1961 and production petered out in 1964 when 43 had been made - fifteen remain on the UK Register.

Variants included a 175 hp. Continental version - the A111 and a lighter less comprehensively equipped version for club use.

Beagle built their aeroplanes to last and owners dote on them - the Airedale (and the rest of the Beagle 'litter') will be around for some time yet!

DATA	IMPERIAL		METRIC	
Span	36.3	ft	11.2	m
Wing area	190	ft²	17.8	m²
Aspect ratio	7		7	
Empty weight	1700	lb	772	kg
Loaded weight	2750	lb	1248	kg
Wing loading	14.5	lb/ft²	70.6	kg/m²
Max speed	141	mph	226	kmh
Cruise speed	133	mph	213	kmh
Stalling speed	50	mph	80	kmh
Climb rate	650	ft/min	200	m/min
Range	560	mls	896	km

CESSNA
MODEL 206

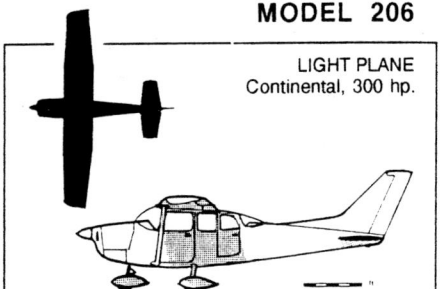

LIGHT PLANE
Continental, 300 hp.

The five seat Model 206 first flew in 1962 and deliveries commenced in 1964; it was a development of the Model 205 as was the retractable gear Model 210 (Which, illogically, flew before the '206, in 1950). The Model 206 is the fixed gear version of the '210 and has run to many variants, 7,500 of which have been built. Amongst the variant types are the P206 Super Skylane six seater, TP206 Super Skylane with turbo-supercharged engine, U206 Super Skywagon, Stationair and Stationair 6 (1978) - to name but a few of the fifteen models. These are all comfortable, fast cruising, metal aircraft with a useful range.

Distinguishing features are down turned wing tips, a lot of cabin windows (3 full ones per side) going well beyond the wing trailing edge.

The Model 207 is even longer with four cabin windows per side but retaining the same wing and tail.

There are 27 model 206s on the UK Register.

DATA	IMPERIAL		METRIC	
Span	36.5	ft	11.24	m
Wing area	176	ft²	16.5	m²
Aspect ratio	7.6		7.6	
Empty weight	1765	lb	801	kg
Loaded weight	3600	lb	1634	kg
Wing loading	10	lb/ft²	48.8	kg/m²
Max speed	174	mph	278	kmh
Cruise speed	164	mph	262	kmh
Stalling speed	50	mph	80	kmh
Climb rate	920	ft/min	283	m/min
Range	800	mls	1280	km

Intended for ease of construction without complicated jigs and using only hand tools, the BN-3 was an ingenious design allowing licence building anywhere in the world.

First flown in 1969 the all-metal two-seat prototype, G-AXFB, was powered by a 115 hp. Lycoming engine; subsequent versions, seating up to four were to have 130 and a60 hp engines.

Clearly a rival to the omnipresent Cessna tribe the brilliant and competitively priced BN-3 inexplicably never sold and is little known to day.

The two spar high aspect ratio wings carried electrically operated plain flaps and were foldable for ease of hangarage. (A big plus over its rivals!).

After its debut at the 1969 Paris Air Show and talk of an Australian order for 100, the Nymph faded away.

In 1981 the ten years stored BN-3 was sold in Scotland, bought back by Desmond Norman later, rebuilt and modified as the NAC-1 Freelance (G-NACI) and flown again in 1984. A second Freelance (G-NACA) has been built..

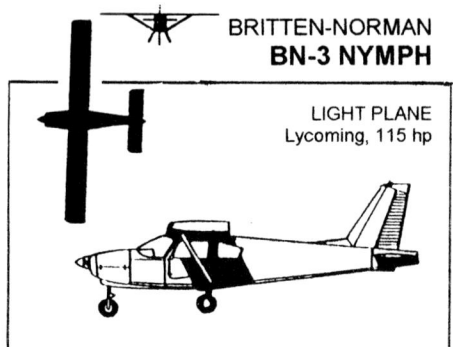

BRITTEN-NORMAN
BN-3 NYMPH

LIGHT PLANE
Lycoming, 115 hp

DATA	IMPERIAL		METRIC	
Span	39	ft	12	m
Wing area	169	sq.ft	16	sq.m
Aspect ratio	9			
Empty wt	1140	lb.	517	kg.
Loaded wt	1925	lb.	874	kg.
Wing loading	28	lb/sq.ft	136	kg/sq.m
Max speed	117	mph	187	kmph
Cruising speed	113	mph	181	kmph
Stall speed	65	mph	104	kmph
Climb	580	fpm	178	mpm
Range	500	mls	800	km

The MW 5 - Sorcerer - was designed by Mike Whittaker in 1983, based on the one off MW 4 which first flew in 1982, and is a single seat microlight under whose extremely simple lines lies a very well engineered airframe.

The MW 5 is sold as 'plans only' and over 40 are currently on the British Register, a fair proportion of which can be seen at the annual MW rally held at Charterhouse.

The tail boom and main spar are of light alloy tube the wing having plywood ribs and leading edge with fabric covering. The tail boom carries an all moving rudder and elevator at one end and the Rotax 477 at the other.(Other Rotax and Robin engines may be fitted)

The main wheels are mounted on leaf springs and may be fitted with spats and brakes. The nose wheel is steerable.

A batch of 18 were built by Aerotech with tapered wings.

This is an enduring little aeroplane with a good safety record, well pleased owners and PFA approval.

WHITTAKER
MW 5

MICROLIGHT
Rotax 477 40 hp

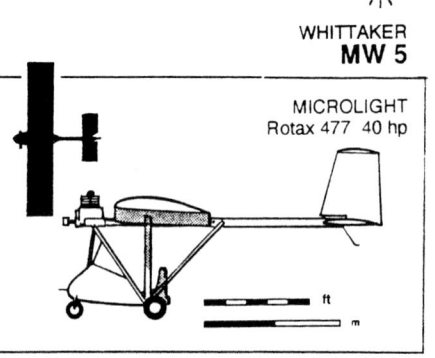

DATA	IMPERIAL		METRIC	
Span	28	ft	8.62	m
Wing area	140	ft^2	13.16	m^2
Aspect ratio	5.6		5.6	
Empty weight	300	lb	136	kg
Loaded weight	625	lb	284	kg
Wing loading	4.46	lb/ft^2	21.8	kg/m^2
Max speed	92	mph	147	kmh
Cruise speed	63	mph	101	kmh
Stalling speed	34	mph	54	kmh
Climb rate	600	ft/min	185	m/min
Range	200	mls	320	km

CYCLONE AIRSPORTS
CYCLONE AX 3

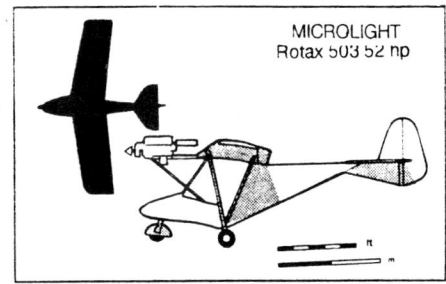

MICROLIGHT
Rotax 503 52 hp

The Cyclone design originated in the USA and has been produced in France since 1982 by Ultralair were it has proved hugely popular -- with over 5000 sold world wide! (Making it the most numerous microlight?)

Produced in this country by Cyclone Airsports near Oxford, the AX3 is being flown by an RAF flying club – quite a feather in its cap!

The structure is of light alloy tubing with Dacron covering the cockpit pod being of GRP with optional side doors. Lateral control is by flaperons the other axes being looked after by a conventional tailplane, elevator, fin and rudder. The tricycle 'gear is sprung and braked with a steerable nose-wheel.

It is available as a kit and is PFA approved.

A development, the AX2000, marketed by Pegasus Aviation has a water cooled Rotax 582.

There are 42 AX3s and 23 AX2000s on the UK Reg.

DATA	IMPERIAL		METRIC	
Span	32	ft	19.8	m
Wing area	175	ft²	16.5	m²
Aspect ratio	5.8		5.8	
Empty weight	429	lb	195	kg
Loaded weight	858	lb	390	kg
Wing loading	4.9	lb/ft²	23.9	kg/m²
Max speed	75	mph	120	kmh
Cruise speed	60	mph	96	kmh
Stalling speed	34	mph	54	kmh
Climb rate	433	ft/min	133	m/min
Range	200	mls	320	km

NOBLE-HARDMAN
SNOWBIRD

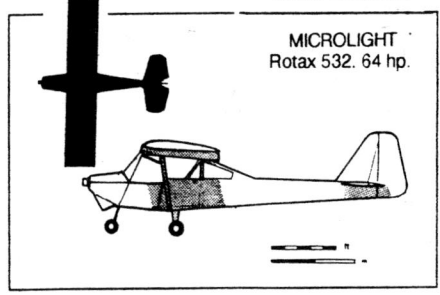

MICROLIGHT
Rotax 532. 64 hp.

This British designed and built microlight two seater was the brainchild of Richard Noble (not the ARV designer) in 1982, and launched as the Noble-Hardman Snowbird. In 1984 it was marketed by the Snowbird Aeroplane Company in Cowbridge, S. Glamorgan run by Ex Snowbird test pilot Marcus Edwards .

This is a factory built aeroplane (no kits yet) with a fully enclosed fuselage constructed of light alloy tubes and covered in Dacron. The two spar wing has, unusually, spoilers on the top surface instead of ailerons. The tricycle undercarriage has a steerable nose wheel and cable operated main wheel brakes - the cable being situated in the cabin roof!

There are 20+ Snowbirds currently on the British Register, most are airworthy and one, G-MVIM, is in the Yorkshire Air Museum.

DATA	IMPERIAL		METRIC	
Span	31	ft	9.5	m
Wing area	186	ft²	17.4	m²
Aspect ratio	5.2		5.2	
Empty weight	399	lb	181	kg
Loaded weight	848	lb	385	kg
Wing loading	4.6	lb/ft²	22.4	kg/m²
Max speed	75	mph	120	kmh
Cruise speed	60	mph	96	kmh
Stalling speed	38	mph	61	kmh
Climb rate	900	ft/min	277	m/min
Range	180	mls	288	km

Designed by Mike Whittaker - as are all the MW range - the MW6 is the two seater of the family, either in tandem (MW6) or side by side (MW6S) - the prototype MW6S being nick-named Fat Boy Flyer.

It is a microlight of simple but soundly engineered construction with large diameter light alloy tubes taking the principle loads in single spar wings and tail boom. The wing has plywood ribs, fabric covering, half span ailerons and is braced to the cockpit 'pod' by a single strut. The constructional configuration is basically the same as the well proven MW 4 & MW 5.

This two seat MW has proved popular, there being 54 or more on the latest British Register. It is a PFA approved design

The tricycle undercarriage main wheels are mounted on leaf springs.

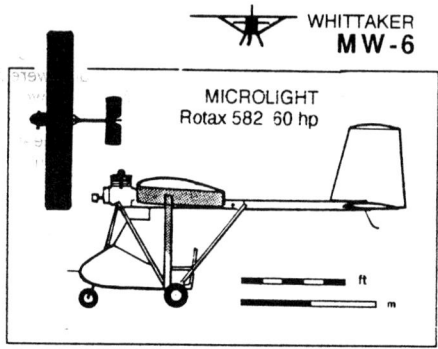

WHITTAKER
MW-6

MICROLIGHT
Rotax 582 60 hp

DATA	IMPERIAL		METRIC	
Span	32.7	ft	10.1	m
Wing area	164	ft^2	15.4	m^2
Aspect ratio	6.5		6.5	
Empty weight	400	lb	182	kg
Loaded weight	858	lb	389	kg
Wing loading	5.2	lb/ft^2	25.4	kg/m^2
Max speed	86	mph	138	kmh
Cruise speed	63	mph	101	kmh
Stalling speed	34	mph	54	kmh
Climb rate	1000	ft/min	308	m/min
Range	150	mls	240	km

This attractive two seat Canadian design has been demonstrated around Europe by various agents and sales now include two, which are on the UK Register. 75+ have been built in the USA and Canada.

The prototype first flew in 1984 and current models offer a range of wingspans and engines. Designed to be assembled from a kit of parts, the Pelican's fuselage is of moulded GRP/Epoxy foam sandwich and the single strut braced wing is all metal (Early models had fabric covered wings).

Both nose wheel and tail-dragger undercarriages are available.

Rotax, Continental and Hapi engines ranging in power from 52 to 115 hp are also options. (Figures below are for the PL version with Rotax 912, 80 hp).

The Pelican, with its high aspect ratio wing has a good cruise speed on modest power using only four gallons of fuel per hour. The roomy cockpit is well appointed and has comprehensive instrumentation.

Agencies for this good looking aeroplane have come and gone – leaving the type currently 'stranded'!

ULTRAVIA
PELICAN

LIGHTPLANE
Rotax 912, 80 hp.

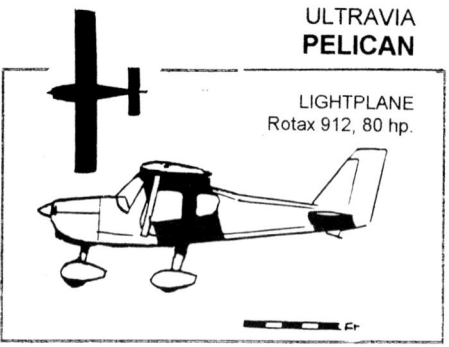

DATA	IMPERIAL		METRIC	
Span	29.5	ft	9.1	m
Wing area	108	sq.ft	10.1	sq.m
Aspect ratio	8			
Empty wt	700	lb.	318	kg.
Loaded wt	1250	lb.	567	kg.
Wing loading	11.5	lb/sq.ft	56	kg/sq.m
Max speed	135	mph	216	kmph
Cruising speed	123	mph	197	kmph
Stall speed	48	mph	77	kmph
Climb	950	fpm	293	mpm
Range	600	mls	960	km

The Canadian, Chris Heintz designed, CH701 STOL first flew in 1986 and is now produced by Zenair in Mexico, Missouri, as an all metal kit plane. Available as a tail-dragger or a nose wheel trike the CH701 is an ultra light two seater with a genuine STOL performance. The wing has full span, Fowler type flaperons plus full span fixed leading edge slats; giving it a single seat stall of 23 mph. – a claimed Lift Coefficient of 3.1.

Power may be supplied by Rotax 503, 532, 912 or other units up to 100 hp.

The CH701 is an approved design in many countries and over 400 have been built worldwide, including six on the UK Register.

PFA approved, the '701 is an ultralight that has a 'real' aeroplane feel about it. The metal structure is stressed for +6 to –3g and is devoid of double curvature panels and is mainly secured by blind rivets (Pop rivets). The main gear is on a leaf spring and the steerable nose wheel is bungee sprung – or as a tail-dragger, a sprung tail wheel.

Zenair and the Czech Aircraft Works have co-operated to build an economic crop duster version.

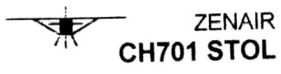
ZENAIR
CH701 STOL

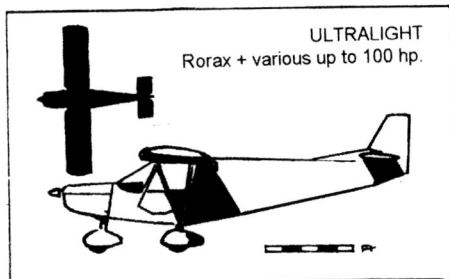
ULTRALIGHT
Rorax + various up to 100 hp.

Data for 52 hp Rotax 503 model.

DATA	IMPERIAL		METRIC	
Span	27	ft	8.3	m
Wing area	122	sq.ft	11.5	sq.m
Aspect ratio	6			
Empty wt	430	lb.	195	kg.
Loaded wt	880	lb.	400	kg.
Wing loading	7.2	lb/sq.ft	35	kg/sq.m
Max speed	82	mph	131	kmph
Cruising speed	74	mph	118	kmph
Stall speed	26	mph	42	kmph
Climb	820	fpm	253	mpm
Range	200	mls	320	km

A gem from Australia! The two seater Jabiru first flew in 1989, was certificated in '91 and is now well established in the UK. An all composites kit, or factory built plane powered by the company's own engine.

This is the first aero engine to be designed and approved in Australia; the Jabiru is a four cylinder, horizontally opposed four stroke with direct drive to the prop via a six bearing crankshaft. In two models, 1600 cc/60 hp and 2200 cc/80 both quiet and efficient they are increasingly sought after.

The wing, braced by a single steel strut, has a 'glass skin over a foam core and composites spar and has generous plain flaps and inset ailerons. The fuselage is built in two halves, top and bottom, and houses the side by side dual control seating, fuel tank (behind seats) and the hydraulically braked tricycle undercarriage.

There are 20+ on the UK Register and others are being built with PFA approval

JABIRU AIRCRAFT
JABIRU ST

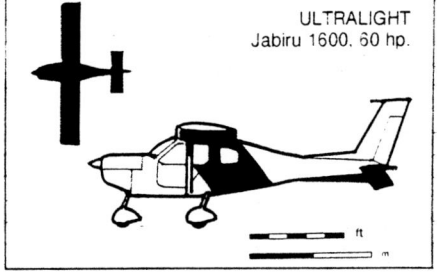
ULTRALIGHT
Jabiru 1600. 60 hp.

DATA	IMPERIAL		METRIC	
Span	26.3	ft	8	m
Wing area	85	ft^2	7.9	m^2
Aspect ratio	8.1		8.1	
Empty weight	517	lb	275	kg
Loaded weight	990	lb	450	kg
Wing loading	11.6	lb/ft^2	56.6	kg/m^2
Max speed	134	mph	214	kmh
Cruise speed	120	mph	192	kmh
Stalling speed	46	mph	73	kmh
Climb rate	800	ft/min	244	m/min
Range	575	mls	920	km

Developed from the single seat Sparrow Sport Special the two seat, side by side, Sparrow 2 is a product of Carlson Aircraft Inc. of East Palestine, Ohio.

This neat microlight/ultralight comes in kit form - factory built models are under consideration - and has a welded steel tube fuselage and tail unit. The wing spars are of extruded light alloy with built up light alloy ribs; all covered in Dacron.

The tricycle undercarriage is bungee sprung and has hydraulic disc brakes on the main wheels.

Dual controls are standard and its short field performance is very good with an initial climb rate of 1000 feet/min.

There are only two on the UK Register currently, the pilots of which report 'excellent handling characteristics with no bad habits'.

CARLSON
SPARROW 2

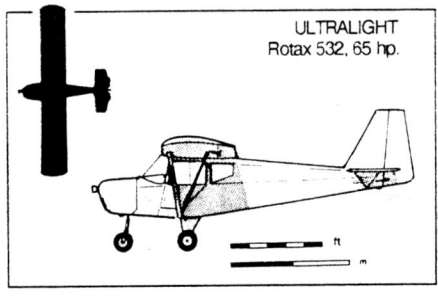

ULTRALIGHT
Rotax 532, 65 hp.

DATA	IMPERIAL		METRIC	
Span	32	ft	9.8	m
Wing area	144	ft^2	13.5	m^2
Aspect ratio	7.1		7.1	
Empty weight	390	lb	177	kg
Loaded weight	945	lb	429	kg
Wing loading	6.5	lb/ft^2	32	kg/m^2
Max speed	90	mph	144	kmh
Cruise speed	70	mph	112	kmh
Stalling speed	30	mph	48	kmh
Climb rate	1000	ft/min	308	m/min
Range	300	mls	480	km

The two seat Rans S6 Coyote, developed from the single seat S4/S5, went into production in 1990 at the Rans Hays factory in Kansas and is available with three motor and three wing options covering its categorisation from microlight to 1100 lb. light aircraft with a 120 mph. cruise.(Shortly to be adapted to the 450 kg microlight category, with Rotax 582).

The kit comprises a welded tube cabin module and bolt together light alloy tubes for the rear fuselage. The wing has two tubular spars and a slip on Dacron covering with light alloy riblets in sewn pockets. It has ailerons and flaps - not flaperons.

Other options are Trike or Taildragger, spats or no spats, and disc or drum brakes. A unusual option is a rocket deployed total aircraft recovery ballistic parachute!

The Coyote is a PFA approved design, with 125 on the Reg. and flying plus 40 odd being built.

Data below is for the 450 kg microlight.

RANS
S6 COYOTE

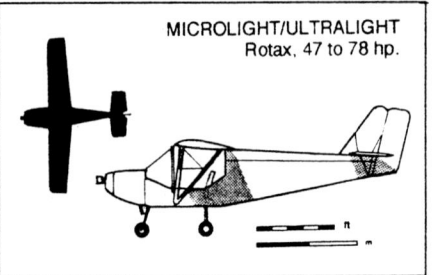

MICROLIGHT/ULTRALIGHT
Rotax, 47 to 78 hp.

DATA	IMPERIAL		METRIC	
Span	34.5	ft	10.6	m
Wing area	155	sq.ft	15.1	sq.m
Aspect ratio	7.6			
Empty wt	499	lb.	227	kg.
Loaded wt	990	lb.	450	kg.
Wing loading	6.4	lb/sq.ft	31.2	kg/sq.m
Max speed	100	mph	160	kmph
Cruising speed	80	mph	128	kmph
Stall speed	34	mph	54	kmph
Climb	1000	fpm	308	mpm
Range	350	mls	560	km

Initially badged as the Partenavia P92 Echo this Pascale brothers design is now produced by Tecnam at their plant near Naples.

A two seat ultralight that first flew in 1993 the Echo has a metal tube and sheet airframe with fabric covering and GRP fairings. It meets JAR/VLA requirements and is stressed for +6/-3g.

The latest model has a re-shaped rear fuselage since the last edition of this book and our drawing here has been suitably modified.

Five version are available all powered by the Rotax 912 of 80 or 100 hp. and the data on these various models is similar – except for the floatplane version, the Seasky, which is, obviously, heavier and slower.

The flaps are electrically operated as is the trim tab on the all-moving tailplane and the fuel tanks are contained in the wing leading edge.

The first one, for PFA approval, is now on the UK Register – MR Aviation of Dorchester, Dorset are the sole UK Distributors.

Data below for 100hp model.

DATA	IMPERIAL		METRIC	
Span	30.6	ft	9.3	m
Wing area	142	sq.ft	13.2	sq.m
Aspect ratio	6.6			
Empty wt	619	lb.	281	kg.
Loaded wt	1212	lb.	550	kg.
Wing loading	8.53	lb/sq.ft	41.6	kg/sq.m
Max speed	135	mph	216	kmph
Cruising speed	117	mph	187	kmph
Stall speed	37	mph	59	kmph
Climb	1260'	fpm	388	mpm
Range	448	mls	717	km

TECNAM
P92 ECHO

ULTRALIGHT
Rotax 912, 80/100 hp.

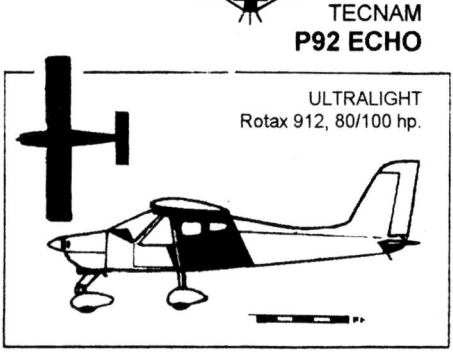

The Light Aircraft Data Book is now in its fourth year and has found a niche in many an enthusiast's library and pilot's glove pocket.
We intend to go on adding to and updating the book.
We are always glad to hear from owners, builders and purveyors of interesting aeroplanes

SMALL PLANE PUBLISHING
Tel/Fax 01963 23423

A Czechoslovakian designed microlight that arrived in the UK in 1993. The Sluka is a single seater, though a two seat version, of almost identical appearance, the ST-4 Aztek has been introduced.

Of standard microlight construction - light alloy tubes and Dacron covering - the Sluka has a neat GRP nacelle with an integral semi-reclining seat.

This is a three axis control aircraft that comes in a very comprehensive kit, complete with engine and all instruments - but the wheel spats are part of a 'speed modification' kit!

A handy feature is the folding wing arrangement making for ease of towing and storage.

Lateral control is by flaperons and the other axes being looked after by the conventional fin/rudder and tailplane/ elevator.

The main 'gear wheels are sprung on a carbon fibre semi-elliptic beam and the nose wheel is stearable.

There are a dozen Slukas currently on the 'Reg. (and 8 being built) but the attractive price and comprehensive kitting should ensure that many more will be added.

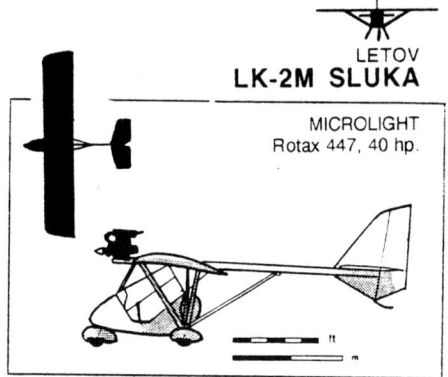

LETOV
LK-2M SLUKA
MICROLIGHT
Rotax 447, 40 hp.

DATA	IMPERIAL		METRIC	
Span	34	ft	10.4	m
Wing area	162	ft²	15.3	m²
Aspect ratio	7.1		7.1	
Empty weight	341	lb	155	kg
Loaded weight	605	lb	275	kg
Wing loading	3.7	lb/ft²	18.2	kg/m²
Max speed	78	mph	125	kmh
Cruise speed	55	mph	88	kmh
Stalling speed	25	mph	40	kmh
Climb rate	700	ft/min	215	m/min
Range	160	mls	256	km

Dan Denney designed the highly successful Kitfox in 1984 and, as Denney Aircraft produced hundreds of kits. The Vixen, to Denney's design, is built by the Skystar Aviation Corp. who have taken over Denney. The Vixen, the first nose-wheeler in this range, took to the air in 1994 and is structurally similar to the Kitfox, ie. welded steel tube fuselage, tubular spar wings with ply' ribs all fabric covered.

The Rotax 912, as fitted to the Kitfox, the Continental IO-200 (100 hp) or the Continental IO-240 (125 hp) are all engine options.

The wings, of 29 or 32 ft. span, fold for ease of towing or storage and are of an improved laminar flow section which combined with the 'Fowler type' flaps improve its characteristics and delay the stall.

Lateral control is by the 80% span flaperons and the tailplane has an electrical trimmer.

None yet on the UK Reg.

SKYSTAR
VIXEN
LIGHT PLANE
Continental IO-240, 125 hp.

DATA	IMPERIAL		METRIC	
Span	32	ft	9.75	m
Wing area	132	ft²	12.2	m²
Aspect ratio	7.75		7.75	
Empty weight	894	lb	406	kg
Loaded weight	1400	lb	635	kg
Wing loading	10.6	lb/ft²	51.8	kg/m²
Max speed	133	mph	213	kmh
Cruise speed	120	mph	192	kmh
Stalling speed	44	mph	71	kmh
Climb rate	800	ft/min	246	m/min
Range	500	mls	800	km

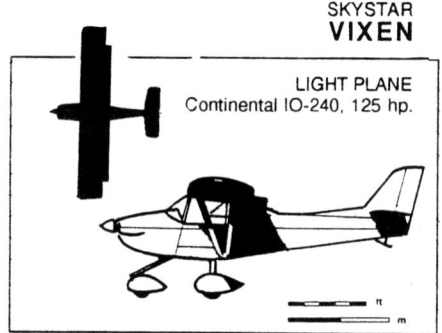

From the same stable as the sleek and fast Glassair the high wing, side by side two seat Glastar is not, in spite of its swoopy lines, an all composites aeroplane like its sister. Construction is mixed, GRP panels cover a welded steel tube forward fuselage - aft of the cabin it is composite - trike or tail-dragger gear can be easily fitted. All flying surfaces are metal and of simple construction - the high aspect ratio wing has only four full chord ribs per side - and is 'Fowler" flapped. (The flaps are manually operated).

The Glastar is fitted with Lycomings of 160 hp and 120 hp – the data below is for the lower powered version.

The Glastar is much compared with the, now venerable, Cessna 150/152 as a trainer, which it out performs in both range and speed. It is roomier and has wings designed to fold alongside the fuselage. A lot of pluses - but can it stand up to the, year in year out, hammering of training that the '150s have?

Wing vortex generators and tailplane cuffs are fitted to later models, making a nice handling aeroplane even nicer.

Five on the 'Register and ten being built.

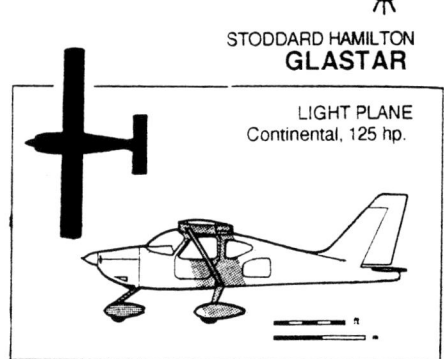

STODDARD HAMILTON
GLASTAR

LIGHT PLANE
Continental, 125 hp.

DATA	IMPERIAL		METRIC	
Span	35	ft	10.8	m
Wing area	116	ft²	10.9	m²
Aspect ratio	10.5		10.5	
Empty weight	1100	lb	500	kg
Loaded weight	1900	lb	862	kg
Wing loading	16.4	lb/ft²	80	kg/m²
Max speed	156	mph	250	kmh
Cruise speed	140	mph	141	kmh
Stalling speed	45	mph	72	kmh
Climb rate	1000	ft/min	308	m/min

The Ukranian Aeroprakt A22 Foxbat is, at the time of writing, being assessed by the PFA for BCAR-S approval. In the 450kg SLA category, the design was originally called the Shark and its designer carries the famous name of Yuri Yakovlev.

The A22 is already approved in Germany (Where it has a control wheel instead of a 'stick) and is marketed in the USA by Spectrum Aircraft Corp as the Valor.

The airframe kit is composed of riveted metal sheet and tube with fabric covering plus GRP panels and fairings. The wings come completely assembled less covering.

Fitted with a Rotax 912-S engine the Foxbat has a real STOL performance, the full span flaperons getting its stall down to 34 mph. and the initial climb is a respectable 1200 fpm.

Identification features include the large glazed area aft of the cabin, the large fin and rudder and the swept forward wings.

Marketed in the UK by The Small Light Aeroplane Co. Ltd. at Otherton Airfield.

AEROPRAKT
A22 FOXBAT

ULTRALIGHT / SLA
Rotax 912-S, 100 hp.

DATA	IMPERIAL		METRIC	
Span	32.4	ft	10	m
Wing area	145	sq.ft	13.7	sq.m
Aspect ratio	7.1			
Empty wt	566	lb.	255	kg.
Loaded wt	991	lb.	450	kg.
Wing loading	6.8	lb/sq.ft	33	kg/sq.m
Max speed	100	mph	160	kmph
Cruising speed	85	mph	136	kmph
Stall speed	34	mph	54	kmph
Climb	1200	fpm	370	mpm
Range	600	mls	960	km

Based on the American Weedhopper design (As are the AX2000 and AX3) the X'AIR is the latest variant – with a difference – it is the *first* UK microlight to be certificated in the new '450 kg' category.

Built in India and shipped to the UK via Rand Kar (France), the Carnelford and Wessex Light Aeroplane Co. in Cornwall are the sole agents in the UK.

The mods required to the basic 'AX' design included an extra jury strut in the wing brace, a more substantial and higher, spring/gas strut undercarriage, a handbrake and a nose-wheel centring spring.

A bolted aluminium tube airframe is covered in a 'suit' of pre-tailored Dacron; simple and strong the Xair has a very short build time,(Has been built in a weekend!).

Though dual controls are standard, the rules do not allow the X'AIR to be used as an official trainer – must be factory built.

Its STOL performance, ease of build and low price should ensure a successful run for this microlight.

450 are flying worlwide, fifteen in the UK – many others being built here.

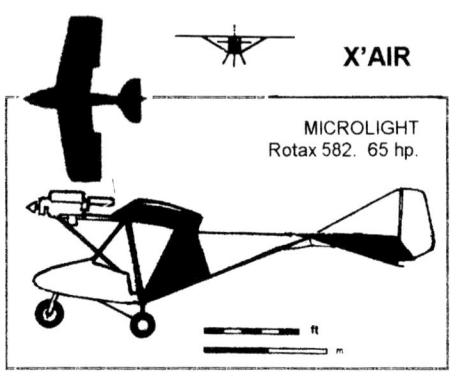

X'AIR

MICROLIGHT
Rotax 582. 65 hp.

DATA	IMPERIAL		METRIC	
Span	32	ft	9.8	m
Wing area	170	sq.ft	16	sq.m
Aspect ratio	6			
Empty wt	522	lb.	237	kg.
Loaded wt	991	lb.	450	kg.
Wing loading	5.8	lb/sq.ft	28	kg/sq.m
Max speed	75	mph	120	kmph
Cruising speed	53	mph	84	kmph
Stall speed	30	mph	48	kmph
Climb	600	fpm	185	mpm
Range	189	mls	302	km

The latest design from German firm Ikarus Comco, producers of the popular tube and fabric C22 microlight, is the C42, of more traditional layout with a sleek composites fuselage and tube and fabric wings.

First deliveries of the C42 began in 1997 and in the 'States, 1998 as the C42 Cyclone, marketed by Flightstar Sportplanes.

The strut braced wings fold for economic hangarage and the tube and fabric 'tail feathers' are also strut braced. The 50% span flaps are electrically operated.

Unusually for a new type the undercarriage is of the three strut split axle type rather than the fashionable cantilever spring leg. 'Speed fairings' are standard on the hydraulically braked wheels.

It is claimed that a ballistic recovery parachute is fitted as *standard* – a brilliant 'non-extra' safety feature.

The side by side seats are reached under upward hinging doors on each side.

Straddling the SLA and 450 kg microlight category the Ikarus C42 looks like a winner.

IKARUS COMCO
C 42

SLA/MICROLIGHT
Rotax 912, 80 hp.

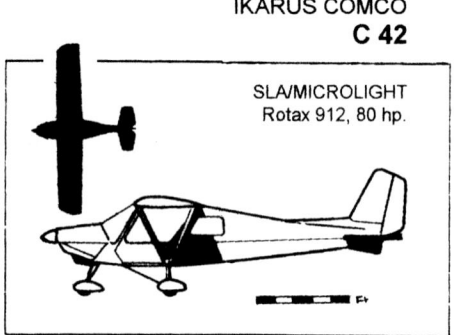

DATA	IMPERIAL		METRIC	
Span	31	ft	9.45	m
Wing area	134	sq.ft	12.5	sq.m
Aspect ratio	7.2			
Empty wt	551	lb.	250	kg.
Loaded wt	992	lb.	450	kg.
Wing loading	7.4	lb/sq.ft	36	kg/sq.m
Max speed	120	mph	192	kmph
Cruising speed	109	mph	175	kmph
Stall speed	40	mph	63	kmph
Climb	1000	fpm	308	mpm
Range	497	mls	800	km

When first flown in 1957 the 210 was a four seater based on the Model 182, with a strut braced wing, but having a retractable tricycle undercarriage and a 260 hp. Continental engine. Various modifications, mainly to windows and cabin rear roof line took the model number up to 210D - when it also became Centurion and acquired two child seats, making it 4+2. (1500 of the 210 to 210D were built).

With the 210G the cantilever wing was introduced and later the 210K became a full adult six seater at an AUW of 3800 lb. Wing tip and stabiliser changes plus nose lights, turbo engines and finally, pressurisation took the type to 210R (325 hp. Continental). Over 7000 of the cantilever 210s were built, the most numerous being the 210L Centurion, with 6 seats nose light and tubular legs instead of spring steel - 2070 of these being built.

The construction is standard Cessna all metal with large cabin doors either side.(The complicated doors fully covering the retracted wheels were dropped in '79) Though weighing in at around two tons, its owners say it handles like a '172 - and furthermore, they are hanging on to them! There are 14 on the UK Register. Figs. for 210N (310 hp.)

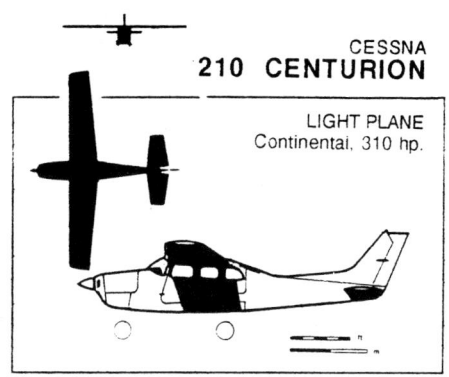

CESSNA 210 CENTURION

LIGHT PLANE
Continental, 310 hp.

DATA	IMPERIAL		METRIC	
Span	36.7	ft	11.3	m
Wing area	175.5	ft²	16.4	m²
Aspect ratio	7.6		7.6	
Empty weight	2303	lb	1045	kg
Loaded weight	4000	lb	1816	kg
Wing loading	22.8	lb/ft²	111	kg/m²
Max speed	235	mph	376	kmh
Cruise speed	221	mph	353	kmh
Stalling speed	67	mph	107	kmh
Climb rate	930	ft/min	286	m/min
Range	1800	mls	2880	km

Introduced in 1967, the Cessna Cardinal, a roomy four seater, had a cantilever wing; though somewhat unusual for the range, this configuration was always a favourite with Clyde Cessna - his first series production 'plane, the Model A of 1927 was, in fact, a high wing cantilever monoplane!

First models of the '177 had 150 hp. Lycomings which were replaced by 180 hp. units in the 177A. The 177B or Cardinal 2 had a fifth (child's) seat, a constant speed prop. and curved down wing tips. The 1978 Cardinal Classic was a de Luxe version of the 177B.

The big step of retracting the undercarriage came in 1970 with the Cardinal RG (Retractable Gear) which also incorporated a 200 hp. Lycoming - the combination adding about 40 mph. to the top speed.

The sleek and slippery RG has a straight tapered wing (like the other cantilever Cessna, the Centurion) electric flaps and an all moving stabilator.

There are 29 Cardinals on the UK Reg. 20 of them RGs. Total production is 4000.

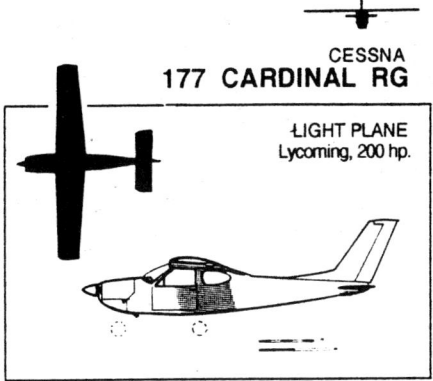

CESSNA 177 CARDINAL RG

LIGHT PLANE
Lycoming, 200 hp.

DATA	IMPERIAL		METRIC	
Span	35 5	ft	11	m
Wing area	174	ft²	16.3	m²
Aspect ratio	7		7	
Empty weight	1707	lb	775	kg
Loaded weight	2800	lb	1271	kg
Wing loading	16.1	lb/ft²	78.6	kg/m²
Max speed	180	mph	290	kmh
Cruise speed	170	mph	273	kmh
Stalling speed	57	mph	92	kmh
Climb rate	925	ft/min	282	m/min
Range	1005	mls	1608	km

American Airlines pilot Tom Cassutt designed and built the first Cassutt Special 1 in 1954 as a small fast and practical aeroplane suitable for home building.

After winning it's class at the National Air Races in 1958 a Cassutt Special 2 was built-- smaller and faster with the pilot 'shoe horned' into a very narrow cockpit -- an out and out racer. And twenty five years after the first flight Cassutt Specials finished 1st, 2nd, and 3rd in the Cleveland Nationals.

2000 plans have been sold world wide and in 1985 at least 125 were flying. 17 are on the UK Reg.

The wooden wing has no incidence, no dihedral and no flaps! --and the spring steel legs carry braked wheels.

The Cassut is a PFA approved design; two are being built.

CASSUTT SPECIAL

ULTRALIGHT
Continental 85 hp

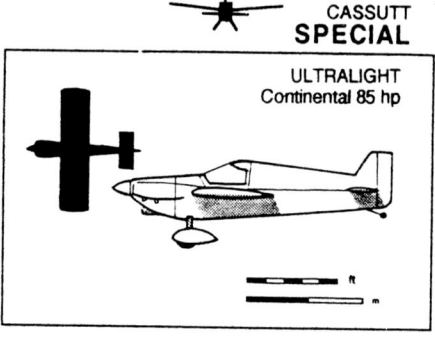

DATA	IMPERIAL		METRIC	
Span	17	ft	5.18	m
Wing area	76.5	ft^2	7.11	m^2
Aspect ratio	3.75		3.75	
Empty weight	500	lb	227	kg
Loaded weight	800	lb	363	kg
Wing loading	10.5	lb/ft^2	51.24	kg/m^2
Max speed	200	mph	322	kmh
Cruise speed	180	mph	290	kmh
Stalling speed	50	mph	80	kmh
Climb rate	3000	ft/min	914	m/min
Range	490	mls	788	km

A plans homebuilt aerobatic single seater, the Akro won the US Championships in 1975 and competed at world level in the mid 70s.

The design is PFA approved and several have been built in the UK – six are on the 'Reg, three airworthy.

The prototype first flew in 1967 and a bigger wing version, the Model B, in 1969. Like most modern aerobats the Akro is without dihedral or incidence and the wooden two-spar wing is built in one piece. The ailerons are fabric covered and have ground adjustable tabs. The fuselage is of welded steel tube construction with Ceconite covering as is the tail unit, which is wire braced. The tailplane and rudder and elevator tabs are ground adjustable.

The cantilever, spring steel tail dragger undercarriage has disc brakes and the sreerable tail-wheel is by Maule. Some early models had a floor window

Fixed pitch or constant speed propellers may be fitted and special fuel tanks for prolonged inverted flying may be fitted.

The Akro has had many variant designs based on it inc. the Extra 230 (Akro Laser) and the Pace Spirit.

STEPHENS AKRO

LIGHTPLANE
Lycoming, 180 hp.

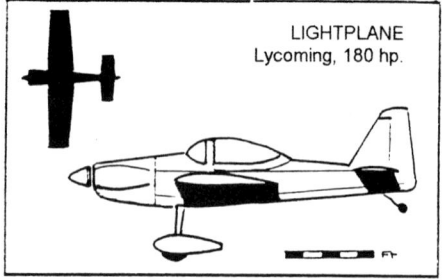

DATA	IMPERIAL		METRIC	
Span	24.5	ft	7.5	m
Wing area	94	sq.ft	8.7	sq.m
Aspect ratio	6.4			
Empty wt	950	lb.	431	kg.
Loaded wt	1300	lb.	589	kg.
Wing loading	13.8	lb/sq.ft	67	kg/sq.m
Max speed	170	mph	274	kmph
Cruising speed	160	mph	257	kmph
Stall speed	55	mph	89	kmph
Climb	4000'	fpm	1220	mpm
Range	350	mls	563	km

MONNET
SONERAI

The small, sleek Sonerai, first flown in 1973, comes in single and two seat versions - Sonerai 1 and 2 respectively.

An American design, the Sonerai is constructed in the American way with a welded steel tube fuselage but has metal cantilever wings, in mid or low wing configuration, which carry full span ailerons.

The standard power unit is the reliable 2200 cc VW of 82 hp giving the Sonerai 2 a top speed of 165 mph.

Marketed ready made or in kit form by Mosler of Hendersonville USA, over 500 have been built stateside and 17 are registered in this country - one being built.

It is a PFA approved design which is also available with tricycle landing gear.

The figures below are for the Sonerai 2.

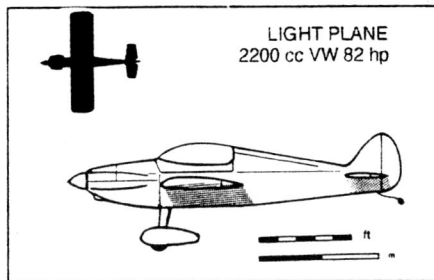

LIGHT PLANE
2200 cc VW 82 hp

DATA	IMPERIAL		METRIC	
Span	18.8	ft	5.69	m
Wing area	84	ft^2	7.5	m^2
Aspect ratio	4.15		4.15	
Empty weight	500	lb	227	kg
Loaded weight	1150	lb	521	kg
Wing loading	13.7	lb/ft^2	66.8	kg/m^2
Max speed	160	mph	257	kmh
Cruise speed	130	mph	209	kmh
Stalling speed	44	mph	71	kmh
Climb rate	500	ft/min	152	m/min
Range	350	mls	563	km

HAPI
CYGNET

The Cygnet, designed and built by ex Boeing 747 captain, Bert Sisler, has had a chequered background. Known first as the Sisler Cygnet, the rights and prototype were sold to HAPI (Homebuilt Aircraft Parts Inc.) in 1983, hence the HAPI Cygnet, only to merge with Mosler in 1992 - so sometimes known as the Mosler Cygnet.

This sturdy, side by side, two seater has, like the ARV 2, a shoulder mounted swept forward wing giving excellent visibility from the high set cockpit.

The all wooden wing, designed to fold for storage, is multi sparred with ply wood ribs, the whole being encased in a geodetic like matrix of spruce laths, giving it great strength in torsion and shear.

The fuselage is built up with welded steel tube with a few wooden formers under the fabric covering.

Rotax, Mosler and VW engines have been fitted, the data below is for the 62 hp. VW model.

The first UK example flew at the 1995 PFA rally, there are now five on the UK Register; it is PFA approved and two are being built.

ULTRALIGHT
VW or Rotax 60 hp.

DATA	IMPERIAL		METRIC	
Span	30	ft	9.2	m
Wing area	120	ft^2	11.3	m^2
Aspect ratio	7		7	
Empty weight	585	lb	266	kg
Loaded weight	1100	lb	500	kg
Wing loading	9.1	lb/ft^2	44	kg/m^2
Max speed	100	mph	160	kmh
Cruise speed	90	mph	144	kmh
Stalling speed	41	mph	66	kmh
Climb rate	600	ft/min	185	m/min
Range	300	mls	480	km

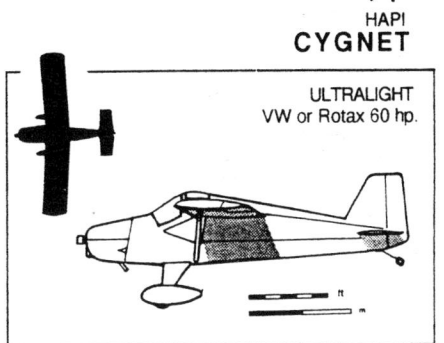

Bearing a Yakovlev family resemblance to the late model YAK 18, the '55, which first flew in 1984 is a smaller aeroplane designed from the start as an aerobat and developed from the YAK 50 of 1975 vintage.

The '55 differs from its predecessor in having a mid wing of symmetrical section with zero dihedral as a opposed to a low wing and a fixed rather than retractable undercarriage giving it a seriously aerobatic look!

Such is the pace of aerobatic aircraft design at World' level that the '55 was never quite as successful as the '50 and subsequently was released on to the open market -   one currently on the UK Register.

The all metal construction makes for a heavier plane than most of its competitors - hence the lighter weight YAK 55M.

With its full span ailerons and big radial engine the YAK 55 is still very competitive and a delight to fly.

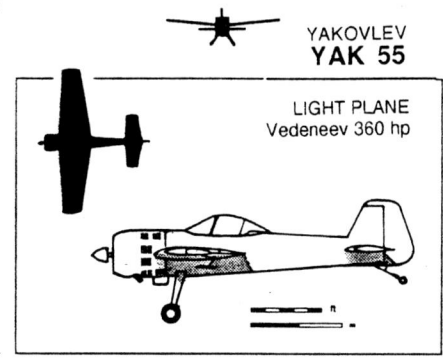

YAKOVLEV YAK 55

LIGHT PLANE
Vedeneev 360 hp

DATA	IMPERIAL		METRIC	
Span	26.5	ft	8.16	m
Wing area	138	ft²	13	m²
Aspect ratio	5.1		5.1	
Empty weight	1594	lb	724	kg
Loaded weight	1894	lb	860	kg
Wing loading	13.8	lb/ft²	67	kg/m²
Max speed	136	mph	218	kmh
Cruise speed	108	mph	172	kmh
Stalling speed	51	mph	82	kmh
Climb rate	3050	ft/min	939	m/min
Range	431	mls	690	km

Built in the USA by Rans Co. and marketed in the UK by Sport Air of Thirsk, Yorkshire, the S10 is available as a kitplane. The kit is PFA approved as non-aerobatic, but is cleared for aerobatics in the USA. (Late news - Brit. agents can check individual a/c during construction for aerobatic clearance.)

The two seat, side by side, accommodation is within a welded steel tube fuselage with a two door centre hinged canopy. The wings have alloy tube spars and ribs and are fabric covered, flaperons run full span and two struts brace the wing to the lower longerons.

The performance, with it s fairly high wing loading, is lively and is not for the tyro.' It's Rotax 65hp. engine gives it a cruising speed of 100 mph and a climb of 500 fpm.

200 have been built in the USA, 28 are on the UK Register and 6 are being built – PFA approved.

RANS S10 SAKOTA

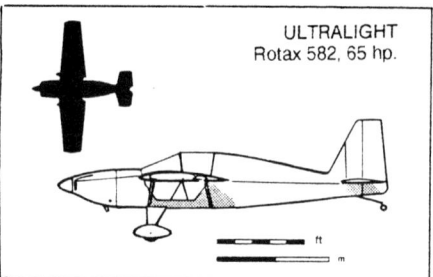

ULTRALIGHT
Rotax 582, 65 hp.

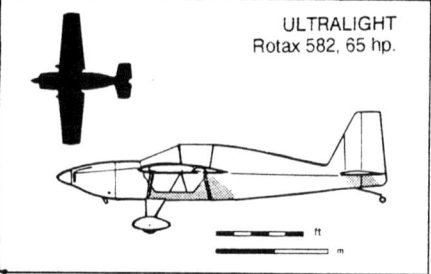

DATA	IMPERIAL		METRIC	
Span	24	ft	7.4	m
Wing area	98	ft²	9.1	m²
Aspect ratio	5.4		5.4	
Empty weight	420	lb	191	kg
Loaded weight	895	lb	406	kg
Wing loading	9.1	lb/ft²	44.5	kg/m²
Max speed	120	mph	192	kmh
Cruise speed	95	mph	152	kmh
Stalling speed	26	mph	42	kmh
Climb rate	500	ft/min	152	m/min
Range	200	mls	320	km

The TEAM bit of Minimax stands for its parent company Tennessee Engineering and Manufacturing Inc. In the UK it was factored by UFM (Ultralight Flying Machines) of Gloucestershire until recently.

First flown in the USA in 1985 and sold as a kit, component built, or plans, the Minimax has sold well and over 500 plans have been purchased to date. In the UK 47 are on the UK Register and ten are being built. Most Minimax have the Rotax 447 engine, an alternative fit is the 40 hp. Mosler (VW based). Data below is for the Rotax version.

Of all wood construction with mainly fabric covering the Minimax has its mainplane strut braced to the unsprung landing gear and full span 'flaperons', which when doing duty as flaps, help achieve its landing speed of 34 mph. As there is no agent or distributor for the aircraft, in the UK, the Minimax Owners Club does a very good job of keeping owners happy.

TEAM MINIMAX

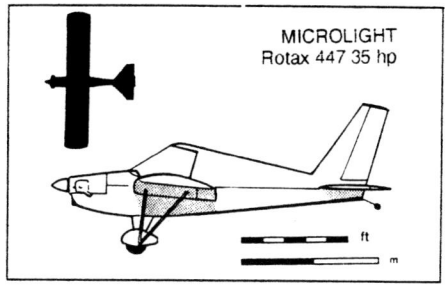

MICROLIGHT
Rotax 447 35 hp

DATA	IMPERIAL		METRIC	
Span	25	ft	7.7	m
Wing area	118	sq.ft	11.6	sq.m
Aspect ratio	5.3			
Empty wt	300	lb.	136	kg.
Loaded wt	560	lb.	254	kg.
Wing loading	4.75	lb/sq.ft	23	kg/sq.m
Max speed	82	mph	131	kmph
Cruising speed	70	mph	112	kmph
Stall speed	34	mph	54	kmph
Climb	1000	fpm	308	mpm
Range	120	mls	192	km

The Sukhoi SU 26 marked a departure from the strictly all sheet metal structures of the preceding Soviet aerobatic aircraft. The SU 26 has a welded steel tube fuselage and 'plastic' wings i.e.. GRP and foam skins over a ribless aerofoil with a carbon fibre spar. The airframe is incredibly strong - +12, -11g - plus a factor of x2! (24g ultimate!).

The SU 26 first flew in 1984 and compared with its compatriot, and rival, the YAK 55, is smaller, lighter, faster and quicker in the climb.

The SU 31 is the export version of the '26 and is generally better finished; the SU 29 is a two seat version of the '26.

The pilots seat is set at approximately 45 degrees, putting the rudder pedals at about shoulder height, this position enabling high g's to be sustained without early black/red out.

Looking rather similar to the YAK 55, the little waist level windows of the Sukhoi are a give away.

There are two SU26s on the UK Register.

SUKHOI SU 26

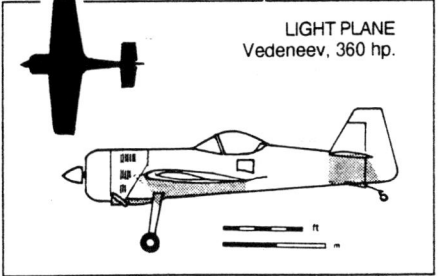

LIGHT PLANE
Vedeneev, 360 hp.

DATA	IMPERIAL		METRIC	
Span	25.3	ft	7.8	m
Wing area	125	ft^2	11.8	m^2
Aspect ratio	5.1		5.1	
Empty weight	1409	lb	640	kg
Loaded weight	2132	lb	968	kg
Wing loading	17	lb/ft^2	83	kg/m^2
Max speed	212	mph	340	kmh
Cruise speed	180	mph	288	kmh
Stalling speed	72	mph	115	kmh
Climb rate	4680	ft/min	1441	m/min
Range (ferry)	935	mls	1500	km

Walter Extra the German designer has created a range of superlative aerobatic monoplanes, both single and two seater. The Extra 300 is the latest model - the suffix indicates the horse power - essentially an aerobat, it is well suited to training and fast touring.

Earlier Extras of similar layout were the single seat Extra 230 and the Extra 260, all acclaimed in the aerobatic world. These earlier models had wooden wings whereas the '300 has a one piece composites wing with carbon fibre spars - the tailplane is of similar construction. The fuselage is of welded steel tube with part fabric and part metal covering - an unusual feature being the windows in the fuselage belly.

This is a factory built aeroplane and at the time of writing there are seven on the UK Register.

EXTRA
300

LIGHT PLANE
Lycoming, 300 hp.

DATA	IMPERIAL		METRIC	
Span	26.25	ft	8.08	m
Wing area	115	ft²	10.8	m²
Aspect ratio	6		6	
Empty weight	1500	lb	681	kg
Loaded weight	2095	lb	951	kg
Wing loading	17.3	lb/ft²	84.4	kg/m²
Max speed	220	mph	352	kmh
Cruise speed	181	mph	289	kmh
Stalling speed	64	mph	102	kmh
Climb rate	2600	ft/min	800	m/min
Range	517	mls	827	km

Scooping three trophies at the 1995 PFA Rally at Cranfield, Barry Smith's sleek little Acro Advanced aerobatic mid winger was the outcome of his quest for a simple, light weight (actually in the microlight weight category!) - aerobat powered by the cheap and reliable Volkswagen engine, thus putting serious aeros within the reach of many more.

The fuselage is of welded steel tube and the wings are wooden with fabric covering and no flaps. The powerful push rod operated balanced ailerons are 60% of the span.

The VW engine modified by Barry Smith for aerobatics - and renamed the Acro Aerobatic - is fuel injected and will run in all attitudes and with negative 'g'.

The cantilever spring legs carry disc braked wheels (of Barry Smith design) - spats, and at the back end a castoring tail wheel.

Only one Acro Advanced exists at the time of writing but production is under consideration and the type has PFA approval.

SMITH
ACRO ADVANCED

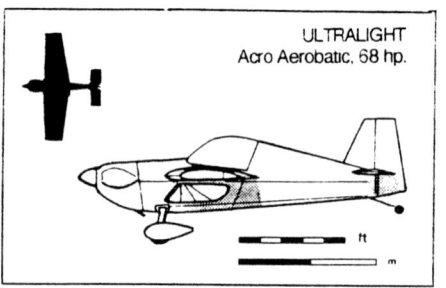

ULTRALIGHT
Acro Aerobatic, 68 hp.

DATA	IMPERIAL		METRIC	
Span	19.8	ft	6.1	m
Wing area	76	ft²	7.1	m²
Aspect ratio	5.1		5.1	
Empty weight	480	lb	218	kg
Loaded weight	750	lb	340	kg
Wing loading	9.8	lb/ft²	48	kg/m²
Max speed	170	mph	272	kmh
Cruise speed	140	mph	224	kmh
Stalling speed	48	mph	77	kmh
Climb rate	1500	ft/min	462	m/min
Range	479	mls	766	km

The original Tipsy Nipper, first flew in 1957 and was designed by E.O.Tips who worked for the Belgian arm of Fairey Aviation. Mks. 1 and 2 were produced in Belgium, as ready built or part kitted, up to 1966 when the manufacturing rights were sold off to various companies, amongst them being Slingsby who produced the Mk3, to suit British Airworthiness requirements.

The wing is a single spar, all wood, cantilever structure with a ply leading edge and fabric covering aft. There are no flaps and wing removal for storage is simple. The fuselage employs a light but strong (+6/-3g) welded steel tube framework with a GRP undertray and fabric covered rear end. The empennage consists of braced wood and fabric horizontal surfaces and a welded tube, fabric covered finless rudder. The rubber sprung legs have disc braked wheels and the nose wheel is steerable, making it very 'ground friendly'.

The Nipper is a PFA approved design and there are 34 on the UK Register.

TIPSY NIPPER

ULTRALIGHT
60 hp. Volkswagen

DATA	IMPERIAL		METRIC	
Span	19.6	ft	6.04	m
Wing area	80.7	ft^2	7.6	m^2
Aspect ratio	4.8		4.8	
Empty weight	465	lb	211	kg
Loaded weight	750	lb	340	kg
Wing loading	9.3	lb/ft^2	45.3	kg/m^2
Max speed	115	mph	184	kmh
Cruise speed	90	mph	144	kmh
Stalling speed	39	mph	62	kmh
Climb rate	650	ft/min	200	m/min
Range	184	mls	294	km

BOLKOW Bo 208 JUNIOR

Built in the USA to the designs of Bjorn Andreasson, and first flown in 1958 as the MFI 9B, the design was taken up by Bolkow in West Germany in 1962 and produced as the Bo 208 Junior, 200 being built in the first seven years.

The Junior seats two, side by side, and is fully aerobatic, its swept forward wing, braced by a single strut, is a distinguishing feature. Its airframe is all light alloy, the wing having the minimum ribs under a heavy gauge skin and the fuselage has unusual external stringers.

Power is supplied by a Rolls Royce Continental four cylinder engine of 100 hp. giving it a useful cruising speed of 125 mph. and a range of nearly 500 miles.

The Junior has a lot of 'modern' features for a 35 year old design - like cantilever spring legs and steerable nose wheel - and still looks good.

There are 19 on the UK Register.

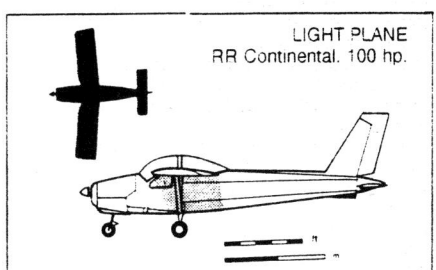

LIGHT PLANE
RR Continental. 100 hp.

DATA	IMP		METRIC	
Span	24.3	ft	7.4	m
Wing area	93.1	ft^2	8.65	m^2
Aspect ratio	6.4		6.4	
Empty weight	740	lb	335	kg
Loaded weight	1256	lb	570	kg
Wing loading	13.5	lb/ft^2	66	kg/m^2
Max speed	140	mph	224	kmh
Cruise speed	125	mph	200	kmh
Stalling speed	45	mph	72	kmh
Climb rate	790	ft/min	240	m/min
Range	510	mls	816	km

A two seat side by side microlight motor glider, the Chevvron in it's first form was a wooden aeroplane that first flew in 1980. Three years later it re-appeared as an all composites airframe.

The Chevvron is not marketed as a kit plane and is manufactured by AMF Microlight Ltd at Membury who also make trailers for gliders – and Chevvrons. (The wings are easily removed for trailer stowage).

At the time of writing 26 Chevvrons are flying and a squadron of enthusiastic Chevvron owners has been formed.

To counter extended landing float, glider type upper surface wing spoilers are fitted to some models.

A well built modern 'plane of original lines with a very quiet engine installation needing only 2 galls fuel per hour.

The Super Chevvron has a 45 hp. Limbach.

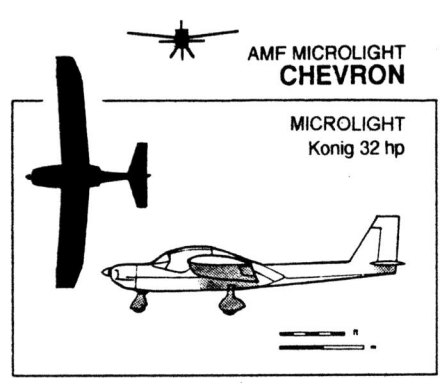

AMF MICROLIGHT
CHEVRON
MICROLIGHT
Konig 32 hp

DATA	IMPERIAL		METRIC	
Span	44	ft	13,5	m
Wing area	189	ft^2	17.7	m^2
Aspect ratio	10		10	
Empty weight	370	lb	167	kg
Loaded weight	842	lb	382	kg
Wing loading	4.32	lb/ft^2	21	kg/m^2
Max speed	92	mph	142	kmh
Cruise speed	64	mph	102	kmh
Stalling speed	31	mph	49	kmh
Climb rate	300	ft/min	92	m/min
Range	232	mls	370	km

Richard Noble, the one time world land speed record This all metal two seater was the brain child of holder; and originally produced on the Isle of Wight in 1986. Powered by a Hewland three cylinder, in line, two stroke engine, specially developed for the ARV. This engine ran into trouble, causing the aircraft to be grounded and the company made bankrupt. Several attempts at reviving the ARV have been made in England, Scotland and Sweden (Opus 2).

Successful engine installations have been, the Rotax 912, the 90 hp. AE 100 rotary, a Norton and the modified Hewland – fitted to the majority still flying.

Sturdily built with a swept forward wing which has a highish loading of 12.6 lb/ft the ARV will cruise at over 100 mph with excellent visibility and a well mannered stall. Thirty have been built, all still on the UK Register, 19 are flying and it is listed as a PFA approved kit.

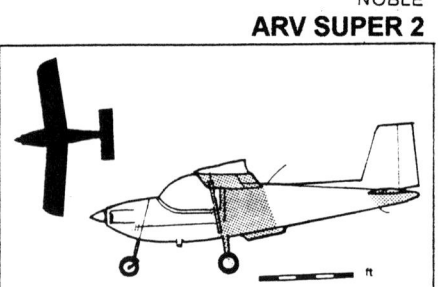

NOBLE
ARV SUPER 2

DATA	IMPERIAL		METRIC	
Span	29.5	ft	9.1	m
Wing area	92.5	ft^2	8.7	m^2
Aspect ratio	9.4		9.4	
Empty weight	715	lb	321	kg
Loaded weight	1100	lb	500	kgz
Wing loading	11.9	lb/ft^2	58	kg/m^2
Max speed	107	mph	171	kmh
Cruise speed	92	mph	147	kmh
Stalling speed	48	mph	77	kmh
Climb rate	750	ft/min	231	m/min
Range	350	mls	560	km

The all composites shoulder wing Lambada is a product of the Czech company Urban Air and when fitted with a Rotax 447 comes within the 450kg microlight category. None in this country at the time of writing, but this could become a popular 'Euro-microlight'. (Ed. One in Irish ownership; Jabiru powered).

The two versions, UFM13 and UFM11 have wing spans of the suffix (appx) in metres; the larger span version with a Rotax 447 is essentially a motor glider, whilst the UFM11 with an HKS700E engine (65hp) is niftier but over the microlight weight limit. A Rotax 912, four stroke, four cylinder engine of 80hp can also be fitted.

The composite wing structure, though beautifully slender, has been tested to +12.5 and –10.5 g.

Views from the side-by-side cockpit are excellent, positioned as it is ahead of the eye level wing and behind a short and not too bulbous nose.

Handling in the air is described as 'easy and forgiving'. The wings quickly detach for ease of storage and a kit version is also available.

Figures below are for the UFM13 (Rotax 447).

DATA	IMPERIAL		METRIC	
Span	39	ft	12.2	m
Wing area	126	sq.ft	11.1	sq.m
Aspect ratio	12			
Empty wt	601	lb.	225	kg.
Loaded wt	991	lb.	450	kg.
Wing loading	7.8	lb/sq.ft	38	kg/sq.m
Max speed	120	mph	192	kmph
Cruising speed	85	mph	136	kmph
Stall speed	40	mph	64	kmph
Climb	470	fpm	144	mpm
Range	280	mls	448	km

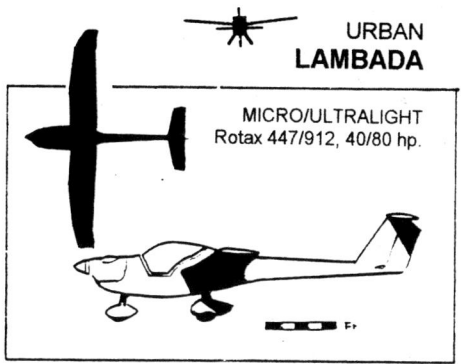

URBAN
LAMBADA

MICRO/ULTRALIGHT
Rotax 447/912, 40/80 hp.

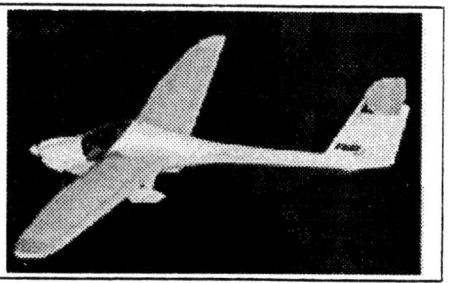

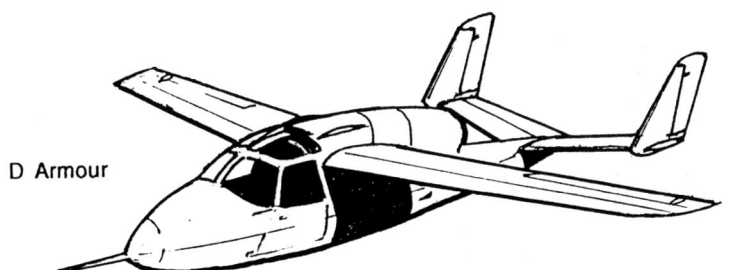

D Armour

Miles Student, see page 151.

This bruiser is a WW2 advanced trainer manufactured by North American Aircraft and powered by a huge 550 hp. Pratt and Whitney single row radial engine.

The prototype, designated NA-26, first flew in 1937 and subsequent production ran to an incredible 15,000 aircraft. It was operated by thirty air forces throughout the world - including both the Luftwaffe and the RAF!

The USAAF designation was AT-6 (becoming T6, post war) and Harvard in the Allied air forces. Production continued up to 1954 including 2000 wartime AT-6s being 're-manufactured' as T-6G Texans.

An all metal heavy-weight with an inward retracting undercarriage, split trailing edge flaps, a swept back mean chord and a long 'glass house' canopy over the tandem cockpits.

The un-geared radial engine and the fast spinning CS prop. produce a very distinctive rasp!

There are about 30 on the UK Register.

NORTH AMERICAN HARVARD

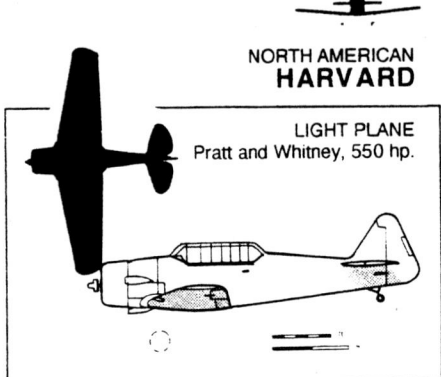

LIGHT PLANE
Pratt and Whitney, 550 hp.

DATA	IMPERIAL		METRIC	
Span	42	ft	13	m
Wing area	254	ft²	24	m²
Aspect ratio	7		7	
Empty weight	4271	lb	1939	kg
Loaded weight	5617	lb	2550	kg
Wing loading	23	lb/ft²	112	kg/m²
Max speed	212	mph	339	kmh
Cruise speed	170	mph	272	kmh
Stalling speed	60	mph	96	kmh
Climb rate	1643	ft/min	502	m/min
Range	870	mls	1392	km

CULVER CADET

With an original Albert Mooney design K K Culver formed the Dart Aircraft Co in the early '30s to produce the two seat Dart Dart. Dart became Culver Aircraft in '39 and the Dart became the Culver Dart. Beech took over in '41 but retained the Culver badge.

The many variants all looked, pretty much, the same and were renowned for their good performance on low power (140 mph on 80 hp is a pretty good two seater).

The Cadet has a wooden semi monocoque fuselage, elliptical wooden cantilever wings with 'letter box' type slots at the tips. The manually retractable gear' folds inwards, with only two turns of the crank!

Civil Cadet production was curtailed by WW2 but over 400 of these pretty aeroplanes were fitted with R/C and trike gear and became target drones!

368 Cadets were built between '39 and '42, 100 of which are still flying. There is one on the UK Register and a 'new' homebuilt version has flown in Kansas.

Various attempts were made to bring the Cadet back 'on stream', including, Lark Aviation's Lark 95 and the Helton Lark from Arizona.

We can learn a thing or two from this 60 year old design.

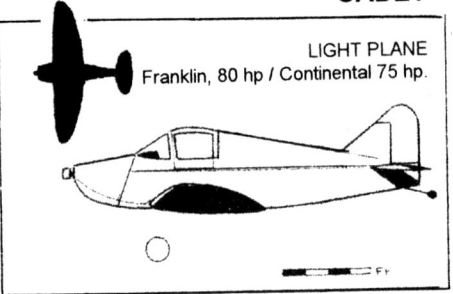

LIGHT PLANE
Franklin, 80 hp / Continental 75 hp.

DATA	IMPERIAL		METRIC	
Span	27	ft	8.1	m
Wing area	120	sq.ft	11.1	sq.m
Aspect ratio	6			
Empty wt	720	lb.	327	kg.
Loaded wt	1305	lb.	592	kg.
Wing loading	10.9	lb/sq.ft	42.2	kg/sq.m
Max speed	140	mph	224	kmph
Cruising speed	120	mph	193	kmph
Stall speed	45	mph	72	kmph
Climb	800'	fpm	244	mpm
Range	600	mls	965	km

An advanced concept, for it's time; it first flew in 1941 as GC-1, and was a fast two seater with side by side seating and a retractable undercarriage.

The prototype had wooden wings and a welded tube fuselage but appeared in 1945 as an all metal aeroplane manufactured by the Globe Aircraft Co. Later, to speed up production, Temco came into the picture until production ceased in 1951 when over 1000 Swifts had been made.

As recently as 1999 plans were being made to re-start production of the Swift by Aviat Inc.

A keen owners club exists in the USA, where several hundred are still flying, and a variety of engines have been fitted - including a turbo-prop!

The undercarriage and flaps are operated by an electro-hydraulic power pack and later model have disc braked main wheels in place of the rather poor drums.

The Swift, being a small aeroplane with a big engine, is fairly fast with fighter like handling - though the range is rather limited.

There are two Swifts on the UK Register.

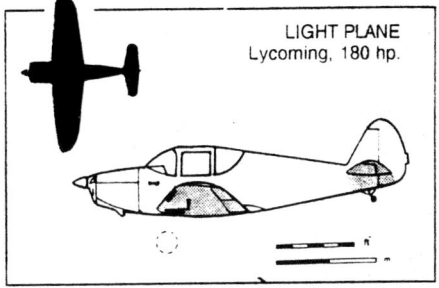

GLOBE
SWIFT

LIGHT PLANE
Lycoming, 180 hp.

DATA	IMPERIAL		METRIC	
Span	29.3	ft	9	m
Wing area	131.2	ft^2	12.3	m^2
Aspect ratio	6.5		6.5	
Empty weight	1110	lb	503	kg
Loaded weight	1710	lb	776	kg
Wing loading	13	lb/ft^2	63.4	kg/m^2
Max speed	185	mph	296	kmh
Cruise speed	156	mph	250	kmh
Stalling speed	60	mph	96	kmh
Climb rate	1000	ft/min	308	m/min
Range	320	mls	512	km

This Swiss 'fighter trainer' first flew in 1945 and only 57 were produced, they served in the Swiss Air Force up to 1981 when they were sold on to the civilian market - five being UK registered.

Messerschmitt Me 109 main gear and tailplane and elevator are incorporated in the design which is of mixed wood and metal construction. The wings are all wood with two box spars, ply ribs and skinning. The fuselage is a metal semi monocoque with a long sliding canopy over the tandem seats and fronted by the long, slim, inverted V12 air cooled Argus engine. An interesting feature is the constant speed prop which is actuated by a vaned spinner.

All the control surfaces and flaps are fabric covered.

Pilatus produce the more famous Porter and were one-time owners of Britten-Norman.

The P2 is popular for film work disguised as a Luftwaffe type.

PILATUS
P 2

LIGHT PLANE
Argus, 370 hp.

DATA	IMPERIAL		METRIC	
Span	36.1	ft	11.1	m
Wing area	183	ft^2	17.2	m^2
Aspect ratio	7		7	
Empty weight	3345	lb	1518	kg
Loaded weight	4335	lb	1968	kg
Wing loading	23.7	lb/ft^2	116	kg/m^2
Max speed	211	mph	337	kmh
Cruise speed	206	mph	329	kmh
Stalling speed	63	mph	101	kmh
Climb rate	1280	ft/min	394	m/min
Range	350	mls	560	km

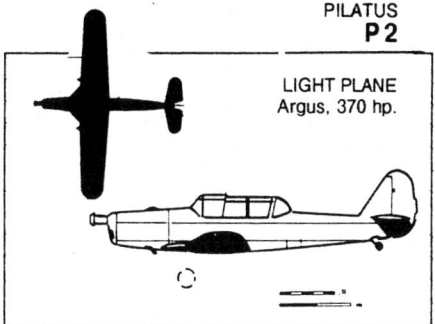

SPORTAVIA/FOURNIER
RF-4 and RF-5

Rene Fournier called his 'motor glider' an Avions Planeur and worked initially with Pierre Robin.

An all wood glider type aeroplane which first flew in 1960 as RF-1 to be followed by the developments RF-2 and RF-3, which flew in 1963 to become in production the RF-4, an aerobatic single seater.

Alpavia, in France, produced the first RF3/4s - 89 of them before the German company Sportavia began building the RF-4 as the RF-4D and the two seat, in tandem, RF-5, which first flew in 1968.

The engines for both models are VW based units including the RF-5s 68 hp. Limbach. An exception being the RF-55 which has a 60 hp. Franklin.

The CFI (Club Fournier International) is the Fournier owners club, active both sides of the Channel. A total of 34 RF-4s and RF-5s are on the UK Register.

Details below are for the single seat RF-4.

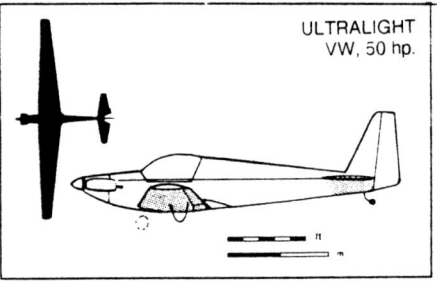

ULTRALIGHT
VW, 50 hp.

DATA	IMPERIAL		METRIC	
Span	37	ft	11.26	m
Wing area	121.7	ft^2	11.3	m^2
Aspect ratio	11.24		11.24	
Empty weight	584	lb	265	kg
Loaded weight	859	lb	390	kg
Wing loading	7.0	lb/ft^2	34	kg/m^2
Max speed	112	mph	180	kmh
Cruise speed	100	mph	160	kmh
Stalling speed	40	mph	64	kmh
Climb rate	690	ft/min	212	m/min
Range	422	mls	680	km

SCHLEICHER
AS-K16

A handsome low winged motor glider from Germany, the two seat, side-by-side AS-K16 first flew in 1971 and was placed third in the First International Motor Glider Competition in 1974.

No longer in production, there are two on the UK register.

Of mixed construction the AS-K16 has a welded steel tube fuselage frame with plywood and GRP fairings. The wings, which are swept forward one degree, have a single wooden spar with a ply' 'D box' nose and fabric covering behind the spar. The ailerons are operated by push rods, no flaps are fitted but upper surface spoilers are. The main undercarriage, with its trouser-like doors, retracts very smartly inwards and has drum braked wheels.

The Limbach (VW conversion) engine drives a VP prop and has an electric starter.

The 52 ft span wing has detachable outer panels as an option.

In many ways similar to the Fournier RF-9, the AS-K16 with its lower aspect ratio wing (13.5 to the RF-9s 16) has a slightly higher gliding angle.

MOTOR GLIDER
Limbach SL1700, 72 hp.

DATA	IMPERIAL		METRIC	
Span	52.5	ft	16	m
Wing area	204	sq.ft	19	sq.m
Aspect ratio	13.5			
Empty wt	1036	lb.	470	kg.
Loaded wt	1543	lb.	700	kg.
Wing loading	7.5	lb/sq.ft	37	kg/sq.m
Max speed	120	mph	200	kmph
Cruising speed	100	mph	160	kmph
Stall speed	41	mph	69	kmph
Climb	200'	fpm	61	mpm
Range	-----	mls	-----	km

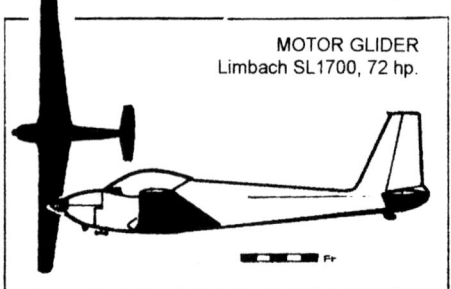

Californians Ken Rand and Stuart Robinson designed and built the single seat KR-1 which first flew in 1972 and had a top speed of 200 mph powered by a 1700 cc. VW. engine.

Kitted in 1974, it proved to be popular with homebuilders and around 200 were built and flying - mainly in the USA.

The KR-1 was followed up by a side by side two seat version, the KR-2 which was also snapped up by the DIY boys and over 300 are now in the air.

Of pioneering mixed wood and 'plastics' construction the KR-2 has wooden spar wings with foam ribs and infill covered in Dynel reinforced epoxy. the outer wing panels detach for ease of storage. The fuselage and tail unit are of similar construction.

65 hp. Continentals and 1600 - 2000 cc. VW's are fitted giving the tiny plane a very nifty performance.

The retractable u/c version is standard but taildragger and nosewheel versions have been devised.

34 are on the Register and it is PFA approved.

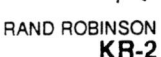

RAND ROBINSON
KR-2

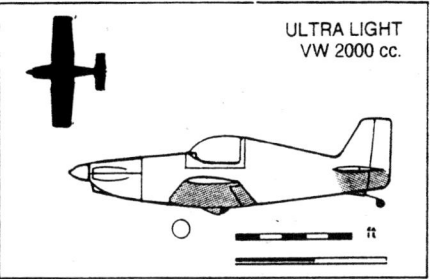

ULTRA LIGHT
VW 2000 cc.

DATA	IMPERIAL		METRIC	
Span	20.6	ft	6.34	m
Wing area	80	ft^2	7.5	m^2
Aspect ratio	5.3		5.3	
Empty weight	440	lb	200	kg
Loaded weight	800	lb	363	kg
Wing loading	10	lb/ft^2	48.8	kg/m^2
Max speed	180	mph	288	kmh
Cruise speed	170	mph	272	kmh
Stalling speed	45	mph	72	kmh
Climb rate	800	ft/min	246	m/min
Range	2000	mls	3200	km

WAR, War Aircraft Replicas, of Santa Paula, California, have produced a range of realistic war bird look-a-likes; starting with the Peter Nieber designed FW190, which first flew in 1973.

The realistic contours are obtained by carving to shape blocks of urethane foam that have been attached to a basic wooden core airframe before the final 'glassing over. The wings have two wooden spars and the foam and ply' sandwich ribs give it the correct plan shape. Just like the real thing, the undercarriage retracts inwards and is electrically operated.

Approximately 2/3 scale, the 'FW190, in its authentic camouflage and markings looks just like its famous 'role model' and it is only when close up that it is seen to be a very small aeroplane - 20' wingspan!

The range includes, Sea Fury, Corsair, Thunder bolt, Mustang and Zero; they are supplied as kits or sets of plans. The type is PFA approved and there are three on the UK Register.

WAR
FW-190

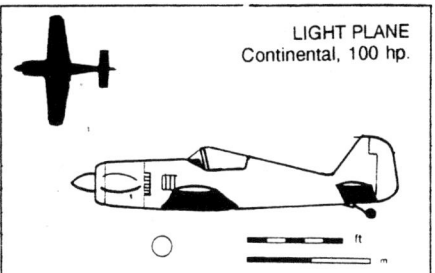

LIGHT PLANE
Continental, 100 hp.

DATA	IMPERIAL		METRIC	
Span	20.5	ft	6.1	m
Wing area	79	ft^2	7.4	m^2
Aspect ratio	5.3		5.3	
Empty weight	650	lb	292	kg
Loaded weight	950	lb	427	kg
Wing loading	12	lb/ft^2	57	kg/m^2
Max speed	195	mph	314	kmh
Cruise speed	125	mph	201	kmh
Stalling speed	55	mph	89	kmh
Climb rate	1000	ft/min	305	m/min
Range	400	mls	643	km

Czechoslovakia - that was - designed and built, like many mid European aeroplane makers, their 'planes to suit many tasks. The Trener is well known in its single seat aerobatic role - a big winner in its day - and as a tourer / trainer with tandem seating; it also does duty as a glider tug.

The Trener nomenclature ranges from Z26, the wooden prototype to the Z726K, first flown in 1973, is all metal and has a 210 hp. supercharged Avia.

The Z326 was the first in the range to have a retractable undercarriage and the aerobatic versions, Z226, Z326, Z526, are all named Akrobat.

In production since 1947 the Trener range has run to over 1400 units. All are distinguished by their swept back main plane leading edge, narrow in-line six cylinder engine and a long 'glass house' canopy (two seaters).

There are 12 of the Z-26 range on the UK Register. The figures below are for the Z526, 180 hp. Avia.

ZLIN Z526 TRENER

LIGHT PLANE
Avia, 180 hp.

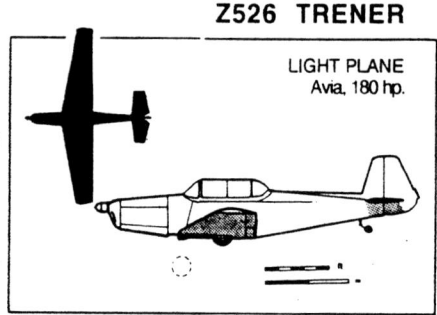

DATA	IMPERIAL		METRIC	
Span	32.5	ft	10	m
Wing area	155	ft^2	14.6	m^2
Aspect ratio	6.8		6.8	
Empty weight	1465	lb	665	kg
Loaded weight	2072	lb	940	kg
Wing loading	13.4	lb/ft^2	65.2	kg/m^2
Max speed	145	mph	232	kmh
Cruise speed	130	mph	210	kmh
Stalling speed	55	mph	88	kmh
Climb rate	1181	ft/min	360	m/min
Range	295	mls	480	km

LOEHLE 5151 MUSTANG

ULTRALIGHT
Rotax 582, 65 hp.

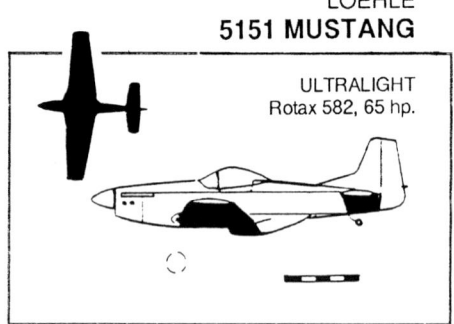

Strikingly similar to the WW2 fighter it is modelled on the Loehle 5151 Mustang is a ¾ scale light plane powered by a Rotax 582 engine.

Designed in 1985 and produced in kit form in the USA by Mike Loehle the Mustang is of all wood construction. The rear fuselage and empenage are of semi-geodetic construction and the two spar wing is fabric covered and devoid of flaps.

Fixed gear or manually retractable models are available; the drag reduction with the latter is minimal at a cruise of 80 mph – but it looks much nicer!

Over 200 kits have been sold in the USA, 30+ are flying and one, built with PFA approval, appears on the UK Register.

Though looking like a really 'hot ship' the 5151 Mustang with its 65 hp engine and 80 mph cruise is a 'pussy cat' – and almost in the microlight category.

The one example of this attractive and interesting aeroplane was in storage at the time of writing.

DATA	IMPERIAL		METRIC	
Span	27.4	ft	8.43	m
Wing area	130	sq.ft	12.2	sq.m
Aspect ratio	5.8			
Empty wt	513	lb.	232	kg.
Loaded wt	885	lb.	401	kg.
Wing loading	6.8	lb/sq.ft	33	kg/sq.m
Max speed	100	mph	160	kmph
Cruising speed	80	mph	128	kmph
Stall speed	30	mph	48	kmph
Climb	1200'	fpm	370	mpm
Range	250	mls	400	km

AEROMOT
SUPER XIMANGO

MOTOR GLIDER
Rotax 912, 80 hp.

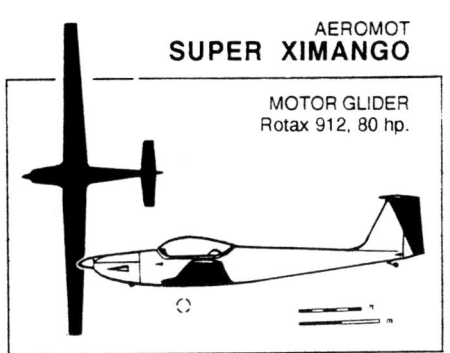

A Rene Fournier design built under licence by Aeromot in Brazil the Super Ximango is the twin of Fourniers RF 10 an all composites high performance motor glider. The AMT100 Ximango which preceded it was Limbach powered whereas the Super' has a Rotax 912 with a three pitch Hoffman prop.

An exceedingly elegant aeroplane with side by side seating under a huge bubble canopy, folding wings (Navy style) and a wide track retractable undercarriage. The AMT200 Super Ximango is an efficient glider and an even more efficient powered aircraft - 152 mph on 80 hp is remarkable! Its low drag profile is enhanced by the clean cowling lines afforded by the water cooled engine,

Fifty AMT 100s were built before switching to the AMT 200 Super Ximango. Four are on the UK Register.

DATA	IMPERIAL		METRIC	
Span	57.5	ft	17.7	m
Wing area	201	ft^2	18.9	m^2
Aspect ratio	16.3		16.3	
Empty weight	1334	lb	605	kg
Loaded weight	1874	lb	851	kg
Wing loading	9.3	lb/ft^2	45	kg/m^2
Max speed	152	mph	243	kmh
Cruise speed	126	mph	201	kmh
Stalling speed	44	mph	70	kmh
Climb rate	600	ft/min	185	m/min
Range	800	mls	1280	km

EUROPA AVIATION
EUROPA

LIGHT PLANE
Rotax 912 80 hp

Designed and built by Ivan Shaw and Don Dykins the Europa first flew in 1992. The aim was to come up with a fast cruising two seater with STOL capabilities suitable for home construction. The kits of pre moulded GRP, foam and carbon fibre are marketed by Europa Aviation at Kirkbymoorside. The de-rigged size enables the completed aeroplane to fit into a domestic garage and be trailered to the air strip, where it is quite happy to operate from grass and will take off in 100 metres and land in 200 m !

The single semi retracting main wheel and wing outriggers are simple, light weight and low drag. Flaps, an all flying tailplane, dual control and a very quiet Rotax 912 double silenced engine are all features of this little beauty.

The Europa must be the most successful UK homebuilt lightplane ever, with over 700 sold in 32 countries (200 on UK Reg.) inc. the taildragger version (p 119) and now the new Liberty XL-2 factory-built.

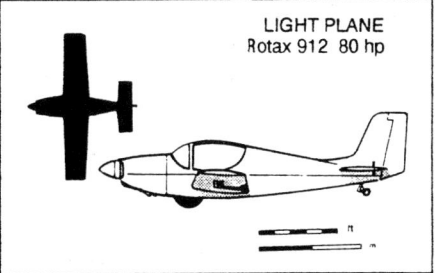

DATA	IMPERIAL		METRIC	
Span	26	ft	8	m
Wing area	95	ft^2	8.9	m^2
Aspect ratio	6.58		6.58	
Empty weight	680	lb	308	kg
Loaded weight	1300	lb	590	kg
Wing loading	13.7	lb/ft^2	66	kg/m^2
Max speed	166	mph	267	kmh
Cruise speed	115	mph	184	kmh
Stalling speed	56	mph	90	kmh
Climb rate	800	ft/min	246	m/min
Range	500	mls	800	km

The T61 Venture is a motor glider originally designed and built, in some numbers, in Germany by Scheibe as the SF25 Falke, which first flew in 1963. Slingsby built 75 T61s before 'moving up a gear' to the T67 Firefly.

The wing is all wood - though late models have a GRP spar - with about 30% fabric covering, the rest being plywood. Welded steel tubes form the fuselage basic frame with plywood formers and stringers under a fabric skin. The mono-wheel undercarriage is braked, the tail-wheel is steerable and there are lift spoilers.

At one time the main ATC trainer but de-commissioned in 1991 and many sold onto the civil market.

A pleasant, docile and cheap aeroplane to operate - 2 galls. per hour!

56 T61s are on the 'Register and 36 SF25's.

SLINGSBY
T61 VENTURE

MOTOR GLIDER
Rollason VW, 55 hp.

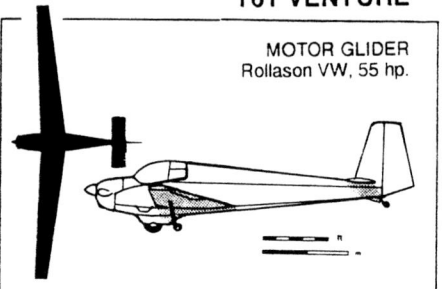

DATA	IMPERIAL		METRIC	
Span	50	ft	15.25	m
Wing area	188	ft²	17.5	m²
Aspect ratio	13.3		13.3	
Empty weight	739	lb	335	kg
Loaded weight	1168	lb	530	kg
Wing loading	6.2	lb/ft²	30.3	kg/m²
Max speed	103	mph	165	kmh
Cruise speed	86	mph	138	kmh
Stalling speed	46	mph	73	kmh
Climb rate	350	ft/min	107	m/m
Range	276	mls	442	km

Monnett are based at the epi-centre of home-building - Oshkosh! After building sailplanes for many years, Monnett turned in 1980 to the Moni power-glider; Monnett call it an Air Recreation Vehicle and it first flew in 1981.

Construction is all metal and several hundred sets of plans and kits have been sold, it is a PFA approved design, though currently, new sets of plans are not available.

The distinctive Moni - which, in spite of being all metal only just misses out on Microlight classification on wing loading! - is powered by a KFM engine of 30 hp. (the prototype had a 22hp. KFM).

A variety of undercarriages may be fitted - the classic glider mono-wheel with small 'tip wheels, tail dragger with cantilever spring legs or these legs plus a nose wheel. A number of span options are also apparent, the parallel chord wing being eminently suitable for chopping off to suit!

There are four Monis on the UK Register - one being built by a school in Sheffield.

MONNETT
MONI

ULTRALIGHT
KFM, 30 hp.

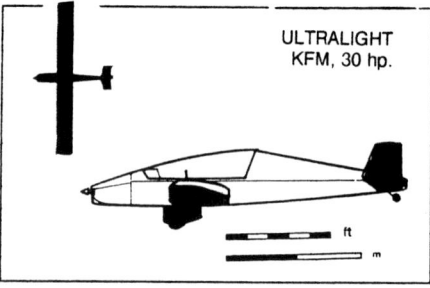

DATA	IMPERIAL		METRIC	
Span	27.5	ft	8.4	m
Wing area	75	ft²	7	m²
Aspect ratio	10		10	
Empty weight	260	lb	118	kg
Loaded weight	500	lb	227	kg
Wing loading	6.7	lb/ft²	32	kg/m²
Max speed	110	mph	177	kmh
Cruise speed	80	mph	128	kmh
Stalling speed	38	mph	62	kmh
Climb rate	500	ft/min	152	m/min
Range	320	mls	515	km

The Humming Bird was built for the Daily Mail Light Aeroplane Trials of 1923 held at Lympne. DH entered two of the little strut braced low wing monoplanes powered by 750 cc Douglas motor cycle engines (appx 15 hp) and though they won no prizes they were considered the best all round performers.

Of all wood construction with ply covered fuselage and fabric covered wings and tail G-EBHX was soon re-engined with a Blackburn Tomtit of 26 hp and so powered flew non stop to Brussels on 10 shillings worth of petrol (50p) – at that time about three gallons!

Surprisingly, no civil orders were forthcoming but the RAF ordered ten for 'communication duties' and five were sold abroad. (3 Australia, 1 Russia, 1 Czech).

In October 1925 a Humming Bird with a hook above the cockpit was dropped from the airship R33 and successfully re attached itself back to the mother ship.

The protype G_EBHX still flies at Old Warden and Continental powered replica is flying in Canada.

De HAVILAND HUMMING BIRD

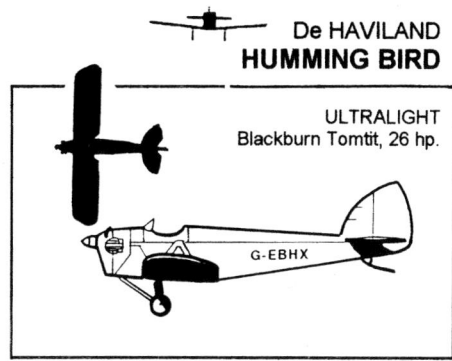

ULTRALIGHT
Blackburn Tomtit, 26 hp.

DATA	IMPERIAL		METRIC	
Span	30	ft	9.2	m
Wing area	125	sq.ft	6	sq.m
Aspect ratio	7		7	
Empty wt	326	lb.	148	kg.
Loaded wt	565	lb.	256	kg.
Wing loading	4.5	lb/sq.ft	22	kg/sq.m
Max speed	73	mph	117	kmph
Cruising speed	50	mph	80	kmph
Stall speed	33	mph	53	kmph
Climb	225	fpm	70	mpm
Range	200	mls	320	km

The BA (British Aircraft Manufacturing Co. Ltd.) Swallow is, essentially, the 1927 German Klemm L25 which was distributed in this country in the thirties powered by a 75 hp. Salmson radial engine. The type proved so popular that the British Klemm Aeroplane Company Ltd. was formed to build them at Hanworth with the Pobjoy radial as an alternative power unit. In 1934 BAM was formed and the Swallow 2 (illustrated) appeared with square cut tail and wing tips, as opposed to the rounded original Klemms, and the engine options included the Cirrus Minor of 90 hp.

Of all wood construction, plywood covered, the Swallow had one of the earliest production light plane cantilever wings.

About 150 were built and very well liked they were by their pilots. 37 survived WW2 and there are still seven on the 'Register including a recently built Klemm L25 and the well known Shuttleworth Swallow.

BRITISH AIRCRAFT BA SWALLOW

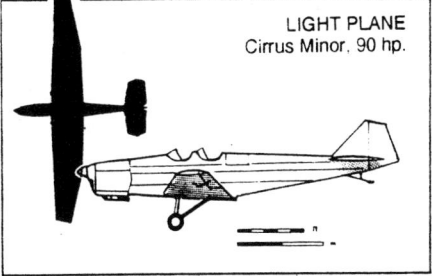

LIGHT PLANE
Cirrus Minor, 90 hp.

DATA	IMPERIAL		METRIC	
Span	42.6	ft	13.1	m
Wing area	219	ft^2	20.6	m^2
Aspect ratio	8.3		8.3	
Empty weight	990	lb	450	kg
Loaded weight	1500	lb	681	kg
Wing loading	6.8	lb/ft^2	33.2	kg/m^2
Max speed	104	mph	166	kmh
Cruise speed	90	mph	144	kmh
Stalling speed	40	mph	64	kmh
Climb rate	800	ft/min	246	m/min
Range	420	mls	672	km

This remarkable little aeroplane was built and first flown in 1927 to further the cause of the monoplane and the Cirrus engine. Faster than many fighters of its day, a short span DH 71, with a 135 hp Gipsy, was capable of nearly 200 mph. and set an official world 100km closed circuit speed record for Class 2 Light Aeroplanes at 186 mph.

Built entirely of wood with fabric covered wings and ply skinned fuselage, the wings were totally wire braced as was the undercarriage, which had internally sprung wheel hubs.

Though entered for several air races the DH 71 – or Tiger Moth, its official name – never carried of any prizes.

Only two were built, one going to Australia, where it crashed and the other, after its 'days in the sun', went into storage at Hatfield and eventually was destroyed by a German bomb in 1940.

Two replicas have been built in the UK, one static, one to fly; but a USA example is flying and alleged to be 'a bit of a handful'! (Though Hubert Broad, the DH test pilot, around whom the aircraft was built, had no complaints). Data below for 'tourer'.

De HAVILAND
DH 71 TIGER MOTH

ULTRALIGHT
Cirrus, 85hp.

DATA	IMPERIAL		METRIC	
Span	22.5	ft	7	m
Wing area	76.5	sq.ft	7.2	sq.m
Aspect ratio	6.6			
Empty wt	618	lb.	308	kg.
Loaded wt	905	lb.	411	kg.
Wing loading	11.8	lb/sq.ft	57.6	kg/sq.m
Max speed	166	mph	265	kmph
Cruising speed	150	mph	240	kmph
Stall speed	60	mph	96	kmph
Climb	1500	fpm	462	mpm
Range	200	mls	320	km

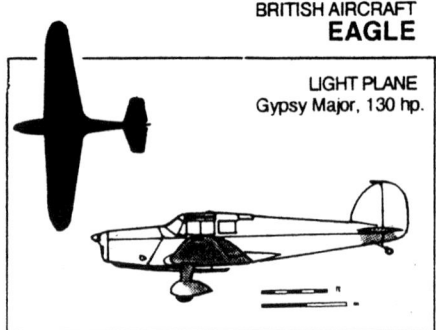

Originally the British Klemm BK1 Eagle, this attractive three seater, became, on the change of company name, the British Aircraft BA Eagle. Klemm, a German company, produced a similar type, the L32, but the BA Eagle was an entirely new design from the 'board of G.H. Handasyde.

First flown in 1934, the Eagle with the pilot in the front seat and the two passengers behind, was ahead of its time in having a retractable undercarriage - albeit manually operated. (and strangely, no flaps!)

The first production model was powered by a 200 hp. Gypsy Six engine and flew in the 1934 Kings Cup air race; subsequent models were 130 hp. Gypsy Major powered.

Much raced and given to breaking point to point records - including a record crossing of the South Atlantic on a delivery flight! - the Eagles boasted many famous pilots, including, Amy Johnson, Tommy Rose and A E Clouston.

The sole remaining Eagle, G-AFAX, is the only one produced with a fixed undercarriage - and it is still flying.

BRITISH AIRCRAFT
EAGLE

LIGHT PLANE
Gypsy Major, 130 hp.

DATA	IMPERIAL		METRIC	
Span	39.2	ft	12.1	m
Wing area	200	ft^2	18.8	m^2
Aspect ratio	7.7		7.7	
Empty weight	1450	lb	658	kg
Loaded weight	2400	lb	1090	kg
Wing loading	12	lb/ft^2	58.5	kg/m^2
Max speed	148	mph	237	kmh
Cruise speed	130	mph	208	kmh
Stalling speed	55	mph	88	kmh
Climb rate	700	ft/min	215	m/min
Range	650	mls	1040	km

PERCIVAL
MEW GULL

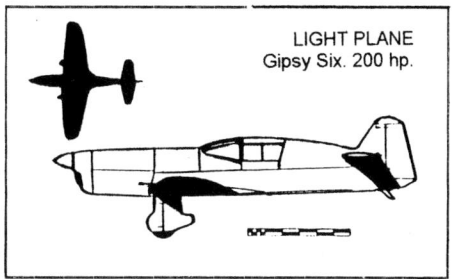
LIGHT PLANE
Gipsy Six. 200 hp.

The Percival Mew Gull, probably the most charismatic British light plane of the pre-war era.

First flown in 1934 the small single seater with the big engine was all wood and initially powered by a Napier Javelin engine of 165 hp. With a Gipsy Six (200 hp.) fitted it flew in the Kings Cup air race, lapping at 191mph, but was handicapped out of prize.

In 1935 the Mew Gull 2 with single leg gear and flaps won many races inc. Deauville – Cannes and Heston – Cardiff at 218 mph. A '2A Mew won the '37 Kings Cup another coming 3rd and in 1938 G-AEXF won the race at an incredible 236 mph!

In 1939 Alex Henshaw, in 'XF made a record dash to Cape Town and back in a gruelling 4 days, 10 hrs.

This aircraft was sold to France where it was stored during the war; it was later repatriated and restored in the UK to fly again in 1950.

Six Mews were built, two were destroyed by enemy bombing, one sold to SA crashed and two were scrapped.

G-AEXF still flies at Old Warden – a joy to behold.

DATA	IMPERIAL		METRIC	
Span	22.7	ft	7	m
Wing area	75	sq.ft	7	sq.m
Aspect ratio	6.8			
Empty wt	1150	lb.	522	kg.
Loaded wt	2125	lb.	963	kg.
Wing loading	28.3	lb/sq.ft	138	kg/sq.m
Max speed	235	mph	376	kmph
Cruising speed	232	mph	371	kmph
Stall speed	70	mph	112	kmph
Climb	1800	fpm	554	mpm
Range	875	mls	1320	km

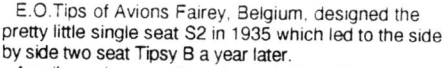
TIPSY
B/TRAINER

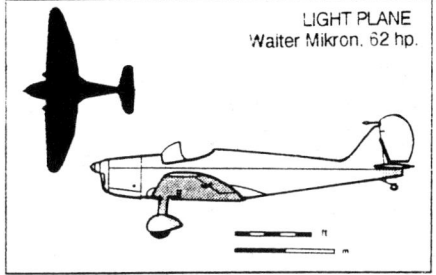
LIGHT PLANE
Walter Mikron. 62 hp.

E.O.Tips of Avions Fairey, Belgium, designed the pretty little single seat S2 in 1935 which led to the side by side two seat Tipsy B a year later.

An all wooden aeroplane, it was built by Tipsy Aircraft Ltd. and was powered by the Czech built Walter Mikron engine. It came at a time when the Civil Air Guard needed trainers and a third of the pre war production of 15 were upgraded to, and named, Trainer.

Ten survived the war, three of which were soon sold overseas, and when production was resumed after the war only three were completed - one having a long and useful life teaching Fairey employees to fly.

The aircraft's apparently elliptical wing is composed of three straight lines at the trailing edge.

Fairey Avions Belge built a cabin version in 1939, which served with distinction throughout the conflict, and a further seven in 1947 named Belfair.

The specification of all three types are similar, the Trainer and Belfair being heavier.

There are eight on the UK Register.

DATA	IMPERIAL		METRIC	
Span	31.2	ft	9.6	m
Wing area	129	ft²	12.1	m²
Aspect ratio	7.5		7.5	
Empty weight	496	lb	225	kg
Loaded weight	992	lb	450	kg
Wing loading	7.7	lb/ft²	37.5	kg/m²
Max speed	124	mph	198	kmh
Cruise speed	100	mph	160	kmh
Stalling speed	42	mph	67	kmh
Climb rate	450	ft/min	139	m/min
Range	450	mls	720	km

The first DW 1 was designed and built by two ex de Haviland Technical School students A. Dalrymple and A. R. Ward in 1937 at Hungerford in Berkshire.

Intended as a cheap easy build single seater with a good performance on low power, the all wood cantilever monoplane achieved remarkable figures-- 112 mph on 32 hp! This was with a Carden Ford engine - a modified water cooled car engine - later to be replaced by a 44 hp Train engine of French manufacture.

Four aircraft were built before the outbreak of WW2, and all survived to be resurrected and flown again. In the 50's the DW 1 was popular in the big air races of those days - with various clean up modifications - G-AFSV, in fact lapped the Kings Cup course in 1957 at 144 mph! (Walter Mikron 62 hp).

A pretty little aeroplane with eight on the 'Register – four originals + one original, completed post war and three new PFA builds.

CHILTON
DW-1 MONOPLANE

ULTRALIGHT
Train, 44 hp.

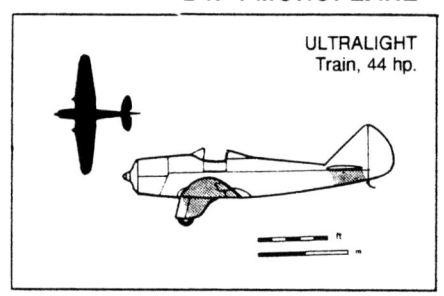

DATA	IMPERIAL		METRIC	
Span	24	ft	7.32	m
Wing area	78	ft^2	7.24	m^2
Aspect ratio	7.4		7.4	
Empty weight	370	lb	168	kg
Loaded weight	650	lb	295	kg
Wing loading	8.4	lb/ft^2	41	kg/m^2
Max speed	112	mph	179	kmh
Cruise speed	100	mph	160	kmh
Stalling speed	35	mph	56	kmh
Climb rate	300	ft/min	198	m/min
Range	500	mls	800	km

The last model produced by Phillips and Powis (later Miles Aircraft) before WW2, it first flew in 1938 and was the first design to be entrusted to F G Miles brother George. Based on the two seat Whitney Straight of 1936 the Monarch was a three seater of similar all wood construction without the 'Straight's folding wing facility but incorporating a unique 'glide control' - a system linking the throttle with the vacuum operated flaps. Only eleven were built, eight carrying UK registrations (though three of these were soon sold abroad). Six were impressed for communications duties during the war and G-AFLW was a camouflaged hack for Rolls Royce. Five returned to 'civvie street' in '46 and three are still on the 'Register. G-AFRZ was registered for a while as G-AIDE and in this guise won the 1956 Goodyear Trophy at an av. 131 mph.(now in storage in Birmingham). G-AFJU is in the Museum of flight at East Fortune.

A desirable aeroplane of its day, fast, comfortable and economical and much praised by the aviation press.

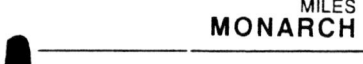

MILES
MONARCH

LIGHT PLANE
Gipsy Major, 130 hp

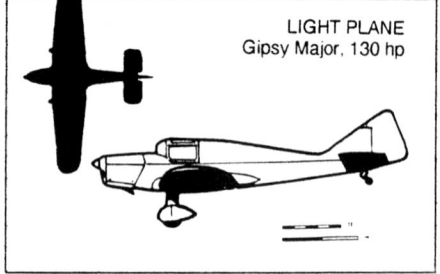

DATA	IMPERIAL		METRIC	
Span	35.5	ft	11	m
Wing area	180	ft^2	17	m^2
Aspect ratio	7		7	
Empty weight	1390	lb	631	kg
Loaded weight	2200	lb	998	kg
Wing loading	12.2	lb/ft^2	58	kg/m^2
Max speed	145	mph	232	kmh
Cruise speed	130	mph	208	kmh
Stalling speed	55	mph	88	kmh
Climb rate	850	ft/min	261	m/min
Range	600	mls	960	km

Following the success of Miles first production aircraft, the tandem two seat Hawk, the first Falcon was a three seat cabin tourer (pilot in the front and two passengers behind) of very clean lines with a Gipsy Major, 130 hp. engine. Hardly out of the workshop this plane made a record breaking Australia - England flight in 1935.

Subsequent models (M3A) had four seats within a wider cabin and the M3B, Falcon Six, with three seats and a Gipsy Six engine of 200 hp., won the Kings Cup Race the same year with Tommy Rose at the controls; later in the same aircraft he broke the England - Cape town record.

The M3C Falcons were full four seaters with dual controls and the Gipsy Six engine.

Of the twenty or so Falcons built pre war only six survived the conflict - and four of these. not for long! Of the two remaining in the UK only one is flying. There is one in Australia and one in Spain,

An advanced design, for its day, cantilever wing, all wood stressed skin structure, split flaps - and no sluggard at 180 mph!

The figures below are for the Falcon Six, a rare and beautiful bird, long may it enthral us.   DA

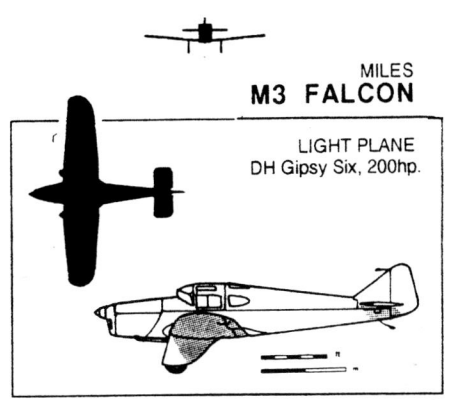

MILES
M3 FALCON

LIGHT PLANE
DH Gipsy Six, 200hp.

DATA	IMPERIAL		METRIC	
Span	35	ft	10.7	m
Wing area	174	ft^2	16.3	m^2
Aspect ratio	7		7	
Empty weight	1550	lb	703	kg
Loaded weight	2350	lb	1066	kg
Wing loading	13.5	lb/ft^2	65	kg/m^2
Max speed	180	mph	288	kmh
Cruise speed	160	mph	256	kmh
Stalling speed	55	mph	88	kmh
Climb rate	1000	ft/min	307	m/min
Range	560	mls	896	km

Built by Dart Aircraft Ltd. at Dunstable and first flown in 1936, the pretty little Dart single seater was designed by Alfred Weyl and was originally powered by a French Ava, two stroke, engine of 27 hp. Of all wood construction with a cantilever wing and single leg undercarriage struts, the prototype was built in four months. The Mk 2 Kitten appeared a year later with revised top decking, stub axles (instead of forks) and the more powerful JAP engine. The Mk 2 Kitten took part in several pre war air races for which it wore spats. Both Kittens were stored during WW2 and flew again after the war; the Mk 1, up to 1952 when it was written off in a crash at Broxbourne. The Mk 2s wings 'went missing' during storage but a rebuild was completed, followed by another crash in '64. The wreck lay in a barn until 1976 when restoration started - it flew again in '85, and is one of the oldest UK Registered aircraft in private hands, still flying.

DART
KITTEN

ULTRALIGHT
JAP, 36 hp.

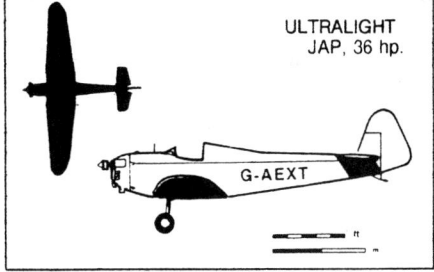

DATA	IMPERIAL		METRIC	
Span	31.7	ft	9.7	m
Wing area	129	ft^2	12.1	m^2
Aspect ratio	7.8		7.8	
Empty weight	510	lb	231	kg
Loaded weight	752	lb	341	kg
Wing loading	5.83	lb/ft^2	28	kg/m^2
Max speed	95	mph	152	kmh
Cruise speed	83	mph	133	kmh
Stalling speed	38	mph	61	kmh
Climb rate	600	ft/min	185	m/min
Range	340	mls	544	km

The main primary trainer of the US Air Forces during WW2 the Fairchild M-62 first flew in 1939 and subsequent production ran to 8000 aircraft. The M-62 was in service with many foreign air forces long after the war, including Paraguay, Haiti, Nicaragua and Honduras.

A tandem two seater with open cockpits or, in the Canadian built version, a long 'greenhouse' enclosing both. The fuselage is of welded steel tube with fabric covering and the wings are wooden. Both Canada and Brazil built M-62s and the Canadian version PT-26 was named Cornell.

Designated PT-19 and PT-26 when fitted with the 200 hp. Ranger engine and PT-23 when powered by the Continental R-640-4 radial engine of 220 hp.

Many are still in existence, over 1000 still on the registers, mainly in the USA where there are about 150 still flying. There are five on the UK Register - one is flying.

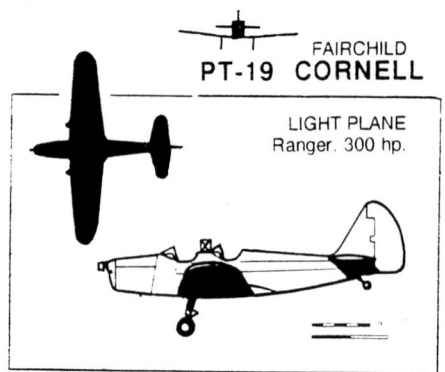

FAIRCHILD PT-19 CORNELL

LIGHT PLANE
Ranger, 300 hp.

DATA	IMPERIAL		METRIC	
Span	36	ft	11.1	m
Wing area	200	ft²	18.8	m²
Aspect ratio	6.5		6.5	
Empty weight	2000	lb	908	kg
Loaded weight	2702	lb	1227	kg
Wing loading	13.5	lb/ft²	66	kg/m²
Max speed	126	mph	202	kmh
Cruise speed	110	mph	176	kmh
Stalling speed	58	mph	93	kmh
Climb rate	690	ft/min	212	m/min
Range	450	mls	720	km

A pre-war Bucker design, adopted as a trainer by the Luftwaffe and produced in considerable numbers - Fokker made 700 of them. After the war Zlin took over manufacture for delivery to the Czech Air Force and the civil market. Over 1000 181s were made and 40 or more are still flying, mainly on the Continent - esp. Germany - others are static in private collections and museums.

In 1947 a Bestmann was registered G-AKAX, and stored at Denham - but was never flown, and finally broken up in 1950. One other remains on the UK Register (G-AMYA) and is, as far as we know, still airworthy and in Luftwaffe markings!

The fuselage consisted of steel tubes forward and plywood monocoque aft, the wooden wings covered in ply and fabric carried trailing edge flaps. A variety of engines were fitted including, Toma and Walter Mikron; the UK example having a 105 hp. Hirth which was standard Zlin fit.

This charming little pre-war side by side two seater is much prized on the Continent and is said to be the 'inspiration' for the SAAB Safir.

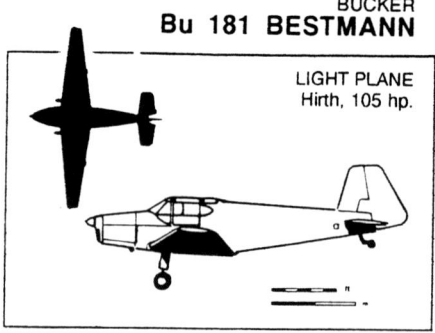

BUCKER Bu 181 BESTMANN

LIGHT PLANE
Hirth, 105 hp.

DATA	IMPERIAL		METRIC	
Span	34.7	ft	10.7	m
Wing area	145.3	ft²	13.6	m²
Aspect ratio	8.3		8.3	
Empty weight	1056	lb	479	kg
Loaded weight	1650	lb	742	kg
Wing loading	11.3	lb/ft²	55	kg/m²
Max speed	133	mph	213	kmh
Cruise speed	121	mph	193	kmh
Stalling speed	60	mph	96	kmh
Climb rate	700	ft/min	215	m/min
Range	497	mls	795	km

RYAN
PT-22 RECRUIT

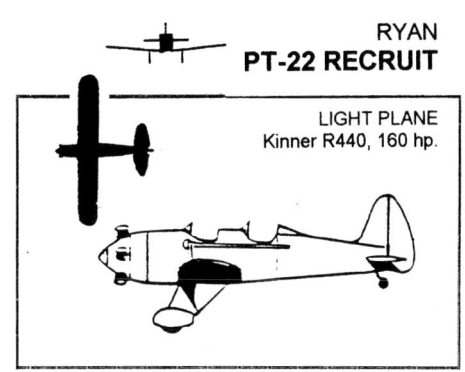

LIGHT PLANE
Kinner R440, 160 hp.

As if loathe to give up the trappings of the biplane the Ryan trainers, the USAAC's first monoplane trainer, had wires, struts, exposed cylinder heads, fixed gear and open cockpits.

First flown in 1939 the PT-22 was developed from the earlier Menasco powered STA and had the more powerful five cylinder 160 hp. Kinner R440 radial engine.

Of mixed construction the PT-22 has a light alloy monocoque fuselage, metal wing ribs and nose skinning – but wooden spars. Manually operated flaps were fitted – rare for the 30's. and the long stroke undercarriage, usually faired, is a wonder to behold when un-faired!

Over 1000 were ordered by the Air Corps, 125 by the USN and an order was received from the Netherlands A.F.

Retired at the end of WW2 500 were sold onto the civil market; many are still flying in the USA, Australia and the UK – where three are airworthy and three are in collections.

DATA	IMPERIAL		METRIC	
Span	30.1	ft	9.2	m
Wing area	134	sq.ft	12.5	sq.m
Aspect ratio	6.7			
Empty wt	1313	lb.	596	kg.
Loaded wt	1860	lb.	844	kg.
Wing loading	13.6	lb/sq.ft	66	kg/sq.m
Max speed	115	mph	184	kmph
Cruising speed	100	mph	160	kmph
Stall speed	60	mph	96	kmph
Climb	1000	fpm	308	mpm
Range	352	mls	766	km

DE HAVILAND
MOTH MINOR

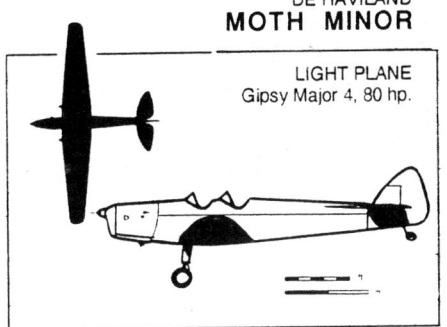

LIGHT PLANE
Gipsy Major 4, 80 hp.

First flown in 1937 and in production by 1939, the all wooden DH94 Moth Minor was intended as a modern low wing replacement for the famous 'Moth biplane series. Owing something to the DH81 Swallow Moth of 1931, the dainty Minor had an open cockpit tandem seating - though a few tandem enclosed cockpit versions were made. Its elegant, ply skinned, high aspect ratio wings folded backwards to save hangar space.

With order books full, 73 were built at Hatfield before production ceased due to the war when all jigs and fixtures were sent to DH Australia and a further 42 were made there.

A dozen, or so, went for export before all civil aircraft were impressed (appx. 35) about half of which returned to civil status in '46. There are 6 currently on the UK Reg.(two airworthy?) whilst in Oz, ten have survived.

DATA	IMPERIAL		METRIC	
Span	36.5	ft	11.2	m
Wing area	162	ft^2	15.2	m^2
Aspect ratio	8		8	
Empty weight	983	lb	446	kg
Loaded weight	1550	lb	704	kg
Wing loading	9.5	lb/ft^2	46.7	kg/m^2
Max speed	118	mph	188	kmh
Cruise speed	100	mph	160	kmh
Stalling speed	47	mph	75	kmh
Climb rate	620	ft/min	191	m/min
Range	300	mls	480	km

Where did they all go? Twelve hundred Magisters were produced for the RAF during WW2 and most of those still serving were released on to the civil market - only *two* are still flying! Several non flying examples are dotted about - some of which may one day become airworthy.   (Three in UK museums). The all wood Magister was in its brief civilian role known as the Hawk Trainer 3, produced at Woodley by the prolific Miles brothers, Fred and George. Mass production of the Magister as the RAF's monoplane *ab initio* trainer and the equally numerous Master boosted Miles fortunes during the war years.

First flown - as the Hawk Trainer - in 1937, it presented quite an advanced design concept with its cantilever wing, split trailing edge flaps and single leg undercarriage.

MILES
MAGISTER
LIGHT PLANE
Gipsy Major, 130 hp.

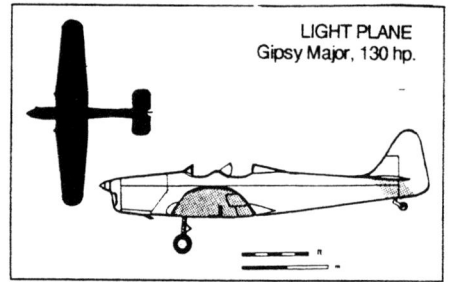

DATA	IMPERIAL		METRIC	
Span	33.8	ft	10.4	m
Wing area	172	ft^2	16.2	m^2
Aspect ratio	6.6		6.6	
Empty weight	1286	lb	584	kg
Loaded weight	1900	lb	863	kg
Wing loading	11	lb/ft^2	54	kg/m^2
Max speed	132	mph	211	kmh
Cruise speed	123	mph	197	kmh
Stalling speed	50	mph	80	kmh
Climb rate	850	ft/min	262	m/min
Range	380	mls	608	km

A militarised version of the, then four year old, P10 Vega Gull, the Proctor, otherwise identical, had revised cabin framing with a four piece blown windscreen. Due to the more comprehensive equipment specification the Proctor 1,2 and 3 carried only three people whilst its civil sister was a four seater.

First flown in 1939 the Proctors structure was all wood, with plywood covering; there were split trailing edge flaps, folding wings and neatly spatted main wheels.

Its performance, 150 mph cruise and 1000 ft/min climb was outstanding for its day.

Mks 4 and 5 appeared in 1943 with a plumper fuselage and four seats.

After the war 225 were civilianised, many being sold abroad - some making the trip under their own power as far as Australia.

Of eight on the 'Register, two are airworthy, three are stored, two are in museums and one is in Australia. (There are 14 in foreign museums).

PERCIVAL
PROCTOR
LIGHT PLANE
Gipsy Queen, 210 hp.

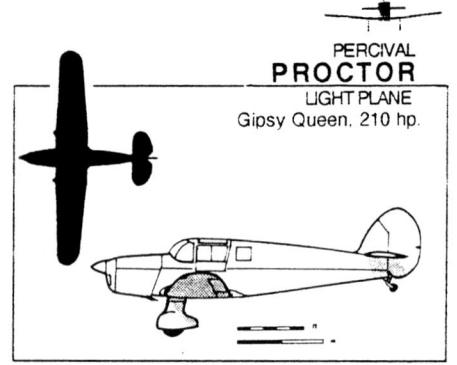

DATA	IMPERIAL		METRIC	
Wing area	197	ft^2	18.5	m^2
Aspect ratio	7.9		7.9	
Empty weight	1875	lb	851	kg
Loaded weight	3250	lb	1475	kg
Wing loading	16.5	lb/ft^2	80.5	kg/m^2
Max speed	165	mph	264	kmh
Cruise speed	150	mph	241	kmh
Stalling speed	60	mph	96	kmh
Climb rate	1020	ft/min	314	m/min
Range	660	mls	1056	km

The all wooden M38 Messenger was designed for small field liaison duties an first flew in 1942. About 25 were delivered to the armed forces - one being General Montgomery's hack - and with the cessation of hostilities production was geared to the civil market, bringing total production figures up to 80. Ex army Messengers also came onto the civil market.

A clean, capacious fuselage, long stroke trailing link undercarriage and fixed Miles trailing edge flaps were all features of this four seat STOL aeroplane.

A Messenger made aviation history in 1947 when, after its engine detached itself from the fuselage (due to prop. failure) it made a safe landing, almost undamaged!

There are currently 13 Messengers on the UK Register, four are flying and four are under restoration.

MILES
M38 MESSENGER

LIGHT PLANE
Gipsy Major, 145 hp.

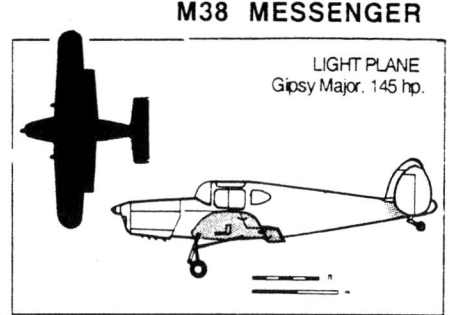

DATA	IMPERIAL		METRIC	
Span	36.2	ft	11.1	m
Wing area	191	ft²	18	m²
Aspect ratio	6.8		6.8	
Empty weight	1360	lb	617	kg
Loaded weight	2400	lb	1089	kg
Wing loading	12.5	lb/ft²	61.3	kg/m²
Max speed	115	mph	184	kmh
Cruise speed	100	mph	160	kmh
Stalling speed	45	mph	72	kmh
Climb rate	1100	ft/min	338	m/min
Range	460	mls	736	km

Designed by E O Tips of Fairey Avions Belge and first flying in 1948, the single seat Junior was one of the first new, post WW2, ultralights.

Two prototypes were built; one powered by a 36 hp. JAP J99 and the other a Walter Micron of 60 hp. Both aircraft were demonstrated in this country and assessed at Boscombe Down in 1950 – the report of this assessment was highly favourable; but no orders were forthcoming.

The Micron powered Belgian registered aircraft, OO-ULA was re-registered to Fairey UK as G-AMVP and later passed into private ownership. It was seen at the '93 PFA Rally in camouflage and is currently undergoing repairs to a damaged undercarriage on the Isle of Wight.

With an all wooden airframe, part ply' and part fabric covered, the Junior, strong and well built, was never offered as a kit – though Tips must have had a sense of 'humour' as the apparently parallel chord wing tapers just 3"! (About half an inch in length per rib!).

The late '40s were lean years for light aviation and the Junior, sadly, 'withered on the vine'.

FAIREY
JUNIOR

ULTRALIGHT
Walter Micron, 60 hp.

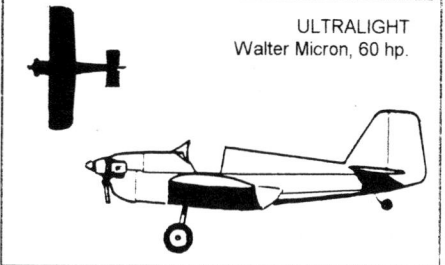

DATA	IMPERIAL		METRIC	
Span	22.6	ft	7	m
Wing area	111	sq.ft	10.4	sq.m
Aspect ratio	4.6			
Empty wt	486	lb	220	kg.
Loaded wt	770	lb	350	kg.
Wing loading	7	lb/sq.ft	34	kg/sq.m
Max speed	108	mph	173	kmph
Cruising speed	98	mph	157	kmph
Stall speed	32	mph	51	kmph
Climb	800	fpm	246	mpm
Range	300	mls	480	km

SIPA S 903

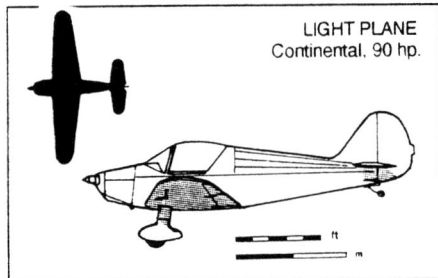

LIGHT PLANE
Continental, 90 hp.

A design competition organised by the Service de -l'Aviation Legere et Sportive in 1946, to promote sport flying in France, produced winners in several classes, one of which was the two seat SIPA S90.

Designed by Yves Gardan, the SIPA S90 was powered by a 75 hp. Mathis engine. Many variants followed, almost identical, but with different engines, i.e. S91, 85 hp. Continental; S93, 75 hp. Salmson; S94, 90 hp. Continental; S901 75 hp. Minie. The S903 with the 90 hp. Continental is the most popular version.

All wooden structure with part fabric covering, rakishly spatted main wheels and steerable tail wheel, the S903 has tapered wings with rounded tips and a similar tailplane. (Its plan silhouette is rather like a Zero!)

Over 100 of the SIPA S903 range were produced of which 11 are on the UK Register.(5 flying).

DATA	IMPERIAL		METRIC	
Span	28.6	ft	8.8	m
Wing area	120.5	ft^2	11.3	m^2
Aspect ratio	6.8		6.8	
Empty weight	895	lb	406	kg
Loaded weight	1390	lb	631	kg
Wing loading	11.5	lb/ft^2	56.3	kg/m^2
Max speed	124	mph	198	kmh
Cruise speed	96	mph	153	kmh
Stalling speed	52	mph	83	kmh
Climb rate	492	ft/min	151	m/min
Range	280	mls	448	km

De HAVILAND CHIPMUNK

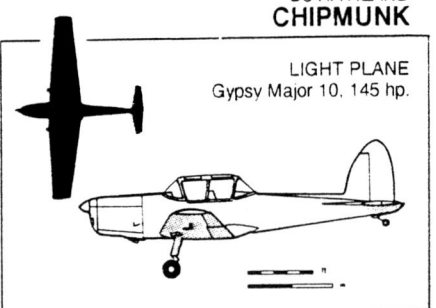

LIGHT PLANE
Gypsy Major 10, 145 hp.

Designed and built by De Haviland Canada Ltd and first flown in 1946, the first Chipmunks were built in Canada (217 off) and subsequently in the UK (1014 off) and by OGMA in Portugal.

Built either as a civilian or RAF tandem two seat trainer (740 for military use) the Chipmunk is of all metal construction and of the 1200+ built, around 140 are still on the British Register - and most of them still working for a living - not bad for a 48 year old aeroplane!

The Gypsy Major 10 is the most common power plant and the long 'greenhouse' canopy is replaced by a one piece blown perspex hood in the Canadian versions. Wheel spats are occasionally fitted.

The slim fully tapered wing, elliptical fin and rudder and the long glazed cockpit cover are all distinctive features.

A few single seat Ag. versions were also built.

DATA	IMPERIAL		METRIC	
Span	34.3	ft	10.6	m
Wing area	172.5	ft^2	16.2	m^2
Aspect ratio	6.8		6.8	
Empty weight	1425	lb	647	kg
Loaded weight	2014	lb	914	kg
Wing loading	11.7	lb/ft^2	55.6	kg/m^2
Max speed	138	mph	221	kmh
Cruise speed	102	mph	163	kmh
Stalling speed	50	mph	80	kmh
Climb rate	840	ft/min	259	m/min
Range	280	mls	448	km

An early post war French design from the drawing board of Roger Druine. It was the first really popular and successful ultralight for the homebuilder to emerge after the dark years of WW2. Many have been built over the last 40 years all over the world, and are *still* being built!

From 1958 Rollason Aircraft of Croydon produced 29 Turbulents and supplied components to home constructors to the PFA drawings.

The Turbulent is of all wood construction, the cantilever wing being ply skinned up to the main spar and fabric aft. The fuselage is ply all over, as are the tailplane and fin, with the control surfaces all fabric covered.

The landing gear has a spring strut and may be braked, plus a steerable tailwheel, or unbraked with a skid.

This rather cheeky little aeroplane is invariably powered by a VW engine of 36 hp. There are 41 on the UK Register + others being built.

DRUINE
TURBULENT

ULTRALIGHT
VW 36 hp

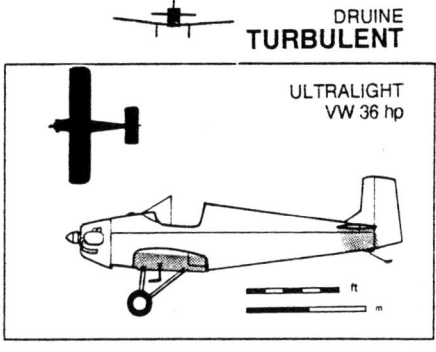

DATA	IMPERIAL		METRIC	
Span	21.4	ft	6.5	m
Wing area	80.7	ft^2	7.5	m^2
Aspect ratio	5.4		5.4	
Empty weight	350	lb	159	kg
Loaded weight	607	lb	275	kg
Wing loading	7.5	lb/ft^2	36.7	kg/m^2
Max speed	87	mph	140	kmh
Cruise speed	75	mph	121	kmh
Stalling speed	25	mph	40	kmh
Climb rate	492	ft/min	150	m/min
Range	180	mls	288	k

One of Fokker's first products after WW2 the side by side S11 was designed as a military trainer, powered by a 190 hp Lycoming 0-435-A, the S11 first flew in 1947. The Netherlands Air Force took delivery of 40, 41 went to the Israeli Defence Force and 150 were built under licence in Italy as the Macchi M416. A further 100 were built in Brazil.

A nose wheel version, the S12, was prototyped in Holland but all production took place in Brazil, where 70 were built.

When the S11 was de-militarised many came on to the civil market – most of them going to Italian clubs – though two are shown on the UK Register – one is stored at Elstree and the other, G-BIYU, is airworthy.

The S11's fuselage is of welded steel tube with fabric covering and the wings are all metal with fabric covered ailerons and manually operated flaps. The tail surfaces have a fabric covered metal structure and the tailplane is strut braced.

The cranked undercarriage legs are distinctive and terminate in hydraulically braked wheels.

FOKKER
S11 INSTRUCTOR

LIGHT PLANE
Lycoming, 190 hp.

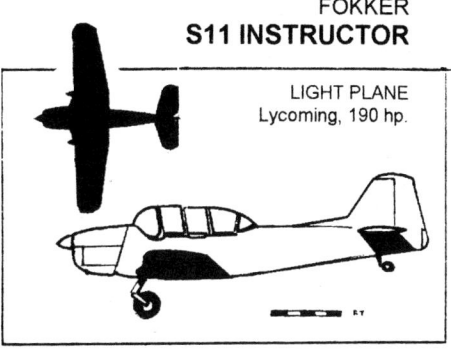

DATA	IMPERIAL		METRIC	
Span	36	ft	11	m
Wing area	199	sq.ft	18.7	sq.m
Aspect ratio	6.5			
Empty wt	1784	lb.	810	kg.
Loaded wt	2426	lb.	1100	kg.
Wing loading	12.2	lb/sq.ft	59.5	kg/sq.m
Max speed	130	mph	209	kmph
Cruising speed	102	mph	164	kmph
Stall speed	55	mph	88	kmph
Climb	650	fpm	200	mpm
Range	400	mls	640	km

Designed and built by Edouard Joly and Jean Delmontez just after WW2 and first flown in 1948, the D9 is the progenitor of the whole family of 'crank wing' Jodels and Robins.

A brilliantly simple design in all wood ideal for the amateur constructor, this little aeroplane - in the microlight weight class - has been built in the hundreds in France and elsewhere with 10 on the UK Register + two being built.

The original D9 had a Poinsard engine - all subsequent D9's had a suffix that denoted the engine type – and the D92 with the VW being the most popular.

The wing, which is stressed for 9g. has a unique main spar, a four 'longeron' ply covered box which takes all the lift, drag and torque loads. The wide parallel chord centre section and tapered, upswept outer panels form a famously efficient wing.

The rudder is aerodynamically balanced and may or may not have a minuscule fixed fin atop the tail plane.

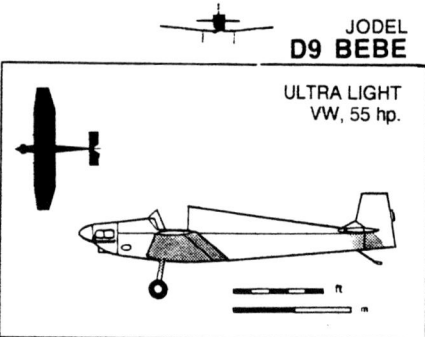

JODEL
D9 BEBE

ULTRA LIGHT
VW, 55 hp.

DATA	IMPERIAL		METRIC	
Span	23	ft	7.1	m
Wing area	97	ft²	9.1	m²
Aspect ratio	5.45		5.45	
Empty weight	435	lb	197	kg
Loaded weight	715	lb	325	kg
Wing loading	7.37	lb/ft²	36	kg/m²
Max speed	103	mph	165	kmh
Cruise speed	85	mph	136	kmh
Stalling speed	36	mph	58	kmh
Climb rate	650	ft/min	200	m/min

Roger Druine's single seat Turbulent was a pioneering plane in the homebuilt movement; he followed it with the two seat, in tandem, Turbi in the late '40s. Though not as numerous as the Turbulent, several were built in the UK.

The prototype was powered by a Beaussier engine of 45 hp. most subsequent models, however, were Walter Mikron (62 hp) powered. Other engines fitted have been, Gipsy Minor, Cirrus Minor, Coventry Victor and Continental A75.

An all wooden aeroplane of simple construction, it is PFA approved and is a 'plans only' build. The flapless wing has two box spars and is fabric covered aft of the main spar, as are the tail surfaces. The undercarriage has rubber block sprung legs and braked wheels with a steerable tail wheel; unbraked models have a steerable tail skid Both open cockpit and coupe versions have been built and the wings have 'letterbox' leading edge slots.

Two of the three UK Turbis are airworthy, the other is 'getting there'! My drawing is based on G-APBO.

DRUINE
D5 TURBI

LIGHT PLANE
Continental, 75 hp

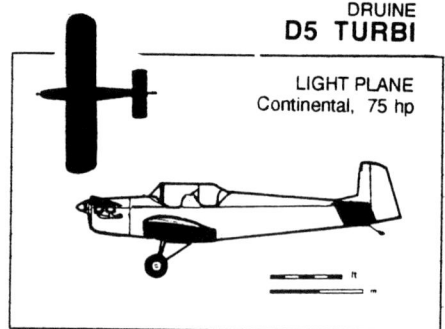

DATA	IMPERIAL		METRIC	
Span	28.7	ft	8.76	m
Wing area	130	ft²	12.9	m²
Aspect ratio	6.3		6.3	
Empty weight	725	lb	330	kg
Loaded weight	1240	lb	562	kg
Wing loading	9.5	lb/ft²	46	kg/m²
Max speed	94	mph	150	kmh
Cruise speed	74	mph	119	kmh
Stalling speed	32	mph	51	kmh
Climb rate	500	ft/min	152	m/min
Range	250	mls	400	km

A French design from the drawing board of Yves Gardan, a lightweight version of the SIPA 90, built by Constructions Aeronautique du Bearn and first flown in 1949. CAB built only a few of the neat little all wood two seater before the drawings and production rights were acquired by A. Orde-Hume who re-designed it to meet UK air worthiness requirements and to enable it to be easily 'homebuildable'.

Sets of plans have been sold world-wide including USA and Australia - where it was the first post war DCA approved plane to fly. It is also approved by the PFA and 17 are currently on the UK register. Various motors (65 - 120 hp) have been fitted - the figures in our table are for the 65 hp Continental model.

A retractable undercarriage version is known as the Gardan GY30 Supercab which has ply covered wings.

GARDAN MINICAB

LIGHT PLANE
Continental 100 hp

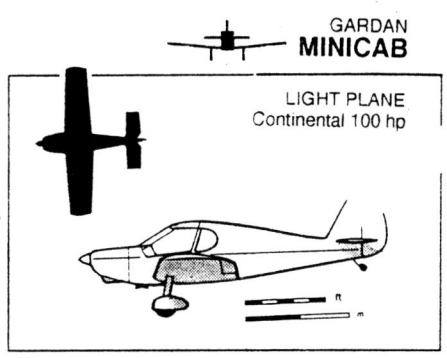

DATA	IMPERIAL		METRIC	
Span	25	ft	17.62	m
Wing area	107.6	ft^2	10	m^2
Aspect ratio	5.8		5.8	
Empty weight	595	lb	270	kg
Loaded weight	1235	lb	560	kg
Wing loading	11.47	lb/ft^2	56	kg/m^2
Max speed	124	mph	200	kmh
Cruise speed	112	mph	180	kmh
Stalling speed	47	mph	76	kmh
Climb rate	680	ft/min	207	m/min
Range	466	mls	750	km

David Long, one time Piper Chief Engineer, designed and built the Midget Mustang, an all metal, single seater for air racing. In 1949 it came 4 th. in the Continental Trophy. Afterwards it languished as a one off homebuilt racer, and David Long died before any further development could take place.

In the early 50's Robert Bushby set about productionising the Midget Mustang parts for kit assembly and by 1959 the re-engineered plane took to the air as the MM-1-85 with a 85 hp. Continental.

The MM-1-125 followed in 1963 with a 125 hp. Continental and then a two seat version, Mustang 2, with a 160 hp. Lycoming. Over 900 sets of plans and kits have been sold.

This pioneering all metal kit plane is PFA approved and there are four on the British Register.

The data below is for the MM-1-125.

BUSHBY MIDGET MUSTANG

LIGHT PLANE
Continental, 125 hp.

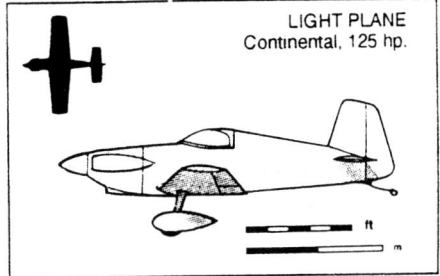

DATA	IMPERIAL		METRIC	
Span	18.5	ft	5.7	m
Wing area	68	ft^2	6.4	m^2
Aspect ratio	5		5	
Empty weight	575	lb	261	kg
Loaded weight	875	lb	397	kg
Wing loading	12.8	lb/ft^2	63	kg/m^2
Max speed	190	mph	304	kmh
Cruise speed	175	mph	280	kmh
Stalling speed	57	mph	91	kmh
Climb rate	1750	ft/min	540	m/min
Range	400	mls	640	km

Designed to AM Spec T16/48, the prototype Provost first flew in 1950 with an AS Cheetah 17 engine. Subsequent production aircraft all had the Leonides 126.

Of all metal construction, the Provost, an *ab initio* to advanced trainer was capable of carrying machine guns and under-wing bombs and was in production for ten years, during which time 461 aircraft were built. These sturdy trainers were supplied to many foreign air forces, including Eire, Burma, Rhodesia, Iraq, Muscat and Sudan. Finally being succeeded by the Jet Provost – though prop and jet models overlapped for two years.

Flaps, brakes and windscreen wipers were operated pneumatically from an engine driven compressor.

Fully aerobatic, a Percival owned and civil registered Provost (G-AMZM) was entered for the 1956 Lockheed aerobatic Contest – however, it failed to gain a place against the specialist 'stunters'.

On 'de-mobilisation' the Provosts were overhauled, stripped of AM gear and sold on to the civil market and to foreign buyers.

12 are currently on the UK Register – 9 of which appear to be airworthy and 8 are static in various UK museums.

DATA	IMPERIAL		METRIC	
Span	35.16	ft	10.8	m
Wing area	214	sq.ft	20.1	sq.m
Aspect ratio	5.8			
Empty wt	3350	lb.	1520	kg.
Loaded wt	4400	lb.	1997	kg.
Wing loading	20.5	lb/sq.ft	100	kg/sq.m
Max speed	195	mph	312	kmph
Cruising speed	177	mph	283	kmph
Stall speed	64	mph	102	kmph
Climb	2200	fpm	677	mpm
Range	450	mls	720	km

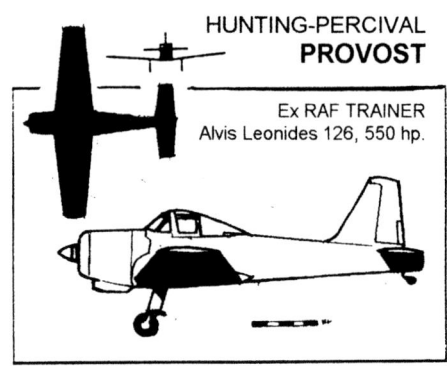

HUNTING-PERCIVAL
PROVOST

Ex RAF TRAINER
Alvis Leonides 126, 550 hp.

Percival's first all metal aeroplane the Prentice replaced the Tiger Moth as the RAF's *ab initio* trainer after the war. With a variable pitch airscrew, flaps, more comprehensive instrumentation, side by side seating and a more powerful engine the Prentice brought training more up to date.

About 400 were delivered between 1948 and '49, many of them built under contract by Blackburn Aircraft Ltd. Replaced by the Provost in 1955 a batch of 250 were sold to Aviation Traders Ltd for conversion to civil use and dispersed at airfields up and down the country. The conversion and subsequent obtaining of C of A took a couple of years and eventually 20 or more made it on to the UK Register. Devoid of military kit four or five seats could be fitted. Some were sold abroad the rest were scrapped!

The sturdy Prentice (stressed for 10g) was, in its early days, a 'spinner' and various tail forms were tried before it was cured.

Eleven are still on the UK Reg. four are flying, (One with the Shuttleworth Trust), six are in UK museums and about the same number in museums abroad. (A flying example exists in the USA).

DATA	IMPERIAL		METRIC	
Span	46	ft	14.2	m
Wing area	305	sq.ft	28.7	sq.m
Aspect ratio	7			
Empty wt	3232	lb.	1055	kg.
Loaded wt	4350	lb.	1975	kg.
Wing loading	14.3	lb/sq.ft	70	kg/sq.m
Max speed	143	mph	229	kmph
Cruising speed	126	mph	202	kmph
Stall speed	55	mph	88	kmph
Climb	650	fpm	200	mpm
Range	350	mls	560	km

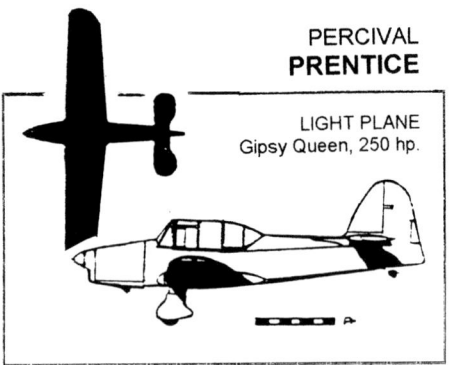

PERCIVAL
PRENTICE

LIGHT PLANE
Gipsy Queen, 250 hp.

The Jodel D.11 of 1950 has spawned a shoal of variants and, logically, if the first two digits are 11 it's of D.11 parentage i.e. D.117, D.119, even D.1190. But the D.120 through to D.126 are also derivants! More than a little confusing! (..plus the D127 and D128 built by EAC with sliding canopies).

The main Jodel 'trade mark', common to all, is its wing: a large parallel chord centre-section with no dihedral and tapered outer planes with pronounced dihedral and considerable wash-out The aerodynamic efficiency of this wing is legendary.

This side by side, all wood, two seater was developed from the pioneering single seat D.9 of 1948 by the designers E. Joly and J. Delemontez.

Jodels are still being built at Dijon and remain popular with homebuilders.

Over 100 of the D.11 tribe are on the UK Register.

JODEL D.112. CLUB

LIGHT PLANE
Continental A65-8, 65 hp.

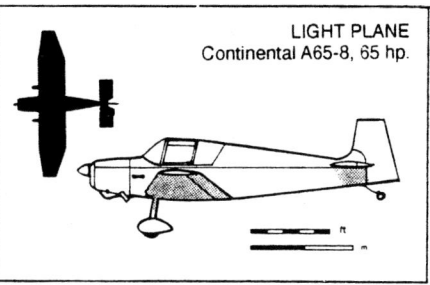

DATA	IMPERIAL		METRIC	
Span	26.8	ft	8.25	m
Wing area	136.7	ft²	12.8	m²
Aspect ratio	5.25		5.25	
Empty weight	600	lb	272	kg
Loaded weight	1145	lb	520	kg
Wing loading	8.4	lb/ft²	41	kg/m²
Max speed	118	mph	189	kmh
Cruise speed	93	mph	149	kmh
Stalling speed	45	mph	72	kmh
Climb rate	632	ft/min	194	m/min
Range	373	mls	597	km

STITS SA-3A PLAYBOY

Ray Stits designed a range of light aircraft for home building, one of the first being the single seat Playboy that first flew in 1953. A pioneer of home building, Stits started by supplying kits but went on to plans only.

Well known now for the covering products, Stits Poly-Fiber Aircraft Coatings, the light plane movement has had a doughty champion in Mr Stits.

A low wing, strut braced single seater with fixed taildragger undercarriage, the Playboy is to be seen with many minor variations of cockpit, strut arrangement, fin shape and engine model.

The fuselage is of welded steel tube and the wings are all wood with a ply' leading edge, the tail is welded tube and the whole is fabric covered.

A two seat Playboy, the SA-3B, with a two foot span increase has also been built in some numbers.

An enduring 47 year old homebuilt with up to 1000 built in the USA and three currently on the UK Register.

ULTRALIGHT
Continental, 85 hp.

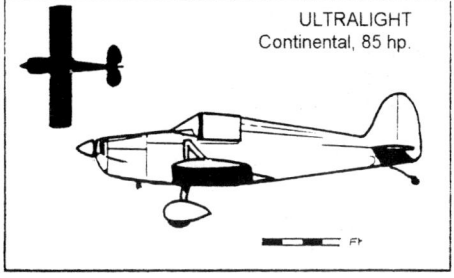

DATA	IMPERIAL		METRIC	
Span	22.1	ft	6.76	m
Wing area	96	sq.ft	8.92	sq.m
Aspect ratio	5.1			
Empty wt	600	lb.	272	kg.
Loaded wt	902	lb.	409	kg.
Wing loading	9	lb/sq.ft	44	kg/sq.m
Max speed	145	mph	232	kmph
Cruising speed	130	mph	209	kmph
Stall speed	45	mph	72	kmph
Climb	1000'	fpm	305	mpm
Range	250	mls	400	km

First flown in 1954 the Nord 3202, developed from the 3200 and 3201 civilian and military trainers, it's role was basic training, aerobatics and blind flying training.

Production ceased in 1961 by which time 100 machines had been made. Subsequently withdrawn from service during '73/75 they were sold on to the civilian market - many going to the USA.

The power unit is a Potez 4D-32 of 240 hp or - in the last batch of 50 - the Potez 4D-34D of 260 hp.

Construction comprises a welded tube fuselage with fabric covering and detachable panels; the wing has a single spar, metal nose sheeting and fabric aft. It is fitted with plain flaps which are fabric covered, as are all the flying control surfaces. The tailplane is braced by a single strut and the trailing link undercarriage legs are a distinctive feature.

Being an ex military type of rather dated construction the '3202 is much prized as a pseudo war bird and there are 3 on the UK Register.

Nord 3202s were flown in the 1966 World Aerobatic Championships by the French team.

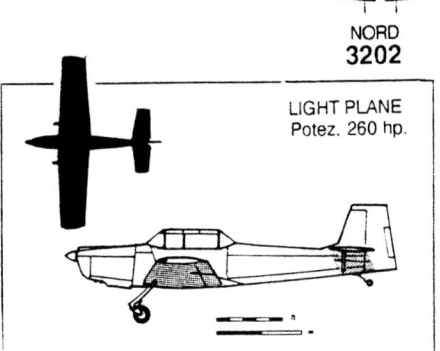

NORD
3202

LIGHT PLANE
Potez. 260 hp.

DATA	IMPERIAL		METRIC	
Span	31.1	ft	9.6	m
Wing area	175	ft^2	16.4	m^2
Aspect ratio	5.5		5.5	
Empty weight	1965	lb	892	kg
Loaded weight	2690	lb	1221	kg
Wing loading	15.4	lb/ft^2	75.1	kg/m^2
Max speed	180	mph	288	kmh
Cruise speed	120	mph	192	kmh
Stalling speed	72	mph	115	kmh
Climb rate	1122	ft/min	345	m/min
Range	575	mls	920	km

French engineer, Claude Piel designed and built the Emeraude in which he and his wife made the first flight in 1954. Since then many variants have appeared with engines ranging from 65hp to 125hp.

Manufactured in ready-made or kit form by Scintex in France, in Germany, as Smaragd, by Schempp Hirth and in the UK by Fairtravel/Garland Bianchi as the Linnet.

Of all wood construction with a semi elliptical wing - sometimes with a cropped tip - the construction is conventional with two spars, ply covering, flaps and inset ailerons (much praised for their effectiveness)

A British built Emeraude won the Best Homebuilt award at the 1990 PFA rally.

The Super Emeraude is identical to look at but is stronger and has a more powerful engine.

A good looking 50 year old aeroplane, much cherished by its owners. 35 on the UK Register.

PIEL
CP301 EMERAUDE

LIGHT PLANE
Continental 90 hp.

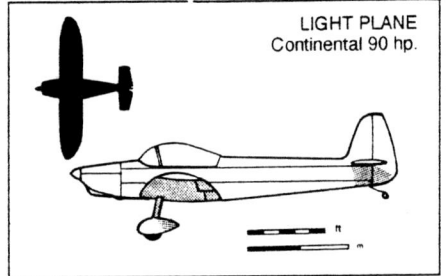

DATA	IMPERIAL		METRIC	
Span	26.5	ft	8.1	m
Wing area	117	ft^2	10.9	m^2
Aspect ratio	6		6	
Empty weight	850	lb	386	kg
Loaded weight	1500	lb	681	kg
Wing loading	12.8	lb/ft^2	62.5	kg/m^2
Max speed	124	mph	198	kmh
Cruise speed	104	mph	166	kmh
Stalling speed	47	mph	75	kmh
Climb rate	700	ft/min	215	m/min
Range	275	mls	440	km

JURCA
MJ-2 TEMPETE

The Tempete, a single seat, aerobatic sport plane which first flew in 1956, is from the drawing board of prolific Romanian/French designer Marcel Jurca.
The prototype specially designed for the amateur constructor, was built by a team from the Courevoie Aero Club and has since been copied in many countries and marketed in N. America by Falconair Aircraft in Canada.
Of all wood construction the Tempete's high rear top decking integral with the fin is a distinctive feature as are the truly half round tips to the wings and tailplane.
The single spar, low aspect ratio wing, with no dihedral, is built in three sections and supports a wide track Jodel D112 taildragger undercarriage.
Engines ranging from 65 to 125 hp. may be fitted - figures below are for the 110 hp. model.
There are two on the UK Register; the type is PFA approved.

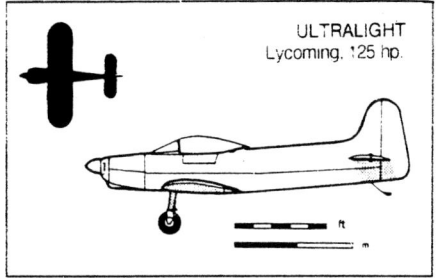

ULTRALIGHT
Lycoming, 125 hp.

DATA	IMPERIAL		METRIC	
Span	19.6	ft	6	m
Wing area	86	ft²	8	m²
Aspect ratio	4.5		4.5	
Empty weight	539	lb	290	kg
Loaded weight	948	lb	430	kg
Wing loading	7.4	lb/ft²	36	kg/m²
Max speed	120	mph	193	kmh
Cruise speed	102	mph	163	kmh
Stalling speed	45	mph	72	kmh
Climb rate	550	ft/min	170	m/min
Range	320	mls	512	km

JODEL
D140 MOUSQUETAIRE

Developed by the Societe Aeronautique Normande, the D140 Mousquetaire (Musketeer) first flew in 1958, a typical 'crank wing' Jodel with very sporty lines and four seats.
The first D140's had an un-Jodel-like triangular fin and horn balanced rudder (as shown on drawing) this soon gave way to a square tipped swept back assembly.
The D140R Abeille (Bee) is a dedicated glider tug version with a bubble canopy.
The structure of both aircraft is all wood with the wings part fabric covered - the D150 has an all moving tail plane.
These Jodels were designed for touring and their generous tankage gives them both a range of about 1000 miles.
There are 12 on the UK Register. It is a PFA approved design and one, at least, is being built.

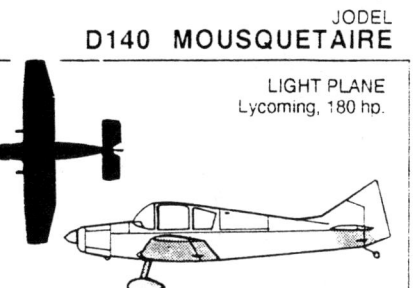

LIGHT PLANE
Lycoming, 180 hp.

DATA	IMPERIAL		METRIC	
Span	33.6	ft	10.3	m
Wing area	192	ft²	18	m²
Aspect ratio	6		6	
Empty weight	1367	lb	621	kg
Loaded weight	2645	lb	1200	kg
Wing loading	14	lb/ft²	68.3	kg/m²
Max speed	150	mph	240	kmh
Cruise speed	115	mph	184	kmh
Stalling speed	52	mph	83	kmh
Climb rate	750	ft/min	231	m/min
Range	870	mls	1393	km

Developed from the Jodel D11 two seater, the DR1050 was built under licence by SAN a close associate of Jodel, and started out as the DR100A with a 90 hp Continental, first flying in 1958. The DR1050 Ambassadeur, which followed, flew in 1959 and with it's close relative, the DR1051 Sicile, had the Potez E4-20 engine as an option to the 100 hp. Continental.

All these models had non swept rudders - with mini fins - and pitch control by tailplane and elevator.

In 1963 the '1051M variants introduced the swept fin and rudder and the one piece tailplane/stabilator.

This highly regarded four seater has the famous Jodel 'crank wing' and a fixed spatted tail dragger undercarriage.

Access to the 41 in. wide cockpit is via half depth car type doors. Construction is all wood, with ply covered fuselage and part fabric covered wings.

Running costs are claimed to be outstanding for a four seat tourer/trainer - said to be 50% lower than average!

There are 80 Jodel DR1050/1051s on the UK Register.

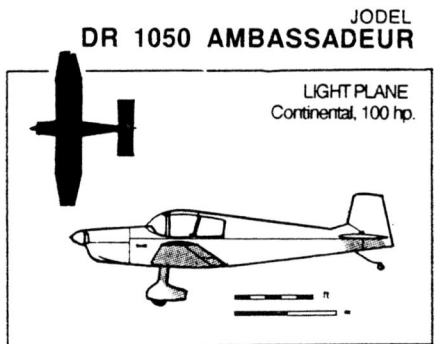

JODEL
DR 1050 AMBASSADEUR

LIGHT PLANE
Continental, 100 hp.

DATA	IMPERIAL		METRIC	
Span	28.5	ft	8.8	m
Wing area	146.4	ft^2	13.7	m^2
Aspect ratio	5.5		5.5	
Empty weight	892	lb	405	kg
Loaded weight	1651	lb	750	kg
Wing loading	11.3	lb/ft^2	55	kg/m^2
Max speed	143	mph	229	kmh
Cruise speed	120	mph	192	kmh
Stalling speed	55	mph	88	kmh
Climb rate	500	ft/min	154	m/min
Range	1000	mls	1600	km

The Taylor JT.1 Monoplane, which first flew in 1959, was one of the first post war all British Ultralights and was designed and built by John Taylor at his home in Ilford. This small and sporty monoplane powered, usually, by a 1600 cc. VW engine, has a world wide following with 100 sets of plans sold and 45 on the UK register.

The airframe is stressed to +9,-9 g and is of all wood construction it has a two spar wing with warren girder ribs, ply leading edge skinning with Dacron aft of the main spar. The fuselage is a four longeron ply covered box with, depending on builder, an open or bubble hooded cockpit. Coil springs take the loads in the main u/c legs and the tail wheel is steerable. Flaps are optional.

The flying qualities of this, now historic, little 'plane are praised by all who have flown her.

The type is PFA approved and one is being built.

TAYLOR
MONOPLANE

ULTRALIGHT
VW, 1600 cc

DATA	IMPERIAL		METRIC	
Span	21	ft	6.5	m
Wing area	76	ft^2	7.14	m^2
Aspect ratio	5.8		5.8	
Empty weight	430	lb	195	kg
Loaded weight	660	lb	300	kg
Wing loading	8.7	lb/ft^2	42.4	kg/m^2
Max speed	115	mph	184	kmh
Cruise speed	100	mph	160	kmh
Stalling speed	40	mph	64	kmh
Climb rate	1000	ft/min	308	m/min
Range	290	mls	464	km

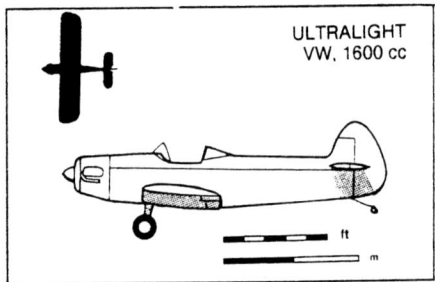

Fred Weick of Texas A&M built the AG-1 agricultural aircraft which first flew in 1950 and crashed in '53. Pipers took Weick on to develop it and the Piper AG-3 flew in 1959, becoming the PA-25 Pawnee, a dedicated single seat agricultural aeroplane which has proved to be probably the most numerous of its class. (Over 5000 made)

Variants are as follows, the Pawnee B, larger hopper and improved spray gear; Pawnee C, (1966) removable rear decking, improved landing gear, cockpit cooling and bigger engine air intake; Pawnee D, wing fuel tanks.

In 1969 the similar Pawnee Brave with a cantilever wing and square swept fin appeared, 938 of these were made, powered by a 285 hp.Continental Tiara engine. (The Pawnee brave, though similar, is a new design hence PA-36 type number).

Later developments had 300 and 375 hp. Lycomings and were named Brave 300 and Brave 375.

Though dedicated all metal aircraft builders, Piper reverted back to welded steel tube and fabric for the Pawnee.

There are 42 PA-25s on the UK Reg. (no 'Braves) - mainly used for glider tug work. Figs. below for 235 hp.

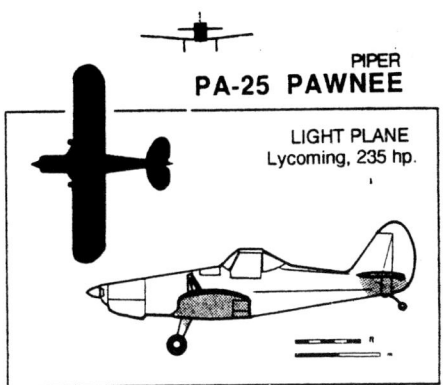

PIPER
PA-25 PAWNEE

LIGHT PLANE
Lycoming, 235 hp.

DATA	IMPERIAL		METRIC	
Span	36.1	ft	11.1	m
Wing area	183	ft²	17.2	m²
Aspect ratio	7.1		7.1	
Empty weight	1488	lb	675	kg
Loaded weight	2900	lb	1316	kg
Wing loading	15.8	lb/ft²	77	kg/m²
Max speed	117	mph	187	kmh
Cruise speed	105	mph	168	kmh
Stalling speed	60	mph	96	kmh
Climb rate	630	ft/min	194	m/min
Range	300	mls	480	km

Designed by Eugene Turner of Oklahoma and first flown in 1961 as a single seater, to be followed in '66 by the two seat version. It is marketed by Turner Aircraft Inc. of Grandview, USA. as a plans built wooden aeroplane of modern appearance.

Variants include, the T40 cabin taildragger, the Super T40A with a blister canopy and the T40B with nose wheel 'gear. G-BRIO, the sole UK aircraft is typed 'Super T40A Modified'; the wing section being drastically modified to cure bad stall characteristics. The wooden two spar wing is in three sections the outer panels attaching to a short centre section from which depends the wide track, cantilever legged undercarriage. The wing has plain flaps and pitch control is by elevon.

This neat side by side, fast cruising, two seater has been built in some numbers in its country of origin.

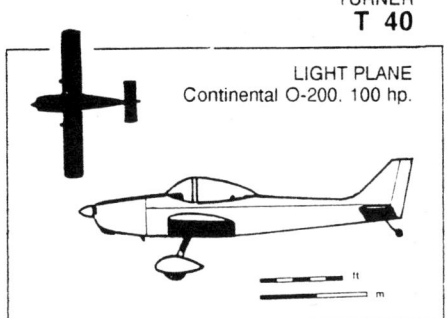

TURNER
T 40

LIGHT PLANE
Continental O-200. 100 hp.

DATA	IMPERIAL		METRIC	
Span	29.5	ft	9.1	m
Wing area	109,4	ft²	10.28	m²
Aspect ratio	7.9		7.9	
Empty weight	1000	lb	454	kg
Loaded weight	1500	lb	681	kg
Wing loading	14.5	lb/ft²	70.7	kg/m²
Max speed	170	mph	214	kmh
Cruise speed	115	mph	184	kmh
Stalling speed	61	mph	97	kmh
Climb rate	700	ft/min	215	m/min
Range	400	mls	640	km

SPEZIO
DAL-1 TUHOLER

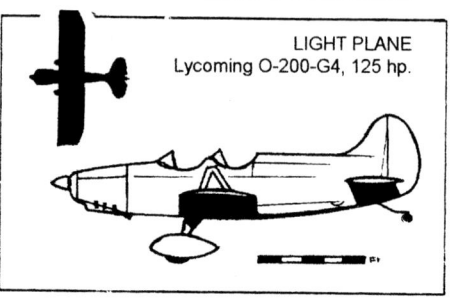

LIGHT PLANE
Lycoming O-200-G4, 125 hp.

Designed by the husband and wife team Tony and Dorothy Spezio, the Tuholer first flew in 1961. (Tuholer being 'USA speak' for two holes – ie two open cockpits).
Designed with home builders in mind, Tuholer plans are available – though not on the PFA approved list as none as yet built in the UK.
With fold-back wings the aeroplane can be stored in a normal garage and road towed on its own wheels; re-assembly at the 'field takes only ten minutes.
The steel tube fuselage is faired with wooden formers and stringers and fabric covered. The all wood, strut braced, two spar wing is fabric covered aft of the plywood nose skin.
Drum braked and spatted wheels are attached to the bungee sprung undercarriage.
With its 125 hp engine the 24 ft span Tuholer is a lively performer with a top speed of 150 mph and an initial climb rate of 2000 fpm.
Two on the UK Register – although one crashed in France, but may be re-built.

DATA	IMPERIAL		METRIC	
Span	24.7	ft	7.55	m
Wing area	115	sq.ft	10.7	sq.m
Aspect ratio	5.3			
Empty wt	810	lb.	367	kg.
Loaded wt	1400	lb.	635	kg.
Wing loading	12	lb/sq.ft	59	kg/sq.m
Max speed	150	mph	241	kmph
Cruising speed	125	mph	200	kmph
Stall speed	40	mph	64	kmph
Climb	2000	fpm	616	mpm
Range	725	mls	1167	km

Following up his successful Turbulent, Roger Druine designed the tandem two seat D61 Turbi and the side by side D62 Condor two seater along the same lines. The D62 A followed immediately powered by a Continental 0-200A engine, first flying in 1963.(A flapless, slightly lighter version the D62B was produced in smaller numbers)
Rollasons of Redhill took on the construction of an 'anglicised' version, eventually producing about 50 by 1974 when production ceased.
The Condor is an all wood aeroplane with a two spar wing which is fabric covered aft of the main spar as are all the control surfaces. The seating is side by side and the cabin hood hinges on its centre line, opening upwards each side. The tail wheel type undercarriage has cantilever main legs with drum brakes on the main wheels.
40 Condors are on the British Register and the type is on the PFA approved list.

DRUINE / ROLLASON
CONDOR

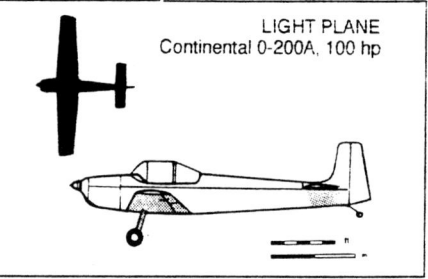

LIGHT PLANE
Continental 0-200A, 100 hp

DATA	IMPERIAL		METRIC	
Span	27.5	ft	8.38	m
Wing area	119	ft²	11.3	m²
Aspect ratio	6.3		6.3	
Empty weight	950	lb	431	kg
Loaded weight	1475	lb	670	kg
Wing loading	14.6	lb/ft²	71.3	kg/m²
Max speed	115	mph	185	kmh
Cruise speed	107	mph	172	kmh
Stalling speed	46	mph	74	kmh
Climb rate	610	ft/min	185	m/min
Range	350	mls	560	km

Peter Bowers of Boeing, an authority on vintage aeroplanes, designed the Fly Baby with the home builder in mind, made it all wood and very simple.

First flown in 1960, the design was also aimed at the EAA homebuilt competition, which it won in 1962.

Over 3000 sets of plans have been sold by Bowers plus those serialised in Sport Aviation magazine.

Its rather retro looks and wire braced wing belie the design's age and its present day popularity - flocks of them in the USA!

A biplane version, the Fly Baby Bi, was designed and built in 1968 - one, at least, modified from the monoplane,- is flying in the UK.

The monoplane's wings are hinged to fold alongside the fuselage for easy 'parking'.

The Fly Baby is a PFA approved design, there are three on the 'Register. + one being built.

BOWERS FLY BABY

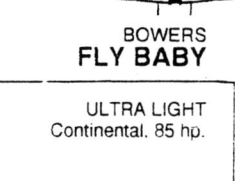

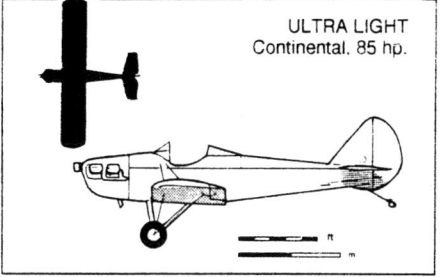

ULTRA LIGHT
Continental. 85 hp.

DATA	IMPERIAL		METRIC	
Span	28	ft	8.6	m
Wing area	120	ft²	11.3	m²
Aspect ratio	6.5		6.5	
Empty weight	605	lb	274	kg
Loaded weight	924	lb	419	kg
Wing loading	7.7	lb/ft²	37.6	kg/m²
Max speed	120	mph	192	kmh
Cruise speed	105	mph	168	kmh
Stalling speed	45	mph	72	kmh
Climb rate	1100	ft/min	338	m/min
Range	320	mls	512	km

The sporty Colibri is the brainchild of the Swiss, Max Brugger, who took the fuselage of a Jodel D9 and wings of a Turbulent as the basis of this neat single seater.

First flown in 1965, the Colibri is of all wood construction with some fabric covering and is stressed for aerobatics.

The preferred engine is the 65hp. Volkswagen.

Wheel spats may or may not be worn and some models have a finless aerodynamically balanced rudder.

It is popular with homebuilders and an example won the Best Plan Built Aircraft award at the 1993 PFA rally.

There are 16 on the UK Register and the design is PFA approved.

BRUGGER MB2 COLIBRI

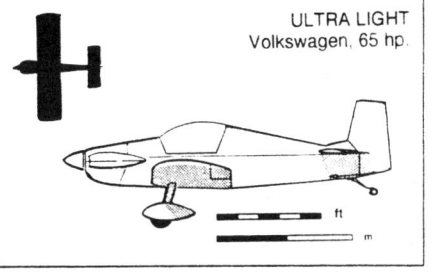

ULTRA LIGHT
Volkswagen, 65 hp.

DATA	IMPERIAL		METRIC	
Span	19.5	ft	6	m
Wing area	89	ft²	8.3	m²
Aspect ratio	4.3		4.3	
Empty weight	474	lb	215	kg
Loaded weight	727	lb	330	kg
Wing loading	8.1	lb/ft²	39.8	kg/m²
Max speed	111	mph	177	kmh
Cruise speed	99	mph	159	kmh
Stalling speed	38	mph	61	kmh
Climb rate	590	ft/min	180	m/min
Range	310	mls	497	km

An American kit plane *par excellence*. the T18 took on the factory built all metal light planes and showed them a clean pair of heels!

Designed by John Thorp, one time employee of Boeing and Lockheed and designer of the Piper Cherokee. The T18 took to the air for the first time in 1966 and was initially a 'plans only' home built. From 1970 kits were available for the all metal plane with its Jodel type 'crank wing' spanning only 21 feet and a cruising speed of 170 mph.

1500 plans and kits have been sold world-wide with, 400 of them now flying.

Several record breaking flights have been made by T18s including, round the world, Australia - England and the North Pole and back non stop. The 1976 round the world plane is now in the EAA museum, it being the first homebuilt to circumnavigate.

PFA approved, three on the Register and two being built.

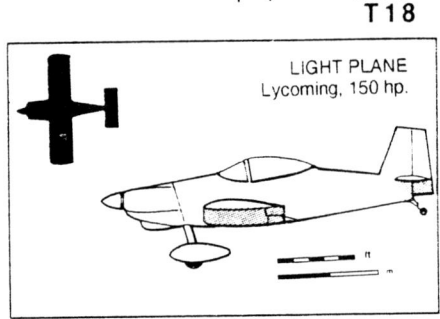

THORP
T 18

LIGHT PLANE
Lycoming, 150 hp.

DATA	IMPERIAL		METRIC	
Span	20.8	ft	6.4	m
Wing area	86	ft^2	8.1	m^2
Aspect ratio	5		5	
Empty weight	900	lb	390	kg
Loaded weight	1200	lb	521	kg
Wing loading	14	lb/ft^2	68	kg/m^2
Max speed	209	mph	334	kmh
Cruise speed	165	mph	264	kmh
Stalling speed	40	mph	64	kmh
Climb rate	1200	ft/min	370	m/min
Range	500	mls	800	km

The Czech LET company's ZX-37 Cmelak was designed as an agricultural aircraft and is of tube and fabric construction – in the Eastern bloc way – strong and simple.

In production from 1966 to 1977 over 700 were made, some fitted with turbo prop engines.

Although basically a single seat Ag-plane it has also been built with dual controls as a trainer an example of which is flying in the UK.

Many countries including Bulgaria, Finland, Germany, Hungary, India operate the Cmelak and Iraq where its rugged construction, big 315 hp nine cylinder engine and large hydraulically operated flaps are ideal for it's demanding role.

One or two have found their way on to the UK Register and although many are still flying world-wide, it is to be found in several aircraft museums.

Not the prettiest of aeroplanes but a good performer with a spray bar and half a ton of chemical or as a semi aerobatic tandem seat trainer.

LET
XZ-37 CMELAK

LIGHT PLANE
M462. 315 hp.

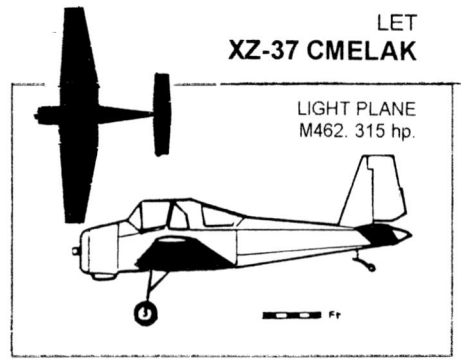

DATA	IMPERIAL		METRIC	
Span	40	ft	12.2	m
Wing area	256	sq.ft	24	sq.m
Aspect ratio	6.2			
Empty wt	2138	lb.	970	kg.
Loaded wt	4080	lb.	1852	kg.
Wing loading	16	lb/sq.ft	78	kg/sq.m
Max speed	124	mph	198	kmph
Cruising speed	112	mph	179	kmph
Stall speed	55	mph	88	kmph
Climb	728'	fpm	224	mpm
Range	370	mls	592	km

TAYLOR
TITCH

John Taylor's first design was the JT-1 Monoplane and was followed by the Titch which first flew in 1967 and had a more powerful engine plus revised easy build structure.

The Titch has proved popular, especially in the USA, its 200 mph. top speed making it a very useful tourer and it is a much admired 'classic' in those parts.

18 are on the UK Register and several are being built – the construction being well thought out for the amateur with limited resources.

A tapered, two spar, wooden wing with part ply and part fabric covering has optional flaps and broad chord ailerons. The fuselage is a ply covered semi monocoque with a bubble canopy and an integral fin.

The main 'gear legs may be the fuselage mounted leaf spring type or wing mounted coil spring legs - both, nearly always, smartly spatted.

It is PFA approved and plans plus enthusiastic backup are available from Terry Taylor at Leigh on Sea, Essex.

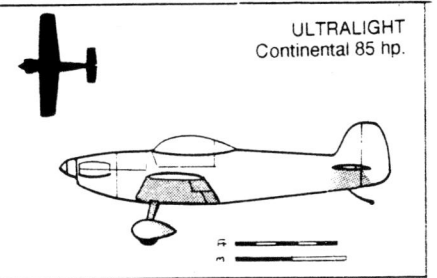

ULTRALIGHT
Continental 85 hp.

DATA	IMPERIAL		METRIC	
Span	18.75	ft	5.8	m
Wing area	68	ft²	6.4	m²
Aspect ratio	5.2		5.2	
Empty weight	505	lb	230	kg
Loaded weight	760	lb	345	kg
Wing loading	11.2	lb/ft²	54.6	kg/m²
Max speed	200	mph	320	kmh
Cruise speed	160	mph	256	kmh
Stalling speed	59	mph	94	kmh
Climb rate	1800	ft/min	554	m/min
Range	380	mls	608	km

STOREY
TSR3 WONDERPLANE

The TSR3 Wonderplane was designed and built by Tom Storey in 1968 – closely followed by PFA approval!

Airmark Ltd, of Pulborough, Sussex, was formed in 1969 to build further TSR3s, but in the end only the prototype, G-AWIV, was ever made. (Airmark went on to build, under licence, Cassutts and Rollason-Luton Betas).

Storey was a well-known racing pilot of the late 60s and early 70s and raced the TSR3, with its distinctive union jack colour scheme, as well as the Cassutts and Betas.

The TSR3 is of all wood construction with plywood and fabric covering, fixed tail-dragger gear with main wheel oleos and a tail skid. The wings have no dihedral and the large blister canopy gives excellent vision to the high-seated pilot. Powered, currently by a Continental PC60 GPU (Modified O-200) giving 100 hp. - + fine pitch prop gives spectacular rate of climb.

The TSR3 is described by its present owner (who rescued it from 10 years storage and restored it over four years) – as, 'Great fun to fly'.

LIGHTPLANE
Continental GPU, 100 hp.

DATA	IMPERIAL		METRIC	
Span	18.5	ft	5.7	m
Wing area	62	sq.ft	6.1	sq.m
Aspect ratio	5.5			
Empty wt	620	lb.	281	kg.
Loaded wt	926	lb.	420	kg.
Wing loading	15	lb/sq.ft	73	kg/sq.m
Max speed	120	mph	192	kmph
Cruising speed	100	mph	160	kmph
Stall speed	50	mph	80	kmph
Climb	1500	fpm	462	mpm
Range	370	mls	582	km

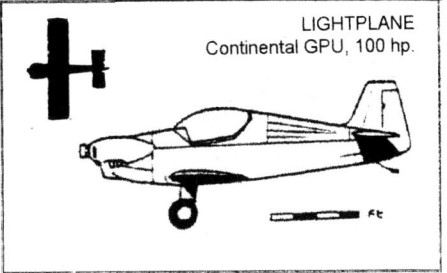

First flown in 1968 and type approved two years later the French CAP 10 is a development of the Piel Emeraude who's designer Claude Piel was a pioneer of the light plane movement in France and was on the Mudry team.

Developed by CAARP the production CAP 10B is more powerful than the Emeraude and is fully aerobatic with dual controls. The Armee de l'Air uses them as aerobatic trainers.

Avions Mudry, formed in 1968, build the all wood Cap 10 with its typical Piel semi elliptical wing and neatly faired tailwheel undercarriage.

A single seat version the CAP 20 appeared in 1973 of very similar appearance but with more horse power and a longer nose.

CAARP ceased production in 1981, but SAN at Bernay still make them.

There are 20 Cap 10s on the British Register.

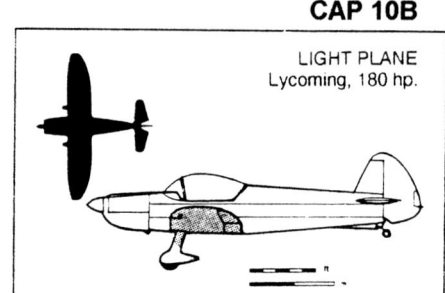

MUDRY
CAP 10B

LIGHT PLANE
Lycoming, 180 hp.

DATA	IMPERIAL		METRIC	
Span	26.5	ft	8.06	m
Wing area	116.8	ft²	10.85	m²
Aspect ratio	6		6	
Empty weight	1168	lb	530	kg
Loaded weight	1666	lb	756	kg
Wing loading	14.2	lb/ft²	69.4	kg/m²
Max speed	168	mph	280	kmh
Cruise speed	149	mph	240	kmh
Stalling speed	55	mph	88	kmh
Climb rate	1180	ft/min	363	m/min
Range	745	mls	1200	km

This delightful little homebuilt first flew in the 1969 in the USA, since then many hundreds have been built, of which 47 are on the UK Register and many are being built to PFA rules.

One of the cheapest and easiest to build of all the 'plan planes', the VP1 has been powered by various engines, the 50 hp. Volkswagen, however, being the most popular.

The all wood airframe avoids fancy curves and has a strut braced low wing, which is mainly fabric, covered; both the tailplane and rudder are 'all moving'.

A cabin or coupe version is available with a higher rear turtle back to blend with a bubble canopy considerably enhancing its rather spartan basic shape.

A side-by-side two-seater model, the VP2 is featured elsewhere in the book.

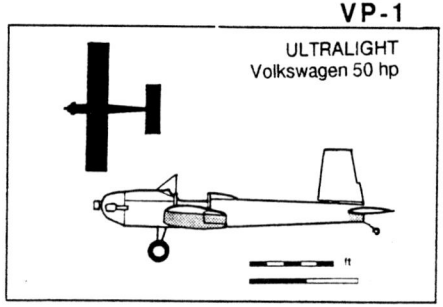

EVANS
VP-1

ULTRALIGHT
Volkswagen 50 hp

DATA	IMPERIAL		METRIC	
Span	24	ft	7.4	m
Wing area	82	ft²	7.7	m2
Aspect ratio	7		7	
Empty weight	475	lb	215	kg
Loaded weight	680	lb	308	kg
Wing loading	8.3	lb/ft²	40	kg/m²
Max speed	88	mph	140	kmh
Cruise speed	70	mph	112	kmh
Stalling speed	42	mph	67	kmh
Climb rate	350	ft/min	107	m/min
Range	232	mls	370	km

The Jodel family are legion and a mass of numbers. Briefly, the single seat D9 spawned the two seat D11 which led to the D111, D112, D113, D114, D115, D117, D118, D119, D120, D121, D122, D123, D124, D125 and D126 - all basically the same airframe with engine and equipment variations and factory or homebuilt status.

The D120 is the D117 built by the French Wassmer company and named the Paris-Nice (the D121 is the homebuilt version of the D120).

An all wooden aeroplane with the famous Jodel crank-wing which is built around a large 'Fokker' type spar which takes all the lift, drag and torsion loads. Fabric covering is employed aft of the main spar.

The, usually spatted, main gear is rubber or oleo sprung and has braked wheels; the tail wheel is steerable. Wassmer went out of business in 1977, some of their work being taken on by Issoire Aviation.

There are about 40 on the UK Register and many more in its home country.

JODEL D 120
LIGHT PLANE
Continental C90. 90 hp.

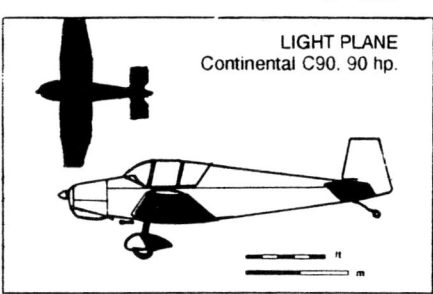

DATA	IMPERIAL		METRIC	
Span	27	ft	8.22	m
Wing area	136	ft²	12.7	m²
Aspect ratio	5.4		5.4	
Empty weight	827	lb	375	kg
Loaded weight	1433	lb	650	kg
Wing loading	10.5	lb/ft²	51.4	kg/m²
Max speed	130	mph	210	kmh
Cruise speed	118	mph	190	kmh
Stalling speed	45	mph	72	kmh
Climb rate	690	ft/min	210	m/min
Range	680	mls	1100	km

Designed and built by George Shield in Yorkshire, the Xyla first flew in 1971 at Helmswell. After several years flying the Xyla suffered an accident in 1980 that led to it being grounded and re-sold. The new owner did not finish restorations and it finished up in the roof of a car spray shop. Bought by Ken Snell (ex Concorde and Vimy pilot!) in 1997 who has painstakingly restored it, enabling it to fly in to the PFA Rally in 1999. 1500 hours work and an eye-catching yellow paint job turned many a head.

Xyla is the Greek word for wood – which is the principal constituent of its airframe. The sturdy basic airframe is ply' covered; the main gear legs and outer wing panels are attached to a short centre section and the control surfaces and rear deck are Ceconite covered.

The engine, an ex-wartime Continental of 100 hp. drove a three bladed prop on the original version but is now fitted with a two blader.

The design is PFA approved and took George Shield ten years to build – it's good to see it flying again.

SHIELD XYLA
ULTRALIGHT
Continental CPU, 100hp.

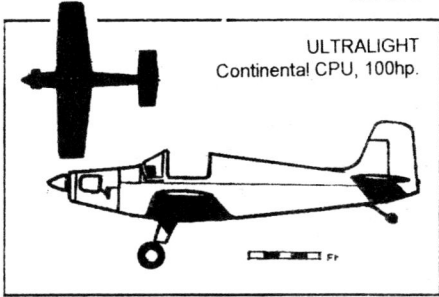

DATA	IMPERIAL		METRIC	
Span	28.2	ft	8.7	m
Wing area	135	sq.ft	12.7	sq.m
Aspect ratio	6			
Empty wt	600	lb.	272	kg.
Loaded wt	1000	lb.	454	kg.
Wing loading	7.4	lb/sq.ft	36	kg/sq.m
Max speed	120	mph	192	kmph
Cruising speed	97	mph	156	kmph
Stall speed	35	mph	56	kmph
Climb	1200'	fpm	370	mpm
Range	450	mls	720	km

PAZMANY
PL-4A

An all metal sport plane from the drawing board of Ladislao Pazmany of San Diego, the PL-4A was preceded by the successful PL-1 and PL-2 which were produced in limited numbers by various Eastern air forces.

The PL-4A is a single seater which was first flown in 1972. It has an all moving 'T' mounted tailplane, cantilever spring steel legs for the taildragger landing gear and a 1600 cc. VW engine developing about 50 hp.

The Canadian Air Force evaluated the PL-4A in 1973 and ordered 200 for cadet training - the order, in fact, never materialised, but other air forces have shown interest.

Its 'T' tail, large canopy, and high ground angle are distinctive features.

PFA approved, the PL-4A is a simple build project and five are flying in the UK.

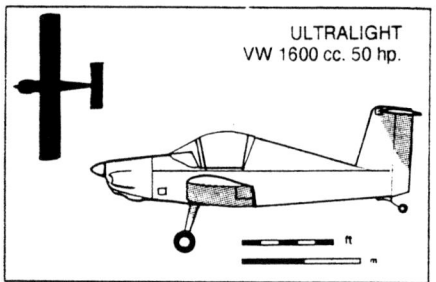

ULTRALIGHT
VW 1600 cc. 50 hp.

DATA	IMPERIAL		METRIC	
Span	26.6	ft	8.1	m
Wing area	89	ft²	8.28	m²
Aspect ratio	8		8	
Empty weight	578	lb	262	kg
Loaded weight	850	lb	386	kg
Wing loading	9.5	lb/ft²	46.6	kg/m²
Max speed	110	mph	173	kmh
Cruise speed	97	mph	156	kmh
Stalling speed	45	mph	72	kmh
Climb rate	650	ft/min	200	m/min
Range	350	mls	560	km

This little charmer from Australia was designed by John Corby and first flew in 1972. It is of all wood construction - the wings being part fabric covered - and the main wheels of the fixed tail dragger undercarriage depend on cantilever spring legs.

The Starlet is the most popular Australian homebuilt with an estimated 100 flying and about the same number under construction. In Australia it is essentially a plans built plane, but is also marketed in the USA by CSN of Fort Lauderdale, who kit some parts.

The Starlet is powered by an aero conversion VW engine of 60 hp. which propels the little single seater at a highly respectable 160 mph and gives it a climb of 1000 fpm. All this and an airframe stressed for aerobatics - no wonder it's popular!

There are two on the UK Register, the design is PFA approved and two are being built.

The drawing shows the enclosed cockpit version, open cockpit models are equally popular.

CORBY
STARLET

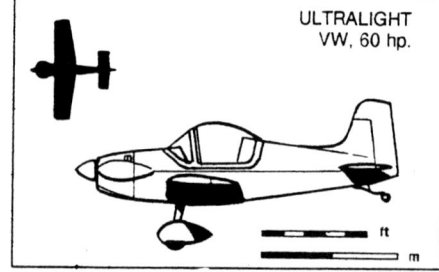

ULTRALIGHT
VW, 60 hp.

DATA	IMPERIAL		METRIC	
Span	18.5	ft	5.7	m
Wing area	68	ft²	6.4	m²
Aspect ratio	5		5	
Empty weight	450	lb	204	kg
Loaded weight	710	lb	322	kg
Wing loading	10.4	lb/ft²	51	kg/m²
Max speed	160	mph	257	kmh
Cruise speed	130	mph	209	kmh
Stalling speed	49	mph	79	kmh
Climb rate	1050	ft/min	320	m/min
Range	266	mls	428	km

Big brother of the single seat VP-1, one of the simplest plans build planes to construct. The two seat side by side VP-2 is generally similar though it has a bigger wing of greater area and 15% chord/depth ratio (VP-1 has 12%) and a variety of cockpit types including, open, large multi glazed canopy or one piece blown hood (as my drawing, based on G-BMSC).
The VPs were designed by W S Evans, an ex Convair man, the VP-1 first flying in 1969; since then many hundreds of plans have been sold and VP-1s are flying or being built al over the world. (The VP comes from Evans original name for the type - the Volksplane).
VP-2 construction is all wood with fabric covered wings and tail surfaces (which are of the all-moving type). The simple alloy plate u/c legs are non shock absorbing (being wire braced) all shocks being taken by the tyres. The type is PFA approved (though new plans are no longer available), there are 25 on the 'Register plus one being built.

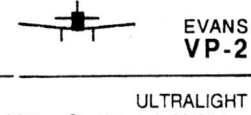

EVANS
VP-2

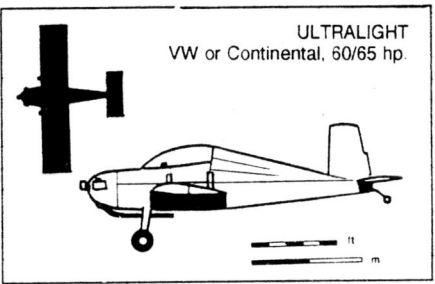

ULTRALIGHT
VW or Continental, 60/65 hp.

DATA	IMPERIAL		METRIC	
Span	27	ft	8.23	m
Wing area	130	ft^2	12.1	m^2
Aspect ratio	5.6		5.6	
Empty weight	640	lb	290	kg
Loaded weight	1040	lb	471	kg
Wing loading	8	lb/ft^2	39	kg/m^2
Max speed	100	mph	161	kmh
Cruise speed	75	mph	121	kmh
Stalling speed	40	mph	64	kmh
Climb rate	400	ft/min	122	m/min
Range	200	mls	320	km

The RV-6 is a side by side two seater designed by Dick van Grunsven and marketed in kit form by Vans Aircraft Inc. of North Plains, Oregon. The company has been supplying kits since 1973 and launched the RV-6 in 1985.
Of all metal construction, the fuselage is a monocoque and the wings, identical to the RV-4, have a light alloy skin on alloy ribs and spars. Half span ailerons and plain flaps are standard.
Non structural fairings etc. are made in GRP and the main wheels are carried on cantilever spring steel legs and have hydraulic brakes.
With a Lycoming engine of 150 or 180 hp. the RV-6 is fast, with a top speed of 202 mph.
Approved by the PFA in 1993 (non aerobatic) there are 37 on the UK Register and many being built.

VANS
RV - 6

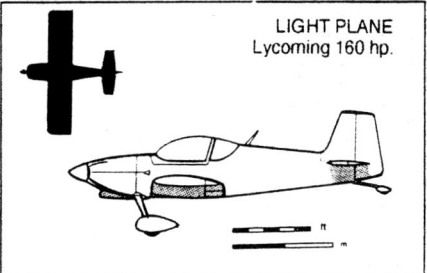

LIGHT PLANE
Lycoming 160 hp.

DATA	IMPERIAL		METRIC	
Span	23	ft	7.1	m
Wing area	110	ft^2	10.3	m^2
Aspect ratio	4.8		4.8	
Empty weight	950	lb	431	kg
Loaded weight	1600	lb	726	kg
Wing loading	14.5	lb/ft^2	70.6	kg/m^2
Max speed	202	mph	373	kmh
Cruise speed	168	mph	268	kmh
Stalling speed	54	mph	86	kmh
Climb rate	1600	ft/min	492	m/min
Range	925	mls	1480	km

ISAACS SPITFIRE

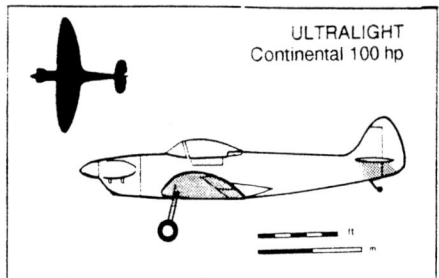

ULTRALIGHT
Continental 100 hp

The Isaacs Spitfire, a 6/10 replica of the famous WW2 fighter, was the brainchild of John Isaacs, who had earlier built a replica Hawker Fury. Isaacs designed and built this little 'classic' with it's all wood cantilever elliptical wing – no mean feat! The ply covered wooden fuselage is a semi-monocoque with a neatly faired 100 hp. Continental in front.

The Spitfire first flew in 1975 and has a sparkling performance, cruising at 134 mph and climbing at 1100 feet a minute.

The main wheels are disc braked but non retracting. It has no flaps but is fully aerobatic and is a PFA approved design.

Painted in PRU blue with RAF markings this little beauty is a 'show stopper' wherever it goes.

There are two on the UK register.

DATA	IMPERIAL		METRIC	
Span	21.12	ft	6.75	m
Wing area	87	ft²	8.1	m²
Aspect ratio	5.6		5.6	
Empty weight	805	lb	366	kg
Loaded weight	1100	lb	499	kg
Wing loading	12.6	lb/ft²	61.5	kg/m²
Max speed	150	mph	240	kmh
Cruise speed	134	mph	215	kmh
Stalling speed	52	mph	84	kmh
Climb rate	1100	ft/min	336	m/min
Range	200	mls	200	km

CRANFIELD A1-200 EAGLE

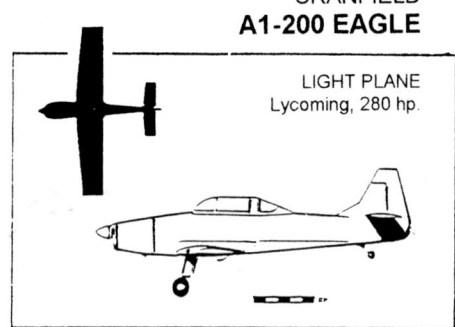

LIGHT PLANE
Lycoming, 280 hp.

Built by the Cranfield College of Technology as a dedicated aerobatic monoplane, the A1 was built to the specification of the late Neil Williams (UK aeros champion) first flew in 1976. Intended to compete at international level with the French and Eastern bloc aerobatic specialists, the A1 (G-BCIT) never quite 'cut the mustard' and went into storage at Cranfield.

In 1995 the aircraft was re-engineered as a two seater with a new canopy, rudder, paint job, registration (G-UAI) and the name Eagle.

The airframe, designed to withstand +7 to –5g, has a welded steel tube fuselage part ply' and part fabric covered and the one piece wing, which is all metal, has mean chord sweepback and 3 degrees of dihedral. The fixed tail dragger undercarriage is from a Chipmunk and the two-place hood from a Schliecher ASK 13.

The A1-200 Eagle first flew in September 1998 and development continues as a joint venture with British Aerospace.

The single seat A1.

DATA	IMPERIAL		METRIC	
Span	32.9	ft	10	m
Wing area	161.5	sq.ft	15	sq.m
Aspect ratio	6.7			
Empty wt	1700	lb.	772	kg.
Loaded wt	2205	lb.	1000	kg.
Wing loading	13.7	lb/sq.ft	67	kg/sq.m
Max speed	170	mph	274	kmph
Cruising speed	150	mph	240	kmph
Stall speed	56	mph	90	kmph
Climb	2255	fpm	688	mpm
Range	124	mls	200	km

Designed by Jean Delemontez and Alain Cauchy and first flown in 1984 the D18 (like the D11) is an all wood and fabric kit aeroplane with a VW engine, ancestrally linked to the little D9.

The proof of concept aircraft the DC01 made its first flight in 1979 and was refined into the D18 and has proved very popular with home builders in Britain and France - hundreds being under construction or flying - the traditional wooden structure is prefered by many builders as is the more affordable VW engine. 13 on the UK register and many more 'on the stocks'.

The rubber sprung undercarriage legs may be in either tail or nose wheel configuration - the latter is typed as the D19. The all flying tailplane/elevator is cable operated and fabric covered.

A neat, tight, light, good looking and efficient aeroplane.

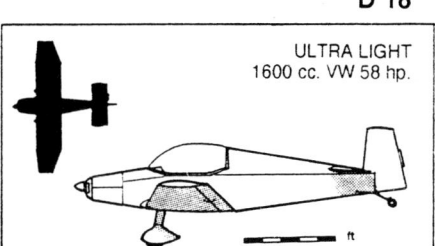

JODEL
D 18

ULTRA LIGHT
1600 cc. VW 58 hp.

DATA	IMPERIAL		METRIC	
Span	24.5	ft	7.5	m
Wing area	105.8	ft^2	9.83	m^2
Aspect ratio	5.7		5.7	
Empty weight	551	lb	250	kg
Loaded weight	1014	lb	460	kg
Wing loading	9.6	lb/ft^2	46.7	kg/m^2
Max speed	118	mph	190	kmh
Cruise speed	105	mph	170	kmh
Stalling speed	46	mph	75	kmh
Climb rate	688	ft/min	212	m/min
Range	350	mls	560	km

This German, side by side, two seat motor glider first flew in 1980 and with its all GRP/composites construction, is a very smooth and handsome aeroplane.

Various motors have been fitted, the later models having a single ignition 80 hp. Limbach SL2000EJ. (The data below is for this model). A two blade, fully feathering, three position, Hoffman prop is standard.

The canopy opens forwards and the un-flapped wings have airbrake/spoilers that are linked to the wheel brakes

The 109B has a 57 ft wing, that folds and gull wing cabin doors.

The RAF took delivery of 53 109Bs for Air Cadet training, naming it the Vigilant T1.

The performance of the Grob compares with that of the Cessna 150 – on less power and fuel.

Over 500 109s have been built of which 25 are on the UK Register

GROB
G 109

MOTOR GLIDER
Limbach 59 hp.

DATA	IMPERIAL		METRIC	
Span	54.5	ft	16.6	m
Wing area	220	sq.ft	20.7	sq.m
Aspect ratio	13.5			
Empty wt	1320	lb.	600	kg.
Loaded wt	1820	lb.	826	kg.
Wing loading	8.3	lb/sq.ft	40	kg/sq.m
Max speed	130	mph	208	kmph
Cruising speed	118	mph	189	kmph
Stall speed	47	mph	75	kmph
Climb	530	fpm	163	mpm
Range	557	mls	892	km

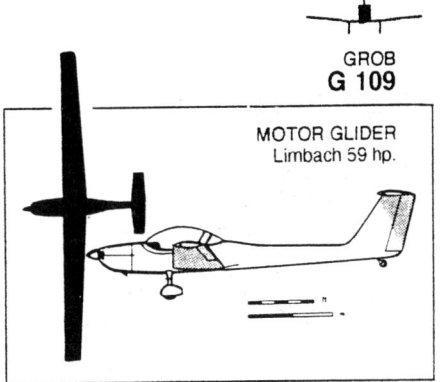

The RV-4 is a tandem two seater designed by Dick van Grunsven and sold in kit form by Vans Aircraft Inc. of North Plains, Oregon. The company has been in the kit plane business since 1973 and introduced the RV-4, it's first two seater, in 1981.

Of all metal construction, the fuselage is a monocoque and the wings have light alloy stressed skin over alloy ribs and spars. Half span ailerons and plain flaps are standard. Non structural fairings etc. are moulded in GRP.

The main wheels are carried on spring steel legs and have hydraulic brakes.

With either a 150 or 180 hp, Lycoming engine the 23 ft. span RV-4 has a slight edge on its sister, RV6, due to its slimmer fuselage

A PFA approved design, there are 15 on the 'Register and several being built.

The RV-8 is a broader, taller version for the taller pilot!

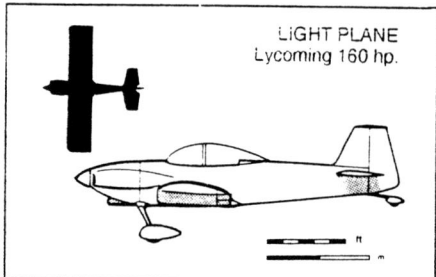

VANS
RV - 4

LIGHT PLANE
Lycoming 160 hp.

DATA	IMPERIAL		METRIC	
Span	23	ft	7.1	m
Wing area	110	ft²	10.3	m²
Aspect ratio	4.8		4.8	
Empty weight	905	lb	410	kg
Loaded weight	1500	lb	681	kg
Wing loading	13.6	lb/ft²	66.4	kg/m²
Max speed	205	mph	378	kmh
Cruise speed	170	mph	272	kmh
Stalling speed	54	mph	86	kmh
Climb rate	1650	ft/min	508	m/min
Range	800	mls	1280	km

A two seat sport plane from France, designed by Henri Nicollier and developed from his single seat HN433 - their lines are almost identical - the HN700 first flew in 1989.

Of all wood construction with plywood and fabric covering the Menestrel (Minstrel in English) is usually powered by a 2000cc. Limbach engine - distantly related to the VW - and popular in powered gliders, develops 77 hp.

The Menestrels fine lines and semi elliptical wing plan enhance its very useful performance - cruising at 112 mph. whilst consuming only 3 gph. - or 40 miles per Gallon!

A PFA approved design with two on the 'Register.

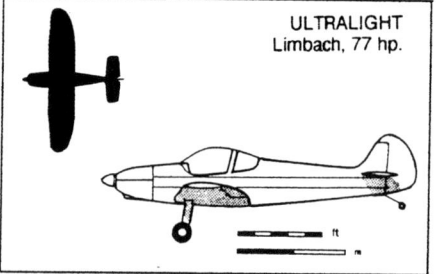

NICOLLIER
HN700 MENESTREL

ULTRALIGHT
Limbach, 77 hp.

DATA	IMPERIAL		METRIC	
Span	25.5	ft	7.8	m
Wing area	105.5	ft²	10	m²
Aspect ratio	6.2		6.2	
Empty weight	622	lb	282	kg
Loaded weight	1103	lb	500	kg
Wing loading	10.45	lb/ft²	51	kg/m²
Max speed	124	mph	198	kmh
Cruise speed	112	mph	179	kmh
Stalling speed	50	mph	80	kmh
Climb rate	1180	ft/min	364	m/min
Range	590	mls	944	km

Auguste Mudry began building the CAP series at Bernay with CAARP in 1958. The CAP 20 and 21 were single seat wooden aerobatic aircraft with elliptical wings developed from the CAP 10 two seater, in turn, developed from the Piel Emeraude. Then came the '231, first flown in 1990, of which 20 were built by 1994 - one of the first going to T. Bianchi, the UK agent, at White Waltham.

The wing, which is stressed for +10,-10 g, has a single spar, is plywood covered and has 80% span ailerons.

The cantilever sprung undercarriage legs, mounted on the welded tube fuselage, are of GRP construction and carry the disc braked wheels.

The CAP EX, first flown in 1991, is the same plane fitted with the German Extra 260 carbon fibre wing. From 1995 Mudry will make their own carbon fibre wings - hence the CAP 232.

The 231 EX climbs faster than the '230 whose data is below, and which won the 1993 World Championships. There is one CAP 231's on the UK Register.

MUDRY CAP 231

LIGHT PLANE
Lycoming, 300 hp.

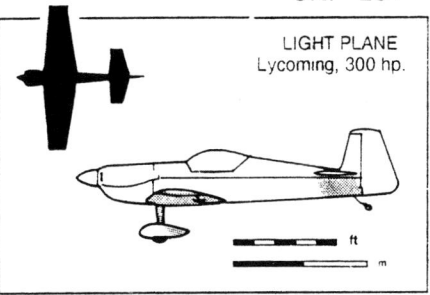

DATA	IMPERIAL		METRIC	
Span	26.5	ft	8.1	m
Wing area	106.1	ft^2	9.86	m^2
Aspect ratio	6.6		6.6	
Empty weight	1389	lb	630	kg
Loaded weight	1609	lb	730	kg
Wing loading	15.2	lb/ft^2	74	kg/m^2
Max speed	205	mph	330	kmh
Cruise speed	186	mph	300	kmh
Stalling speed	56	mph	90	kmh
Climb rate	3150	ft/min	960	m/min
Range	223	mls	360	km

A ghost - from Small Plane Publishing's archives.

Heston Phoenix

The Heston Aircraft Co. Ltd was formed in 1934, taking over the assets of Comper Aircraft Ltd and the Phoenix was its first venture. A bulky five seater - pilot and four passengers - the Phoenix was powered by a 200 hp Gipsy Six engine (later models had the Series 2 with VP airscrew) and it first flew in 1935.

Of all wood construction with fabric covered flying surfaces the Phoenix was remarkable, for its time, for its retractable undercarriage, a Dowty designed hydraulic assembly which folded the wheels inwards into the stub wing to which the wing bracing struts were attached. The square section cabin module faired into a semi monocoque rear fuselage of elliptical form sporting a spatted tailwheel.

The Phoenix cruised at 125 mph. Its occupants housed in a roomy cabin of exceptional quietness whilst their luggage was stowed in a separate compartment in the rear fuselage.

The second aircraft was bought by an Australian operator for air line work in that country and after having flown to its new home it was struck by lightning and crashed within a few months of its arrival.

Another Phoenix was used extensively by Standard Telephone and Cable for air radio development work.

Six were built altogether, three being impressed in 1940 as communications aircraft. G-AESV the ex Standard Telephones aircraft survived its impressement to become a civil aircraft again and was flying up to 1952 when it collided with a French mountain and thus extinguished the breed.

Authors note : As a boy in '38, I built a flying model Phoenix from a Frog(?) kit. Big things must have been expected of the Phoenix for a company to tool up, produce and market such a model.

© D Armour

Span	40.3ft (12.4 m)	Wing loading,	12.7 lb/ft^2 (62 kg/)
Length	30.1ft (9.3 m)	V max,	145 mph (232 kmh)
Wing Area	260 ft^2 (24 m^2)	V cruise,	125 mph (200 k
Aspect ratio	6.24	V min,	60 mph (96 k
Empty wt,	2000 lb (908 kg)	Climb,	650 ft min (200 m/min)
Loaded wt,	3300 lb (1498 kg)	Range,	500 mls (800km)

BEECH
BONANZA

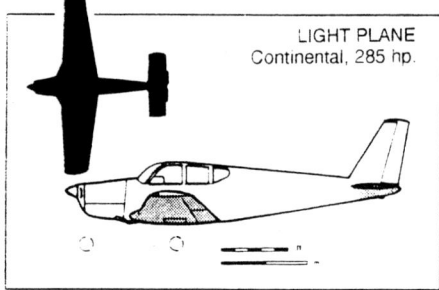

LIGHT PLANE
Continental, 285 hp.

The Model 35 Bonanza, which first flew in 1945, and its variants have been in continous production since 1947 - some 14000 models built and still sought after.

Its continuing popularity and almost cult status is down to its high performance - 200 mph. cruise - rugged and superb build, its 4/5 seats and its deserved tag of 'the Rolls Royce of its class'.

The Bonanza is famous (and for a while - infamous) for its 'V' tail, though the later models, still in production, have convential tails.

The first Bonanzas had 185 hp. Continentals and four seats, the specification has crept up to 260 hp. and six seats. The Model 33 was originaly named the Debonair but became Bonanza in 1967 - the current 'Bonanza", the six seat A36 is essentially a single engined Baron.

Well equiped, with a luxury interior, the Bonanza is not a cheap aeroplane - but one much drooled over!
There are 25 on the UK Register. .(inc. 10 'V' tails).

DATA	IMPERIAL		METRIC	
Span	33.5	ft	15.2	m
Wing area	181	ft^2	17	m^2
Aspect ratio	6.2		6.2	
Empty weight	1885	lb	836	kg
Loaded weight	3300	lb	1498	kg
Wing loading	18.2	lb/ft^2	89	kg/m^2
Max speed	212	mph	339	kmh
Cruise speed	205	mph	328	kmh
Stalling speed	62	mph	99	kmh
Climb rate	1200	ft/min	369	m/min
Range	1145	mls	1832	km

YAKOVLEV
YAK 18

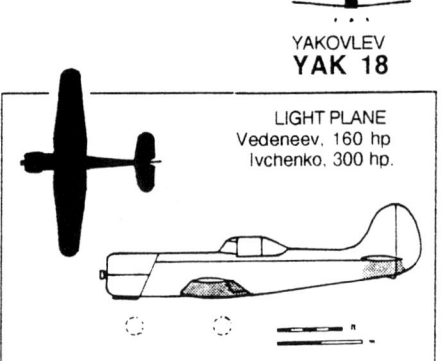

LIGHT PLANE
Vedeneev, 160 hp
Ivchenko, 300 hp.

This Russian plane, well known for its record in top class aerobatics, started life as tandem seat military trainer in 1947. Practically the whole Red Air Force was trained on it - including Yuri Gagarin; and many hundreds were exported to Eastern bloc countries, even being productionised in China.

In 1960 '18's ' became available on the civil market and it's possibilities as an aerobat were soon realised.

All the early models had rearward retracting undercarriages, with the '18 P came inward retraction and a 260 hp. engine, soon to give way to the 'PM (data below) with less dihedral and a rearward sited cockpit. The lightweight 18 M, though maintaining its metal structure, was largely fabric covered and had upped the power with a 300 hp. Ivchenko.

In 1966 YAK 18 PM's took the first four places in the World Aerobatic Championships.

Though based on the YAK 18 series the latest YAK aerobats, the 50 & 55, are totally new, smaller airframes.
There are six YAK 18s on the UK Register.

DATA	IMPERIAL		METRIC	
Span	35	ft	10.6	m
Wing area	183	ft^2	17.2	m^2
Aspect ratio	6.7		6.7	
Empty weight	1819	lb	825	kg
Loaded weight	2425	lb	1100	kg
Wing loading	13.2	lb/ft^2	64.6	kg/m^2
Max speed	196	mph	313	kmh
Cruise speed	175	mph	280	kmh
Stalling speed	58	mph	93	kmh
Climb rate	1968	ft/min	606	m/min
Range	100	mls	160	km

Two seat trainer

The Yak 18T is the last in a long line of Yakolev 18s (see elsewhere in book) which go back to 1947. The early trainers were produced in huge numbers - 8000 of the tandem two seater tail dragger with the long 'greenhouse' canopy. With the '18U came a retracting tricycle undercarriage and the '18A, also a trike, had the 260 hp. Ivchenko engine. The '18P was the single seat aerobat and the 'PM had a rear sited cockpit and a 300 hp Ivchenko - the 'PS was the same aircraft with a tail dragger undercarriage

The four seat cabin Yak 18T first flew in 1967 and with its big radial engine, stalky landing gear and substantial cabin framing, has a vaguely vintage look.

Production officially ceased in 1989 when 200 had been made - but limited production re-started in 1993. Powered by a growling Vedneyev VOKBM M-14P nine cylinder radial of 335 hp the '18T is unique, for a four seater, in being fully aerobatic.

There are eleven in the Register - mainly still bearing their Russian registrations.

YAKOLEV 18 T

LIGHT PLANE
Vedneyev. 335 hp.

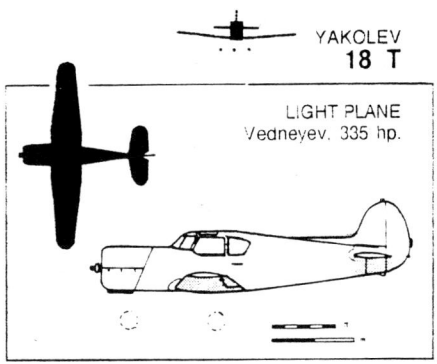

DATA	IMPERIAL		METRIC	
Span	36.6	ft	11.3	m
Wing area	202	ft^2	19	m^2
Aspect ratio	6.6		6.6	
Empty weight	2676	lb	1214	kg
Loaded weight	3637	lb	1650	kg
Wing loading	18	lb/ft^2	88	kg/m^2
Max speed	184	mph	294	kmh
Cruise speed	126	mph	202	kmh
Stalling speed	68	mph	108	kmh
Climb rate	985	ft/min	303	m/min
Range	562	mls	900	km

The original M20 was of part wooden construction - pressure bonded laminated spruce - and first flew in 1953. It was a four seat touring aeroplane with a retractable tricycle undercarriage, and distinguished from similar low wing cabin types by its raked forward fin (actually vertical) - with a tailplane of similar geometry.

In 1961 it was re-engineered as an all metal aeroplane and a year later the M20D flew with fixed undercarriage - one of many variants.

Other models flew with different engines and standard of equipment fit after Butler Aviation, and finally Republic Steel Corp. took over production. The M20 range continued in production up to 1976 when over 7000 had been produced. Some variants (M20C, M20E) have a small 'acorn' fairing at the top of the fin and a five seat pressurised version, the M22 has three cabin windows.

Latest models, TLS and Ovation have longer fuselages and windows plus turbo charged power.

56 M20's are on the UK Register.

MOONEY M20 CHAPARALL

LIGHT PLANE
Lycoming, 180 hp.

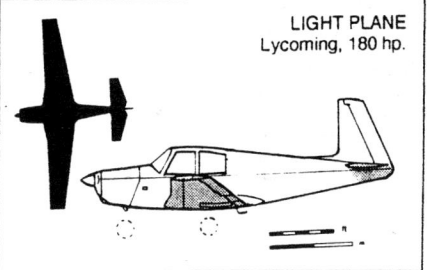

DATA	IMPERIAL		METRIC	
Span	35	ft	10.67	m
Wing area	167	ft^2	15.5	m^2
Aspect ratio	7.3		7.3	
Empty weight	1525	lb	691	kg
Loaded weight	2575	lb	1168	kg
Wing loading	15.4	lb/ft^2	75.2	kg/m^2
Max speed	185	mph	296	kmh
Cruise speed	159	mph	254	kmh
Stalling speed	58	mph	93	kmh
Climb rate	800	ft/min	246	m/min
Range	800	mls	1128	km

SEQUOIA/FRATI
F8L FALCO

LIGHT PLANE
Lycoming, 160 hp.

Italian designer, Stelio Frati, a post war light plane pioneer, designed the sleek, two seat Falco which first flew in 1955. Licence built in small numbers by various firms the Falco became available in kit form, from Sequoia, from 1980.

The all wood airframe is stressed for +6-3g, is cleared for basic aerobatics, and carries the PFA 'seal of approval' - indeed winning the Best Homebuilt award at the PFA rally in 1989.

The bubble canopy, unswept fin and rudder with long ventral fin, straight tapered wings, are all identifying features as, in the air, are the retractable tricycle wheels.

A fast mover which has gained favour as a racing aircraft - 212 mph.- with faultless flying characteristics.

Falcos are built by four companies, Aviamilano, Aeromere, Laverda and kitted by Sequoia in the USA. There are 13 on the UK Register plus others being built.

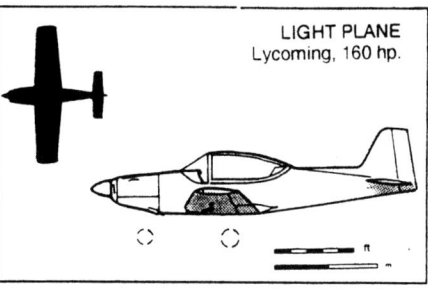

DATA	IMPERIAL		METRIC	
Span	26.25	ft	8.1	m
Wing area	107.5	ft²	10.1	m²
Aspect ratio	6.4		6.4	
Empty weight	1212	lb	550	kg
Loaded weight	1880	lb	853	kg
Wing loading	17.5	lb/ft²	85.4	kg/m²
Max speed	212	mph	340	kmh
Cruise speed	170	mph	272	kmh
Stalling speed	65	mph	104	kmh
Climb rate	1140	ft/min	371	m/min
Range	850	mls	1360	km

First flown in 1956, powered by a 180 hp. Lycoming, the four seat PA24 Comanche was soon up-engined to a Lycoming of 250 hp. - this model the PA 24- 250 soon became the standard production model.

Advanced for its time, this all metal tourer was the predecessor of the Cherokee, which at first it appears to resemble. The more powerful Comanche is much heavier than the Cherokee and faster; its tapered wing and tailplane plus the retracting gear sort it out from the standard PA28.

Some 5000 Comanches have been built - a great number - but a long way off the 30,000 its best selling brother the Cherokee has clocked up.

The PA 30 Twin Comanche is virtually a PA 24 Comanche with two 160 hp. Lycomings; structural interchangeability being kept to a maximum.

There are 33 PA 24 Comanches on the UK Register

PIPER
PA 24 COMANCHE

LIGHT PLANE
Lycoming, 250 hp.

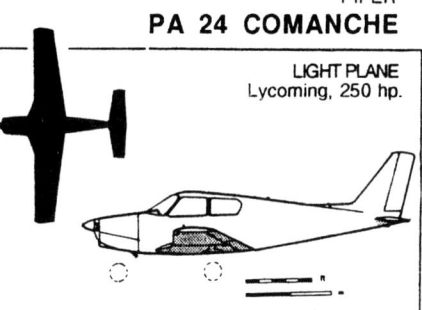

DATA	IMPERIAL		METRIC	
Span	36	ft	11.1	m
Wing area	178	ft²	16.7	m²
Aspect ratio	7.3		7.3	
Empty weight	1690	lb	767	kg
Loaded weight	2900	lb	1316	kg
Wing loading	16.3	lb/ft²	79.5	kg/m²
Max speed	190	mph	304	kmh
Cruise speed	181	mph	289	kmh
Stalling speed	62	mph	99	kmh
Climb rate	1350	ft/min	415	m/min
Range	1650	mls	2640	km

A French design from the drawing board of Yves Gardan who has been responsible for several light planes including the Minicab.

The Horizon, which first flew in 1960, is a four seater of all metal construction with a retractable tricycle undercarriage.

Design rights were sold in 1962 to Sud Aviation and pruduction continued under the SOCATA banner, 260 or more beeing built in the sixties. First run models were powered by a 160 hp. Lycoming and under SOCATA the 180 Lycoming was offered.

An improved version the Super Horizon or ST 10 Diplomate with a 200 hp. Lycoming, longer fuselage, redesigned tail nit and roomier cabin appeared in 1967 but had only a limited production run.

There are 15 Horizons on the UK Register.

GARDAN
GY80 HORIZON

LIGHT PLANE
Lycoming, 160 hp.

DATA	IMPERIAL		METRIC	
Span	31.8	ft	9.7	m
Wing area	140	ft²	13	m²
Aspect ratio	7.2		7.2	
Empty weight	1367	lb	620	kg
Loaded weight	2425	lb	1100	kg
Wing loading	17.3	lb/ft²	84.5	kg/m²
Max speed	149	mph	240	kmh
Cruise speed	145	mph	234	kmh
Stalling speed	60	mph	96	kmh
Climb rate	690	ft/min	212	m/min
Range	590	mls	950	km

First flown in 1970 the Commander 112 is powered by a 200 hp. Lycoming and the Commander 114, which followed in 1976 has a Lycoming of 260 hp.

This rakishly good looking all metal aeroplane with a retractable tricycle undercarriage cruises at 175 mph., climbs at 1000 ft/min. and has a range of over 1000 miles - a very useful performance for a well equipped four seater with plenty of shoulder room.

The tailplane is, unusually mounted half way up the fin and the straight mainplane leading edge can appear to be swept forward due to the swept back root extensions.

Access to the cabin is via car type doors on either side.

Made now by Commander Aircraft, production figures are, Commander 112, 726 off and Commander 114, 429 off. (Still in production).

They are prettv well represented on the UK Register with 70 showing at the last count.

Figures below are for the Commander 112.

ROCKWELL
COMMANDER 112

LIGHT PLANE
Lycoming, 210 hp.

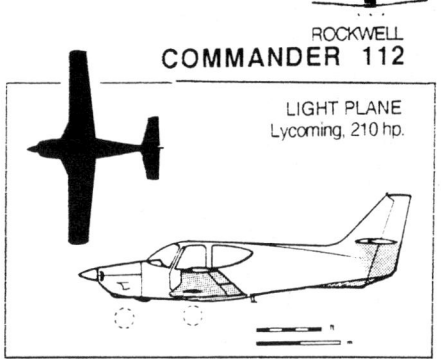

DATA	IMPERIAL		METRIC	
Span	35.5	ft	11	m
Wing area	160	ft²	15	m²
Aspect ratio	7.8		7.8	
Empty weight	1530	lb	694	kg
Loaded weight	2550	lb	1157	kg
Wing loading	16	lb/ft²	78	kg/m²
Max speed	190	mph	304	kmh
Cruise speed	175	mph	281	kmh
Stalling speed	58	mph	93	kmh
Climb rate	1000	ft/min	305	m/min
Range	1130	mls	1808	km

The HR 100 is one of the all metal Robins, and though similar to the HR 200, it is a bigger aeroplane, carrying up to five people, and unlike the wooden Robins, does not have a crank wing.

First flown in 1972 the HR 100 - in the French manner - comes in many variants. The first 31 aircraft, designated HR 100/200, were four seaters with a retractable tricycle undercarriage. (The suffix indicates horse power). This was followed by the fixed 'gear version, the HR 100/210, 78 of which were made. In late '72 the Tiara (illustrated) was a retracting gear five seater with more horse power - hence HR 100/285. A six seater with extended cabin glazing appeared in 1975 as the HR 100/4+2 (change of nomenclature here!) having a 320 hp. Lycoming which booted its cruise up to 168 mph.

On all variants the windscreen has a central glazing bar - divided windscreen.

There are 18 Robin HR 100's on the UK Reg.

(Ed. HR stands for Heintz-Robin).

ROBIN
HR 100

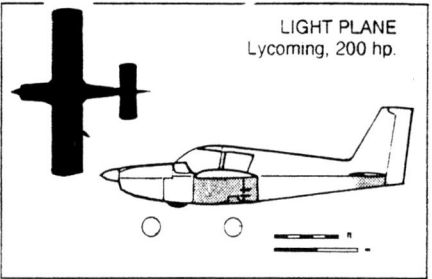
LIGHT PLANE
Lycoming, 200 hp.

DATA	IMPERIAL		METRIC	
Span	29/8	ft	9.08	m
Wing area	163.6	ft²	15.2	m²
Aspect ratio	5.42		5.42	
Empty weight	1609	lb	730	kg
Loaded weight	2755	lb	1250	kg
Wing loading	16.8	lb/ft²	82.3	kg/m²
Max speed	171	mph	275	kmh
Cruise speed	154	mph	248	kmh
Stalling speed	66	mph	106	kmh
Climb rate	885	ft/min	270	m/min
Range	845	mls	1360	km

The Russian design philosophy is 'make 'em simple, make 'em strong, and make a lot of them (like the Kalashnikov); so it is with the YAK 18 - 52 series of airframes. Though bearing a family resemblance to the YAK 18, they are structurally different inasmuch that the YAK 50 series have fully monocoque fuselages.

The YAK 50 was a single seat aerobatic aircraft with backward retracting tail-wheel undercarriage (World Champion first in 1976 and '82) and the YAK 52 a tandem two seater with the same airframe and engine (Vedeneyev M-14P) but forward retracting main wheels and rearward nose-wheel retraction. All flying controls are push rod or cable operated and the split trailing edge flaps are pneumatic. Immensely strong (+7, -5g) the YAK 52 is fully aerobatic.

Production of the YAK 52 was taken over by IAv Bacau, the Romanian company in the late '70s - the Bacau built prototype first flying in 1978. In the following ten years over 1500 were built. There are 60 on the UK Register, many with Eastern Bloc markings - inc. in service markings, the R N Flying Clubs.

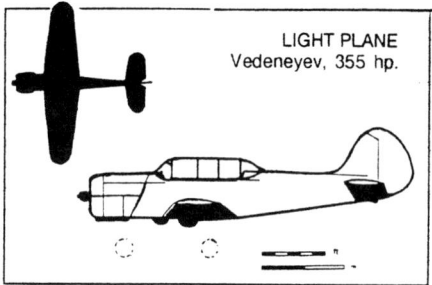
YAKOLEV
52

LIGHT PLANE
Vedeneyev, 355 hp.

DATA	IMPERIAL		METRIC	
Span	30.5	ft	9.3	m
Wing area	161.5	ft²	15	m²
Aspect ratio	5.8		5.8	
Empty weight	2204	lb	1000	kg
Loaded weight	2844	lb	1290	kg
Wing loading	17.6	lb/ft²	86	kg/m²
Max speed	186	mph	300	kmh
Cruise speed	160	mph	256	kmh
Stalling speed	56	mph	90	kmh
Climb rate	1476	ft/min	450	m/min
Range	341	mls	550	km

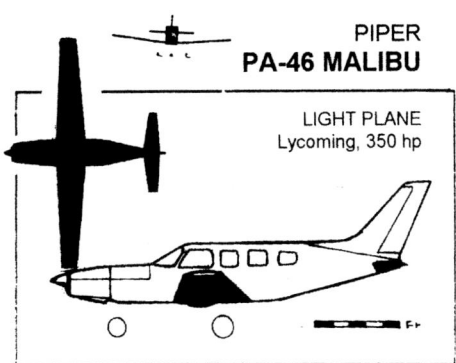

PIPER
PA-46 MALIBU

LIGHT PLANE
Lycoming, 350 hp

First flown in 1979, the Malibu was claimed to be the first cabin class, pressurised piston powered aircraft. Over 700 of these big singles have been sold to date – nine are on the UK Register – and the latest variant the Malibu Mirage, is currently in production.

The first Malibu, the PA-46-310P, had a straight tapered high aspect ratio wing and a 310 hp. turbo charged continental engine; the following PA-46-350P Malibu Mirage was re-engined with a 350 hp. Lycoming.

In 1999 the Malibu Meridian flew with a 400 shp. Pratt and Whitney turboprop engine and a new wing with swept back inboard 'cuffs'. (Latest 'Mirages have this wing – without the 'cuffs').

The seating is for five passengers and a pilot in a cabin pressurised to maintain 8,000 ft level up to 25,000 ft.

The inward retracting main wheels and the 90 degree twisting and rearward retracting nose wheel are hydraulically operated, as are the flaps and brakes.

Pneumatic de-icing boots on the wing and tail leading edges are optional.

Details below for the Malibu Mirage

DATA	IMPERIAL		METRIC	
Span	43	ft	13.1	m
Wing area	175	sq.ft	16.3	sq.m
Aspect ratio	10			
Empty wt	3157	lb.	1433	kg.
Loaded wt	4340	lb.	1970	kg.
Wing loading	24.8	lb/sq.ft	121	kg/sq.m
Max speed	253	mph	405	kmph
Cruising speed	245	mph	391	kmph
Stall speed	67	mph	107	kmph
Climb	1218	fpm	375	mpm
Range	1213	mls	1941	km

The two seat Lancair 320 (pronounced Lance-air) is developed from Lancair types 200 and 250, first flown in 1984; the type numbers referring to the model of Continental motor used. The 160 hp Lancair 320 took to the air in 1986 and immediately made a big first impression with its sleek lines and fighter like performance - 250 mph max. level speed.

Constructed of pre moulded and part assembled units of high strength composites giving a very smooth skin finish, which combined with the retractable tricycle undercarriage, electrically operated flaps and constant speed airscrew enhance its remarkable performance figures.

Four seat kit Lancairs are now flying, the Lancair IV and the Columbia.

1600 kits have been sold, worldwide; it is PFA approved, eight are on the UK Register and three are being built.

NEICO
LANCAIR

LIGHTPLANE
Continental 320 160 hp

DATA	IMPERIAL		METRIC	
Span	23.5	ft	7.2	m
Wing area	76	ft^2	7.1	m^2
Aspect ratio	7.2		7.2	
Empty weight	1000	lb	454	kg
Loaded weight	1685	lb	765	kg
Wing loading	22.2	lb/ft^2	108	kg/m^2
Max speed	250	mph	400	kmh
Cruise speed	241	mph	385	kmh
Stalling speed	61	mph	98	kmh
Climb rate	1650	ft/min	508	m/min
Range	1140	mls	1824	km

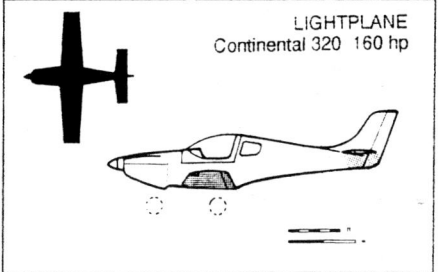

A neat two seater from Switzerland, designed by Max Brandli and first flown in 1982.

The BX-2 is of mixed wood, foam and GRP construction - a basic wooden load bearing structure with GRP covered foam for the curved bits.

In 1885 Max Brandli was awarded the Henri Mignet Diploma by the FAI for his work on the Cherry - praise indeed. Many hours of test flying went into the development of the Cherry and by 1991 the prototype had logged 1100 hours.

Light for a two seater, the BX-2 enjoys the low drag bonus of a retractable tricycle undercarriage as its 125 mph. cruise on 65 hp. reflects – and only 3 gph. fuel consumption.

Brandli produces no kits but plans are available - over 150 being sold to date. The design is PFA approved, three are under construction and one is already flying.

BRANDLI
BX-2 CHERRY

LIGHT PLANE
Continental, 65 hp.

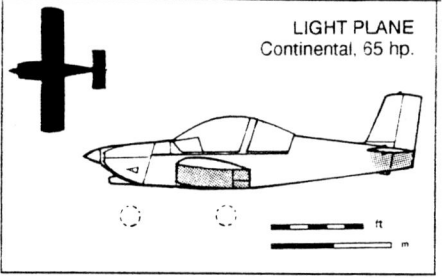

DATA	IMPERIAL		METRIC	
Span	23	ft	7.02	m
Wing area	90	ft²	8.37	m²
Aspect ratio	5.9		5.9	
Empty weight	683	lb	310	kg
Loaded weight	1212	lb	550	kg
Wing loading	13.5	lb/ft²	65.7	kg/m²
Max speed	140	mph	225	kmh
Cruise speed	125	mph	201	kmh
Stalling speed	55	mph	88	kmh
Climb rate	680	ft/min	207	m/min
Range	575	mls	920	km

Designed and built by George Periera in Sacramento, California, the GP 4 is a sleek two seater first flown in 1984 by Pereira, who later in the same year flew it the 2000 miles to Oshkosh where it won Outstanding New Design.

With the looks of a 'state of the art' carbon/GRP/foam speedster it is, at first, surprising to find that the GP 4 is a wooden aeroplane!

Built for +8 to -6g loads the sleek lines, without double curvature, disguise its orthodox ply covered fuselage and the one piece wing, again all wood, with its massive main spar taking all the lift loads.

Unusual for a kit plane the GP 4 has a retractable tricycle undercarriage with steerable nose wheel. The 'gear is manually operated though the flaps are electric as are the trimmers.

You will have to hop a '747 if you want to see this stunning 265 mph speedster - none on the UK Register.

PEREIRA
GP-4

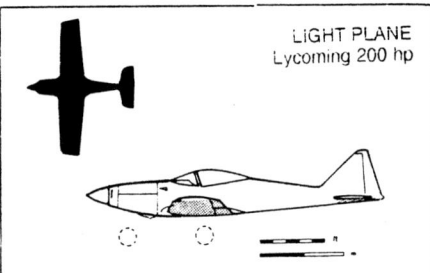

LIGHT PLANE
Lycoming 200 hp

DATA	IMPERIAL		METRIC	
Span	24.6	ft	7.6	m
Wing area	104	ft²	9.8	m²
Aspect ratio	5.54		5.54	
Empty weight	1248	lb	566	kg
Loaded weight	1985	lb	901	kg
Wing loading	19.1	lb/ft²	93.2	kg/m²
Max speed	265	mph	424	kmh
Cruise speed	240	mph	384	kmh
Stalling speed	65	mph	104	kmh
Climb rate	1500	ft/min	462	m/min
Range	1250	mls	2000	km

An all composites four seater from Germany, the prototype first flew in 1988 and was FAA approved in 1994. Features include gull wing cabin doors, trailing link main gear, four bladed prop and 'wet wing' fuel tanks. Initially powered by a Porsche aero engine of 212 hp., but replaced by a Textron Lycoming 10-540 (230 hp) when the Porsche venture failed. Production, originally at Melle has moved to Dessau where other variants are being developed; the IO-360 (180 hp) powered fixed undercarriage R90-180FG and a turbo charged version the R90-300T-RG which is planned for 1998. There is also a R90 Aerobat and a top of the range, 400 hp. Allison turboprop powered R90-420T - this (the R90 prototype re-engined) first flew in 1993.
An R95 pressurised five seater is on the drawing board. A quiet and comfortable aeroplane that matches up well to its US competitors on less power. (Two on the UK Reg)

RUSCHMEYER R 90

LIGHT PLANE
Textron Lycoming, 230 hp.

DATA	IMPERIAL		METRIC	
Span	30.8	ft	9.5	m
Wing area	140	ft²	13	m²
Aspect ratio	6.8		6.8	
Empty weight	1977	lb	898	kg
Loaded weight	2973	lb	1350	kg
Wing loading	21.3	lb/ft²	104	kg/m²
Max speed	202	mph	323	kmh
Cruise speed	190	mph	304	kmh
Stalling speed	70	mph	112	kmh
Climb rate	1140	ft/min	351	m/min
Range	689	mls	1103	km

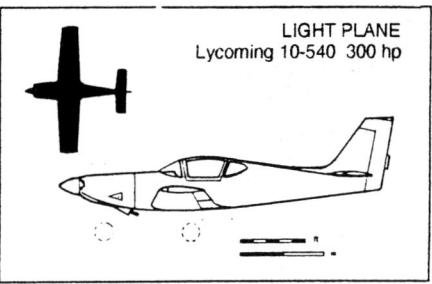

This legendary kit plane is manufactured by Stoddard Hamilton of Arlington, Washington; who have sold over 1500 Glasair kits, 100 of which are flying. One winning the 'Custom Built Champion' at Oshkosh in 1990.
This aeroplane has fighter like performance and is not for novices, though in the hands of the experts it is said to be 'impeccable at all speeds'.
Earlier versions came with lower powered engines, tail wheel gear, fixed or retracting trikes and long or short fuselages and wings.
The fully retracting undercarriage has a castoring nose wheel and, essentially, braked main wheels as it lands at about 90 mph.
The type is PFA approved, two are being built and 14 are flying.

STODDART HAMILTON GLASAIR

LIGHT PLANE
Lycoming 10-540 300 hp

DATA	IMPERIAL		METRIC	
Span	23.25	ft	7.16	m
Wing area	90	ft²	8.5	m²
Aspect ratio	6		6	
Empty weight	1550	lb	704	kg
Loaded weight	2400	lb	1089	kg
Wing loading	26	lb/ft²	127	kg/m²
Max speed	335	mph	536	kmh
Cruise speed	284	mph	454	kmh
Stalling speed	74	mph	118	kmh
Climb rate	2400	ft/min	740	m/min
Range	1500	mls	2400	km

The side by side two seat Cygnet of 1936 was the first all metal stressed skin light aeroplane built in this country. Designed and built initially by C W Aircraft the Cygnet was taken on by General Aircraft Ltd of Hanworth when CWA folded.

GAL fitted the twin fins and rudders, increased the dihedral and, in production aircraft, cantilever undercarriage legs in place of the prototype's strutted ones. The Cygnet 1 had a Gipsy Major, 130 hp and the Cygnet 2 a Cirrus Major 150 hp.

Nine were produced up to 1941, several being exported to S. America and five were impressed for the duration for communications and tricycle u/c training. Four survived the war and became well known in the post war civil scene, taking part in several air races – in one, notably piloted by the famous flyer Jim Mollison.

By 1955 two had crashed, one kept flying until 1969 when it to met its end in France. The sole survivor is on display at East Fortune.

An advanced and good-looking aeroplane that would not look out of place today. (They are making Luscombe Silvaires again – how about Cygnets?).

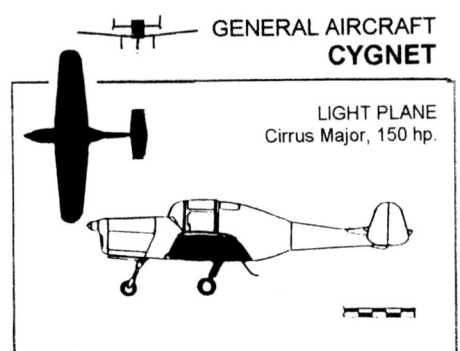

GENERAL AIRCRAFT
CYGNET

LIGHT PLANE
Cirrus Major, 150 hp.

DA TA (Mk 2)	IMPERIAL		METRIC	
Span	34.5	ft	10.6	m
Wing area	179	sq.ft	16.8	sq.m
Aspect ratio	6.6			
Empty wt	1475	lb.	670	kg.
Loaded wt	2200	lb.	998	kg.
Wing loading	12.3	lb/sq.ft	60	kg/sq.m
Max speed	135	mph	216	kmph
Cruising speed	115	mph	184	kmph
Stall speed	55	mph	88	kmph
Climb	800	fpm	246	mpm
Range	445	mls	712	km

A product of Engineering and Research Corp. the Ercoupe first flew as long ago as 1937. It was in production at ERCO up to 1955 when the design rights were taken up by various other manufacturers including Forney, Alon and Mooney; the latter adding a fin of typical Mooney shape. There are still many hundreds flying in the States and 13 on the British Register.

The all metal Ercoupe has dual controls, side-by-side seating and is one of the first production light planes to have a nose-wheel undercarriage. The ailerons run full span (no flaps) on the much 'dihedralled' wing – which on early models was fabric covered.

Initially a car type wheel was the only control – no rudder pedals – but later models had the more traditional arrangement.

There are 13 on the UK Register, four are in world museums. Back in 1941 an Ercoupe became the first plane to take-off successfully under rocket power!

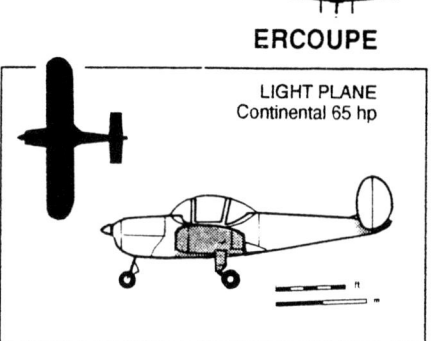

ERCOUPE

LIGHT PLANE
Continental 65 hp

DATA	IMPERIAL		METRIC	
Span	30	ft	9.15	m
Wing area	142	ft^2	13.2	m^2
Aspect ratio	6.3		6.3	
Empty weight	725	lb	329	kg
Loaded weight	1260	lb	572	kg
Wing loading	8.8	lb/ft^2	42.9	kg/m^2
Max speed	117	mph	187	kmh
Cruise speed	105	mph	168	kmh
Stalling speed	42	mph	67	kmh
Climb rate	700	ft/min	352	m/min
Range	525	mls	840	km

A sde-by-side two seat trainer/tourer from the drawing board of John Thorp – who designed the Piper Cherokee – the T211 is an all metal aeroplane of simple and robust design that first flew as the Sky Scooter in 1946. Since then it has been produced by several companies and been in and out of production.

The airframe makes much use of ribbed skinning to reduce internal framing, the wing (with only three ribs!) the rudder and stabilator are all built this way.

Economy of maintenance and low fuel consumption are big plusses for the T211; the kits for which are currently being produced in the USA and distributed in the UK by DM Aerospace, Manchester who see them as replacements for the, now aging Cessna 150 fleets.

As a kit it is PFA approved – two are being built and three are currently on the UK Register.

THORP
T211

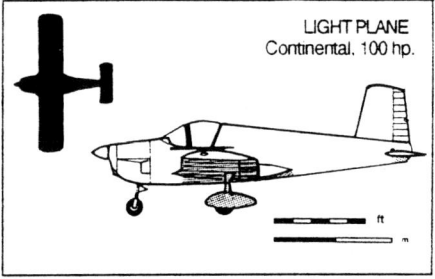

LIGHT PLANE
Continental. 100 hp.

DATA	IMPERIAL		METRIC	
Span	25	ft	7.7	m
Wing area	104.6	ft²	9.83	m²
Aspect ratio	6		6	
Empty weight	775	lb	352	kg
Loaded weight	1270	lb	576	kg
Wing loading	12.2	lb/ft²	59.6	kg/m²
Max speed	142	mph	227	kmh
Cruise speed	123	mph	197	kmh
Stalling speed	45	mph	72	kmh
Climb rate	750	ft/min	231	m/min
Range	364	mls	583	km

As the Morane Saulnier MS 880 Rallye, this all metal French three seater first flew in 1959 with an unswept fin, powered by a 90 hp Continental.

Variants with more powerful engines - up to the 150 hp. Lycoming - and with four seats have produced a spate of type numbers for 'look-a-like' aeroplanes with low parallel chord wings of pronounced dihedral with full span leading edge slots, tubby cabins and fixed trike undercarriages.

Nearly 600 were produced by Morane Saulnier before SOCATA took over in 1966.

The SOCATA built Rallyes type numbers indicate the engine power - ie. Rallye 100T and Rallye 235GT have 100 hp. and 235 hp. respectively.

SOCATA have outstripped MS. production with over 2000 Rallyes built to date. (180 on UK Register)

The SOCATA Caribbean range, in some ways similar is a more recent design.

Data below is for the MS 893, 180 hp.

SOCATA
RALLYE

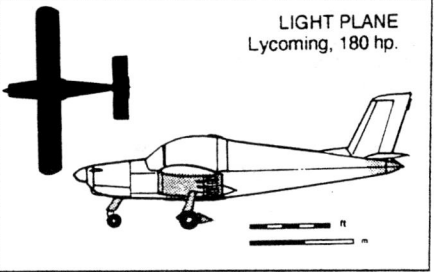

LIGHT PLANE
Lycoming, 180 hp.

DATA	IMPERIAL		METRIC	
Span	31.5	ft	9.7	m
Wing area	132	ft²	12.4	m²
Aspect ratio	7.5		7.5	
Empty weight	1265	lb	574	kg
Loaded weight	2315	lb	1051	kg
Wing loading	17.5	lb/ft²	85.4	kg/m²
Max speed	142	mph	227	kmh
Cruise speed	128	mph	205	kmh
Stalling speed	50	mph	80	kmh
Climb rate	800	ft/min	308	m/min
Range	620	mls	992	km

This chunky little two seater was the winner of the 1953 Royal Aero Club of Great Britain light aircraft design competition. It went into production in Australia un 1959 an all wood prototype first flying in 1959. Production aircraft were all metal trainer/tourers. A modified and 'up motored' version was produced by AESL, 96 being delivered to the armed forces.

Production by Victa and AESL, in New Zealand, has placed 250 on the civil market.

Designer Henry Millicer went on to create a four seat version, the Aircruiser which never went into production. Both these aircraft have highly efficient, low drag, laminar flow wings which combined with the small span and dumpy, but clean fuselage, give the Airtourer a good performance on 100 hp.

Various models acquired more power, up to 210 hp. Production ceased in 1966 (though plans are a-foot to re-start production); there are 6 on the UK Register. The data below is for the 100 hp. Airtourer AT100.

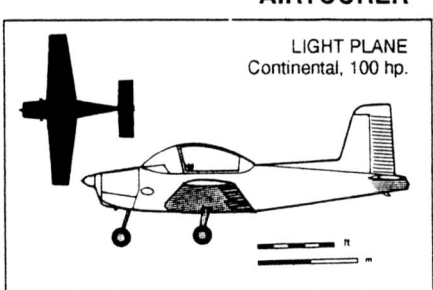

VICTA AIRTOURER

LIGHT PLANE
Continental, 100 hp.

DATA	IMPERIAL		METRIC	
Span	26	ft	8	m
Wing area	120	ft^2	11.3	m^2
Aspect ratio	5.6		5.6	
Empty weight	1058	lb	480	kg
Loaded weight	1650	lb	749	kg
Wing loading	13.8	lb/ft^2	67	kg/m^2
Max speed	137	mph	219	kmh
Cruise speed	116	mph	185	kmh
Stalling speed	50	mph	80	kmh
Climb rate	600	ft/min	185	m/min
Range	900	mls	1440	km

The Sundowner 180 has evolved from the Model 23 Musketeer which first flew in 1961 and had four seats, a fixed tricycle undercarriage and a 160 hp. Lycoming engine. The 5th variant, the C23, re-named Sundowner 180, proved the most popular with over 1000 being made. Close relatives, the Model 24s, include the Sierra 200 and Musketeer Super R, all with retract u/c and 4/6 seats.

The airframe is all metal incorporating bonded aluminium honeycomb in the wing structure, a roomy cabin and wide track tricycle undercarriage. The elevator is of the all moving, or stabilator type, and cabin access is via car type doors front and rear.

There are 18 aircraft in this range on the UK Register, many more in the 'States where over 4500 have been made.

BEECH SUNDOWNER 180

LIGHT PLANE
Lycoming, 180 hp.

DATA	IMPERIAL		METRIC	
Span	32.7	ft	10.1	m
Wing area	146	ft^2	13.7	m^2
Aspect ratio	7.3		7.3	
Empty weight	1375	lb	624	kg
Loaded weight	2400	lb	1089	kg
Wing loading	16.4	lb/ft^2	80	kg/m^2
Max speed	154	mph	246	kmh
Cruise speed	146	mph	233	kmh
Stalling speed	60	mph	96	kmh
Climb rate	805	ft/min	248	m/min
Range	678	mls	1085	km

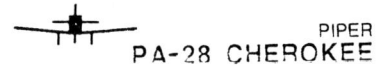

PIPER PA-28 CHEROKEE

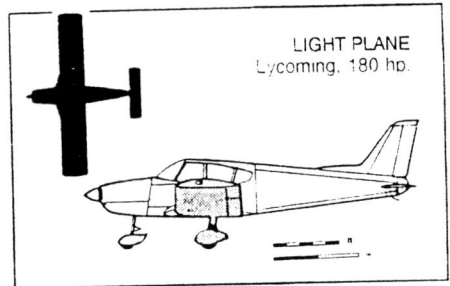

LIGHT PLANE
Lycoming. 180 hp.

With over 30,000 fixed undercarriage P-28s built since 1961, the Cherokee tribe must be considered one of the most successful series of aeroplanes ever produced. The prototype, an all metal aircraft, designed by John Thorp and Fred Weick, first flew in 1960, had four seats and a fixed nose-wheel undercarriage; production followed a year later.
More than 40 variants have been produced, involving engine changes, seating, cockpit equipment, windows and wing plan and span changes. The main *visible* changes are, as follows - 180 Cherokee D, introduced three side windows; 180 Challenger, increased wing span and fuselage length plus stabilator (renamed Archer in '74);151 Warrior, tapered outer wing panels; 181 Archer 2, tapered wing and new u/c fairings; the Archer 3 had re-styled engine air intakes;
NB- the suffix numbers are indicative of the model's engine horse power throughout the range.
The PA28-235 Charger had a longer fuselage and bigger stabilator; PA28R-180 Cherokee Arrow had a retractable undercarriage and parallel chord wing; the PA28R-201 Arrow 4 had a 'T' tail and tapered wing (6600 of the retractable PA28R models have been built - making it the most popular light 'retractable'.)
Two seat versions have been made, primarily for the training role, including the PA28-140 of 1964, the 140 Flite Line and the unusual Pillan with two seats in tandem under a big bubble canopy. (only two Piper built - 120 kitted for the Chilean Air Force).
Turbo Arrows 3 and 4 were the first in the range to be turbo-supercharged in 1976.
In 1978 the PA28-236 Dakota became turbo-supercharged as the '201T Turbo Dakota with a 200 hp Lycoming.
There are over 1000 PA28s on the UK Register making it our most numerous light plane.
Although named *Cherokee 6*, the PA32 is an entirely new design, hence the change in prefix.
The order in which some of the different types appear is shown below -

PA28-150/160/180	1961	PA28-151 Warrior	1972
PA28-235	1963	PA28-180 Archer 2	1973
PA28R-180 Arrow	1967	PA28R-201 Arrow 3	1975
PA28-235 Charger	1972	PA28R-201 Arrow 4	1976
PA28-180 Challenger	1972	PA28-236 Dakota	1978

The photograph is of a PA28-181 Archer 2 and the sketches beneath show a few of the variants - a bit like 'Spot the difference'!

The figures below are for the PA28-140B.

DATA	IMPERIAL		METRIC	
Span	30	ft	9.24	m
Wing area	160	ft^2	15	m^2
Aspect ratio	5.6		5.6	
Empty weight	1180	lb	535	kg
Loaded weight	1950	lb	885	kg
Wing loading	12.2	lb/ft^2	59.5	kg/m^2
Max speed	144	mph	230	kmh
Cruise speed	134	mph	214	kmh
Stalling speed	54	mph	86	kmh
Climb rate	820	ft/min	259	m/min
Range	700	mls	1120	km

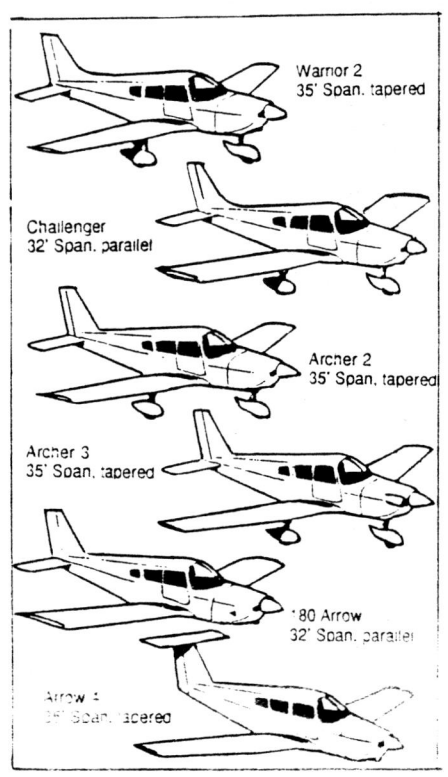

Warrior 2
35' Span, tapered

Challenger
32' Span, parallel

Archer 2
35' Span, tapered

Archer 3
35' Span, tapered

180 Arrow
32' Span, parallel

Arrow 4
35' Span, tapered

Jim Bede the innovative designer of the BD4, BD5 etc. designed the original AA1 Yankee as the BD1, which first flew in 1963. Production followed and 461 were built by the American Aviation Corporation.

The Trainer model, AA-1A, with dual controls was produced in quantity, 500 being made up to 1973.

At this point Grumman Aerospace acquired American Aviation and continued production under the new badge of Grumman American - later to become the Gulfstream American Corporation.

This all metal two seater spans only 24.5 ft. whilst its look-a-like brother, the four seat AA5 Traveller has a 32.5 ft. wing. (See elsewhere in the book). Construction embodies metal-to-metal bonding, aluminium honeycomb elements and GRP undercarriage legs. The unusual nose wheel leg is distinguishing feature

There are 17 AA1s on the UK Register

GULFSTREAM AMERICAN
AA1 YANKEE

LIGHT PLANE
Lycoming, 108 hp.

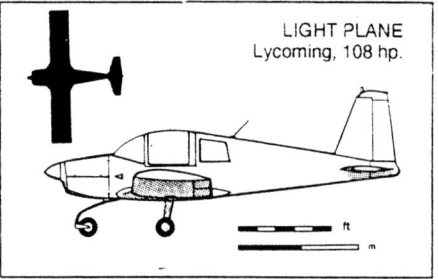

DATA	IMPERIAL		METRIC	
Span	24.5	ft	7.54	m
Wing area	101	ft²	9.5	m²
Aspect ratio	6		6	
Empty weight	963	lb	437	kg
Loaded weight	1500	lb	681	kg
Wing loading	14.8	lb/ft²	72.2	kg/m²
Max speed	134	mph	214	kmh
Cruise speed	114	mph	182	kmh
Stalling speed	55	mph	88	kmh
Climb rate	720	ft/min	221	m/min
Range	515	mls	824	km

A six/seven seat partner to the hugely popular, 2/4 seat PA28 Cherokee became available in 1965, the PA32 Cherokee Six, in three fit standards, Custom, Executive and Sportsman. These early model PA32s all had the 32' span, parallel chord PA28 wing and 260 or 300 hp. Lycoming engines.

In 1974 an extra side window was introduced (making four per side) and in '75 the retractable gear PA32R-300 Cherokee Lance was added to the range (becoming just Lance in '77). The PA32RT-300 was the retractable u/c Lance with a 'T' tail and parallel chord wings (turbo model, PA32RT-300T).

The 36' span, semi tapered wing, based on the Warrior, lifted the 1980 Saratoga, PA32-301 into the range and was followed by the PA32-301T, turbo version and the retractable u/c version PA32R-301. There are about 100 of these fast six seaters on the UK Register, which is still in production and has included in its variants floatplane and COIN versions.

The figures below are for the PA32-300 Cherokee Six.

PIPER
PA 32 CHEROKEE SIX

LIGHT PLANE
Lycoming, 260/300 hp.

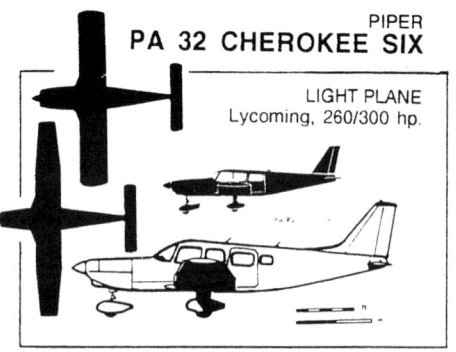

DATA	IMPERIAL		METRIC	
Span	32.75	ft	10	m
Wing area	174.5	ft²	16.4	m²
Aspect ratio	6.1		6.1	
Empty weight	1818	lb	825	kg
Loaded weight	3394	lb	1541	kg
Wing loading	19.4	lb/ft²	95	kg/m²
Max speed	174	mph	278	kmh
Cruise speed	168	mph	269	kmh
Stalling speed	63	mph	101	kmh
Climb rate	1050	ft/min	323	m/min
Range	850	mls	1360	km

First flown in 1965 the Fuji FA-200 Subaru is one of the few Japanese light planes flying in this country.

When production ceased in 1986 a total of 274 had been produced, about a dozen making it onto the British Register.

The Subaru is of all metal construction and can carry four people - though in this mode its range is somewhat restricted and the FA200-160 with a 160 hp Lycoming is a mite underpowered, hence the later FA200-180 with 180 hp Lycoming.

A reliable and well mannered aeroplane comparable to the small Cessnas. Stressed for +6,-3g the Subaru is capable of limited aerobatics at a weight limitation of 1940 lb.

Rather like a Piper Tomahawk, without the 'T' tail! the Fuji, a ten year older design has a marginaly inferior performance to the Piper.

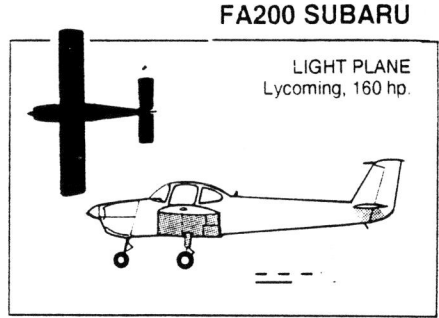

FUJI
FA200 SUBARU

LIGHT PLANE
Lycoming, 160 hp.

DATA	IMPERIAL		METRIC	
Span	30.9	ft	9.5	m
Wing area	150	ft^2	14.1	m^2
Aspect ratio	6		6	
Empty weight	1497	lb	680	kg
Loaded weight	2137	lb	970	kg
Wing loading	14.2	lb/ft^2	69.3	kg/m^2
Max speed	120	mph	192	kmh
Cruise speed	95	mph	152	kmh
Stalling speed	58	mph	93	kmh
Climb rate	600	ft/min	185	m/min
Range	300	mls	480	km

An all metal four seater from Italy, looking a little like an early model Cherokee, the SIAI-Marchetti S205-18F, first flew in 1965 in fixed undercarriage form with a 180 hp. Lycoming; a 200 hp. retractable gear version, the S205-20R followed.

An agreement was reached with the Waco Aircraft Company to assemble 205s at their Pottstown, Pa. plant and 60 aircraft were completed and marketed as the 220 Sirius, powered by a 220 hp. Franklin engine. A five seat version with retracting gear and a 260 hp Lycoming appeared in 1967 as the S208; 85 of these being built.

All 205/208 production ceased in 1972 but was restarted in '77 with an order for 40 from the Aero Club d'Italia which was completed by 1979.

SIAI-Marchetti are an old established firm who make parts for the Panavia Tornado and the Airbus A310 and have their own fighter trainer, the S211A.

There are five S205s on the UK Register.

Data for S205- 18F.

SIAI-MARCHETTI
S 205

LIGHT PLANE
Lycoming, 180 hp.

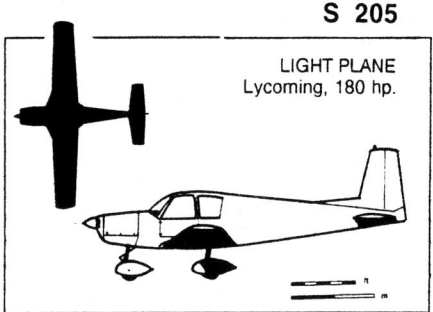

DATA	IMPERIAL		METRIC	
Span	34.9	ft	10.7	m
Wing area	173	ft^2	16.2	m^2
Aspect ratio	7		7	
Empty weight	1490	lb	655	kg
Loaded weight	2645	lb	1163	kg
Wing loading	15.3	lb/ft^2	74.6	kg/m^2
Max speed	147	mph	235	kmh
Cruise speed	134	mph	214	kmh
Stalling speed	66	mph	105.6	kmh
Climb rate	787	ft/min	242	m/min
Range	745	mls	1192	km

An all metal American utralight designed by Leon Davis the DA-2 is now produced, ready made or in kit form, by D2 Incorporated. It was first flown in 1966 and in the same year collected awards at the EAA Fly-In at Rockford for Outstanding Design and Popularity.

Of simple all metal construction (no double curvature panels) with an unusual all moving 'butterfly' tail, the two seat DA-2 has a fixed and spatted undercarriage with spring steel cantilever legs. Unusual, again, for a small low wing cabin monoplane entry is made through a car type side door.

Though fitted, as standard, with a 65 hp. Continental, the airframe is stressed for other motors up to 100 hp.

An official PFA approved design in the UK, there are over 100 flying in the USA. (one on UK Reg.)

DAVIS DA-2

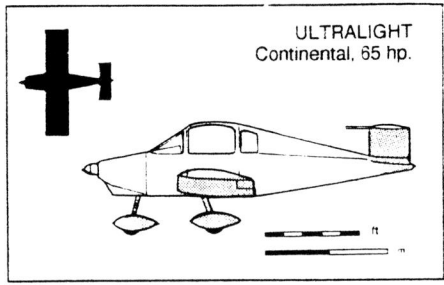

ULTRALIGHT
Continental, 65 hp.

DATA	IMPERIAL		METRIC	
Span	19.25	ft	5.86	m
Wing area	82.5	ft²	7.66	m²
Aspect ratio	4.5		4.5	
Empty weight	610	lb	277	kg
Loaded weight	1125	lb	510	kg
Wing loading	13.6	lb/ft²	66.5	kg/m²
Max speed	120	mph	193	kmh
Cruise speed	115	mph	185	kmh
Stalling speed	55	mph	88	kmh
Climb rate	900	ft/min	277	m/min
Range	450	mls	725	km

First flown in 1967 the DR400 is one of Pierre Robin's designs and is a four seater of all wood construction.

Robin not only designs the Robin range of light planes, he has been a well known air race pilot and founder of the Centre Est Aeronautique in 1957 (Changed to Societe des Avions Pierre Robin in 1969) which produces the planes that bear his name - all based on the Jodel wing.

The DR400 is a highly successful aeroplane on the continent with 1400+ produced to date.

Variants include the DR400-100, a two seat trainer, the DR400-140, with forward sliding canopy, the DR400-180R, a glider tug and the DR400-180 Regent - featured here.

The second of the Robins to feature a tricycle undercarriage, the elegant and efficient DR400 has proved popular in the UK with over 100 on the Register.

ROBIN DR400 REGENT

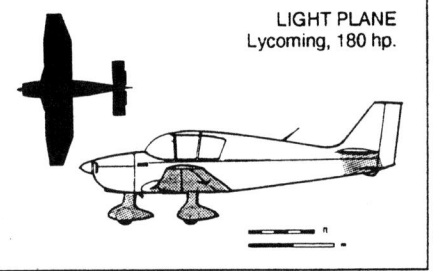

LIGHT PLANE
Lycoming, 180 hp.

DATA	IMPERIAL		METRIC	
Span	28.6	ft	8.72	m
Wing area	146	ft²	13.6	m²
Aspect ratio	5.6		5.6	
Empty weight	1301	lb	590	kg
Loaded weight	2425	lb	1100	kg
Wing loading	16.5	lb/ft²	80.5	kg/m²
Max speed	164	mph	264	kmh
Cruise speed	134	mph	215	kmh
Stalling speed	60	mph	96	kmh
Climb rate	825	ft/min	1320	m/min
Range	913	mls	1470	km

Zlinska Letecka, the pre war Czech company became Moravia after WW2 but the aircraft were still typed as Zlin. The most famous being the Trener, many hundreds of which were made right up to 1973.

In 1967 the Z42 first flew, a two seat aerobatic cabin monoplane, later, with a new canopy and engine it became the Z142 - which in turn, became the Z242 in 1990 with the installation of a 200 hp. Lycoming driving a three blade Hoffman c/s prop. and straight parallel chord wings with upturned tip trailing edges. The construction is all metal with some GRP fairings and the fixed, spatted, tricycle undercarriage has cantilever steel spring main legs and a steerable nose-wheel.

The well stocked panel includes a gauge reading gas pressure within the main wing spar - loss of pressure = crack in spar! (some helicopters have this safety feature on their rotor spars).

UK flight tests have declared the cockpit, comfortable with parachute recesses in seats, good visibility and handling all combined in a very tough airframe.

There are three Z242s on the UK Register.

ZLIN
Z 242

LIGHT PLANE
Lycoming, 200 hp.

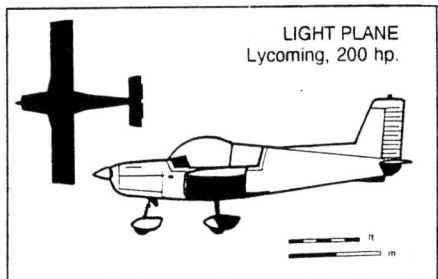

DATA	IMPERIAL		METRIC	
Span	30.6	ft	9.4	m
Wing area	147	ft^2	13.3	m^2
Aspect ratio	6.6		6.6	
Empty weight	1609	lb	730	kg
Loaded weight	2400	lb	1089	kg
Wing loading	17	lb/ft^2	82	kg/m^2
Max speed	198	mph	316	kmh
Cruise speed	173	mph	278	kmh
Stalling speed	58	mph	94	kmh
Climb rate	1200	ft/min	370	m/min
Range	425	mls	680	km

The original Pup was a two seater, developed from the Miles M117, with a 100 hp. Continental engine and the series 2, which followed was powered by a 150 hp. Lycoming and was a 3/4 seater. The Pup is an all metal aeroplane that was originally designed for composites construction.

Built like a battleship, the Pup has a keen following and an owners club, the 70 or so aircraft being much prized.

The Pup features, well harmonized controls, sweet handling, an aerobatic capability, and a commodious and well laid out cockpit.

When Beagle folded in 1969 it dealt a body blow to the UK volume light aircraft industry from which it has never fully recovered. This aeroplane shows just what could be done, along with its sister, the twin engined 206 (See elsewhere in book).which is a big hit in the USA.

The RAF trainer version – bigger + more power – the Bulldog, built by Scottish Aviation, is being decommissioned and three are on the civil UK Register.

BEAGLE
PUP, SERIES 2

LIGHT PLANE
Lycoming 150 hp

DATA	IMPERIAL		METRIC	
Span	31	ft	9.5	m
Wing area	110	ft^2	10.3	m^2
Aspect ratio	8.7		8.7	
Empty weight	1265	lb	574	kg
Loaded weight	1925	lb	874	kg
Wing loading	17.5	lb/ft^2	85.4	kg/m^2
Max speed	140	mph	224	kmh
Cruise speed	120	mph	192	kmh
Stalling speed	57	mph	91	kmh
Climb rate	750	ft/min	231	m/min
Range	287	mls	460	km

An all metal single seater intended for sport flying and glider tugging, the Kittiwake was the brain child of Dr C Mitchell and Roy and Ann Proctor. It first flew in 1967 and the second one, built by Navy apprentices at Yeovilton and Lee-on-Solent, took to the air in 1971.

The Mitchell-proctor team split up in 1968 and Proctor Aircraft Associates along with Yorkshire Sailplanes took on the marketing of plans and kit parts.

The construction is simple and self jigging with a single spar wing which has extruded light alloy booms. The fuselage is a four longeron LA box and the cantilever undercarriage legs are spring steel with disc braked wheels. The nose wheel leg is rubber sprung on some versions and cantilevered on others. Fuel is carried in a tank integral with the wing leading edge structure.

A two seat version with a more powerful engine, the Petrel, was built by BAC apprentices and first flew in 1978

There are four Kittiwakes on the UK Register.

MITCHELL-PROCTOR
KITTIWAKE

LIGHT PLANE
Continental, 100 hp.

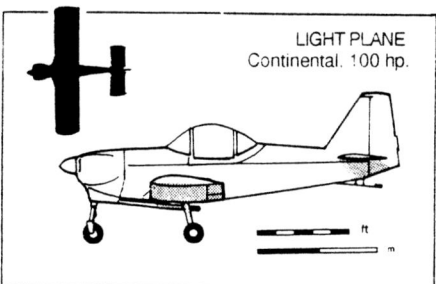

DATA	IMPERIAL		METRIC	
Span	24	ft	7.32	m
Wing area	105	ft^2	9.75	m^2
Aspect ratio	5.3		5.3	
Empty weight	910	lb	413	kg
Loaded weight	1350	lb	612	kg
Wing loading	12.9	lb/ft^2	63	kg/m^2
Max speed	131	mph	211	kmh
Cruise speed	122	mph	196	kmh
Stalling speed	55	mph	88	kmh
Climb rate	1050	ft/min	320	m/min
Range	490	mls	790	km

Designed by J Smyth of Indiana, the Sidewinder, an all metal side-by-side two seater, first flew in 1969 and in that year it won the 'Outstanding Design' award at the EAA Fly In.

Intended for home building, the Sidewinder embodies a Thorp T18 canopy assembly and Wittman main gear. Engines of from 90 to 180 hp. may be fitted; the prototype having a 125 hp. Lycoming as has the only UK representative, G-BRVH, which was built in the UK by its owner.

The wings are of two spar stressed skin construction and the fuselage has a welded steel tube framework with LA formers and skin. All skinning is flush riveted. An unusual feature is the electrically operated under fuselage 'speed brake' or perforated flap – no wing flaps are fitted. Stabilator, ailerons and rudder have electrically operated trimmers and the Wittman spring undercarriage legs carry hydraulically braked wheels, the nose wheel being a steerable oleo.

The pretty Sidewinder, a PFA approved design, with its distinctive very swept fin, is a compact two seater with good performance and luggage space.

SMYTH
SIDEWINDER

LIGHTPLANE
Lycoming O-290, 125 hp.

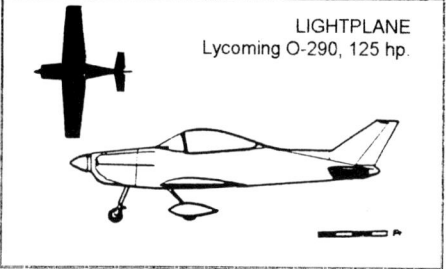

DATA	IMPERIAL		METRIC	
Span	24.8	ft	7.57	m
Wing area	96	sq.ft	8.92	sq.m
Aspect ratio	6.85			
Empty wt	998	lb.	453	kg.
Loaded wt	1450	lb.	657	kg.
Wing loading	15.8	lb/sq.ft	77	kg/sq.m
Max speed	185	mph	321	kmph
Cruising speed	134	mph	214	kmph
Stall speed	59	mph	95	kmph
Climb	1000	fpm	308	mpm
Range	336	mls	537	km

Designed and built, initially, by SIAI in Italy and the Swiss firm FFA; the Italians made the wings and the Swiss made the rest. This arrangement did not last and FFA (later FWA) made the whole aeroplane.

The Bravo is a semi aerobatic 2/3 seat trainer of all metal construction with a fixed tricycle undercarriage. The wing has light alloy spars and ribs under a sheet and honeycomb sandwich skin, with slotted flaps over 60% of the span. The undercarriage is rubber sprung with hydraulic brakes and a steerable nose-wheel.

Motors range from 115 hp to 180 hp – the higher powered versions having the extra seat.

Around 250 Bravos have been made, going to several foreign air forces including Indonesia, Iraq and Oman. Ten were delivered in 1987 to BAe training at Prestwick – where it is called the Wren – these are now being sold on.

Figures below are for the 150 hp AS202/15.

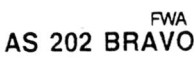

FWA
AS 202 BRAVO

LIGHT PLANE
Lycoming, 115 or 150 hp.

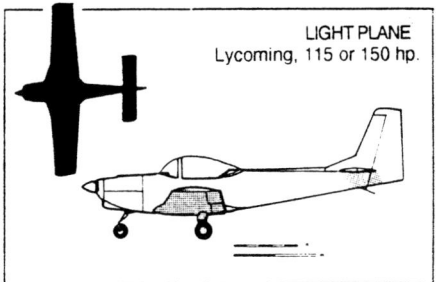

DATA	IMPERIAL		METRIC	
Span	32	ft	9.8	m
Wing area	149	ft²	14	m²
Aspect ratio	6.5		6.5	
Empty weight	1388	lb	630	kg
Loaded weight	2000	lb	908	kg
Wing loading	14.8	lb/ft²	72.2	kg/m²
Max speed	131	mph	209	kmh
Cruise speed	126	mph	201	kmh
Stalling speed	56	mph	90	kmh
Climb rate	633	ft/min	195	m/min
Range	574	mls	918	km

Virtually, a four seat version of the two seat AA-1 Yankee of 1970, the AA-5 first flew in the same year and was type named, Traveller and had a smaller rear window and dorsal fin than later models.

Over 800 of the Traveller version were built to be superseded by the de Luxe AA-5A Cheetah (900 built) which introduced the longer fin and window.

The AA-5B Tiger, which first flew in 1974, stepped up the power from 150 hp. to 180 hp (Lycoming 0-360-4AK) and is currently back in production with over 1300 produced.

The original design was by American Aviation which then became, successively, Grumman American, Gulfstream American and - to date, American General Aircraft Corporation!

The airframe is all metal, but differs from the norm in being 'rivetless' - the major part of the structure being glued together. The single main wing spar is a massive aluminium tube.

The unusual nose wheel leg is very distictive.

150 are on the UK Register

GULFSTREAM AMERICAN
AA-5 TIGER

LIGHT PLANE
Lycoming, 180 hp.

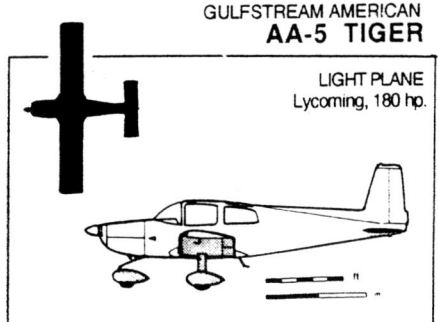

DATA	IMPERIAL		METRIC	
Span	31.5	ft	9.7	m
Wing area	145	ft²	13.6	m²
Aspect ratio	6.8		6.8	
Empty weight	1311	lb	595	kg
Loaded weight	2400	lb	1089	kg
Wing loading	16.6	lb/ft²	81	kg/m²
Max speed	170	mph	272	kmh
Cruise speed	164	mph	262	kmh
Stalling speed	64	mph	102	kmh
Climb rate	850	ft/min	262	m/min
Range	600	mls	960	km

First flown in 1971 the two seat HR 200 is contemporary with the HR 100, a look-alike four seater. Both aeroplanes are all metal, unlike the 'DR' Robin range of wooden 'crank wings'.

The HR 200 has an extensive blown and tinted canopy which slides forward to open and distinguishes it from the HR 100 which has a 'roof and windows'.

With full dual controls and comprehensive instrumentation the '200 is an ideal club trainer in the same category as the Cessna 152, compared to which it is smaller and faster, with a greater range.

Variants are, HR 200/100 S, the basic version, and the HR 200/100 Club, with wheel fairings and Hoffman airscrew, HR 200/120 has 118 hp. Lycoming and HR 200/160 has a 160 hp. Lycoming.

Production ceased in 1981 when 200 had been built - however - it went back into production again in 1993 with a 118 hp. Lycoming. (Details below for this version) There are 18 on the UK Register.

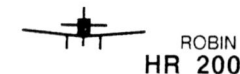

ROBIN
HR 200

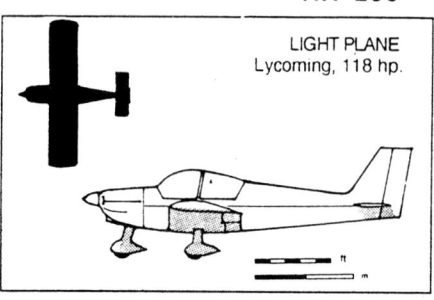

LIGHT PLANE
Lycoming, 118 hp.

DATA	IMPERIAL		METRIC	
Span	27.5	ft	8.4	m
Wing area	135	ft²	12.7	m²
Aspect ratio	5.5		5.5	
Empty weight	1158	lb	502	kg
Loaded weight	1720	lb	746	kg
Wing loading	12.7	lb/ft²	62	kg/m²
Max speed	145	mph	232	kmh
Cruise speed	138	mph	220	kmh
Stalling speed	57	mph	91	kmh
Climb rate	770	ft/min	237	m/min
Range	650	mls	1040	km

Marketed in the USA by Macfam and in Canada by K and S (Kay and Stan Mc Leod) the Cavalier 102.5 is a side by side two seater of all wood construction. Listed as 'plans only' for homebuild, parts and back up are available

The design is based on the Gardan Minicab, of 1949, with modifications, which include, a nose wheel tricycle undercarriage in place of the original taildragger gear, a swept back fin and rudder, and a canopy that slides bodily forward in place of the forward and upward pivoting original. There is also additional cabin glazing aft of the main hood.

An unusual feature, and a boon to spotters, are the upswept wing tip fuel tanks which hold *all* the aircraft's fuel.

Some of the early models were built as tail draggers and later modified to trikes.

There are nine on the UK Reg. It is PFA approved.

Various engines are fitted, from 85 to 135 hp. - the figures below are for the 100 hp. model.

K and S
CAVALIER 102.5

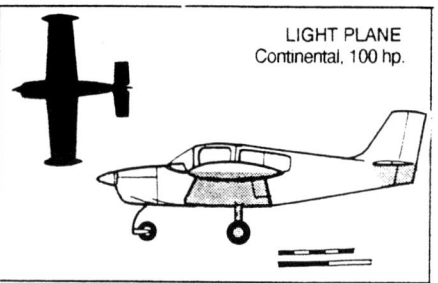

LIGHT PLANE
Continental, 100 hp.

DATA	IMPERIAL		METRIC	
Span	27.6	ft	8.39	m
Wing area	118	ft²	10.9	m²
Aspect ratio	6.4		6.4	
Empty weight	950	lb	431	kg
Loaded weight	1800	lb	817	kg
Wing loading	15.3	lb/ft²	74.4	kg/m²
Max speed	150	mph	240	kmh
Cruise speed	138	mph	222	kmh
Stalling speed	50	mph	80	kmh
Climb rate	1200	ft/min	366	m/min
Range	830	mls	1328	km

The all metal PA 38 Tomahawk has been produced in considerable numbers - over 2500 - and is a hardworking and durable trainer, with 170 flying in this country.

Introduced in 1978 (first flew 1977), the Tomahawk's high mounted tailplane and all round vision canopy are identification features, as is the fairly high aspect ratio wing.

Of all metal construction, the Tomahawk is fully aerobatic

It has a striking similarity to the Beechcraft Skipper (not in this book) - but if you see a Skipper it is almost certainly a Tomahawk as there are none of the former on the UK Register.

The fashion for 'T' tails comes and goes, the claimed advantage being improved rudder control at high angles and better spin recovery.

PIPER
PA 38 TOMAHAWK

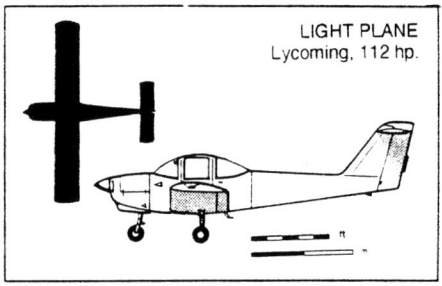

LIGHT PLANE
Lycoming, 112 hp.

DATA	IMPERIAL		METRIC	
Span	34	ft	10.36	m
Wing area	124.7	ft²	11.6	m²
Aspect ratio	9.3		9.3	
Empty weight	1128	lb	512	kg
Loaded weight	1670	lb	757	kg
Wing loading	13.4	lb/ft²	65.4	kg/m²
Max speed	126	mph	202	kmh
Cruise speed	124	mph	200	kmh
Stalling speed	60	mph	96	kmh
Climb rate	725	ft/min	221	m/min
Range	520	mls	838	km

An unusual and innovative design with a good performance, initiated by the PILOT magazine in 1968. It was an all metal two seater intended for kit construction.

The prototype was built by P. Burril over a period of years - '69-'76 - to the designs of Lloyd Jenkinson and Peter Sharman and then taken on by Practavia Ltd at Wycombe Air Park, Booker. The first flight being made in 1976.

During the following years 150 kits were sold - eight of them eventually flying with six still on the UK Register.

Practavia were geared up to sell the Sprite ready made when they went out of business in 1982.

The wing, constructed in three units had leading edge fuel tanks on production models, the home-builts having tip tanks. The semi-monocoque fuselage had no double curvature panels, the u/c legs were rubber sprung and the brakes were hydraulic.

Another lost opportunity for the British light aircraft industry.

PRACTAVIA
PILOT SPRITE

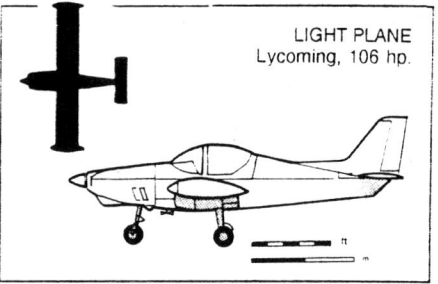

LIGHT PLANE
Lycoming, 106 hp.

DATA	IMPERIAL		METRIC	
Span	27	ft	8.23	m
Wing area	108	ft²	10.03	m²
Aspect ratio	6.75		6.75	
Empty weight	1050	lb	476	kg
Loaded weight	1650	lb	748	kg
Wing loading	15.3	lb/ft²	74.7	kg/m²
Max speed	139	mph	224	kmh
Cruise speed	124	mph	200	kmh
Stalling speed	56	mph	91	kmh
Climb rate	720	ft/min	219	m/min
Range	625	mls	1006	km

Related to the Christophe Heintz designed Robin HR 200 and the R 2100 Super Club, the R2160 is an all metal two seat aerobatic/ trainer, certificated in 1978. 107 were sold before production ceased in 1984. Avions Pierre Robin of Canada being involved in the assembly of some of these. In 1993 production was resumed.

The R 2160, distinctive for its long ventral fin, is an all metal aeroplane powered by a 160 hp. Lycoming. The flying control surfaces comprise an 'all moving' tailplane, horn balanced rudder and balanced slotted ailerons plus electrically operated flaps. The well faired tricycle undercarriage is oleo sprung with disc brakes and a steering nose wheel.

When not aerobatting the R 2160 is a useful fast tourer with a well equipped panel and a range of nearly 600 miles at 150 mph.

There are five on the UK Register. Distributed in the UK by Mistral Aviation of Gloucester Airport.

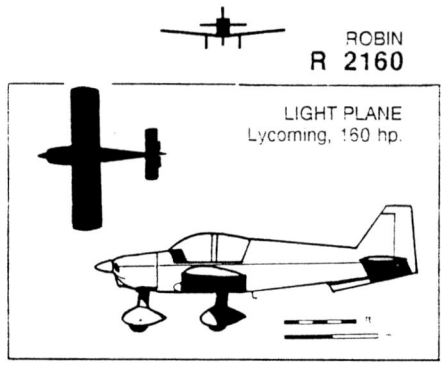

ROBIN
R 2160

LIGHT PLANE
Lycoming, 160 hp.

DATA	IMPERIAL		METRIC	
Span	26.3	ft	8.33	m
Wing area	140	ft²	13.01	m²
Aspect ratio	5.33		5.33	
Empty weight	1235	lb	560	kg
Loaded weight	1764	lb	800	kg
Wing loading	12.6	lb/ft²	61.5	kg/m²
Max speed	160	mph	257	kmh
Cruise speed	150	mph	241	kmh
Stalling speed	60	mph	96	kmh
Climb rate	1025	ft/min	312	m/min
Range	590	mls	950	km

Dart Kitten, see page 65.

This smart 4 seat tourer from France has proved to be a best seller with over a 1000 of the Tobago and its variants - Tampico, Trinidad etc.- produced to date.

From the same stable as the Rallye, the Tobago is a completely new and more streamlined airframe.

The Trinidad TB 20 is the retractable undercarriage version of the Tobago and the TB 200 version, illustrated, Has a 200 hp. Lycoming as opposed to the standard TB 10 Tobago's 180 hp.

The prototype first flew in 1977 and steady refining of the design has ensured an ever full order book.

The airframe is all aluminium alloy with parallel chord wings of fairly pronounced dihedral, a much swept large fin and rudder and an all moving tailplane.

A pair of belly strakes just aft of the wing are an unusual feature.

There are about 120 of the Tobago family on the UK Register - and it's still in production.

SOCATA
TB 10 TOBAGO

LIGHT PLANE
Lycoming, 200 hp.

DATA	IMPERIAL		METRIC	
Span	31.7	ft	9.76	m
Wing area	135	ft²	12.7	m²
Aspect ratio	7.5		7.5	
Empty weight	1576	lb	715	kg
Loaded weight	2535	lb	1146	kg
Wing loading	18.8	lb/ft²	91.6	kg/m²
Max speed	161	mph	257	kmh
Cruise speed	150	mph	240	kmh
Stalling speed	61	mph	98	kmh
Climb rate	940	ft/min	290	m/min
Range	745	mls	1192	km

An advanced design from Avions Pierre Robin that has not, as yet, made its mark on this side of the channel.

The design team set out to produce a cheap, light weight, two seat trainer - in the best Jodel tradition.

After two years work the prototype ATL first flew in 1983 powered by a 47 hp. JPX PAL engine - a three cylinder air cooled unit. The power was soon increased to 56 hp. using a JPX/VW unit and in its initial production form a 65 hp. unit was installed. necessitating a swept forward wing to accommodate the, now, more forward CG position due to the heavier motor.

Deliveries began in 1985 - 30 were ordered - but all were recalled within a year for 'full certification mods'.

Full certification being obtained in 1986.

A German built version was powered by a 70 hp. Limbach engine and this became the standard production version in France, where it is defined as the ATL Club 89 - being certificated in 1989.

The wings and 'V' tail are wooden with fabric covering and the pod and boom fuselage is of GRP/composites.

Over 150 have been delivered - but only one appears on our Register.

ROBIN
ATL

Limbach, 70 hp.

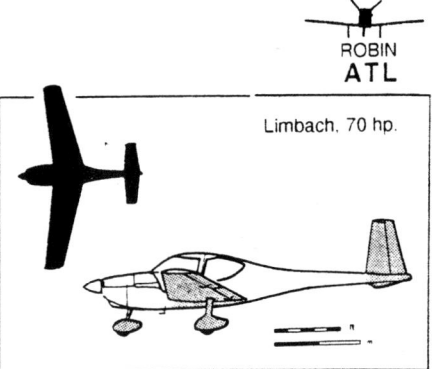

DATA	IMPERIAL		METRIC	
Span	33.6	ft	10.25	m
Wing area	130.8	ft²	12.15	m²
Aspect ratio	8.65		8.65	
Empty weight	794	lb	360	kg
Loaded weight	1278	lb	580	kg
Wing loading	9.8	lb/ft²	47.7	kg/m²
Max speed	121	mph	195	kmh
Cruise speed	104	mph	167	kmh
Stalling speed	47	mph	75	kmh
Climb rate	600	ft/min	183	m/min
Range	624	mls	1004	km

Designed by S.A.Holloway - its initial designation was SAH-1 - and built at Bodmin, the Sprint trainer first flew in 1983. Originally funded by Trago Mills Super markets, the aeroplane has had a chequered history since TMS pulled out.
The Sprint- at one time named Orca - has been much praised by all who have flown it, including RAF Central Flying School and pilots from various foreign firms.
In 1998 FLS sold off the rights, jigs etc for the Sprint to Mike Woodley at N. Weald, with production in mind.
All metal construction, it has manually operated slotted flaps, steerable nose wheel, and cantilever spring legs.
Comparisons with its nearest rivals, the Cessna 152 and the Tomahawk, show it to be roomier, carry more, fly further and faster and out climb them. Why, then, are we not making thousands of them?
Two versions are flying; one with a 118 hp motor and the other has 160 hp. There are six Sprints on the UK Register.

FLS AEROSPACE SPRINT

LIGHT PLANE
Lycoming, 160 hp.

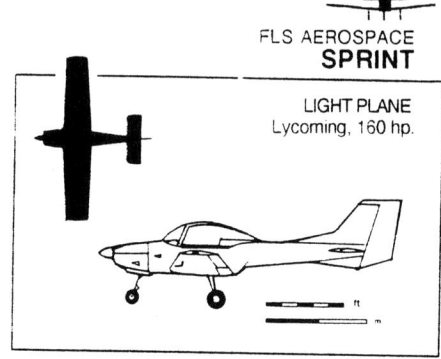

DATA	IMPERIAL		METRIC	
Span	30.6	ft	9.4	m
Wing area	120	ft^2	11.3	m^2
Aspect ratio	7.8		7.8	
Empty weight	1100	lb	500	kg
Loaded weight	1750	lb	794	kg
Wing loading	14.5	lb/ft^2	71.1	kg/m^2
Max speed	140	mph	224	kmh
Cruise speed	138	mph	221	kmh
Stalling speed	53	mph	85	kmh
Climb rate	815	ft/min	251	m/min
Range	713	mls	1141	km

Aero Designs Inc of Texas produced a prize winning single seater for Oshkosh 1983 from which designer Mark Brown developed the two seater Pulsar using the same construction methods, composites fuselage and ply covered wooden spar wing with foam ribs at 8" (20cm) spacing.
First flown in 1989 the Pulsar's stylish lines and lively performance on only 64 hp make this a very desirable kit plane. Launched in kit form in 1991 over 100 were sold in the first two years.
A Rotax 912 (80 hp) version is now available giving an even more spectacular performance combined with the lower noise/vibration level of the four cylinder water cooled engine.
The Pulsar is a PFA approved design and is available As a trike or a tail-dragger – 27 are on the UK Register and six are being built.

AERO DESIGNS PULSAR

ULTRALIGHT
Rotax 582 xx hp

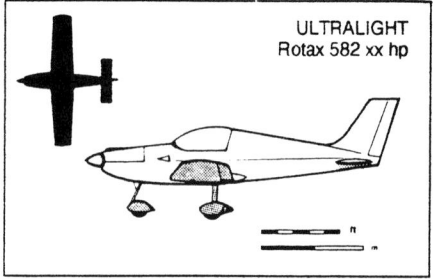

DATA	IMPERIAL		METRIC	
Span	25	ft	7.7	m
Wing area	104	ft^2	9.8	m^2
Aspect ratio	6		6	
Empty weight	430	lb	195	kg
Loaded weight	870	lb	395	kg
Wing loading	8.4	lb/ft^2	41	kg/m^2
Max speed	150	mph	240	kmh
Cruise speed	130	mph	208	kmh
Stalling speed	40	mph	64	kmh
Climb rate	1200	ft/min	370	m/min
Range	400	mls	640	km

French Canadian Chris Heintz designed the Zenair Zodiac CH601, a small but nippy metal two seater, for ease of construction by home builders.

The ease of construction was well demonstrated at the Sun and Fun Rally 1993 when one was completed and flown within the week! There is no double curvature forming of the skins which are attached using mainly 'pop' blind rivets.

The thick single spar wing has a constant chord and the rudder / fin is all moving.

The prototype first flew in 1984 and the first 200 Zodiacs were powered by 65 hp. VW engines and were either trike or taildragger. Later models had Rotax units. The CH 601 HDS has a tapered wing and a claimed cruise of 140 mph.

The CH 601 UL is an ultralight model grossing at under 1000 lb.

There are 12 CH601's on the UK Register and the type is on the PFA approved list

HEINTZ / ZENAIR
CH 601 ZODIAC

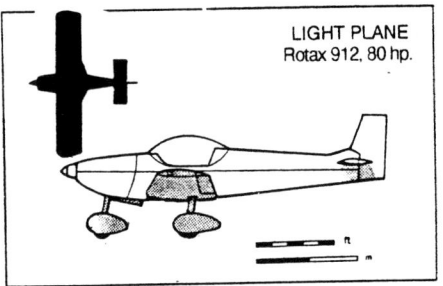

LIGHT PLANE
Rotax 912, 80 hp.

DATA	IMPERIAL		METRIC	
Span	27	ft	8.32	m
Wing area	130	ft²	12.2	m²
Aspect ratio	5.6		5.6	
Empty weight	550	lb	250	kg
Loaded weight	1058	lb	480	kg
Wing loading	8.1	lb/ft²	39.7	kg/m²
Max speed	140	mph	224	kmh
Cruise speed	120	mph	192	kmh
Stalling speed	50	mph	80	kmh
Climb rate	1200	ft/min	370	m/min
Range	550	mls	880	km

A product of TRI-R Technologies of California - KIS stands for keep it simple - was at one time marketed in the UK by ABC Aviation, it is a neat, two seat, side by side kit plane with GRP and Carbon Fibre pre moulded components on honeycomb cores, the metal parts are all pre-formed and welded.

The stateside KIS was powered either by a Limbach L2000 or a 125 hp Continental. The UK prototype has a modified Honda Civic car engine, the CAM 100 (100 hp). but Lycomings and Continentals are now more usual.

A cool performer the KIS cruises at 170 mph and climbs at 1600 feet a minute (solo).

The spatted tricycle gear is non retracting and the upturned 'vortex control' wing tips are a distinguishing feature. It may also be seen as a taildragger.

There are nine flying in the UK and several are under construction with PFA blessing. (Ed. Plus a four seater on the way)

TRI-R
KIS

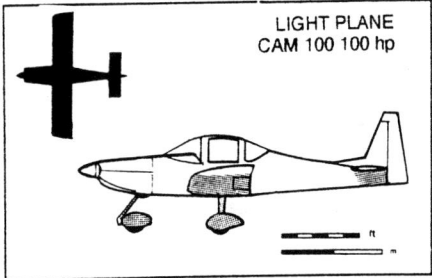

LIGHT PLANE
CAM 100 100 hp

DATA	IMP		METRIC	
Span	23	ft	7.1	m
Wing area	88	ft²	8.3	m²
Aspect ratio	6		6	
Empty weight	680	lb	308	kg
Loaded weight	1400	lb	635	kg
Wing loading	16	lb/ft²	77.6	kg/m²
Max speed	180	mph	288	kmh
Cruise speed	170	mph	272	kmh
Stalling speed	50	mph	80	kmh
Climb rate	1600	ft/min	492	m/min
Range	600	mls	960	km

A product of the German company Burkhart Grob Luft und Raumfahrt, well known for their high performance GRP gliders. The G115 is no power glider though, with its 170 mph. top speed and 180 hp. motor.

The latest model of the G115 - the G115D - differs from the earlier models in having simpler canopy framing, a more swept back fin and rudder. and a more powerful fuel injected engine.

The Royal Navy, through Airwork, are replacing some of their Chipmunks with the G115D (the Navy will call it the Heron), and other orders have been received from flying clubs in Australia and the USA.

The earlier models are flying with UK clubs, giving well instrumented side by side tuition. 18 on UK Register. In RAF service the G115 is the Tutor.

The G115 is an all composites aeroplane that looks set for a successful future.

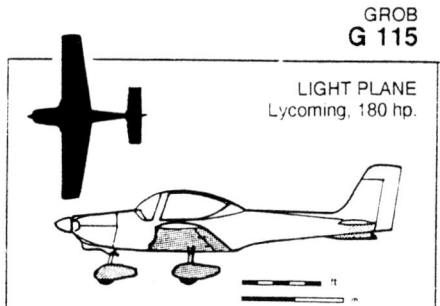

GROB
G 115

LIGHT PLANE
Lycoming, 180 hp.

DATA	IMPERIAL		METRIC	
Span	30.6	ft	9.42	m
Wing area	129	ft^2	12.1	m^2
Aspect ratio	7.25		7.25	
Empty weight	1630	lb	740	kg
Loaded weight	2182	lb	990	kg
Wing loading	17	lb/ft^2	83	kg/m^2
Max speed	168	mph	268	kmh
Cruise speed	135	mph	248	kmh
Stalling speed	53	mph	85	kmh
Climb rate	1350	ft/min	416	m/min
Range	600	mls	960	km

The origins of the Firefly lay in the Fournier RF-6B, an all wood French design of 1971, built under licence by Slingsby. Slingsby re-engineered the Fournier giving it a wider GRP fuselage and all composites wing and tail surfaces. Later developments include more powerful engines and constant speed prop.

Fully aerobatic at +6, -3g, the Firefly has an inverted fuel system, fully comprehensive instrumentation and avionics making it a pretty expensive aeroplane for the average weekend flyer though maintenance costs they say are low. There are 80 on the UK Register.

In 1994 the design won the British Design Council Award - specifically for the T3A version ordered by the USAF - it is the world's first training aircraft to be made largely from GRP and the first GRP 'plane to get Transport Category certification from the CAA.

The American order for 113 aircraft in, conjunction with Northrop Aircraft is worth £37 million.

The T3 was grounded by the USAF in '97 after a spate of crashes and though modified it has been dropped.

SLINGSBY
T67 FIREFLY

TRAINER
Lycoming 160 hp.

DATA	IMPERIAL		METRIC	
Span	34.7	ft	10.6	m
Wing area	136	ft^2	12.6	m^2
Aspect ratio	8.9		8.9	
Empty weight	1543	lb	700	kg
Loaded weight	2250	lb	1020	kg
Wing loading	16.5	lb/ft^2	80.5	kg/m^2
Max speed	161	mph	259	kmh
Cruise speed	149	mph	240	kmh
Stalling speed	45	mph	72	kmh
Climb rate	1150	ft/min	350	m/min
Range	518	mls	833	km

Rene Fournier started in the aviation business in the '60s by producing a range of highly popular motor gliders. Turning to a higher powered trainer/tourer in 1974 with the RF-6, an all wood trike two seater. After only 43 had been made the Fournier factory was in financial trouble and split up (Slingsby at this stage obtained the rights to build the RF-6, which was later to become the successful Firefly).

When Fournier, restructured, got going again the RF-47 appeared in 1993 - at first glance similar to the RF-6, it is a smaller, lighter and lower powered aeroplane. Prototypes were all wood, but subsequent models have included composites (ie. for main spar) but retain part fabric covering.

Stressed for +4.4,-2.2, the RF-47 is semi aerobatic and has superb visibility through its backwards and upwards opening canopy.

Re-badged as Arc Atlantique Aviation, the RF-47 is a works built aeroplane.

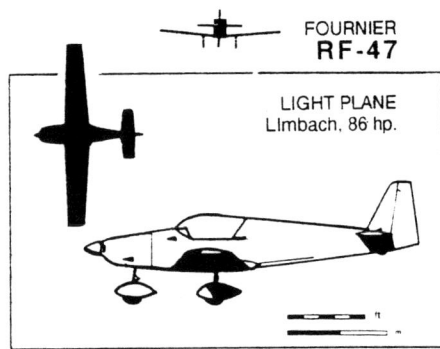

FOURNIER RF-47
LIGHT PLANE
Limbach, 86 hp.

DATA	IMPERIAL		METRIC	
Span	32.8	ft	10	m
Wing area	117.6	ft^2	10.9	m^2
Aspect ratio	9.2		9.2	
Empty weight	870	lb	395	kg
Loaded weight	1376	lb	620	kg
Wing loading	11.6	lb/ft^2	57	kg/m^2
Max speed	124	mph	200	kmh
Cruise speed	112	mph	180	kmh
Stalling speed	49	mph	78	kmh
Climb rate	787	ft/min	240	m/min
Range	616	mls	985	km

This 'up and coming' two seater from France is based on the all metal Colomban Ban Bi, designed by Michel Colomban, which first flew in 1994.

The MCR 01 is of mixed construction, composites fuselage and a wing with alloy skin over foam ribs and carbon and plywood spars. It is manufactured by Dyn Aero whose director is Christophe Robin son of the famous Pierre Robin, he of the delightful Robin range of light aircraft.

The three main versions of the MCR-01 are, the VLA, short span, 100 hp Rotax, capable of an incredible 190 mph., the Club, seen as a' trainer', bigger wing, flies and lands slower than the 'hot' VLA, but is just outside the SLA category, into which the MCR 01 SLA falls, which has more wing and less weight. The SLA has full span double slotted Fowler flaps and a stalling speed of 40 mph.

Half a dozen are on the UK Register at the time of writing – but I have a hunch we'll see many more.

Data below is for the MCR-01 SLA.

DYN AERO MCR 01
SLA/ULTRALIGHT
Rotax 60/100 hp

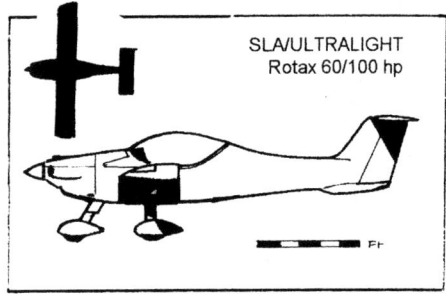

DATA	IMPERIAL		METRIC	
Span	25.5	ft	7.8	m
Wing area	80.7	sq.ft	7.5	sq.m
Aspect ratio	8			
Empty wt	528	lb.	240	kg.
Loaded wt	991	lb.	450	kg.
Wing loading	12.3	lb/sq.ft	60	kg/sq.m
Max speed	111	mph	178	kmph
Cruising speed	95	mph	152	kmph
Stall speed	40	mph	63	kmph
Climb	800	fpm	246	mpm
Range	400	mls	640	km

This sleek modern two seater designed and built by the Austrian company HOAC (also made by Diamond Aircraft in Canada) is marketed in this country by Diamond Aircraft UK who are based at Staverton.

Of all-composites construction, the Katana is powered by the economical Rotax 912 a four cylinder, four stroke which employs both air and water cooling.

The Katana, with it's low operating costs, low maintenance and docile handling is seen by many as the way ahead in the mass training field - i.e.. a long overdue replacement for the omnipresent, but ageing, Cessna 150/152 and Tomahawk.

Based on the Super Dimona powered glider, with its aspect ratio of ten, up-turned wing tips, pod and boom fuselage and 'T' tail, the Katana is easily identified.

Already in use at some flying schools, it is much praised by instructors who find that student dual time to solo can be as little as six hours.

A well stocked instrument panel, constant speed prop., and a very low noise level are all part of the package. (A four seat version is being developed)

Katana sales have burgeoned since our first edition and there are now 32 on the UK Register.

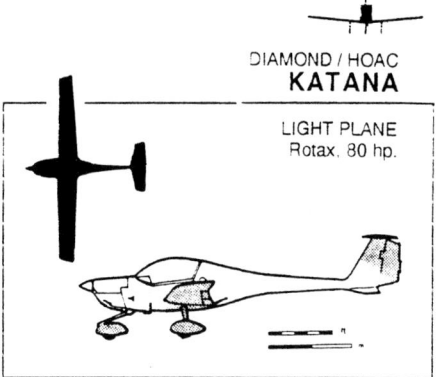

DIAMOND / HOAC
KATANA
LIGHT PLANE
Rotax, 80 hp.

DATA	IMPERIAL		METRIC	
Span	31.1	ft	10.8	m
Wing area	114.8	ft²	11.6	m²
Aspect ratio	10		10	
Empty weight	1090	lb	494	kg
Loaded weight	1610	lb	730	kg
Wing loading	14.1	lb/ft²	70	kg/m²
Max speed	160	mph	256	kmh
Cruise speed	137	mph	219	kmh
Stalling speed	57	mph	91	kmh
Climb rate	730	ft/min	225	m/min
Range	600	mls	962	km

Michel Colomban, the French designer of the innovative and minuscule Cri Cri has turned his hand to a rather more traditional configuration. The Banbi is a side by side two seater with a fixed tricycle undercarriage and a 'T' tail. The prototype aircraft are of all metal construction - and a metal kit is available - but a composites kit version is produced by Messrs Robin.

The Banbi first flew in 1994 and has been well liked by the pundits - especially its 190 mph (304 km p h) on 80 hp, supplied by a water cooled Rotax 912.

It is a small aeroplane 21ft (6.6 m) span and almost qualifies as a microlight weight-wise.

The smooth skin finish is achieved by much of the skin being bonded to the structure instead of riveting. The large flaps are electrically operated and reduce the stall from 64 mph (102 kmh) to 52 mph (83 kmh).

With its high wing loading the, as yet non-aerobatic, Banbi is not for the tyro, but a joy for the more experienced pilot.

PFA approval pending.

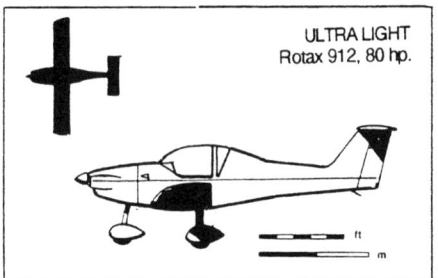

COLOMBAN
MC 100 BANBI
ULTRA LIGHT
Rotax 912, 80 hp.

DATA	IMPERIAL		METRIC	
Span	21.6	ft	6.6	m
Wing area	56	ft²	5.2	m²
Aspect ratio	8.3		8.3	
Empty weight	444	lb	201	kg
Loaded weight	946	lb	429	kg
Wing loading	16.8	lb/ft²	82	kg/m²
Max speed	190	mph	304	kmh
Cruise speed	181	mph	289	kmh
Stalling speed	64	mph	102	kmh
Climb rate	980	ft/min	301	m/min
Range	500	mls	800	km

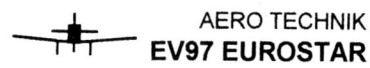

AERO TECHNIK
EV97 EUROSTAR

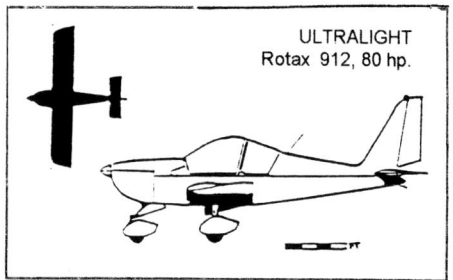

ULTRALIGHT
Rotax 912, 80 hp.

This Czech designed ultralight kitplane is a two seat development of the Pottier P220S three seater.

Hordes of modern, simple and economic light planes exist on the Continent but most are kept from the UK builder/owner by rigorous BCAR requirements. The Eurostar looks like breaking through the 'red tape - the PFA are reviewing the design and one has been built and is flying in the UK.

Of all metal construction, the Eurostar prototype first flew in 1997 and the type has since received certification in most Euro-countries.

The fixed tricycle gear has GRP cantilever legs with hydraulically braked wheels and a steerable or castoring nose-wheel. The wings - optional folding - carry three position flaps. (Another option is a Ballistic parachute).

A two bladed wooden propeller is driven by a Rotax 912 of 80 hp.

The kit comes pre-formed and ready to rivet together with the front and rear fuselages already part assembled.

The 'chamfered' lower edge of the rudder is a distinctive feature.

DATA	IMPERIAL		METRIC	
Span	26.5	ft	8.1	m
Wing area	106	sq.ft	6.0	sq.m
Aspect ratio	6.6			
Empty wt	577	lb.	262	kg.
Loaded wt	992	lb.	450	kg.
Wing loading	9.37	lb/sq.ft	45.7	kg/sq.m
Max speed	141	mph	225	kmph
Cruising speed	113	mph	180	kmph
Stall speed	41	mph	65	kmph
Climb	1079	fpm	332	mpm
Range	435	mls	700	km

EUROPA AVIATION
EUROPA TRI-GEAR

LIGHT PLANE
Rotax 912, 80 hp.

Europa's have gone from strength to strength with over 400 flying or in build since the '97 edition of this book. The model covered here is the tri-gear version - in place of the original model's mono-wheel (the mono-wheel option is still available).

The more familiar 'trike' will appeal to many - the mono still being an undercarriage rarity, which, although good for rough strips, needs special take off and crosswind techniques.

The penalty for having three long legs is a reduction in maximum speed, in the order of 15 mph. Flight handling is just as good as the earlier model, and in the cockpit a wider seat is possible as the mono' housing is empty.

Europa kits are renowned for their quality as is the factory back-up. Ivan Shaw and his team have put British light planes 'on the map' with sales world-wide.

A big winged motor-glider model and the 200 mph XS (new wing and clean up) are the latest Europas.

Deliveries of a factory built model the Liberty XL-2 are scheduled for 2000.

DATA	IMPERIAL		METRIC	
Span	19.2	ft	5.9	m
Wing area	95	ft^2	8.9	m^2
Aspect ratio	6.6		6.6	
Empty weight	730	lb	331	kg
Loaded weight	1370	lb	622	kg
Wing loading	14.4	lb/ft^2	70.3	kg/m^2
Max speed	150	mph	240	kmh
Cruise speed	103	mph	168	kmh
Stalling speed	56	mph	89	kmh
Climb rate	600	ft/min	185	m/min
Range	575	mls	920	km

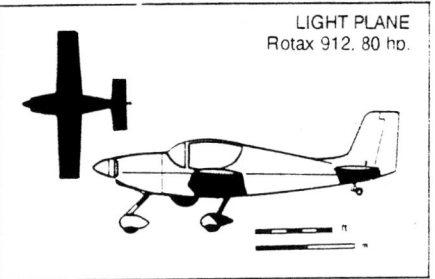

Designed by Hermann Mylius when Bolkow was part of the Messerschmit-Bolkow-Blohm organization, the Monsun is essentially a low wing version of the BO208 Junior. First flown as the MHK 101 in 1967 the BO209 production version flew in 1969.

A clean, all metal, two seat aeroplane with a square section rear fuselage, all flying tailplane, a retractable nose wheel option and wings that fold alongside the fuselage for storage. (This feature is not available on all models)

Semi - aerobatic, a pleasant, viceless aeroplane to fly the Monsun is much coveted by its ten UK Registered owners - 102 were built.

Production was resumed in 1979 by Monsun Flugzeubau at Weiden.

Figures below are for the 150 hp. Lycoming version.

BOLKOW
BO209 MONSUN

LIGHT PLANE
Lycoming, 150 hp.

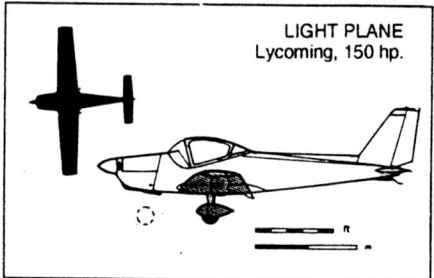

DATA	IMPERIAL		METRIC	
Span	27.5	ft	8.4	m
Wing area	110	ft^2	10.22	m^2
Aspect ratio	6.9		6.9	
Empty weight	1045	lb	474	kg
Loaded weight	1808	lb	820	kg
Wing loading	16.4	lb/ft^2	80.2	kg/m^2
Max speed	146	mph	233	kmh
Cruise speed	127	mph	203	kmh
Stalling speed	57	mph	91	kmh
Climb rate	896	ft/min	276	m/min
Range	618	mls	990	km

The most numerous flying machines in our skies, the flex - wing (some say 'powered hang glider') comes in many models and variants - too many, I fear, for us to cover in this small book. I have, therefore, picked a Mainair Blade as typical of the breed.

Developed in the 70's from the Rogallo foldable wing glider developed by NASA for the safe earth landing of space vehicles, the wing plan was rather like a capital letter 'A'. The modern wing plan is of a much higher aspect ratio with subsequent higher efficiency .

An essential difference between flexible and stiff wings is that the flex-wing dispenses with three axis controls and relies on pilot weight shift via a hanging control yoke.

Many remarkable distance flights have been made by these minimalist flying machines which represent the cheapest form of powered flying in both single and two seat forms.

The BMAA (British Microlight Aircraft Association) is the controlling body for the close-knit flex wing fraternity.

FLEX - WINGS
Represented by Mainair Blade

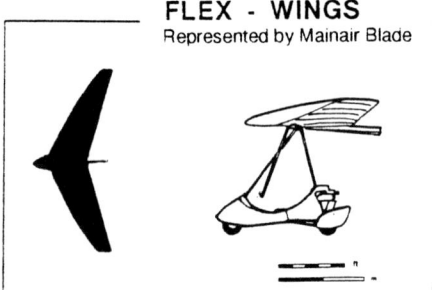

DATA	IMPERIAL		METRIC	
Span	34	ft	10.6	m
Wing area	164	ft^2	15.4	m^2
Aspect ratio	7.2		7.2	
Empty weight	381	lb	173	kg
Loaded weight	858	lb	390	kg
Wing loading	5.12	lb/ft^2	25	kg/m^2
Max speed	101	mph	176	kmh
Cruise speed	70	mph	112	kmh
Stalling speed	30	mph	48	kmh
Climb rate	800	ft/min	246	m/min
Range	300	mls	480	km

FOKKER
Dr1 TRI-PLANE

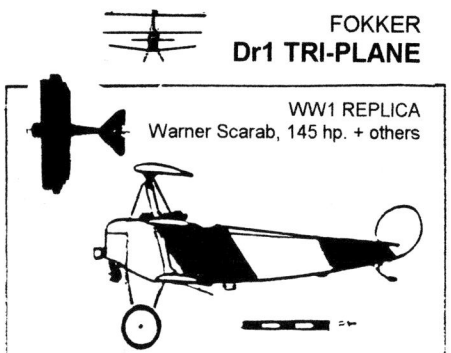

WW1 REPLICA
Warner Scarab, 145 hp. + others

A popular choice for a WW1 replica, the Dr1 has been built many times – there are two on the UK Register and others in many parts of the world.

A small and fairly simple aeroplane, the Tri-plane is usually built actual size using the same construction as that drawn by Anthony Fokker and Reinhold Platz. Various engines are used (none rotaries!?) but the Warner Scarab of 145 hp. seems to fit it like a glove – performance figs below are for this combination.

A favourite mount of Baron Von Richtofen – in fact, his last mount – the Triplane is, by modern standards, a difficult aeroplane to fly and with its original 104 hp engine was not half as agile as our film makers would let us believe! Manoeuvrable, yes, but with limitations.

The fact that the performance and physical characteristics are similar to the 'real thing' engenders respect from today's pilots for the men who flew for their lives in such machines in that far-away war.

There are five replicas in UK museums.

DATA	IMPERIAL		METRIC	
Span	19	ft	5.8	m
Wing area	202	sq.ft	18.8	sq.m
Aspect ratio top	5			
Empty wt	1112	lb.	505	kg.
Loaded wt	1456	lb.	661	kg.
Wing loading	7.2	lb/sq.ft	35.2	kg/sq.m
Max speed	*135*	mph	*216*	kmph
Cruising speed	100	mph	161	kmph
Stall speed	*40*	mph	*64*	kmph
Climb	2000	fpm	610	km
Range	*170*	mls	*272*	km

NIEUPORT
17/23 SCOUT

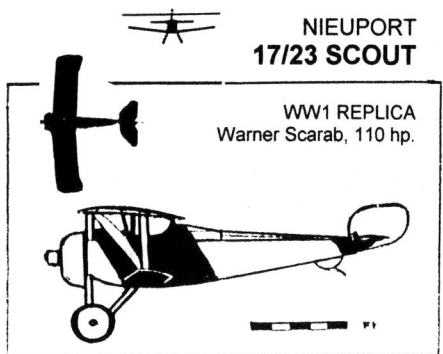

WW1 REPLICA
Warner Scarab, 110 hp.

The original Nieuport single seat fighter of WW1 was extensively used by the RFC and many of our aces flew this French 'V strutter', including Ball, Bishop and Mannock.

The Germans, at one stage in the war, were so impressed with the Nieuport that they started to build them by copying captured aircraft; but none saw action.

Several full size replicas have been built – one flying in the UK and another nearing completion. Original aircraft exist in museums in France, Italy and the USA.

The first Nieuports had a novel trimming device – the high aspect ratio lower wing, pivoting on the 'V' strut, was adjustable in incidence in flight!

The UK replica has a welded steel tube fuselage, instead of wood, but the wings are as original wood and fabric. For safety's sake and to aid manoeuvring, the spoked wheels contain drum brakes, unlike the unbraked original.

The Scarab develops 110 hp with the bespoke prop, is about the right size and is more reliable!

Data for replica below is very similar to original.

DATA	IMPERIAL		METRIC	
Span	27	ft	8.3	m
Wing area	159	sq.ft	15	sq.m
Aspect ratio (av)	9			
Empty wt	1085	lb.	492	kg.
Loaded wt	1380	lb.	626	kg.
Wing loading	8.7	lb/sq.ft	42	kg/sq.m
Max speed	110	mph	176	kmph
Cruising speed	92	mph	147	kmph
Stall speed	52	mph	83	kmph
Climb	800`	fpm	246	mpm
Range	*180*	mls	*288*	km

SE 5

There are many replicas of this famous WW1 fighter worldwide – 13 are on the UK Register, half a dozen of which are airworthy; others are static display replicas in museums. Three originals exist in collection, including, the one at Old Warden – still flying after 82 years!

Many SE5s, redundant after the war, came on to the civil market and were used for banner towing, skywriting and, two seat versions, for joy riding.

The UK replicas are built to the Slingsby design, based on the all wood Currie Wot (used in several films on WW1), or the Canadian Replica Plans version.

Replicas are usually 7/8 scale, about half the weight of the original and powered by Lycoming engines of around 100 hp. – half the power.

The modern engine, being much lighter than the WW1 unit, makes a longer than scale nose necessary to achieve the correct cg. – but the general appearance of these olive green replicas is very authentic – they even seem to sound right!

The Replica Plans version is a PFA approved design (PFA-20F) and two, at least, are under construction.

Data below is typical for this replica.

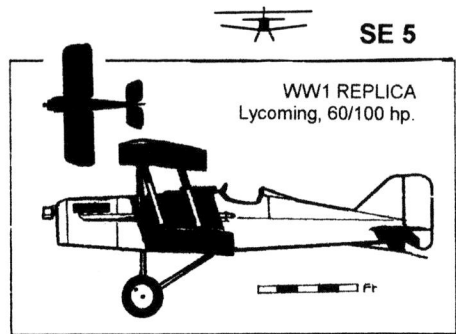

WW1 REPLICA
Lycoming, 60/100 hp.

DATA	IMPERIAL		METRIC	
Span	22	ft	6.7	m
Wing area	180	sq.ft	16.2	sq.m
Aspect ratio top	5.4			
Empty wt	850	lb.	385	kg.
Loaded wt	1200	lb.	545	kg.
Wing loading	6.6	lb/sq.ft	32	kg/sq.m
Max speed	100	mph	160	kmph
Cruising speed	85	mph	136	kmph
Stall speed	40	mph	64	kmph
Climb	500`	fpm	154	mpm
Range	300	mls	480	km

AVRO 504 K

One of the most successful and long lived of aeroplanes. The original A.V.Roe design the 504 became the classic 504K in 1913, serving in the RFC as night fighter, trainer and occasional bomber.

After the '14-18 war 319 504Ks were sold on to the civil market where they served as trainers, joy riders, banner towers and wing walker mounts.

The structure was the wire braced wooden girder type with fabric covering. (Some later models had welded tube fuselages). Power was supplied by a rotary engine. (100 hp Gnome. 110 hp Le Rhone, 150 hp Bentley).

At a time when lateral control was achieved in many cases by wing warping the 504 had the luxury of ailerons on all wings!

The single skid, or 'toothpick', between the main wheels to prevent nosing over, is unique feature.

8000 504's were built, the RAF kept theirs until 1932 and seven were impressed at the start of WW2.

One is still flying with the Shuttleworth Trust; two originals are in UK museums (6 abroad) and four replicas.

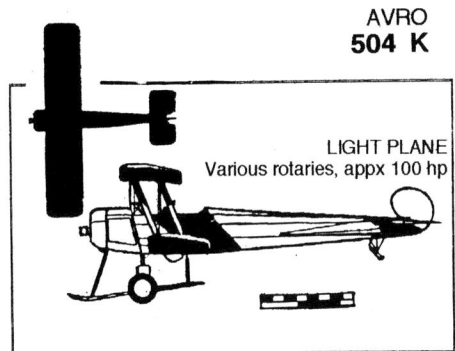

LIGHT PLANE
Various rotaries, appx 100 hp

DATA	IMPERIAL		METRIC	
Span	36	ft	11.1	m
Wing area	330	ft^2	31	m^2
Aspect ratio	7.8		7.8	
Empty weight	1231	lb	559	kg
Loaded weight	1829	lb	830	kg
Wing loading	5.5	lb/ft^2	27	kg/m^2
Max speed	95	mph	152	kmh
Cruise speed	75	mph	120	kmh
Stalling speed	30	mph	48	kmh
Climb rate	700	ft/min	215	m/min
Range	225	mls	360	km

Two Hawker Cygnets were built for the Lympne Light Aeroplane Trials of 1924, they were two seat ultralight biplanes, one powered by a 30 hp. ABC Scorpion and the other by a Bristol Cherub of 32 hp. Let down by erratic engine performance on their first appearance in the '24 Trials, they both won prizes at the Lympne Trials in 1926.

One, G-EBMB, survives to this day in the RAF Museum at Hendon, the other, G-EBJH was destroyed in a crash at Lympne in 1927.

Unlike many 'replica' aeroplanes that are compromises of scale and proportion, the Cygnet is a true replica, not only in scale but in its construction - in fact the replicas have been built, largely, from original Hawker drawings. The design, which is a bit marginal in flight as a two seater, is PFA approved - Sydney Camm would have turned in his grave if it hadn't been!

Two of these charming little replicas have been built, powered by 35hp. Mosler engines - one appropriately registered G-CAMM.

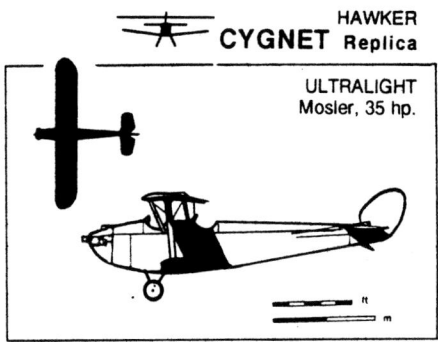

HAWKER
CYGNET Replica

ULTRALIGHT
Mosler, 35 hp.

DATA	IMPERIAL		METRIC	
Span	28	ft	8.6	m
Wing area	172	ft²	16	m²
Aspect ratio	6.6		6.6	
Empty weight	373	lb	169	kg
Loaded weight	730	lb	331	kg
Wing loading	4.2	lb/ft²	20.5	kg/m²
Max speed	82	mph	131	kmh
Cruise speed	60	mph	96	kmh
Stalling speed	30	mph	48	kmh
Climb rate	275	ft/min	85	m/min
Range	400	mls	640	km

The first DH60 Moth, with an upright Cirrus engine, flew in 1925, subsequently the upright Gypsy Major engined DH60g Moth was launched three years later. This father of the famous DH82 Tiger Moth was a sensation in it's day, winning many races and setting class records for speed, altitude, and engine reliability. Jean Batten, Amy Johnson and Francis Chichester all became famous flying the '60 Moth - Amy's *Jason* is in the Science Museum in London.

The '60G Moth was all wood with fabric covered wings and control surfaces and a plywood skinned fuselage, many hundreds being manufactured up to the advent of the Tiger Moth.

The '60M. had a welded steel tube fuselage with fabric covering over wooden stringers - a (close up!) recognition give away.

The success of the '60 Moths boosted De Haviland's fortunes who in 1930 opened a new factory at Hatfield and issued licences for overseas manufacturers. There are 23 '60 Moths on the 'Register, 13 of which are triumphantly airworthy.

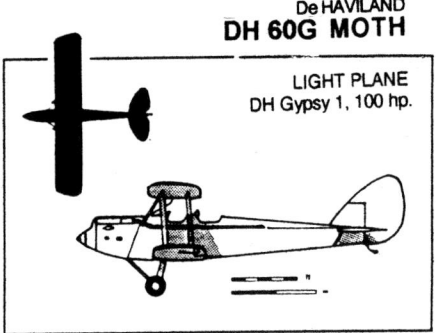

De HAVILAND
DH 60G MOTH

LIGHT PLANE
DH Gypsy 1, 100 hp.

DATA	IMPERIAL		METRIC	
Span	30	ft	9.24	m
Wing area	243	ft²	22.8	m²
Aspect ratio	7.4		7.4	
Empty weight	962	lb	437	kg
Loaded weight	1650	lb	749	kg
Wing loading	6.8	lb/ft²	33.2	kg/m²
Max speed	98	mph	157	kmh
Cruise speed	83	mph	133	kmh
Stalling speed	40	mph	64	kmh
Climb rate	700	ft/min	215	m/min
Range	290	mls	464	km

The two seat Avro 594 Avian was designed and built for the 1926 Lymne Light Aeroplane Trials and was powered by a 75hp. AS Genet engine.

Though only moderately successful at Lymne, eighteen months later Bert Hinkler flew one from Croydon to Darwin in a record 15 days. Avians made other long distance flights in the late '20s and in 1930 an Avian Mk3 won the Kings Cup air race.

Various marks and model numbers covered engine changes, wing tip shapes and undercarriage configuration. The main engines fitted were the Genet (75hp), Cirrus 2 (85hp), and Cirrus 3 (95hp).

About 80 Avians were built, many surviving up to WW2, when they were impressed – four survived the conflict. One is still flying – restored by Lang Kirby in Australia and air freighted to the UK. Whilst flying in the UK it crashed badly, but was rebuilt in two months and flown back to Oz by Kirby.

Three are on the UK Reg. Two in museums and one on long-term restoration.

AVRO AVIAN

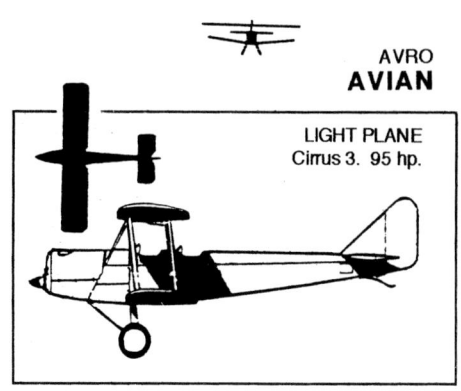

LIGHT PLANE
Cirrus 3. 95 hp.

DATA (Cirrus 2)	IMPERIAL		METRIC	
Span	28	ft	8.6	m
Wing area	245	ft^2	23	m^2
Aspect ratio (Top)	6.4		6.4	
Empty weight	907	lb	411	kg
Loaded weight	1467	lb	666	kg
Wing loading	6.0	lb/ft^2	29.3	kg/
Max speed	98	mph	157	kmh
Cruise speed	82	mph	131	kmh
Stalling speed	30	mph	48	kmh
Climb rate	650	ft/min	200	m/m
Range	325	mls	520	km

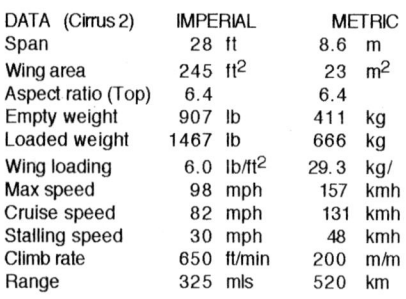

Simmonds Aircraft Ltd built the Spartan two-seat biplane in 1928 with symmetrical section wings interchangeable for ease of manufacture and spares holding. Though fairly successful there was a prejudice against the symmetrical wing section – so Simmonds, re-named Spartan Aircraft Ltd, built a Clark Y section winged model called the Spartan Arrow. Interchangeability continued with the rudder doubling as half an elevator. (A Napier Javelin test bed version (G-ABST) had a non-standard fin and rudder).

All wood with fabric covered wings that folded backwards the Arrow first flew in 1930 and was usually powered by a Hermes 105 hp engine.

Although raced in several Kings Cup races the Arrow was never well placed.

Fifteen Arrows were built all either being sold abroad or destroyed before WW2 – except one! G-ABWP, bought in '36 by Shuttleworth, stored for many years, it is now privately owned and airworthy

SPARTAN ARROW

LIGHT PLANE
Cirrus Hermes, 105 hp.

DATA	IMPERIAL		METRIC	
Span	30.6	ft	9.4	m
Wing area	251	sq.ft	23.6	sq.m
Aspect ratio	7.4			
Empty wt	965	lb.	438	kg.
Loaded wt	1750	lb.	794	kg.
Wing loading	7	lb/sq.ft	34.2	kg/sq.m
Max speed	106	mph	170	kmph
Cruising speed	92	mph	147	kmph
Stall speed	40	mph	64	kmph
Climb	830	fpm	255	mpm
Range	432	mls	691	km

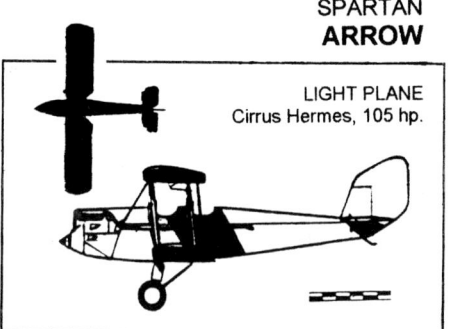

Though, strictly speaking, not a light civil aeroplane, there were several with civil registrations, one of which still exists.

A famous RAF fighter, in its day, the Bulldog first flew in 1928 and was powered by a Bristol Jupiter VII engine. The structure was all metal, both steel and light alloy, the whole being fabric covered, apart from detachable panels between firewall and cockpit. A pair of Vickers machine guns were fitted either side of the forward fuselage.

346 of the chunky Bulldogs (inc. two seat trainer versions) equipped a dozen squadrons in the late 20's and early 30's. Many more were exported.

Four aircraft were civil registered by Bristol's, as demonstrators and engine test beds; two crashed, one transferred to the RAF and one, G-ABBB, survives. This one had a disastrous crash at the SBAC show in 1964, and though a 'write off' it has been miraculously rebuilt by Skysport Engineering and is now on display at the RAF Museum.

One other exists in a museum in Finland.

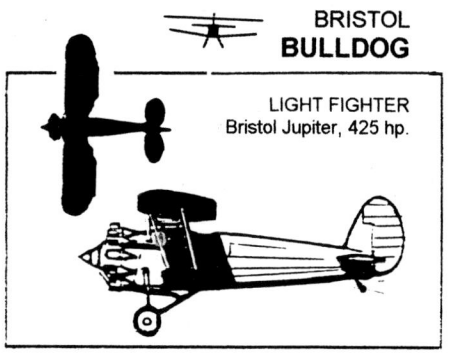

BRISTOL
BULLDOG

LIGHT FIGHTER
Bristol Jupiter, 425 hp.

DATA	IMPERIAL		METRIC	
Span	33.9	ft	10.44	m
Wing area	307	sq.ft	28.8	sq.m
Aspect ratio top	6			
Empty wt	2200	lb.	999	kg.
Loaded wt	3490	lb.	1584	kg.
Wing loading	11.4	lb/sq.ft	55.6	kg/sq.m
Max speed	174	mph	278	kmph
Cruising speed	145	mph	232	kmph
Stall speed	50	mph	80	kmph
Climb	2000	fpm	616	mpm
Range	400	mls	640	km

One of F G Miles first ventures when starting out at Shoreham in 1929 was the conversion of a 1918 Avro Baby into a Southern Martlet. The Baby's fuselage and wings were retained and a new tail, undercarriage and engine were fitted, plus detail improvements produced a lively aerobatic biplane – which was initially called the Hornet Baby.

Six Martlets were built with a variety of engines. The prototype, with an ABC Hornet (85hp) and others included. AS Genet 2 (80hp), Genet Major (100hp), Gipsy 1 (100hp) and Gipsy 2 (120hp).

The only surviving Martlet, G-AAYX, recently restored to airworthy condition at Old Warden, was stored throughout WW2, bought by Billy Butlin in 1947 and restored by Miles, at Woodley, and used to give aerobatic displays at his holiday camps. Alan Cobham's National Air Displays owned one as a workhorse and Mrs F G Miles as a hack – the latter was given to the ATC in 1940.

A final version, the Metal Martlet, had a steel tube fuselage frame and a split axle undercarriage; it was flown in 1931 and (inexplicably!?) scrapped the following year.

Details below for Genet 2 version.

SOUTHERN
MARTLET

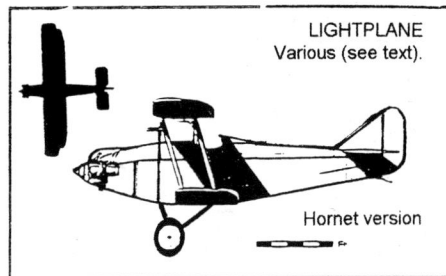

LIGHTPLANE
Various (see text).

Hornet version

DATA	IMPERIAL		METRIC	
Span	25	ft	7.6	m
Wing area	180	sq.ft	17	sq.m
Aspect ratio	7			
Empty wt	705	lb.	320	kg.
Loaded wt	1030	lb.	467	kg.
Wing loading	5.7	lb/sq.ft	28	kg/sq.m
Max speed	112	mph	180	kmph
Cruising speed	95	mph	152	kmph
Stall speed	35	mph	56	kmph
Climb	1100	fpm	339	mpm
Range	280	mls	448	km

Designed as a replacement for the venerable Avro 504 the Tutor first flew in 1929. Fabric covered, it had a steel tube fuselage, single piece LA wing ribs over steel spars. The usual power plant was a seven cylinder, 240 hp. Lynx – which was originally uncowled.

It became the standard RAF trainer, about 200 being delivered and 19 were civil registered. (Several sold abroad inc. Irish and Greek air forces). The famous pre-war Alan Cobham Circus had two Tutors in its fleet.

Three of the civil Tutors were impressed in 1939 and were not seen again – but three ex RAF models were civilianised after the conflict, one of which, G-AHSA, is still flying with the Shuttleworth Trust.

Replaced, finally, by the more economic Tiger Moth the Tutor is a fine example of a typical '30's biplane and long may it enthral us at Old Warden.

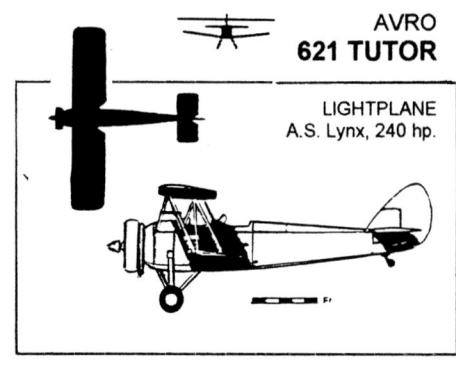

AVRO
621 TUTOR

LIGHTPLANE
A.S. Lynx, 240 hp.

DATA	IMPERIAL		METRIC	
Span	34	ft	10.5	m
Wing area	300	sq.ft	28.2	sq.m
Aspect ratio	7.7		7.7	
Empty wt	1722	lb.	781	kg.
Loaded wt	2380	lb.	1080	kg.
Wing loading	7.9	lb/sq.ft	38.5	kg/sq.m
Max speed	116	mph	185	kmph
Cruising speed	100	mph	160	kmph
Stall speed	48	mph	77	kmph
Climb	1000	fpm	308	mpm
Range	300	mls	480	km

Designed as a trainer for the RAF the Tomtit first flew in 1929 some being sold onto the civil market, plus four to the RNZAF.

An all-metal airframe with fabric covering, heavily staggered wings and a 150 hp. Mongoose engine the Tomtit competed in several Kings Cup air races.

In 1935 the Tomtit was phased out of RAF service and nine were 'civilianised' – one being operated by Campbell Black's British Empire Air Displays.

During WW2 six Tomtits operated on vital communications work, camouflaged and with civil markings, but were never officially 'impressed'. Alex Henshaw, the famous test pilot, had a Tomtit as his personal hack during that war.

Three seem to have survived the conflict, one crashed one was scrapped and one (G-AFTA) survives at that Valhalla for historic aeroplanes, Old Warden, where it is maintained in an airworthy condition.

Other engines fitted were, Cirrus Hermes, Wolseley AR9, Aquarius and Aries (225 hp).

HAWKER
TOMTIT

LIGHT PLANE
A.S. Mongoose III, 150 hp.

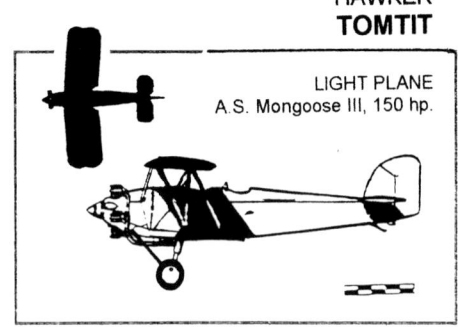

DATA	IMPERIAL		METRIC	
Span	28.5	ft	8.8	m
Wing area	238	sq.ft	22.4	sq.m
Aspect ratio	6.8			
Empty wt	1100	lb.	500	kg.
Loaded wt	2100	lb.	953	kg.
Wing loading	8.8	lb/sq.ft	43	kg/sq.m
Max speed	124	mph	198	kmph
Cruising speed	105	mph	168	kmph
Stall speed	45	mph	72	kmph
Climb	1000	fpm	308	mpm
Range	350	mls	560	km

First flown in 1930, the all wood Redwing was a side- by-side two seater powered by an air cooled flat four ABC Hornet of 75 hp. The fuselage was plywood covered, the rest of the airframe fabric. The sturdy divided axle undercarriage had long shock struts, which were attached to the top longerons.

The Mk 2 Redwing was fitted with a Genet 2A of 80 hp. – all subsequent models used this unit. The Mk 3 with reduced span and spatted wheels was built but never certificated and later converted to a Mk 2.

Twelve Redwings in all were built between 1930/33.

In 1934 a Mrs K Miller attempted to fly from Croydon to Cape Town but came to grief after a creditable flight across the Sahara when it was wrecked in a forced landing in Dahomey after a flight of 10,000 miles.

G-ABNX, a privately owned Redwing, was stored throughout the war and has been in its current ownership for four years, flies at intervals and is currently airworthy

With its 250 sq. ft. of wing the Redwing has stately flying characteristics and a slow landing speed and with its sociable seating it is a true 'gentleman's aerial carriage'.

ROBINSON REDWING

LIGHTPLANE
AS Genet 2, 80hp.

DATA	IMPERIAL		METRIC	
Span	30.5	ft	9.3	m
Wing area	250	sq.ft	23.2	sq.m
Aspect ratio	7			
Empty wt	870	lb.	395	kg.
Loaded wt	1450	lb.	658	kg.
Wing loading	5.8	lb/sq.ft	28.3	kg/sq.m
Max speed	95	mph	153	kmph
Cruising speed	85	mph	137	kmph
Stall speed	35	mph	56	kmph
Climb	800'	fpm	244	mpm
Range	275	mls	442	km

The Tiger Moth, De Havilands 82nd design, first flew in 1931. It was the mainstay of the pre war flying clubs and with the advent of WW2 it got into camouflage and became the RAF's main ab initio trainer - practically every pilot who flew in the war learned his basic skills on this aeroplane.

8,500 Tigers were built, mainly in Britain (4000 during the war). There were also production units in Canada, New Zealand and Australia.

A four seat version with enclosed cockpit, called the Jackaroo, was produced at Thruxton in limited numbers, using ex RAF models.

Some Canadian models were powered by a Menasco Pirate engine of 160 hp.

The wings are a fabric covered wooden structure and the fuselage is ply covered welded steel tube.

64 years old, and still going strong! 200 still on the UK Register.

De HAVILAND TIGER MOTH

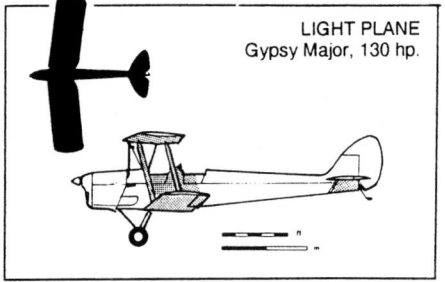

LIGHT PLANE
Gypsy Major, 130 hp.

DATA	IMPERIAL		METRIC	
Span	29.3	ft	9.02	m
Wing area	239	ft^2	22.5	m^2
Aspect ratio	7.2		7.2	
Empty weight	1115	lb	506	kg
Loaded weight	1825	lb	828	kg
Wing loading	7.6	lb/ft^2	37.1	kg/m^2
Max speed	109	mph	174	kmh
Cruise speed	90	mph	144	kmh
Stalling speed	40	mph	64	kmh
Climb rate	673	ft/min	305	m/min
Range	285	mls	456	km

First flown in 1932 the De Haviland Fox Moth embodied many Tiger Moth components - wings, tail unit and undercarriage. It could carry four passengers + pilot on short flights and three passengers on longer journeys. .An early production version with a Gipsy 3A engine (later named Gipsy Major) won the 1933 Kings Cup Air Race at an average speed of 124 mph.
The Prince of Wales owned one, briefly, before it was sold to Belgium as OO-ENC.
98 Fox Moths were built at Stag Lane, 49 were Brit. Reg. and production was also undertaken at DH's Toronto works. Several small airlines used them as well as air display companies, who used them for joy-riding and one was attached to the 1933 British Everest Flight Expedition.
Eleven of the Brit. Reg. Foxes that were around in 1939 were impressed, mainly for ATA taxi work; none of these survived. Today there are four on the UK Reg. two airworthy and two being restored, other examples exist in Switzerland, Australia, New Zealand and Canada.
The Fox Moth with its 120/130 hp. engine was a fine performer, cruising with five people at nearly 100 mph.

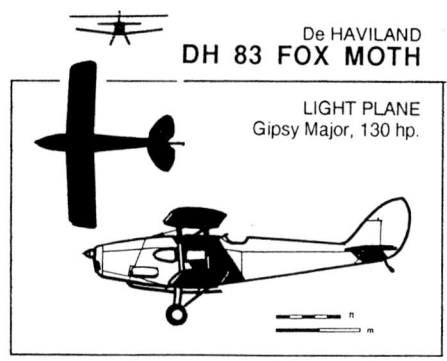

De HAVILAND
DH 83 FOX MOTH

LIGHT PLANE
Gipsy Major, 130 hp.

DATA	IMPERIAL		METRIC	
Span	30.9	ft	9.5	m
Wing area	261	ft²	24.5	m²
Aspect ratio	7.3		7.3	
Empty weight	1100	lb	499	kg
Loaded weight	2070	lb	939	kg
Wing loading	7.9	lb/ft²	38	kg/m²
Max speed	113	mph	181	kmh
Cruise speed	90	mph	144	kmh
Stalling speed	45	mph	72	kmh
Climb rate	492	ft/min	151	m/min
Range	360	mls	576	km

The two seat, side by side, B2 was developed from the Bluebird IV of 1929, both metal framed biplanes with fabric covering. First flown in 1932 the B2 had a redesigned fin and rudder and Alclad covered fuselage. Cirrus Hermes IV engines were usually fitted though other installations included Gipsy III and Gipsy Major.
Entered for the 1932 and 1934 Kings Cup Air Races, G-ACAH finished fourth in '34.
The B2 was taken up by several flying schools and the RAF, doing sterling service as a trainer in the early war years.
Thirty six were built, but by 1942 they had been relegated to 'instructional airframes' and 24 were distributed to ATC squadrons. Seven were written off in crashes before 1942.
There are still three on the UK Register, G-AEBJ airworthy and still flying, two others stored and (hopefully) under restoration. (I wonder if any of the 24 that went to ATC huts up and down the country in1942 still exist, whole or in pieces?)

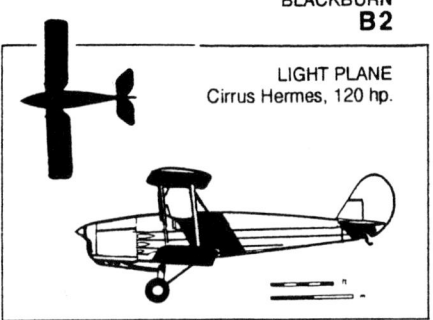

BLACKBURN
B2

LIGHT PLANE
Cirrus Hermes, 120 hp.

DATA	IMPERIAL		METRIC	
Span	30.1	ft	9.3	m
Wing area	246	ft²	23.1	m²
Aspect ratio	7.3		7.3	
Empty weight	1175	lb	528	kg
Loaded weight	1850	lb	840	kg
Wing loading	7.5	lb/ft²	36.7	kg/m²
Max speed	112	mph	179	kmh
Cruise speed	95	mph	152	kmh
Stalling speed	45	mph	72	kmh
Climb rate	700	ft/min	215	m/min
Range	320	mls	512	km

A heavyweight for this book, but a truly classic 'light plane'.

The Beech 17 was the first design to come out of Walter Beech's own factory at Wichita, Kansas in 1932. his previous designs were under the Travel Air label. The prototypes had a fixed undercarriage (the retractable gear coming a year later) and five seats, and by 1934 production had reached a modest 18.

But the back staggered biplane with the big engine had proved an extremely nifty performer and clocked up a lot of air race wins and further enhanced production.

During WW2 the '17 was ordered in quantity by the USAAF and USN as a personnel and utility transport, and with the peace a short run of improved civilian models were produced.

So here we have a 60 year old biplane that cruises at 200 mph., climbs at 1500 fpm., has a range of nearly 1000 miles and a cabin like a limo'! (It makes you think!) At one time there were 12 on the UK Register (including one Amy Johnson) there are now 2 with UK Reg. and 2 with USA registration based here.

Look out for this lovely 'gas guzzler'.

BEECH 17 ('STAGGERWING')

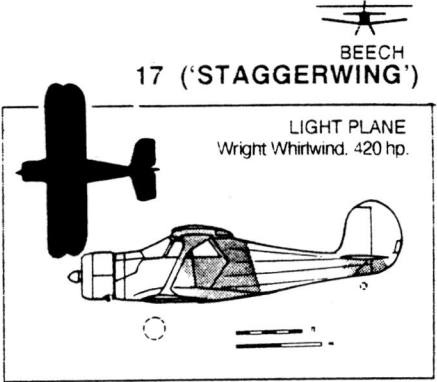

LIGHT PLANE
Wright Whirlwind. 420 hp.

DATA	IMPERIAL		METRIC	
Span	32	ft	9,24	m
Wing area	267	ft^2	25.1	m^2
Aspect ratio	7.7		7.7	
Empty weight	2226	lb	1011	kg
Loaded weight	3900	lb	1771	kg
Wing loading	14.6	lb/ft^2	71.25	kg/m^2
Max speed	230	mph	368	kmh
Cruise speed	202	mph	323	kmh
Stalling speed	55	mph	88	kmh
Climb rate	1500	ft/min	462	m/min
Range	700	mls	1120	km

Co-designed by Jean Stampe, the DH agent in Belgium; this Tiger Moth look-a-like first flew in 1933 and was adopted by the Belgian and French air forces as their *ab initio* trainer.

Production ceased until after the war when production was undertaken by Nord and 700 were built. Stampe, himself, formed Stampe et Renard and continued a small production run in Belgium.

Very popular in post war aerobatic circles right up to the advent of the more specialised Pitts and Zlins.

Made famous in the sixties by the daring Rothman Aerobatic Team the Stampe is still a useful aerobat and there are 50 or more on the British Register.

The Stampe SV-4B's rounded wing tips help in sorting it out from the Tiger Moth!

Both Renault and de Haviland Gypsy Major engines are fitted. (Ed. Plus some Lycoming 150/180 hp.).

STAMPE SV 4

LIGHT PLANE
Renault, 130 hp.

DATA	IMPERIAL		METRIC	
Span	27.5	ft	8.4	m
Wing area	194	ft^2	18	m^2
Aspect ratio	7.8		7.8	
Empty weight	1056	lb	480	kg
Loaded weight	1716	lb	780	kg
Wing loading	8.8	lb/ft^2	43.2	kg/m^2
Max speed	127	mph	204	kmh
Cruise speed	109	mph	175	kmh
Stalling speed	45	mph	72	kmh
Climb rate	900	ft/min	277	m/min
Range	250	mls	400	km

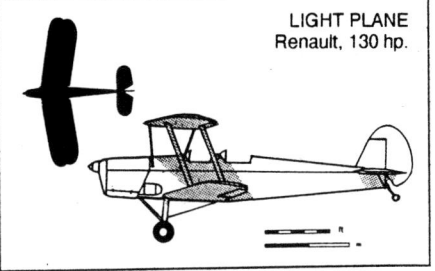

In 1934 Alex Henshaw, air racer and famous Spitfire test pilot, bought a Mk 1 Arrow Active and proceeded to teach himself aerobatics. He liked the little biplane and claimed that he 'learned more about flying in it than any other aeroplane.

Only two Actives were built by Arrow Aircraft Ltd at Yeadon during 1931/32, the airframe was all metal and the covering mainly fabric.

The Mk 1 (G-ABIX) had a 115 hp. Cirrus Hermes engine and the Mk 2 a 120 hp. Gipsy Major 3; the other difference was the Mk I's top plane was attached to the fuselage by a pylon and the Mk 2's by struts.

Both Arrows raced in the 1932 Kings Cup and the Mk2 in the 1933 race. Two years later the Mk1 caught fire in the air and crashed, Henshaw parachuted to safety.

The Mk 2 (G-ASVE) survives, having been discovered in a loft at the Slingsby works in 1957, and is still airworthy at Old Warden.

A tough little aerobatic biplane, which, had it been developed could have become the British Pitts!

ARROW ACTIVE

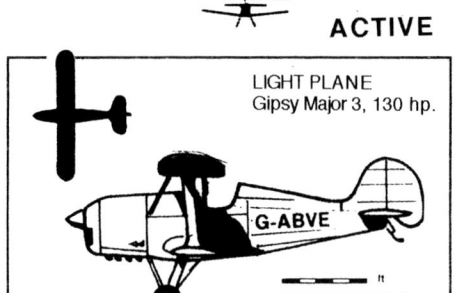

LIGHT PLANE
Gipsy Major 3, 130 hp.

DATA	IMPERIAL		METRIC	
Span	24	ft	7.4	m
Wing area	120	ft^2	11.3	m^2
Aspect ratio (Top wing) 8.2			8.2	
Empty weight	825	lb	420	kg
Loaded weight	1325	lb	602	kg
Wing loading	11.1	lb/ft^2	54	kg/m^2
Max speed	144	mph	230	kmh
Cruise speed	129	mph	206	kmh
Stalling speed	55	mph	88	kmh
Climb rate	1000	ft/min	454	m/min
Range	420	mls	772	km

This pre WW2 German trainer which first flew in 1934, a close contemporary of our Tiger Moth, has been built under licence in various countries and is, in a single seat form, the Jungmeister, a popular aerobat. (The Jungmeister differs in as much that its fuselage is of a completely different design)

Having retained its appeal over the years, limited production was resumed in 1956 by CASA in Spain. It has also been built in Czechoslovakia and Switzerland. In 1968 a production line was set up in West Germany and it looks as if it's going to go on forever! (Total production = 1000 appx)

Fitted either with a Hirth inverted or Tigre in-line engine (CASA). The Jungman's structure is of mixed wood and metal (welded tube fuselage) and is largely fabric covered.

The swept back bi-plane wings and raked forward, leggy, undercarriage are distinctive features

There are 33 on the British Register.

BUCKER JUNGMANN

LIGHT PLANE
Hirth, 105 hp.

DATA	IMPERIAL		METRIC	
Span	24.25	ft	7.5	m
Wing area	145	ft^2	13.6	m^2
Aspect ratio	8.3		8.3	
Empty weight	836	lb	380	kg
Loaded weight	1474	lb	670	kg
Wing loading	10.2	lb/ft^2	49.6	kg/m^2
Max speed	115	mph	184	kmh
Cruise speed	106	mph	170	kmh
Stalling speed	45	mph	72	kmh
Climb rate	600	ft/min	184	m/min
Range	400	mls	640	km

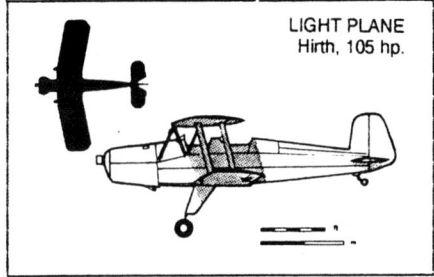

Starting out as the Stearman 75 Kaydet in 1934 this venerable biplane became the classic wartime trainer of the USAF, and was produced in considerable numbers as the Boeing Stearman 75 - 10,000 being the final total.
Still to be seen working for it's living as a stunt plane, carrying wing walkers and joy riding; there are over thirty on the UK Register.
Of rugged construction, with sharply staggered wings, wire braced and 'N' strutted, the '75 has a clean single leg oleo undercarriage, open cockpits (of course!) and an often uncowled radial engine. The engine type varies; Lycoming, Continental, Jacobs and Pratt and Whitney have all been fitted.
In the post war years many of the trainers found work as crop dusters - for which metal fuselage panels replace the fabric covering.
Single seat versions have appeared and a closed cockpit version for the RCAF.
This chunky classic with the big radial growl is a star!

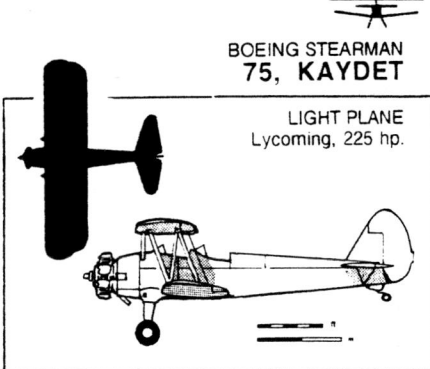

BOEING STEARMAN 75, KAYDET

LIGHT PLANE
Lycoming, 225 hp.

DATA	IMPERIAL		METRIC	
Span	32.15	ft	9.8	m
Wing area	297.4	ft²	27.6	m²
Aspect ratio	7		7	
Empty weight	1931	lb	876	kg
Loaded weight	2635	lb	1196	kg
Wing loading	8.9	lb/ft²	43.3	kg/m²
Max speed	124	mph	200	kmh
Cruise speed	106	mph	170	kmh
Stalling speed	48	mph	77	kmh
Climb rate	1000	ft/min	308	m/min
Range	375	mls	600	km

Next to the Tiger Moth the Hornet is the greatest survivor of the pre WW2 de Havilands. First flown in 1934 as an experimental aircraft for biplane wing research, it had elliptical wings and side by side seating in a well upholstered cabin.
The construction is all wood with mainly fabric covering; the rear fuselage is fabric covered over a conventional ply covered box structure to give a more pleasing/streamlined section.
In production by 1935 it was shortly modified to have square tipped, slightly tapered wings and sub typed as the DH 87B - as drawing.
The elliptical/tapered wings had some nasty habits and owners were invited to trade them in for square ones.
165 were eventually made and most were pressed into military service - three were, in fact, delivered new to the RAF - 24 survived to become 'civilians' again and today I count 15 on the Register.
A quiet and gentle aeroplane and accepted as a valuable touring aircraft.

De HAVILAND
DH 87B HORNET MOTH

LIGHT PLANE
Gypsy Major, 130 hp.

DATA	IMPERIAL		METRIC	
Span	32	ft	9.8	m
Wing area	244.5	ft²	23	m²
Aspect ratio	8.4		8.4	
Empty weight	1304	lb	592	kg
Loaded weight	2000	lb	908	kg
Wing loading	8.2	lb/ft²	40	kg/m²
Max speed	124	mph	198	kmh
Cruise speed	105	mph	168	kmh
Stalling speed	45	mph	72	kmh
Climb rate	690	ft/min	212	m/min
Range	620	mls	992	km

Two Wots powered by Aeronca JAP engines were built to the design of J.R.Currie at Lympne in 1937 and were operated by Cinque Ports Aviation until both were destroyed by enemy bombing in WW2.

The Hampshire Aero Club, in 1958, resurrected Currie's design and built the third Wot, and then a fourth powered by a Walter Mikron engine of 60 hp. Having given the Wot new life, plans were put on the market for home builders and there are now 20 on the British Register, plus others being built.

The Wot is a sturdy good looking biplane with aerobatic strength and has been variously powered by VW, Continental and even, experimentaly, with a Rover gas turbine.

Various scale SE5A replicas are based on the Wot airframe.

Of conventional wood and fabric construction the Wot carries the PFA 'seal of approval'.

CURRIE WOT

ULTRALIGHT
Volkswagen 1600 cc

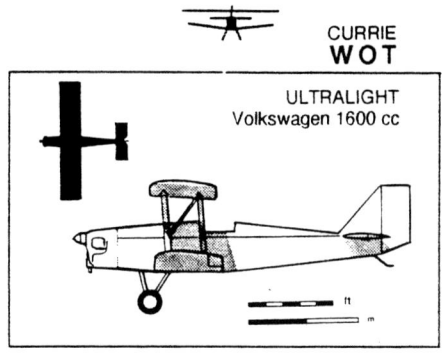

DATA	IMPERIAL		METRIC	
Span	22.1	ft	6.73	m
Wing area	140	ft²	13	m²
Aspect ratio	7		7	
Empty weight	550	lb	250	kg
Loaded weight	900	lb	408	kg
Wing loading	6.4	lb/ft²	31.3	kg/m²
Max speed	95	mph	153	kmh
Cruise speed	90	mph	145	kmh
Stalling speed	40	mph	65	kmh
Climb rate	600	ft/min	183	m/min
Range	240	mls	385	km

Designed and first flown in 1945 by Curtis Pitts the Special is an out and out aerobat, that's what Pitts built it for and that's what it does best.

Originally only available in plans or kit form, the little biplane went into formal production in 1970 and to date in the region of 2000 are flying world-wide.

The main changes, over the years, have been to engine size, in 1945 the prototype had a 55 hp. motor and in 1994 some are flying with 260 hp. Lycomings! the most common power plant, however, is the 180 hp. Lycoming.

Of standard American construction, all wood wings with metal or ply nosing and fabric covering aft of the main spar, welded steel tube fuselage also fabric covered. The landing gear is bungee sprung with disc braked wheels.

A PFA approved type with 100 on the UK Register inc. the S2, two seater.

PITTS S1 SPECIAL

LIGHTPLANE
180 hp. Lycoming

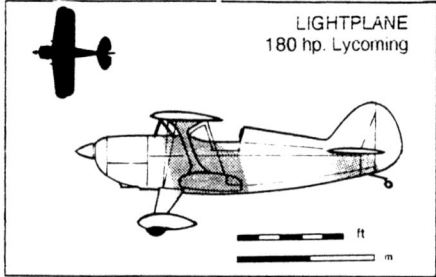

DATA	IMPERIAL		METRIC	
Span	17.4	ft	5.4	m
Wing area	96	ft²	9	m²
Aspect ratio	6.2		6.2	
Empty weight	720	lb	327	kg
Loaded weight	1050	lb	477	kg
Wing loading	11	lb/ft²	54	kg/m²
Max speed	165	mph	264	kmh
Cruise speed	145	mph	232	kmh
Stalling speed	57	mph	91	kmh
Climb rate	3000	ft/min	1362	m/min
Range	120	mls	192	km

The first Starduster was designed by Lou Stolp and George Adams for the homebuilt market in the 50's. A two seat aerobatic 'sport' biplane of the type that the Americans are rather good at. (The fully aerobatic scaled down version is called the Acroduster)

Traditional USA construction, welded steel tube fuselage, wooden two spar wings of elliptical plan (bit of a builders headache all those ribs of different length!) - all fabric covered.

Ailerons may be fitted to both planes or lower plane only, in the former layout the interconnecting operating strut is apparent.

The tailplane is fully wire braced and the large vertical surfaces are a distinct feature.

The Starduster is PFA approved, 14 are on the UK Register, mainly the Starduster Too.

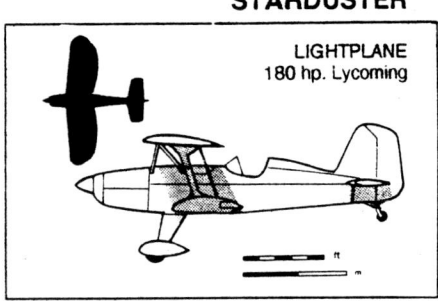

STOLP STARDUSTER

LIGHTPLANE
180 hp. Lycoming

DATA	IMPERIAL		METRIC	
Span	24	ft	7.4	m
Wing area	165	ft²	15.5	m²
Aspect ratio	7		7	
Empty weight	1000	lb	454	kg
Loaded weight	1704	lb	773	kg
Wing loading	10.3	lb/ft²	50	kg/m²
Max speed	148	mph	237	kmh
Cruise speed	104	mph	166	kmh
Stalling speed	50	mph	90	kmh
Climb rate	1500	ft/min	462	m/min
Range	250	mls	400	km

John Isaacs, one time of Supermarine, designed and built this 7/10 scale replica of the RAF's famous Fury single seat fighter of the 1930's. It first flew at Thruxton in 1963 with a 65 hp Walter Mikron engine which rather spoiled the pointed cowling lines. Later a flat four Lycoming engine allowed the classic fine fuselage lines to be more closely represented.

Of all wood construction with fabric covered wings the Fury has ailerons on the top plane only and like its forebear, no flaps. The landing gear is bungee sprung at the axle 'V' strut intersection.

Fully aerobatic, the plans have been sold world-wide and completed aircraft are flying in Australia and the USA.

It is a PFA approved design and 14 are on the UK Register.

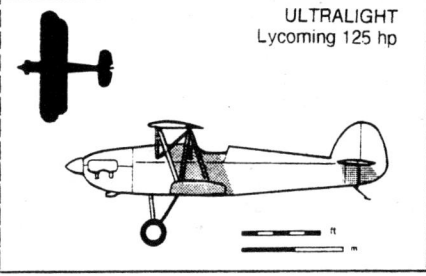

ISAACS FURY

ULTRALIGHT
Lycoming 125 hp

DATA	IMPERIAL		METRIC	
Span	21	ft	6.4	m
Wing area	124	ft²	11.5	m²
Aspect ratio	6		6	
Empty weight	710	lb	382	kg
Loaded weight	1000	lb	450	kg
Wing loading	8.1	lb/ft²	39.3	kg/m²
Max speed	115	mph	185	kmh
Cruise speed	98	mph	157	kmh
Stalling speed	38	mph	61	kmh
Climb rate	1600	ft/min	488	m/min
Range	170	mls	272	km

OLDFIELD
BABY GREAT LAKES

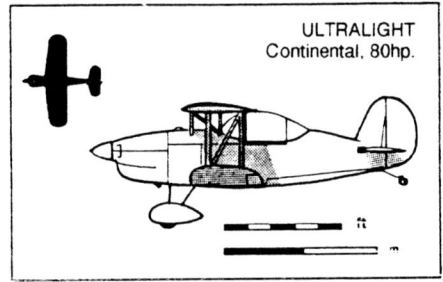

ULTRALIGHT
Continental, 80hp.

The prototype Baby Great Lakes single seat biplane first flew in 1964 and is a scaled down version of the Great Lakes Sport Trainer of 1929 vintage - which went back into limited production in 1980.

It was designed by Andrew Oldfield of Great Lakes Airplanes in the traditional manner - welded steel tube fuselage, wooden wings and fabric covering - and when he died in 1970 the operation was taken over by Barney Oldfield and the company renamed Barney Oldfield Aircraft Co.

This tiny biplane is a nimble performer on its 80 hp., cruising at nearly 120 mph. and an initial climb rate of 2000 ft/min.

Limited aerobatics are permitted on the standard 'Baby' but a Super Baby Great Lakes, first flown in 1976, is fully aerobatic and has a 115 hp. Continental engine.

The design is PFA approved, ten are on the 'Register.

DATA	IMPERIAL		METRIC	
Span	16.6	ft	5.1	m
Wing area	86	ft²	8.1	m²
Aspect ratio	6.4		6.4	
Empty weight	475	lb	216	kg
Loaded weight	850	lb	386	kg
Wing loading	9.9	lb/ft²	48.2	kg/m²
Max speed	135	mph	216	kmh
Cruise speed	118	mph	189	kmh
Stalling speed	50	mph	80	kmh
Climb rate	2000	ft/min	616	m/min
Range	250	mls	400	km

ANDREASSON
BA-4

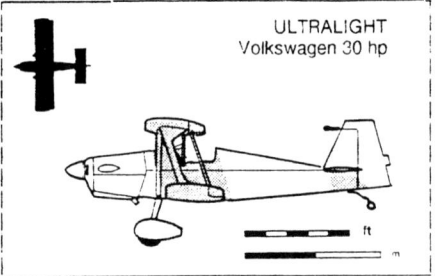

ULTRALIGHT
Volkswagen 30 hp

Designed by Bjorn Andreasson, the prototype was built by students at Malmo Flygindustri, Sweden and first flew in 1965.

A very small aerobatic biplane powered by a Lycoming or Continental engine of 100/150 hp, the BA-4 has a sparkling performance, with a spectacular rate of climb of 2000 feet a minute and a cruising speed of 120 mph.

The metal fuselage can be married to wooden or metal wings which are spaced by a single 'I' strut. Both the upper and lower wings carry ailerons for maximum roll rate. Spatted wheels are standard and later variants have a bubble canopy over the previously open cockpit

Sound design and good record have earned the BA-4 PFA approval. Three examples of the UK licensed built Crosby BA-4 flew in 1970 and several plans built machines are current.

DATA	IMPERIAL		METRIC	
Span	17.6	ft	5.42	m
Wing area	89.3	ft²	8.4	m²
Aspect ratio	7		7	
Empty weight	500	lb	227	kg
Wing loading	9.26	lb/ft²	45	kg/m
Loaded weight	827	lb	375	kgz²
Max speed	140	mph	224	kmh
Cruise speed	120	mph	142	kmn
Stalling speed	45	mph	72	kmh
Climb rate	2000	ft/min	616	m/min
Range	200	mls	320	km

First flown in 1968, the two seat CB-1 is a PFA approved plans-built biplane, three of which are on the UK Register and others are under construction.

The fabric covered, 'N' strut braced, wings are of all wood construction. There are ailerons on all wings, no flaps and the top plane has zero dihedral. The fuselage is of welded steel tube with fabric covering, as is the tail unit, which is wire braced.

A Piper J3, bungee sprung, undercarriage is employed in the tail-dragger configuration with a sreerable tail-wheel. The main wheels contain Piper J3 brakes, are usually spatted and many have the u/c 'V' struts faired together.

The style of the CB-1 is distinctly 'retro' and it is extremely popular in the USA where many are flying and a thriving Hatz CB-1 association – and web site – supplies plans, advice and news.

The prototype was powered by a Continental C85 of 85 hp. but the design is cleared for engines up to 150 hp. (Figures below for 150 hp. model).

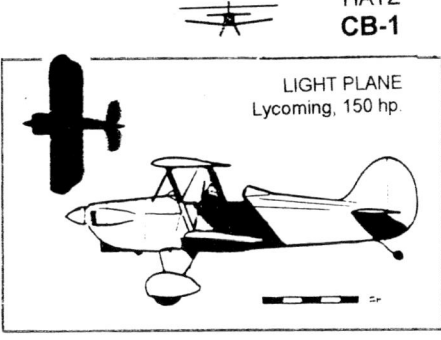

HATZ
CB-1

LIGHT PLANE
Lycoming, 150 hp.

DATA	IMPERIAL		METRIC	
Span	26	ft	7.9	m
Wing area	190	sq.ft	17.6	sq.m
Aspect ratio, top. 6.7				
Empty wt	966	lb.	438	kg.
Loaded wt	1600	lb.	726	kg.
Wing loading	8.4	lb/sq.ft	41	kg/sq.m
Max speed	130	mph	208	kmph
Cruising speed	87	mph	100	kmph
Stall speed	45	mph	72	kmph
Climb	1200	fpm	366	mpm
Range	270	mls	434	km

Designed by Ed Marquart in the USA and first flown in 1970, the MA-5 Charger is a 'classic' American bi-plane with a welded steel tube fuselage. twin solid wood wing spars and fabric covering. The neat undercarriage comprises a steel box leg with rubber in compression blocks within the fuselage.

It is a plans-only aeroplane and not for the first time builder, but when completed it is a beautiful two seater with aerobatic capability.

All the wings are swept back. in the manner of a Bucker, and mount four ailerons which are push rod operated, as are the elevators - the rudder relies on cable operation.

Toe brakes and a steerable tail-wheel make for ease of taxying.

A range of engines have been fitted to the hundred, or so, that have been built with powers of 125 to 180 hp. There are two on the UK Register and two being built.

MARQUART
MA-5 CHARGER

LIGHT PLANE
Lycoming, 125 hp.

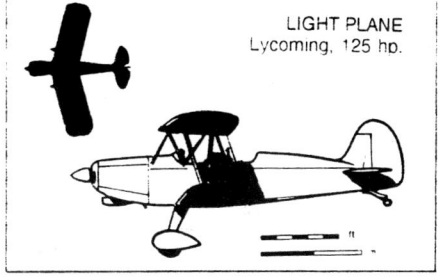

DATA	IMPERIAL		METRIC	
Span	24	ft	7.4	m
Wing area	172	ft²	16.1	m²
Aspect ratio	5		5	
Empty weight	1000	lb	454	kg
Loaded weight	1550	lb	704	kg
Wing loading	10.6	lb/ft²	52	kg/m²
Max speed	125	mph	200	kmh
Cruise speed	116	mph	185	kmh
Stalling speed	43	mph	69	kmh
Climb rate	1000	ft/min	308	m/min
Range	345	mls	552	km

STEEN SKYBOLT

Lamar Steen, an aerospace teacher in Denver, Colorado, designed the Skybolt in 1968 - as a project for his students! The resulting two seater aerobatic biplane first took to the air in 1970 with a 180 hp. Lycoming and an airframe stressed for +12 / -10 g. It was, in fact, the first two seat aerobatic plane to get type approval.

The construction is typical American Classic - welded steel tube fuselage with fabric covering, two spar wooden wing with aluminium leading edge and fabric covering aft of the front spar and ailerons on upper and lower planes. The wheels are bungee sprung and hydraulically braked with spats as standard fit.

Steen claims that 600 Skybolts are flying in 22 countries and that includes 11 in the UK where it is PFA approved

LIGHTPLANE
180 hp. Lycoming

DATA	IMPERIAL		METRIC	
Span	24	ft	7.4	m
Wing area	152	ft^2	14.3	m^2
Aspect ratio	7.5		7.5	
Empty weight	1250	lb	567	kg
Loaded weight	1800	lb	817	kg
Wing loading	11.8	lb/ft^2	58	kg/m^2
Max speed	145	mph	232	kmh
Cruise speed	115	mph	184	kmh
Stalling speed	55	mph	88	kmh
Climb rate	1600	ft/min	493	m/min
Range	250	mls	400	km

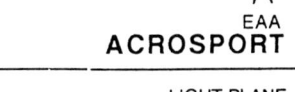

EAA ACROSPORT

Paul Poberezny, founder of the Experimental Aircraft Association (EAA), designed the Acrosport as an easy build aerobatic single seater the prototype flying in 1972 - this aeroplane is now in the Air Adventure Museum at Oshkosh.

Many Acrosports were subsequently built, mainly in the USA, including the two seat Acrosport 2 - slightly bigger but virtually identical in appearance. Ten are on the UK Register

The construction is 'standard American' i.e.. welded steel tube fuselage with light wooden fabric covered fairings, wooden spar wings with wood and metal ribs all fabric covered. There are inset ailerons on both upper and lower planes, linked by a strut, and the two fuel tanks have a capacity of 27 gall.(85 Lt).

The upper plane has an extensive cut out to improve upward vision.

Data below is for the 180 hp. single seat version, note the spectacular rate of climb!

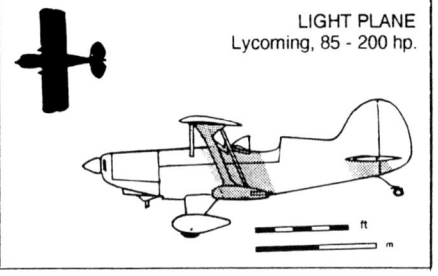

LIGHT PLANE
Lycoming, 85 - 200 hp.

DATA	IMPERIAL		METRIC	
Span	19.6	ft	6	m
Wing area	115	ft^2	10.8	m^2
Aspect ratio	6.6		6.6	
Empty weight	739	lb	335	kg
Loaded weight	1178	lb	534	kg
Wing loading	10.2	lb/ft^2	49.7	kg/m^2
Max speed	150	mph	240	kmh
Cruise speed	130	mph	208	kmh
Stalling speed	55	mph	88	kmh
Climb rate	3500	ft/min	1078	m/min
Range	400	mls	640	km

The all metal Scamp is manufactured and kitted in the USA by Aerosport Ltd and is a NASAD (National Association Sport Aircraft Designers) approved design.
First flown in 1973, its simple construction soon gained many fans and by 1985 over 800 plans had been sold, 36 were flying in the USA, three on the UK Reg. and one bring built to PFA OK.
Designed to operate from grass strips it has light alloy cantilever sprung main wheels and the whole ship is stressed to +6, -3g giving it a limited aerobatic category. A crop sprayer version, the Scamp B, was put into production in Colombia in 1983.
The all metal biplane wings are wire braced, the centre section being supported by a single sturdy strut It has no flaps or trim tabs.

AEROSPORT SCAMP

ULTRALIGHT
Volkswagen, 60 hp.

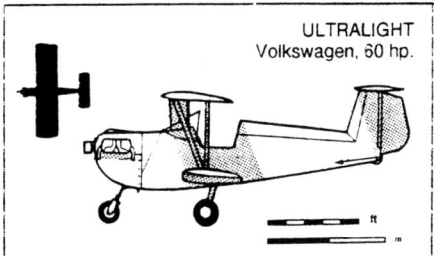

DATA	IMPERIAL		METRIC	
Span	17.5	ft	5.4	m
Wing area	105	ft²	9.8	m²
Aspect ratio	5.8		5.8	
Empty weight	530	lb	240	kg
Loaded weight	780	lb	354	kg
Wing loading	7.4	lb/ft²	36	kg/m²
Max speed	105	mph	168	kmh
Cruise speed	90	mph	144	kmh
Stalling speed	45	mph	72	kmh
Climb rate	800	ft/min	246	m/min
Range	125	mls	200	km

Developed from a range of light biplanes the SN7 is the kit plane version of the SN6 which was a design prize winner at Oshkosh in 1973, the year the prototype SN7 first flew.
The fuselage is of welded steel tube with fabric and GRP panel covering, as is the empennage. The back-staggered wings are all wood with ply' skin; the inter-plane struts are steel.
The landing gear has spring steel Wittman legs and disc brakes, the stearable tail wheel is by Maule.
Metal flaperons are fitted to both planes and are operated by torque tubes from the standard dual controls. The fuselage tapers in side view but is untapered in plan. The tailplane shape is reminiscent of Concorde!
A fast cruising biplane of distinctive lines, only one of which is on the British Register - many more in the States.

SORRELL SN-7 HIPERBIPE

LIGHT PLANE
Lycoming, 180 hp.

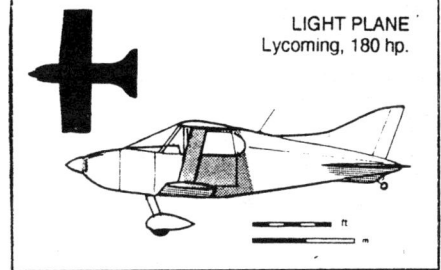

DATA	IMPERIAL		METRIC	
Span	22.8	ft	9.76	m
Wing area	135	ft²	12.7	m²
Aspect ratio	7.5		7.5	
Empty weight	1576	lb	715	kg
Loaded weight	2535	lb	1146	kg
Wing loading	18.8	lb/ft²	91.6	kg/m²
Max speed	161	mph	257	kmh
Cruise speed	150	mph	240	kmh
Stalling speed	61	mph	98	kmh
Climb rate	940	ft/min	290	m/min
Range	745	mls	1192	km

First flown in 1977 and supplied in kit form from that year, the Eagle, a two seat aerobatic biplane, was developed from the single seat Eagle 1.

The designer Frank Christensen of Wyoming, who later acquired the Pitts company, had a Pitts replacement in mind when he draughted the Eagle specifically for the home build market

The structure of the Eagle is conventional American, i.e.. welded steel tube fuselage, part metal and part fabric covered; the wings have wooden spars and ribs, metal leading and trailing edges and is all fabric covered.

The interplane 'I' struts are steel as are the undercarriage legs.

Christensen manufactured both Pitts and Eagle kits in to the mid eighties.

Over 700 kits have been sold, half of which are flying. The type is a PFA approved design with eight on the UK Register.

CHRISTEN EAGLE 2

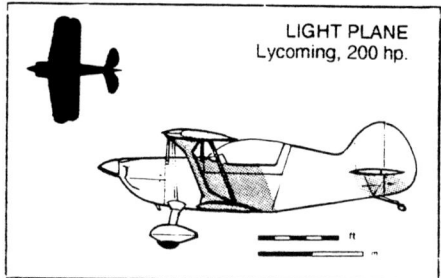

LIGHT PLANE
Lycoming, 200 hp.

DATA	IMPERIAL		METRIC	
Span	19.9	ft	6.13	m
Wing area	125	ft²	11.7	m²
Aspect ratio	6.3		6.3	
Empty weight	1081	lb	491	kg
Loaded weight	1600	lb	726	kg
Wing loading	12.8	lb/ft²	62.6	kg/m²
Max speed	184	mph	294	kmh
Cruise speed	165	mph	264	kmh
Stalling speed	58	mph	93	kmh
Climb rate	2100	ft/min	647	m/min
Range	380	mls	608	km

One of the earlier UK microlights, the Tiger Cub was designed by Tom Wright and originally known as the Micro Bipe.

Initially powered by a 35 hp. Fuji Robin engine the Tiger Cub was a single seat tail dragger as shown in the drawing. Two seat and tricycle undercarriage versions were projected - some of the latter, in fact, flying, but the company, Micro Biplane Aviation of Nottingham went into liquidation in 1984 after 150 kits had been sold.

An export version failed, initially, to meet foreign airworthiness requirements resulting in much delay and aeronautical *angst*.

The wings have light alloy spars with a foam aerofoil section infill, the whole being covered in heat shrink 'fabric', giving smooth and stiff wings.

On early models an all moving tailplane and rudder were fitted with ailerons on the lower plane only.

later models had flapperons on the lower plane and ailerons on the top and a large fin in front of the rudder but retained the all moving tailplane.

There are 46 on the UK Register – only one of which appears to be airworthy.

MBA TIGER CUB

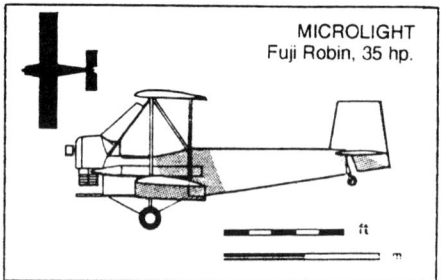

MICROLIGHT
Fuji Robin, 35 hp.

DATA	IMPERIAL		METRIC	
Wing area	140	ft²	13	m²
Aspect ratio	6.6		6.6	
Empty weight	284	lb	129	kg
Loaded weight	551	lb	250	kg
Wing loading	3.9	lb/ft²	19.2	kg/m²
Max speed	69	mph	111	kmh
Cruise speed	52	mph	83	kmh
Stalling speed	29	mph	47	kmh
Climb rate	490	ft/min	150	m/min
Range	75	mls	120	km

Developed from the Renegade 2, the Spirit is a Canadian design that has found a firm following in the UK.

Surprisingly, for such a sturdy (+10,-6g) two seat biplane the Spirit is a microlight! (But only when fitted with the Rotax 503. The Rotax 912 engined Renegade falls outside the microlight limit).

The airframe is all metal with riveted light alloy tubes incorporating patented extruded alloy joints. Alloy tube main spars with pressed alloy ribs form the wings, the whole being covered in Stits fabric.

There are ailerons on both sets of wings linked by a connecting strut and the landing gear has a steerable tail wheel and braked wheels.

A Subaru car engined version has recently flown in the USA.

There are 35 on the 'Register and four being built.

MURPHY
RENEGADE SPIRIT

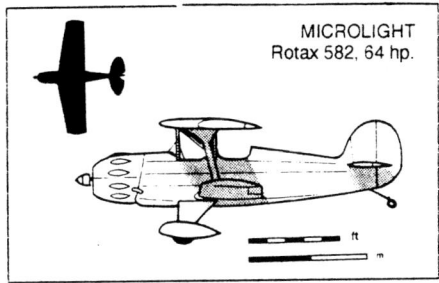

MICROLIGHT
Rotax 582, 64 hp.

DATA	IMPERIAL		METRIC	
Span	24.5	ft	7.54	m
Wing area	172	ft²	16.2	m²
Aspect ratio	7		7	
Empty weight	390	lb	177	kg
Loaded weight	850	lb	386	kg
Wing loading	5.0	lb/ft²	24.4	kg/m²
Max speed	90	mph	144	kmh
Cruise speed	80	mph	128	kmh
Stalling speed	33	mph	53	kmh
Climb rate	1300	ft/min	400	m/min
Range	240	mls	384	km

The BGP-1 is an all wood single seat sport biplane, designed and built by Barry Plumb of Leighton Buzzard, Bedfordshire. The prototype aircraft was first flown in 1986 and received a full Permit to Fly in 1987. The aircraft was powered by a 55 hp. 1834cc. Volkswagen until a 80 hp. Jabiru engine was installed. The aircraft has an open cockpit and a small luggage bay behind the pilot's seat. Ailerons are fitted to the top wing only and all controls are sensitive and well harmonised. An unusual feature is the single lift strut in place of conventional wire bracing for the wings. Construction is all wood with birch ply and fabric covering to the fuselage and fabric covering of the open structure flying surfaces.

A second example is currently under construction in Cornwall, being built from updated drawings. The updated aircraft has increased span but retains the same wing area and general appearance as the prototype. The updated design is currently undergoing approval scrutiny by the PFA, following which plans will be made available.

PLUMB
BGP-1 BIPLANE

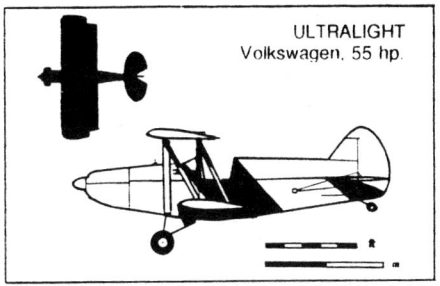

ULTRALIGHT
Volkswagen, 55 hp.

DATA	IMPERIAL		METRIC	
Span	16	ft	4.9	m
Wing area	100	ft²	9.8	m²
Aspect ratio	4.6		4.6	
Empty weight	525	lb	231	kg
Loaded weight	800	lb	363	kg
Wing loading	8	lb/ft²	39	kg/m²
Max speed	103	mph	165	kmh
Cruise speed	78	mph	125	kmh
Stalling speed	45	mph	72	kmh
Climb rate	650	ft/min	200	m/min
Range	150	mls	240	km

AVIASUD
MISTRAL

ULTRALIGHT
Rotax 532 63 hp

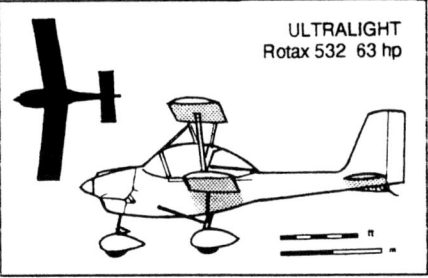

A popular ultra light in France with eleven now on the UK Register.

The extremely short build time (due to many pre-assembled units) caused it to be de-classified as a kit plane in 1993. In its home country 200 or more are flying, not only as ARV, but being capable of cropdusting, aerial TV and police work.

Of unusual appearance, the Mistral has swept forward wings, spatted tricycle undercarriage and an un-biplane-like pod and boom fuselage and an enclosed cockpit.

The wings have Dural spars, wooden ribs and Dacron covering, the lower planes are all-moving and act as ailerons. The tailplane/elevator is all-moving and of similar construction. GRP and composites are used for the pod and boom, which houses the 3 axis controls. The landing gear is sprung and braked.

DATA	IMPERIAL		METRIC	
Span	30.8	ft	9.4	m
Wing area	192.7	ft^2	17.9	m^2
Aspect ratio	9.3		9.3	
Empty weight	383	lb	174	kg
Loaded weight	882	lb	400	kgz
Wing loading	4.58	lb/ft^2	22.3	kg/m^2
Max speed	93	mph	150	kmh
Cruise speed	84	mph	135	kmh
Stalling speed	38	mph	60	kmh
Climb rate	785	ft/min	240	m/min
Range	310	mls	500	km

The all British Sherwood Ranger, developed by Russell Light of TCD Ltd. at Larkfield, South Yorkshire, first flew in 1993, and is a very tidy biplane of vintage - yet modern lines.

Available in the microlight category as the LW and the more powerful and heavier ST ultralight. Both are two seaters, though single seat versions are available in both types. A further model, the XP, which is fully aerobatic, is currently under development.

SHERWOOD
RANGER

MICRO/ULTRALUGHT
Rotax, 503,582,618

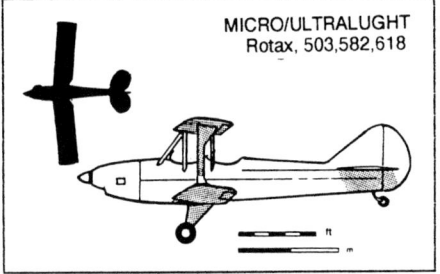

The Ranger's fuselage is built up with light alloy tubing, the joining fish plates and brackets being secured with 'pop' rivets. A fabric skin is smoothly streamlined over light wooden formers. The wings, have light alloy spars and plywood ribs, and are fabric covered, with ailerons on both upper and lower planes.

The wings fold, a la 'Moth, alongside the fuselage and re-rigging takes only three minutes!

The undercarriage is bungee sprung and has differentially braked wheels plus a castoring tail wheel.

The prototype, G-MWND, is shortly to be joined by several homebuilt - one of which is flying in the USA. Five are on the UK Register.

DATA (for LW)	IMPERIAL		METRIC	
Span	26	ft	8	m
Wing area	168	ft^2	15.8	m^2
Aspect ratio	8		8	
Empty weight	400	lb	181	kg
Loaded weight	860	lb	390	kg
Wing loading	5.1	lb/ft^2	24.8	kg/m^2
Max speed	80	mph	107	kmh
Cruise speed	67	mph	107	kmh
Stalling speed	40	mph	64	kmh
Climb rate	650	ft/min	200	m/min
Range	350	mls	560	km

Designed by Lynn Williams and built by Sky Craft Ltd, the Flitzer first flew in 1995 powered by a 1600 cc. VW engine. William's aim was to design a 'vintage' looking aeroplane of simple construction unrestrained by the slavish following of true scale/replica work. This has been achieved in the truly distinctive shape of the Flitzer, which is badged as *Staaken*, the WW1 German aircraft manufacturer.

The Flitzer is powered by a 1834 cc. VW engine (prototype had the 1600) and has the 'registration' D692 displayed on its wings and fuselage - its official UK registration is G-BVAW. A second aircraft is being built with Bell Aeromarine backing at time of writing, and another privately.

The wooden structure with fabric covering has the minimum of metal fittings and has, with its single 'I' struts , 'A' frame cabane and unswept wings, simple rigging requirements. The stalky 'gear is 'classic', three axles, two fixed and one moving with bungee wrap around.

STAAKEN FLITZER

ULTRALIGHT
Volkswagen 1834 cc.

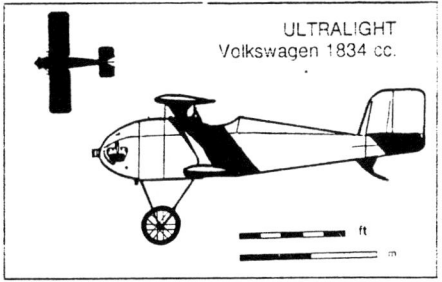

DATA	IMPERIAL		METRIC	
Span	18	ft	5.5	m
Wing area	97	ft^2	9.1	m^2
Aspect ratio	6.5		6,5	
Empty weight	480	lb	218	kg
Loaded weight	750	lb	337	kg
Wing loading	7.5	lb/ft^2	36.6	kg/m^2
Max speed	86	mph	138	kmh
Cruise speed	75	mph	120	kmh
Stalling speed	42	mph	67	kmh
Climb rate	700	ft/min	216	m/min
Range	300	mls	480	km

141

An early British light twin, the Monospar evolved around the novel monospar wing designed by the Swiss H J Stieger. The first version, the ST3 was built by Gloster's for the Monospar Wing Co in 1929. The ST3 was encouraging and General Aircraft was formed to build Monospars, based briefly at Croydon and finally at Hanworth.

The subsequent models were all rather similar except for the ST6 and ST11 which had retractable undercarriages and an experimental model with a, fixed nose wheel, tricycle undercarriage. The last in the range the ST25 had twin fins.

The Monospars were four seaters of mixed wood and metal construction with fabric covering and the engines were usually Pobjoy radials though the ST12 had Gipsy Majors.

Used by small airlines and taxi firms, 57 of the distinctive and sturdy Monospars were built – about half of them going abroad. With WW2 twelve assorted Monospars were impressed but did not survive the war.

In 1961 an Australian ST12 made an epic flight back to the UK and now, after many years storage, is being restored at Newark. (In museums, Denmark 1, NZ 1).

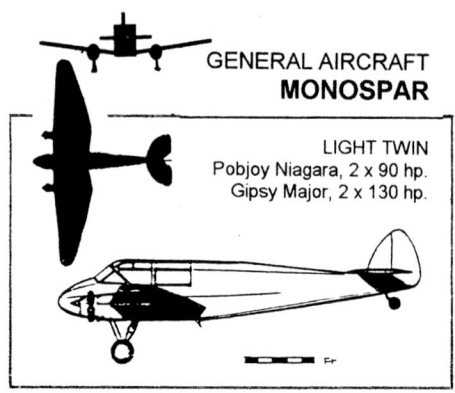

GENERAL AIRCRAFT
MONOSPAR

LIGHT TWIN
Pobjoy Niagara, 2 x 90 hp.
Gipsy Major, 2 x 130 hp.

Data for ST12.
DATA	IMPERIAL		METRIC	
Span	40.16	ft	12.3	m
Wing area	217	sq.ft	20.4	sq.m
Aspect ratio	7.4			
Empty wt	1840	lb.	835	kg.
Loaded wt	2875	lb.	1305	kg.
Wing loading	13.2	lb/sq.ft	64	kg/sq.m
Max speed	158	mph	253	kmph
Cruising speed	142	mph	227	kmph
Stall speed	55	mph	88	kmph
Climb	1233	fpm	380	mpm
Range	410	mls	656	km

A light twin from the '30s, the 6/8 seat Dragon is the same weight as a Piper Seneca.

First flown in 1932 the big wood and fabric biplane with high aspect ratio wings has two Gipsy Major engines and was the mainstay of many of the UK's smaller airlines. Over 100 were built at Hatfield and somewhat fewer at DH in Australia. The Mk 2 had faired main-wheels and separate cabin windows – and was slightly faster than the MK 1.

In 1933 Jim and Amy Mollison used a Dragon for an attempt on the World Long Distance Record, but after flying across the Atlantic, crashed in Connecticut. The rebuilt Dragon was flown back to the UK by J. Ayling and L. Reid and became the first aircraft to fly non-stop from Canada to Great Britain.

Twenty Dragons were impressed at the outbreak of WW2, very few survived – one actually being shot down by a German aircraft.

One Dublin based Dragon is still flying, one other is being restored, two are in UK museums plus three in museums abroad (Oz, NZ, USA).

Figures below are for the Mk 2.

DE HAVILAND
DH84 DRAGON

7 SEAT LIGHT TWIN
2 X Gipsy Major, 130 hp.

DATA	IMPERIAL		METRIC	
Span	47.3	ft	14.6	m
Wing area	376	sq.ft	35.3	sq.m
Aspect ratio	12			
Empty wt	2336	lb.	1060	kg.
Loaded wt	4500	lb.	2043	kg.
Wing loading	12	lb/sq.ft	58.5	kg/sq.m
Max speed	134	mph	214	kmph
Cruising speed	114	mph	182	kmph
Stall speed	50	mph	80	kmph
Climb	565	fpm	174	mpm
Range	545	mls	872	km

The Percival P16 Q6 a pre war light twin carried four or five passengers and a crew of two; it was of all wood construction and beautiful lines.

First flown in 1937, the Q6 had a trousered undercarriage, split trailing edge flaps, VP airscrews and radio as standard. Four of the 22 aircraft built had retractable undercarriages resulting in a very sleek and crisp performer (183 mph cruise).

Five Q6s were sold abroad, two going to Lithuania and others to India, Iraq and Belgium. (French and Australian registrations were taken out for two but these were never delivered).

The Q6s had just about got into service with various companies and small charter airlines when war broke out and most were impressed for RAF and Navy communications work. They later acquired military marks and were referred to as the Petrel – this appellation was, it is said, never 'official').

Three 'Petrels' survived the war plus four others, but their numbers quickly diminished, the last 'flyer' retiring in 1954. One, G-AFFD, has been resurrected and is on long-term restoration on the Isle of Man. (Two others, or parts thereof, may exist in storage).

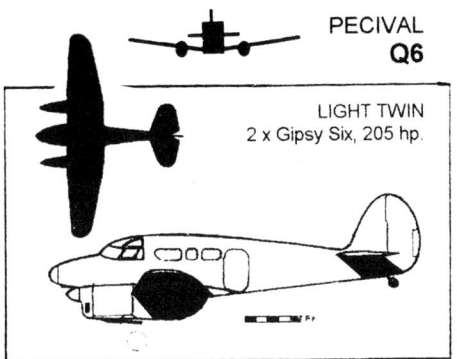

PECIVAL
Q6

LIGHT TWIN
2 x Gipsy Six, 205 hp.

The data below is for the fixed gear version.

DATA	IMPERIAL		METRIC	
Span	46.6	ft	14.3	m
Wing area	278	sq.ft	26	sq.m
Aspect ratio	7.8			
Empty wt	3500	lb.	1569	kg.
Loaded wt	5500	lb.	2497	kg.
Wing loading	19.8	lb/sq.ft	96	kg/sq.m
Max speed	195	mph	312	kmph
Cruising speed	175	mph	280	kmph
Stall speed	50	mph	80	kmph
Climb	1150`	fpm	354	mpm
Range	750	mls	1200	km

When the Miles M65 Gemini prototype first flew in 1945, powered by a 100 hp. Cirrus Minor, fast four seat civil twins were thin on the ground - the American twin invasion being some years in the future.

In the region of 160 Geminis - virtually a twin engined M28 Messenger - were built at Reading, many of them being exported world wide.

Of all wooden construction the Gemini had an electrically operated retractable undercarriage, auxiliary aerofoil flaps and twin fins combined with a luxurious cabin interior.

Many large companies bought them (including Shell) and it was the executive fast twin of it's day - fast indeed, G-AKDC won the 1949 Kings Cup at 165 mph.

Various engines were fitted including the 125 hp Continental C-125-2 and the Cirrus Major of 155 hp.

Ten are still shown on the UK Register - two still flying as a reminder of a ground breaking design by a company of brilliant designers and not so brilliant book keepers. (Miles folded in 1948)

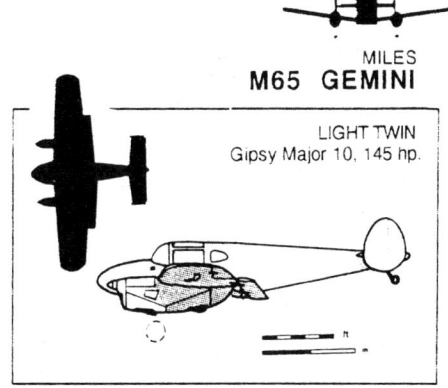

MILES
M65 GEMINI

LIGHT TWIN
Gipsy Major 10, 145 hp.

DATA	IMPERIAL		METRIC	
Span	36.2	ft	11.1	m
Wing area	191	ft^2	17.9	m^2
Aspect ratio	6.8		6.8	
Empty weight	1896	lb	860	kg
Loaded weight	3000	lb	1362	kg
Wing loading	15.7	lb/ft^2	76.6	kg/m^2
Max speed	140	mph	224	kmh
Cruise speed	125	mph	200	kmh
Stalling speed	50	mph	80	kmh
Climb rate	550	ft/min	170	m/min
Range	820	mls	1312	km

A Czechoslovakian twin designed to replace the ageing tail-dragger the Aero 145 (first flew 1947).
The LET 200A first flew in 1969 powered by 160 hp. Walter Minors; after 160 had been built the engine was changed to the more powerful Walter M337 of 210 hp. this remained the standard power unit for the rest of the production run of 1000. These later aircraft were designated LET 200D.
The Morava is a distinctive twin, having inverted in-line engines, Dornier-like twin fins and a retractable tricycle undercarriage. The substantially framed dome-like cabin houses a pilot and 'co-pilot' in the front seats and three passengers on a rear bench seat. There is also an arrangement for loading two stretcher cases.
The construction is all metal, the wing has a high-ish aspect ratio and the 200Ds have three blade constant speed props.
Supplied in some quantity to Aeroflot and built under licence in Yugoslavia, there are two on the UK Reg.

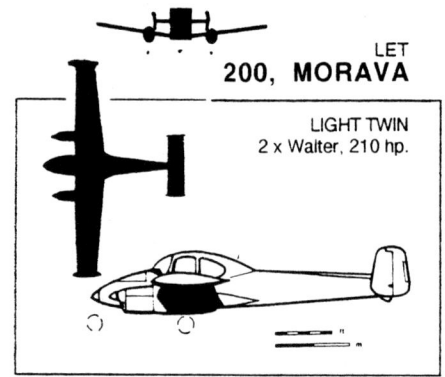

**LET
200, MORAVA**

LIGHT TWIN
2 x Walter, 210 hp.

DATA	IMPERIAL		METRIC	
Span	40.5	ft	12.3	m
Wing area	186	ft^2	17.3	m^2
Aspect ratio	8.8		8.8	
Empty weight	2932	lb	1330	kg
Loaded weight	4300	lb	1950	kg
Wing loading	23.1	lb/ft^2	113	kg/m^2
Max speed	157	mph	290	kmh
Cruise speed	138	mph	256	kmh
Stalling speed	60	mph	96	kmh
Climb rate	1260	ft/min	388	m/min
Range	1068	mls	1710	km

Developed from the Twin Stinson, the Apache is a senior member of the light American twin fraternity having first flown in 1952. It was Pipers first twin and had a 'rag and pipe' fuselage and a fixed tricycle undercarriage. Production models were all metal stressed skin construction and powered by 160 hp. Lycoming O-320s.
Apache models followed with the suffix denoting engine horse power (though not always!) i.e., the PA-23-160 appearing in 1959 and the most powerful PA-23-235 coming in 1962.
The Apache is a four seater with provision for an occasional fifth, a cruising speed of 200 mph. and a production tally of 2000+, twenty of which are on the UK Register.
The Apache, re-engined, became the PA 23 Aztec, with a swept fin and rudder.
The Aztec developed a longer nose and could carry up to six people - all Aztecs have higher powered engines, including turbo charged versions, and have overtaken the Apache with 5000 produced - over 100 being on the UK Register. (Figs. below for PA-23-235 Aztec)

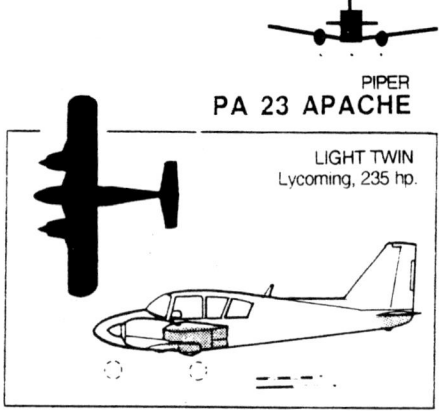

**PIPER
PA 23 APACHE**

LIGHT TWIN
Lycoming, 235 hp.

Span	37.1	ft	11.4	m
Wing area	207	ft^2	19.5	m^2
Aspect ratio	6.6		6.6	
Empty weight	2735	lb	1241	kg
Loaded weight	4800	lb	2179	kg
Wing loading	23.2	lb/ft^2	113	kg/m^2
Max speed	202	mph	323	kmh
Cruise speed	191	mph	305	kmh
Stalling speed	70	mph	112	kmh
Climb rate	1485	ft/min	446	m/min
Range	1185	mls	1896	km

Another classic American twin, the Beech 55 Baron which first flew in 1960 was developed from the Model 95 Travel Air of 1956, which, though similar, had a vertical fin and rudder and the lower powered 180 hp. Lycomings. In 1962 the improved A55 appeared, followed in '64 by the B55 with lengthened fuselage. In 1965 came the C55 with 285 hp. 3 blade prop, Continentals, which is illustrated here.
A military version, designated T42 A, serves in the USAAF as an instrument trainer.
The Baron is all metal and can carry 5 to 6 passengers (plus pilot), can cruise at 230 mph. and has had a production run of over 6000 - including all variants. Variants are, the A56 Turbo Baron, the model 58 with longer cabin and the 58P, which is pressurised.
There are 40+ Barons (inc. three model 95 Travel Airs) on the UK Register flying as company or taxi aircraft.
Very similar to the Piper PA 30 Navajo and PA 31 Twin Comanche, the Baron has a slightly lower aspect ratio fin and rudder.

BEECH
C55 BARON

LIGHT TWIN
2 x Continental, 260 hp.

DATA	IMPERIAL		METRIC	
Span	37.8	ft	11.6	m
Wing area	199.2	ft^2	18.7	m^2
Aspect ratio	7.2		7.2	
Empty weight	3025	lb	1373	kg
Loaded weight	5300	lb	2406	kg
Wing loading	26.6	lb/ft^2	130	kg/m^2
Max speed	242	mph	387	kmh
Cruise speed	230	mph	368	kmh
Stalling speed	70	mph	112	kmh
Climb rate	1670	ft/min	514	m/min
Range	1143	mls	1828	km

Since the prototype first flew in 1953 (forty six years ago!) 10,000 had been made when production ceased in 1981, many thousands of which are still flying world wide; one of the all time successful private light twins. Of all metal construction, the first '310s had a vertical fin and rudder, 240 hp. Continental 0-470-B engines, five seats and wing tip tanks. The 310 D followed, introducing the swept fin and rudder; the 310 G was a six seater and introduced the 310's 'trade mark' - the upswept tip tanks. The 310 G has a longer nose baggage compartment.
The six seat versions have an extra window at the rear. Looking similar, the '320 Skyknight is a stretched six seater with turbocharged engines and the '340 is pressurised - easily identified by its circular cabin windows.
Military versions in service with the USAAF are typed as U3-A and U3-B.
Access is by a car type door on the starboard side, full dual control and lavish instrumentation, split flaps plus the smooth American automobile interior finish make this a real little airliner.
There are around 60 on the UK Register.

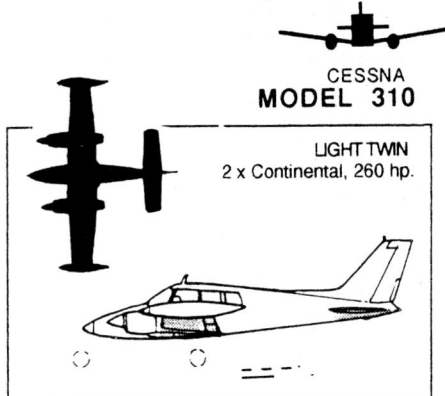

CESSNA
MODEL 310

LIGHT TWIN
2 x Continental, 260 hp.

DATA	IMPERIAL		METRIC	
Span	36.7	ft	11.3	m
Wing area	179	ft^2	16.8	m^2
Aspect ratio	7.5		7.5	
Empty weight	3125	lb	1418	kg
Loaded weight	5200	lb	2360	kg
Wing loading	29	lb/ft^2	141.7	kg/m^2
Max speed	222	mph	355	kmh
Cruise speed	179	mph	286	kmh
Stalling speed	74	mph	118	kmh
Climb rate	1540	ft/min	474	m/min
Range	966	mls	1545	km

Beagle were formed in 1960, combining Pressed Steel Co, Auster and F G Miles Ltd. The Miles design team came up with the slick B206, a 5/7 seater which first flew at Shoreham in 1961. A military version, the B206R Bassett was built alongside the civil versions some of which were the turbo charged B206S. 57 civil aircraft were built and a further 22 for the RAF.

The B206 cruised at over 200 mph. and had a range of 1500 miles, comparing favourably with the 'American twins that were being developed at about the same time. The '206 may have been somewhat 'over-engineered', (in other words, it was a quality product) and in the climate of the time it was under-funded and eventually dropped. The assets of Beagle (after a brief period of State ownership) were transferred to Scottish Aviation in 1969.

An 'American fan of the '206 reputedly bought the entire stock of airframes and spares from Scottish Aviation and set up a stateside '206 'agency'!

There are 6 on the UK Reg. two airworthy, the others in collections.

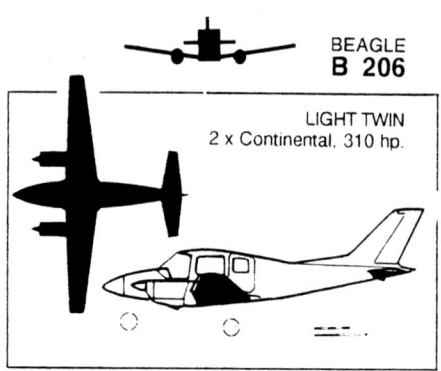

BEAGLE
B 206

LIGHT TWIN
2 x Continental, 310 hp.

DATA	IMPERIAL		METRIC	
Span	45.7	ft	14	m
Wing area	213	ft²	20	m²
Aspect ratio	9.8		9.8	
Empty weight	4444	lb	2017	kg
Loaded weight	7500	lb	3405	kg
Wing loading	35.2	lb/ft²	172	kg/m²
Max speed	220	mph	352	kmh
Cruise speed	214	mph	342	kmh
Stalling speed	77	mph	123	kmh
Climb rate	1170	ft/min	360	m/min
Range	1645	mls	3632	km

117

First flown in 1962 the PA 30 was a twin engined version of the PA 24 single engined Comanche and used many of the PA 24 jigs and fixtures, it was a 4 to 6 seater and ran to many variants.

The PA30 was the initial production version and was a four seater, the PA 30 B, of 1965, the 'Twin Comanche B', had extended cabin glazing and provision for six seats and was available as the Standard, Custom or Sportsman depending on equipment fit as were the Executive 222 and the Professional 422.

The PA 30 C had the improved Lycoming O-320 engines and the Comanche C/R had contra rotating props. and tip tanks as standard (optional on earlier models).

Over 2000 of these all metal twins have been produced and there are currently 50+ on the UK Register. Somewhat lighter and lower powered than other American Twins the PA 30 still cruises at nearly 200 mph. and has fuel for 1000 miles.

A modified PA-30, the PA-39 Twin Comanche went in to production in 1971

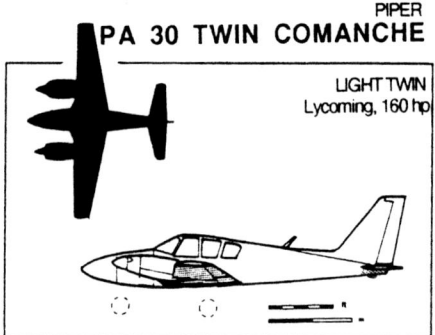

PIPER
PA 30 TWIN COMANCHE

LIGHT TWIN
Lycoming, 160 hp

DATA	IMPERIAL		METRIC	
Span	36	ft	11.1	m
Wing area	178	ft²	16.1	m²
Aspect ratio	7.3		7.3	
Empty weight	2160	lb	980	kg
Loaded weight	3600	lb	1634	kg
Wing loading	20.2	lb/ft²	98.6	kg/m²
Max speed	205	mph	328	kmh
Cruise speed	181	mph	290	kmh
Stalling speed	68	mph	109	kmh
Climb rate	1460	ft/min	450	m/min
Range	1025	mls	1640	km

PIPER
PA31 NAVAJO

LIGHT TWIN
Various

A fast 6/8 seat twin from the Piper stable, first flown in 1964, as the Inca, it was the largest type produced by the firm at the time. The type was certificated in 1966 and remained in production until 1985 by which time 5000 PA31 variants had been built, including the Chieftain, Mojave and Cheyenne.

Variants too numerous to detail in this box include pressurised cabin, turbo props, stretched fuselages and wings — the final, top of the range model the Cheyenne 3 has a 'T' tail, 1000 shp Garrett turbo props and a maximum speed of 335 mph. (Much advanced from the original PA31, the Cheyenne 3 is re-typed as the PA42).

The pilot compartment is separated by a bulkhead from the passengers, who, in the executive version, enjoy the facilities of a bar and WC.

Ten and 15 passengers are carried in certain short haul, high density versions.

Schafer Aircraft of Waco convert pressurised PA31s to turbo prop power with increased tankage and rename them Comancheros.

Data below for PA31T Cheyenne, 620 shp Lycoming

DATA	IMPERIAL		METRIC	
Span	42.6	ft	13	m
Wing area	229	sq.ft	21.3	sq.m
Aspect ratio	7.9			
Empty wt	4983	lb.	2260	kg.
Loaded wt	9000	lb.	4082	kg.
Wing loading	39	lb/sq.ft	191	kg/sq.m
Max speed	322	mph	516	kmph
Cruising speed	282	mph	452	kmph
Stall speed	70	mph	112	kmph
Climb	1750	fpm	540	mpm
Range	1620	mls	2608	km

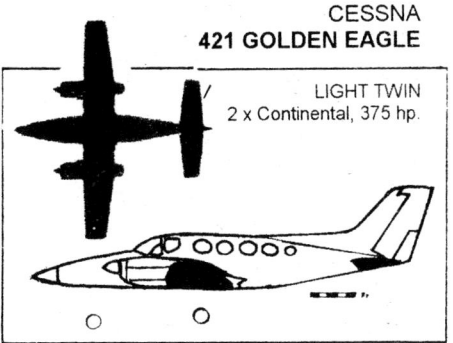

Cessna twins are legion — and all, pretty much, alike! The model 421 Golden Eagle has, however, a good foothold in the UK with 33 on the Register.

First flown in 1965, the '421 was developed from the 401 and the 411, with the difference that its new fuselage was pressurised.

Deliveries of production aircraft did not begin until 1967 and nearly 2000 were made before production ceased in 1984.

Four variants were made, the 421 and the 421A, 358 built; the 421B had an increased span, a longer fuselage, a fifth window and 600lb AUW increase. (699 built). The 421C has a higher aspect ratio fin/rudder, 'wet' wings and no tip tanks — 859 of these were made, powered by Continental GTS10-520N flat six engines developing 375 hp each.

A purposeful 6/10 seater, all except the 421C, having distinctive upturned wing tip fuel tanks, the latter having plain square wing tips.

These aircraft cruise at nearly 300 mph and have an enormous range.

CESSNA
421 GOLDEN EAGLE

LIGHT TWIN
2 x Continental, 375 hp.

Details below for 421C.

DATA	IMPERIAL		METRIC	
Span	41.1	ft	12.5	m
Wing area	215	sq.ft	19.9	sq.m
Aspect ratio	7.9			
Empty wt	4640	lb.	2105	kg.
Loaded wt	7450	lb.	3379	kg.
Wing loading	34.6	lb/sq.ft	169	kg/sq.m
Max speed	297	mph	478	kmph
Cruising speed	279	mph	450	kmph
Stall speed	70	mph	112	kmph
Climb	1940	fpm	591	mpm
Range	1710	mls	2752	km

One of the most popular of the American light twins, the prototype Seneca first flew in 1968. Introduced in 1971, over 4,500 have been produced and they are manufactured under licence in Poland for the Eastern European market - the power units for these versions being PZL- Franklins instead of the USA's turbo - charged Continentals.
Of all metal construction, the Seneca has Three bladed fully feathering airscrews, electrically operated slotted flaps and retractable tricycle undercarriage. Frise type ailerons, comprehensive instrumentation and radio aids.
The wings and empennage have de-icing boots - essential for its ability to cruise up to 25,000 ft.
Pitch control is by a stabilator positioned slightly aft of the rudder.
Much admired for it's wide cabin and comfortable seating, there are in the region of 150 on the UK Reg

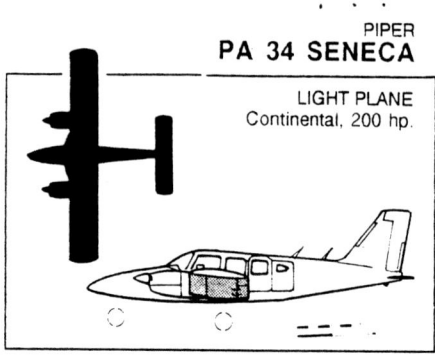

PIPER
PA 34 SENECA

LIGHT PLANE
Continental, 200 hp.

DATA	IMPERIAL		METRIC	
Span	38.9	ft	12	m
Wing area	208.7	ft^2	19.6	m^2
Aspect ratio	7.2		7.2	
Empty weight	3333	lb	1513	kg
Loaded weight	4513	lb	2049	kg
Wing loading	21.7	lb/ft^2	106	kg/m^2
Max speed	225	mph	360	kmh
Cruise speed	205	mph	329	kmh
Stalling speed	73	mph	118	kmh
Climb rate	1400	ft/min	431	m/min
Range	1040	mls	1661	km

Italian company Partenavia's first twin the P68 Victor first flew in 1969 and was aimed to compete with the flood of US twins. Competing with but not imitating the USA product, Partenavia went for a high wing and fixed undercarriage.
Employed in many tasks including aerial survey, met and police work plus charter and taxi, the P68 has been exported in quantity.
400+ aircraft had been produced by the mid 1970's and a part-kitted version is built in India.
Of metal and composites construction the Victor is a clean good looking aeroplane with a useful performance, carrying six passengers 1000 miles at nearly 200 mph.
200 hp Lycomings are the standard fit but variants have 210 hp turbo charged Lycomings and the Spartacus version has 330 hp Allison turbo-props and a retractable undercarriage.
There are 16 on the UK Register.
Performance figures are for the 200 hp version.

PARTENAVIA
P 68 VICTOR

LIGHT TWIN
Lycoming, 200 hp

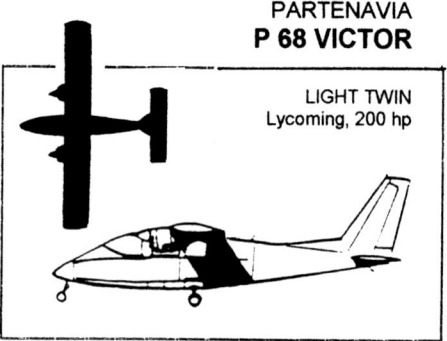

DATA	IMPERIAL		METRIC	
Span	39.3	ft	12	m
Wing area	200	sq.ft	18.6	sq.m
Aspect ratio	7.7			
Empty wt	2425	lb.	1100	kg.
Loaded wt	4100	lb.	1860	kg.
Wing loading	20.5	lb/sq.ft	100	kg/sq.m
Max speed	208	mph	334	kmph
Cruising speed	186	mph	299	kmph
Stall speed	60	mph	96	kmph
Climb	1700'	fpm	523	mpm
Range	1045	mls	1681	km

This remarkable aeroplane designed by Aerospatiale aerodynamacist M.Colomban in 1972 is minute - smaller than the Flying Flea and certainly the smallest twin engined 'plane! With a wing span of 16 ft and 2ft chord the Cri Cri's wing is about the size of a large model glider!

Early aircraft were powered by various chain saw engines but the latest models are powered by the JPX PUL 212 engines specially developed for it.

The Cri Cri won the Design Award at Oshkosh in 1981 and by 1984 360 plans had been sold, 30 of which were soon flying. The design has proved popular all over the world and there are five currently on the British Register.

Of all metal, ultra simple construction, the Cri Cri is PFA approved and two are being built.

A twin jet version has flown recently; the coffee pot sized jets being started with a cigarette lighter!

COLOMBAN
CRI CRI

MICROLIGHT
JPX PUL 212

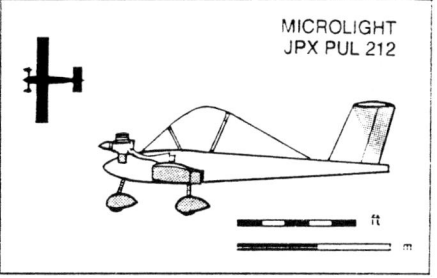

DATA	IMPERIAL		METRIC	
Span	16	ft	14.9	m
Wing area	33.4	ft²	3.1	m²
Aspect ratio	7.75		7.75	
Empty weight	165	lb	74.9	kg
Loaded weight	375	lb	170	kg
Wing loading	11.2	lb/ft²	54.8	kg/m²
Max speed	137	mph	219	kmh
Cruise speed	124	mph	198	kmh
Stalling speed	45	mph	72	kmh
Climb rate	1280	ft/min	394	m/min
Range	248	mls	396	km

Grumman Aircraft's first civil twin, the GA7 first flew in 1974; it can seat four/six people and is in operation as an executive transport and trainer.

Although the prototype first flew in 1974 it was not until 1977 that the production model was finalised, considerable re-design having gone into the Cougar in the intervening three years.

An all metal design that was taken over by Gulfstream American, it has an outward retracting undercarriage, a parallel chord wing and a tapered, in plan, tailplane (which distinguishes it from the similar Seneca).

The all metal construction is rivetless, most joints being glue/bonded. The wing has two spars and electrically operated Fowler type flaps, the gear retracts hydraulically and the nose wheel is steerable.

Production appears to be in the region of 120 - of which 20 are on the UK Register.

GULFSTREAM AMERICAN
GA7 COUGAR

LIGHT PLANE
Lycoming, 160 hp.

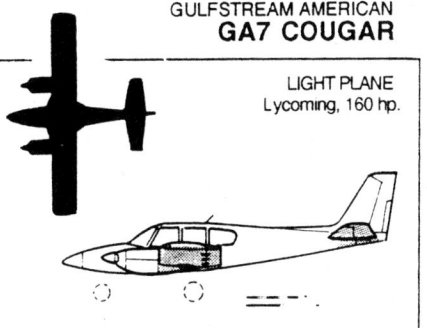

DATA	IMPERIAL		METRIC	
Span	36.9	ft	11.4	m
Wing area	184	ft²	17.3	m²
Aspect ratio	7.4		7.4	
Empty weight	2515	lb	1142	kg
Loaded weight	3800	lb	1725	kg
Wing loading	20.65	lb/ft²	100.8	kg/m²
Max speed	193	mph	309	kmh
Cruise speed	184	mph	294	kmh
Stalling speed	82	mph	131	kmh
Climb rate	1200	ft/min	370	m/min
Range	1336	mls	2137	km

First flown in 1977, the Duchess is a four seat all metal twin with pleasing lines, a retractable tricycle undercarriage and counter rotating propellers.

The high aspect ratio wing has a commonalty with the single engined Sierra and the tailplane is mounted on top of the large chord fin and rudder.

The parallel chord wing helps distinguish the Duchess from other 'T' tailed twins, ie. Seminole, Cheyenne, King Air - which all have tapered wing plans.

At the lower powered end of the small twin range, the Duchess still manages a respectable cruise of nearly 190 mph. and a climb of over 1000 fpm.

As well as 'pilot doors either side, the Duchess has a baggage door aft of the trailing edge on the port side. Slotted flaps run for 75% of the span and the Frise type ailerons are of metal/honeycomb construction. The u/c, flaps and brakes are operated by an electro-hydraulic system.

400 have been made and there are 25 on our 'Reg.

BEECHCRAFT '76 DUCHESS

LIGHT PLANE
2x Lycoming, 180 hp.

DATA	IMPERIAL		METRIC	
Span	38	ft	11.6	m
Wing area	181	ft²	16.8	m²
Aspect ratio	8		8	
Empty weight	2466	lb	1119	kg
Loaded weight	3900	lb	1769	kg
Wing loading	21.5	lb/ft²	105.2	kg/m²
Max speed	197	mph	317	kmh
Cruise speed	182	mph	293	kmh
Stalling speed	81	mph	130	kmh
Climb rate	1248	ft/min	384	m/min
Range	717	mls	1155	km

Designed by the late Peter Phillips, ex RAF and Britten Norman test pilot, the Speedtwin first flew in 1992 after many years of development - carried out with some degree of secrecy. Its debut was at the Biggin Hill Air Fair in '92 where its rakish, new appearance caused quite a stir.

Handled by Speedtwin Developments Ltd. of Monmouth, the Aircraft is of all metal construction, the mainplane being based on a Victa Airtourer wing and the fixed tail-dragger undercarriage being that of a Chipmunk. The twin engines are Continental O-200s of 100 hp. with fixed pitch propellors; a Mk 2 is listed with Textron Lycomings of 160 hp.

Designed for kit building the airframe is stressed for +6,-3g and is cleared for aerobatics - the only light twin to be so. Small for a twin- 26 ft span - the Speedtwin has a short take off run, a high rate of climb and a range of over 1000 ml. at 160 mph.

Three are on the UK Register.

PHILLIPS SPEEDTWIN

LIGHT TWIN
Continental O-200, 100 hp.

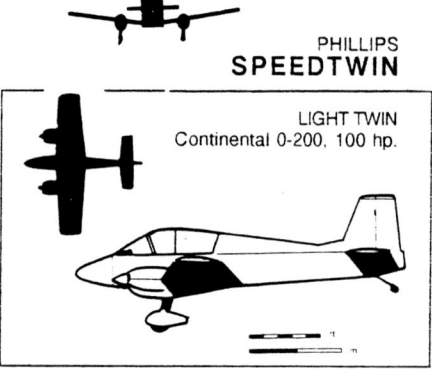

DATA	IMPERIAL		METRIC	
Span	26	ft	8	m
Wing area	120	ft²	11.3	m²
Aspect ratio	5.6		5.6	
Empty weight	1410	lb	640	kg
Loaded weight	2250	lb	1020	kg
Wing loading	18.8	lb/ft²	91.5	kg/m²
Max speed	178	mph	286	kmh
Cruise speed	160	mph	257	kmh
Stalling speed	68	mph	110	kmh
Climb rate	1200	ft/min	366	m/min
Range	1129	mls	2092	km

The British Aircraft Co. of Maidstone manufactured gliders before WW2, and in 1932 C.H. Lowe-Wylde, their designer director fitted one with wheels and a pylon mounted pusher engine and called it the Planette. This early powered glider proved to be a docile performer over its 15 to 40 mph. speed range and more were built - 28 in all before the firm closed down in 1937. A year before this one was flown from Croydon to Berlin in eleven hours at the cost of £1.25!

Several were de-motored and reverted to gliders, others became popular performers at the pre war air shows - and thence in to storage 'for the duration'.

Eight Drones came out of storage, and three flew again - though none currently.

Two are still in existence; at least one being restored.

The Douglas motor cycle engine that powered the prototype was developed into a small aero engine, the Sprite, which developed 23 hp.- very noisily!

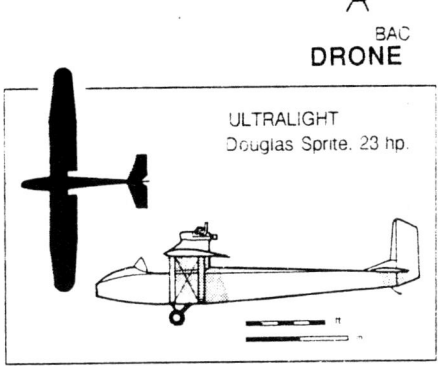

BAC DRONE

ULTRALIGHT
Douglas Sprite. 23 hp.

DATA	IMPERIAL		METRIC	
Span	39.6	ft	12.2	m
Wing area	172	ft^2	16.2	m^2
Aspect ratio	9.1		9.1	
Empty weight	390	lb	177	kg
Loaded weight	460	lb	209	kg
Wing loading	2.7	lb/ft^2	13.0	kg/m^2
Max speed	70	mph	112	kmh
Cruise speed	60	mph	96	kmh
Stalling speed	20	mph	32	kmh
Climb rate	380	ft/min	117	m/min
Range	300	mls	480	km

After Miles Aircraft folded at Woodley in 1947 the Miles brothers, Fred and George, set up in business at Shoreham – where they had started twenty years earlier! It was here that they designed and built the Student, which first flew in 1957, a 300 mph, all metal, two seat jet trainer. Well ahead of its time – we have yet to see another British, small two seat private jet!

Built as a private venture the Student lost out to the Hunting Percival Provost – which cost twice as much.

The Student put on some brilliant aerobatic displays at the SBAC shows where its excellent forward vision and low ground clearance were also admired.

In 1964 the prototype became the Mk 2 with a more powerful Marbore (1,540 lb thrust), which put its top speed up to 400 mph. A four seat version was planned as an 'executive jet' and with funds running low a deal to build it in South Africa looked attractive but this was scuttled by the, then, arms embargo.

Still an attractive and practical aeroplane the Student had all the bad breaks.

Currently being restored by the Berkshire Museum of Aviation, after a forced landing in '85, we may yet see this historic jet airborne again.

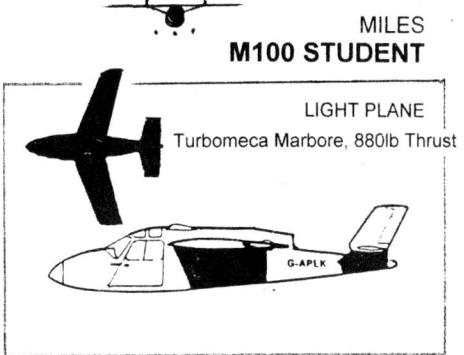

MILES M100 STUDENT

LIGHT PLANE
Turbomeca Marbore, 880lb Thrust

DATA (Mk 1)	IMPERIAL		METRIC	
Span	29	ft	9	m
Wing area	144	sq.ft	13.5	sq.m
Aspect ratio	5.9			
Empty wt	2400	lb	1090	kg.
Loaded wt	3600	lb	1634	kg.
Wing loading	25	lb/sq.ft	122	kg/sq.m
Max speed	300	mph	478	kmph
Cruising speed	260	mph	416	kmph
Stall speed	70	mph	112	kmph
Climb	1780	fpm	548	mpm
Range	444	mls	710	km

When is a twin not a twin? The push/pull one behind the other engines of the Skymaster eliminate the asymmetric thrust hazard peculiar to wing engined twins. Although over 2000 Skymasters were made between 1964 and '80 this was considered disappointing by Cessna standards.

Preceded by the Model 336 Skymaster, which had fixed gear, the 337 Super Skymaster is all metal, has six seats and retractable undercarriage and was first flown in 1964. A dozen variants followed, the main ones being, the 337P pressurised (identified by row of smaller windows), the 337B with belly pannier and the M337 military version, designated USAF O-2A (513 of these were made). About 200 Skymasters were built in France by Reims, mainly the military FTB337G.
Most models are powered by Continental 10-360 engines of 210 hp. with 225 hp. turbo option.
22 Super Skymasters and 3 Skymasters are on 'Reg.

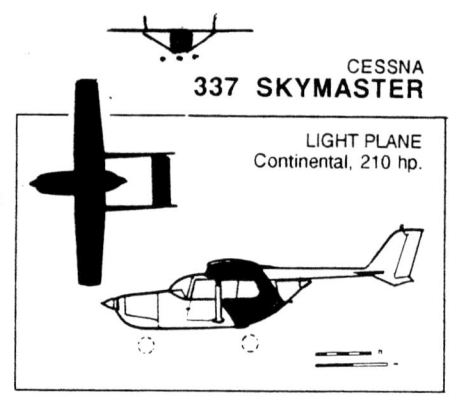

CESSNA
337 SKYMASTER

LIGHT PLANE
Continental, 210 hp.

DATA	IMPERIAL		METRIC	
Span	38.1	ft	11.7	m
Wing area	201	ft^2	18.9	m^2
Aspect ratio	7.2		7.2	
Empty weight	2695	lb	1223	kg
Loaded weight	4630	lb	2102	kg
Wing loading	23	lb/ft^2	112	kg/m^2
Max speed	199	mph	318	kmh
Cruise speed	180	mph	288	kmh
Stalling speed	70	mph	112	kmh
Climb rate	1100	ft/min	339	m/min
Range	600/1300	mls	960/2080	km

Figures for standard 337, the turbo 337P is faster.

The Woody Pusher is named after it's designer H.L.Woods, formerly of Bensen Aircraft Corp. Woods also founded Aerosport, the company that builds the 'Pusher.

The 'Pusher first flew in 1970 with an all wood fuselage, later changed to welded steel tube with fabric covering over wooden formers. The wing has two wooden spars and ribs, fabric covered aft of the main spar; the 'nose' is skinned with aluminium sheet. Flaps are standard and the undercarriage legs are spring steel, the spats are optional.

Engines of from 65 hp. to 85 hp. give it a cruising speed of about 87 mph.

Many hundreds are flying in the USA but ,as yet, few I have appeared in the UK – three on the 'Register.

This sturdy two seater, in the ultralight category, is well liked by those who have flown it and maintain it.

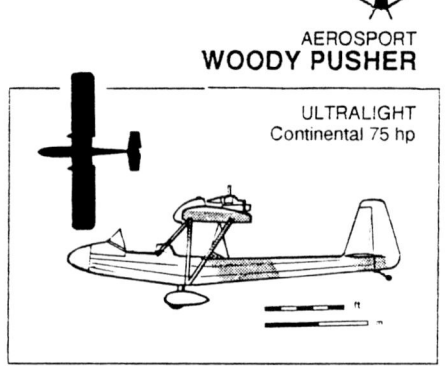

AEROSPORT
WOODY PUSHER

ULTRALIGHT
Continental 75 hp

DATA	IMPERIAL		METRIC	
Span	29	ft	8.84	m
Wing area	130	ft^2	12,1	m^2
Aspect ratio	6.5		6.5	
Empty weight	630	lb	285	kg
Loaded weight	1150	lb	522	kg
Wing loading	8.8	lb/ft^2	43	kg/m^2
Max speed	98	mph	158	kmh
Cruise speed	87	mph	140	kmh
Stalling speed	45	mph	72	kmh
Climb rate	600	ft/min	183	m/min
Range	225	mls	360	km

Designed by Bob Hovey in the USA (he also designed the Whing Ding) the Beta Bird is an aeroplane you sit *on*, rather than *in*!

Of wooden construction with strut braced fabric covered wings - an aluminium tube within the box tail boom carries the empennage. Bungee sprung main wheels with brakes and a steerable tail-wheel comprise the tail-dragger undercarriage.

A rare luxury for a microlight is the large landing light in the nose and wing tip navigation lights.

The controls comprise a normal joystick for elevator and flaperons and external pedals for the rudder and brakes.

The exposed pilot position was considered 'spooky' and almost impractical when it first appeared in the late '70s; but since then 'exposed' flex wing and gyrocopter pilots have become legion.

The Beta Bird is PFA approved and is 'plans only', there is one on the UK Register.

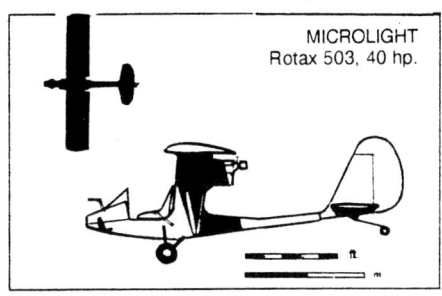

HOVEY
BETA BIRD

MICROLIGHT
Rotax 503, 40 hp.

DATA	IMPERIAL		METRIC	
Span	25.5	ft	7.8	m
Wing area	88	ft^2	8.3	m^2
Aspect ratio	7.4		7.4	
Empty weight	405	lb	184	kg
Loaded weight	650	lb	295	kg
Wing loading	7.4	lb/ft^2	36	kg/m^2
Max speed	90	mph	144	kmh
Cruise speed	80	mph	128	kmh
Stalling speed	40	mph	64	kmh
Climb rate	700	ft/min	215	m/min
Range	160	mls	256	km

First flown in 1971 the diminutive, single seat, BD-5, the brain child of *avant garde* designer Jim Bede had a stormy launch into the world of homebuilding. The type having been certificated was offered on the North American market - over 6000 factory built models were ordered and 3000 kits - vast sums of money flowed in in the form of deposits; but though parts of kits were delivered, no one got a complete set! Engine and sub contract problems plus mismanagement caused the BD-5 bubble to burst in 1979 when the company went bankrupt.

Fifty or so BD-5's were eventually built by persevering adherents of the type – there are six on the UK Register. (Ed. All now grounded!).

The mainly metal aeroplane with a retractable tricycle undercarriage was only 13 feet (4m) long and flew like a dream, cruising at 200 mph (320 kph) - but hitting 'the numbers' at 80 mph+(128 kph)!.

An early model, had a butterfly tail and a jet powered version, the BD-5J, is on the air show circuit.

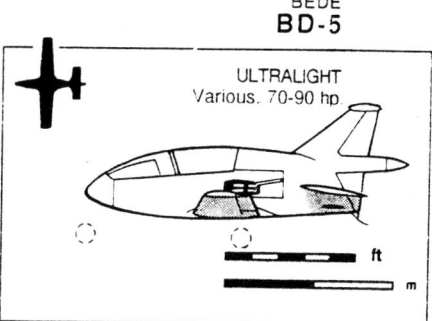

BEDE
BD-5

ULTRALIGHT
Various. 70-90 hp.

DATA	IMPERIAL		METRIC	
Span	17	ft	5.23	m
Wing area	38	ft^2	3.6	m^2
Aspect ratio	7.6		7.6	
Empty weight	410	lb	186	kg
Loaded weight	850	lb	386	kg
Wing loading	22.4	lb/ft^2	109	kg/m^2
Max speed	230	mph	368	kmh
Cruise speed	200	mph	320	kmh
Stalling speed	70	mph	112	kmh
Climb rate	1400	ft/min	431	m/min
Range	1130	mls	1808	km

EIPPER
QUICKSILVER

MICROLIGHT
Rotax 377 33hp

One of the very first 3 axis control Microlights, having taken to the air in 1972. Quicksilver, designed by American Bob Lovejoy set a standard which was immediately copied by other manufacturers - some under licence and some by derivation, and there are now literally thousands of the type flying world-wide.

The 'stick' controls pitch and yaw and a side lever looks after roll -,though conventional 3 axis control is available as an option.

The wings are wire braced via a kingpost and have only a single surface section. Wheels are all torsion bar sprung and the nose wheel is braked. An extension shaft drives the airscrew from the under wing mounted motor.

There are 38 on the UK Register. (Ed. In the USA a 'Police Interceptor' version has a searchlight, radio and siren!).

DATA	IMPERIAL		METRIC	
Span	32	ft	15.5	m
Wing area	160	ft^2	115	m^2
Aspect ratio	6.4		6.4	
Empty weight	230	lb	108	kg
Loaded weight	525	lb	238	kg
Wing loading	3,28	lb/ft^2	16	kg/m^2
Max speed	52	mph	84	kmh
Cruise speed	46	mph	74	kmh
Stalling speed	24	mph	38	kmh
Climb rate	800	ft/min	246	m/min
Range	95	mls	153	km

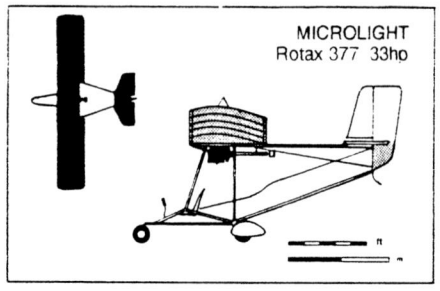

LOVAUX/FLS/ AEROSPACE
OPTICA

LIGHT PLANE
Lycoming, 160 hp.

The three seat Optica made its debut at the 1980 SBAC Show and stunned everyone with its originality and unusual configuration. Designed by John Edgley, who with a few friends began construction in Islington in 1976m moving later to Cranfield. Of all metal construction the Optica, which first flew in 1979, has a mid engine driving a five bladed prop/fan within an annular duct behind the helicopter-like cabin pod and twin booms to carry the twin fins and high mounted tailplane.

The Optica is designed for slow speed, helicopter type observation work (Police/Army) without the high operating costs of the rotorcraft.

The crash of the first delivered 'plane, followed by insolvency then re-birth, followed by a factory fire have hampered the Opticas progress; but 20+ have been made, six on the UK Reg. One is flying in the USA, where plans for Far East production are a-foot.

DATA	IMPERIAL		METRIC	
Span	39.3	ft	12	m
Wing area	170	ft^2	15.8	m^2
Aspect ratio	9		9	
Empty weight	2090	lb	948	kg
Loaded weight	2899	lb	1316	kg
Wing loading	17	lb/ft^2	83	kg/m^2
Max speed	132	mph	211	kmh
Cruise speed	118	mph	189	kmh
Stalling speed	67	mph	107	kmh
Climb rate	810	ft/min	250	m/min
Range	655	mls	1048	km

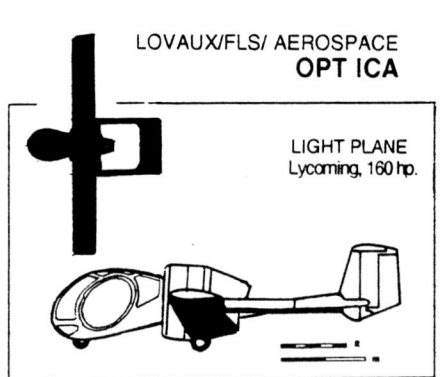

Jean Grinvalds began the design of this all composites 2+2 seater in 1975 - a very early example of this type of construction. It first flew in 1981 as the G801 to be followed in 1983 by the kit version G802.
The three blade pusher constant speed prop is shaft driven by a turbocharged, fan cooled Lycoming T10-350 mounted mid-ships. With its trike gear tucked away this super slippery homebuilt clocks up over 200 mph on its 200 hp! The deep glazed cabin provides, helicopter-like superb 200° visibility and an enthusiast/builders club- Club Orion - exists in France. A company set up in the USA to kit G802s in a big way folded after Grinvalds died in the crash of the prototype in 1985.
This groovy looking speedster is reputed to be complicated and difficult to build - but its *got* to be worth it!
Two are flying in Belgium, 2 in the USA and 6 in France. A PFA Rally visitor. The data below is for the G802.

GRINVALDS
G802 ORION

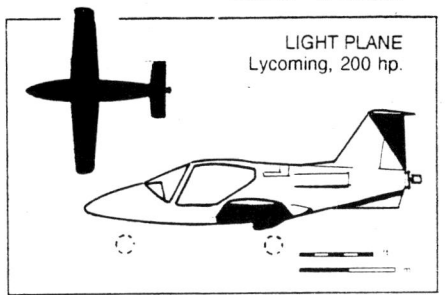

LIGHT PLANE
Lycoming, 200 hp.

DATA	IMPERIAL		METRIC	
Span	29.5	ft	9.1	m
Wing area	122	ft²	11.5	m²
Aspect ratio	7.1		7.1	
Empty weight	1340	lb	608	kg
Loaded weight	2310	lb	1049	kg
Wing loading	19.0	lb/ft²	92.4	kg/m²
Max speed	205	mph	328	kmh
Cruise speed	186	mph	298	kmh
Stalling speed	70	mph	112	kmh
Climb rate	885	ft/min	272	m/min
Range	1864	mls	2984	km

This sleek four seater designed by CMC, under Ian Chichester-Miles back in 1982, progressed through the mock-up stage to prototype first flight in 1988. The first prototype, powered by Noel Penny jets, was superseded by a second development aircraft with Williams FXJ-1, 700 lb. thrust units plus cabin pressurisation and airframe liquid de-icing. The Leopard has no ailerons, roll control being effected by the differential incidence tailplane.
Of all composites construction, the CMC Leopard made a big impression at the 1996 Farnborough air show and is currently undergoing staged flight trials at Cranfield, speeds up to 300 mph. being completed - the next stage, up to its full potential of 500 mph, are pending. In production form, with the new Williams FJX-2 engines its incredible performance figures will include a range of 2000 mls at 45.000 ft. cruising at 500 mph. and a fighter like climb of over 6000 fpm!
The electrifying Leopard is probably the most exciting British light plane since the DH 88 Comet – let's hope its world-beating potential is recognised.

CHICHESTER-MILES
LEOPARD

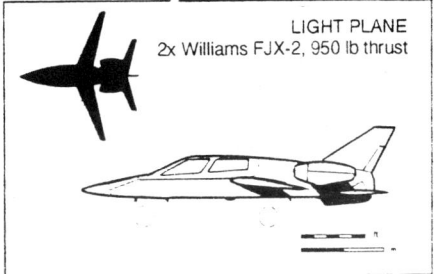

LIGHT PLANE
2x Williams FJX-2, 950 lb thrust

DATA	IMPERIAL		METRIC	
Span	23.5	ft	7.16	m
Wing area	62.9	ft²	5.9	m²
Aspect ratio	8.7		8.7	
Empty weight	2200	lb	1000	kg
Loaded weight	4000	lb	1815	kg
Wing loading	63.5	lb/ft²	310	kg/m²
Max speed	525	mph	840	kmh
Cruise speed	500	mph	804	kmh
Stalling speed	100	mph	160	kmh
Climb rate	6430	ft/min	1980	m/min
Range	1725	mls	2760	km

The Kolb company of Phoenixville, Penn. started in the microlight business in 1970 - one of the earliest to do so.

First flown at Oshkosh in 1982 the TwinStar side by side two seater may be adapted to fly in the ultra light or microlight category. The '82 model was a front engined tractor but later changed to the present pusher set up, and an enclosed cabin was added.

A useful 'garaging' feature are the quick folding wings - completed in minutes without the aid of tools ! The all round visibility from the cockpit is impressive, as is the generous width of 45 inches. It is fitted with dual controls.

The construction is conventional tube, both steel and light alloy - a 6 inch diameter tube being used for the wing main spar which has Stits fabric covering. The large flaps and wide track undercarriage are noteworthy features. PFA approved, 20 are on the 'Register and four are being built.

KOLB - MAINAIR
TWINSTAR

MICROLIGHT
Rotax 503 50 hp

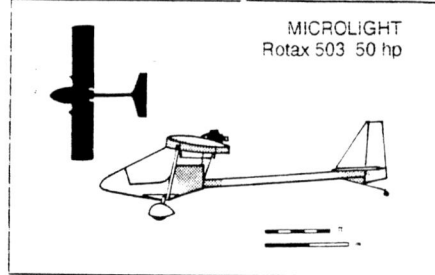

DATA	IMPERIAL		METRIC	
Span	30.16	ft	9.3	m
Wing area	163	ft²	15.3	m²
Aspect ratio	5.6		5.6	
Empty weight	378	lb	172	kg
Loaded weight	1000	lb	454	kg
Wing loading	6.1	lb/ft²	30	kg/m²
Max speed	85	mph	136	kmh
Cruise speed	65	mph	104	kmh
Stalling speed	30	mph	48	kmh
Climb rate	850	ft/min	262	m/min
Range	150	mls	240	km

The two seat Arrow Hawk microlight first flew in 1982 and is very popular in its country of origin, the USA, where most of the 1200 built are flying (one on the UK Register). The UK version of the Arrow Hawk is pretty spartan due to the 390 kg microlight weight limit. It has all fabric covering (including zip-up cabin sides!) minimum instrumentation and a single carb. Rotax 503. The basic structure is aluminium tube and the wings and all flying surfaces are supplied assembled and ready for covering in the kit. The rest of the airframe is riveted or bolted together - no 'gluing' or welding.

Apart from being a 'pussy cat' to fly, the Arrow Hawk's other pluses include, composites leaf spring main legs, +6,-4 g limits, stearable nose-wheel, braked main wheels, 3 notch flaps, 3 axis controls and quick set up from 'knock-down'.

A tail-dragger version is available as is a float plane amphibian.

A tried and trusted design which will benefit from the 450 kg rule.

CGS
HAWK ARROW

MICROLIGHT
Rotax 503. 40 hp.

DATA	IMPERIAL		METRIC	
Span	34	ft	10.5	m
Wing area	160	ft²	15	m²
Aspect ratio	7.2		7.2	
Empty weight	420	lb	191	kg
Loaded weight	820	lb	372	kg
Wing loading	5.1	lb/ft²	25	kg/m²
Max speed	90	mph	144	kmh
Cruise speed	60	mph	96	kmh
Stalling speed	30	mph	48	kmh
Climb rate	1000	ft/min	308	m/min
Range	100	mls	160	km

First flown in 1983 this rugged and good-looking British designed tandem seat microlight is constructed with composites and aluminium tube and is sold as a kit or factory-made. It is designed by pioneer 'microlighter' David Cook. (CFM = Cook Flying Machine)

Shadows have made many notable long-distance flights including England-Australia. Thanks to the very clean aerodynamics, performance is outstanding with a top speed of over 100 mph and climb of 1200 ft/min, at an economic 30 mpg.

Manufactured by CFM Aircraft of Leiston, Suffolk, the Shadow, it is claimed, may be built in 500 hours using simple DIY tools.

The Streak Shadow, with a Rotax 582 engine has been added to the range - but is outside the microlight category.

The Shadow and Shadow Streak have been highly successful with over 300 on the UK Register and 16 being built with PFA approval.

A version is being built, under licence, in the USA by Laron Aviation Technologies.

CFM
SHADOW STREAK

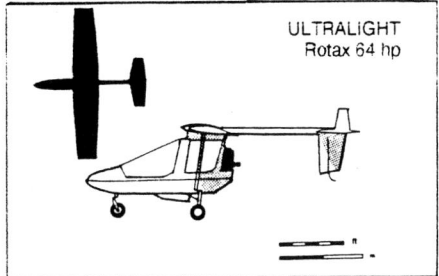

ULTRALIGHT
Rotax 64 hp

DATA	IMPERIAL		METRIC	
Span	28	ft	8.62	m
Wing area	140	ft²	13.2	m²
Aspect ratio	5.6		5.6	
Empty weight	388	lb	176	kg
Loaded weight	900	lb	408	kg
Wing loading	6.4	lb/ft²	31.3	kg/m²
Max speed	140	mph	224	kmh
Cruise speed	87	mph	140	kmh
Stalling speed	31	mph	50	kmh
Climb rate	1200	ft/min	370	m/min
Range	400	mls	640	km

Originating in the USA the Quad City Challenger is a microlight two seater, 500 of which have been built Stateside. The tandem seating enclosed cockpit gives a slim, smooth fuselage - the low drag of which enables it's 55 hp motor to haul the Challenger through the air at a cruise of 75 mph - and using only 2.5 gallons of fuel an hour.

The construction is of light alloy tube with Stits fabric covering and the makers claim it can be put together in 500 hours.

The Challenger is a tough, good looking aeroplane which is easy to maintain and repair.

Full span ailerons or 'flaperons give good roll control, in flight trim and impressive short field landings - 200

With 36 on the 'Register and a dozen being built, the Challenger seems to be a 'hit'.

built, the Quad City Challenger is a PFA approved design.

QUAD CITY
CHALLENGER

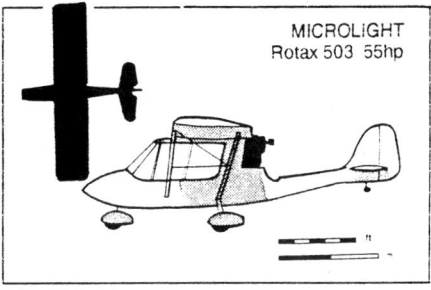

MICROLIGHT
Rotax 503 55hp

DATA	IMPERIAL		METRIC	
Span	31	ft	9.5	m
Wing area	200	ft²	19	m²
Aspect ratio	4.8		4.8	
Empty weight	350	lb	159	kg
Loaded weight	840	lb	381	kg
Wing loading	4.2	lb/ft²	20.5	kg/m²
Max speed	85	mph	136	kmh
Cruise speed	75	mph	120	kmh
Stalling speed	25	mph	40	kmh
Climb rate	500	ft/min	154	m/min
Range	250	mls	400	km

Designed by Boeing engineer Chuck Herbst, the two seat Sparrowhawk first flew in 1986 as a product of Aero Dynamics of Arlington, Washington.

Sold in kit form, the Sparrowhawk has an all composites vacuum formed cockpit pod consisting mainly of Kevlar and foam. The tail booms are of similar construction whilst the wings are metal with fabric covering. The wing roots out to the boom intersection are integral with the fuselage pod, the outer sections are detachable for ease of storage.

The fixed, spatted undercarriage is rugged and practical - but is a retractable gear version 'on the cards'? It's already cool lines and good performance would be enhanced enormously.

The airframe is stressed for +6-4g and will take engines from 60 to 100 hp. (Data below for the 63 hp Rotax)
There is one UK Registered Sparrowhawk and two here with US markings.

AERO DYNAMICS
SPARROWHAWK

LIGHT PLANE
Rotax 532, 63 hp.

DATA	IMPERIAL		METRIC	
Span	34.5	ft	10.5	m
Wing area	143	ft^2	13.3	m^2
Aspect ratio	8.3		8.3	
Empty weight	700	lb	318	kg
Loaded weight	1400	lb	635	kg
Wing loading	10	lb/ft^2	48.8	kg/m^2
Max speed	120	mph	193	kmh
Cruise speed	100	mph	160	kmh
Stalling speed	36	mph	58	kmh
Climb rate	750	ft/min	229	m/min
Range	700	mls	1120	km

The side by side two seat RANS S12 Airaile is the first pod and boom pusher from RANS Aircraft of Kansas USA .and has been available since 1994 (the look alike S14 - also named Airaile - is a single seater).
Three engine options are available, Rotax 503 (47 hp.), Rotax 582 (63 hp.) and the four cylinder water cooled Rotax 912 (80 hp.)
The aircraft which is FAA approved as a 51% kit plane is also PFA approved and one is being built.
The wings, which fold, are built around two tubular spars and are fabric covered, 'V' strut braced and have flaps and ailerons, the latter being push rod operated - as are the elevators. The main gear wheels are braked and sprung on steel cantilever legs, the nose wheel steers. Cabin glazing may be fully enclosed or windscreen only - both versions have a 'perspex' nose cone.
The empenage is carried on a 5 in. diameter tube with a nominal tail skid on to which it descends when 'empty'.
Data below for Rotax 912 version.

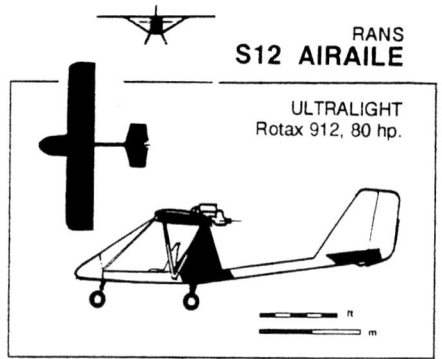

RANS
S12 AIRAILE

ULTRALIGHT
Rotax 912, 80 hp.

DATA	IMPERIAL		METRIC	
Span	31	ft	9.5	m
Wing area	152	ft^2	14.3	m^2
Aspect ratio	6.3		6.3	
Empty weight	525	lb	238	kg
Loaded weight	1094	lb	497	kg
Wing loading	7.2	lb/ft^2	35	kg/m^2
Max speed	100	mph	160	kmh
Cruise speed	80	mph	128	kmh
Stalling speed	32	mph	51	kmh
Climb rate	1000	ft/min	308	m/min
Range	205	mls	328	km

In 1971 Grob began making a series of GRP sailplanes, graduating to motor-gliders in 1980 and in '82 to their first fully powered tourer/trainer the G109 - variants of which ran up to the G115. In 1991 Grob made a quantum leap and came up with the GF 200, a 4/5 seat all composites pusher with a retractable undercarriage a 'T' tail and 270 hp.
The Fowler flapped wing is of unusual plan form with a double swept back leading edge and tip fin/winglets. The tall, small wheeled, undercarriage is necessary to give the prop clearance at high ground angles and retracts inwards, the nose-wheel forwards.
The engine on production models will be the 310 hp, water cooled, Continental as used in the globe circling Voyager. Only one GF 200 is flying, as I write. Other projected versions include the GF 300, pressurised, and the GF 350 with twin turbo shaft engines.
This fast, long legged, advanced aeroplane could be the shape of the future.

GROB
GF-200

LIGHT PLANE
Continental, 310 hp

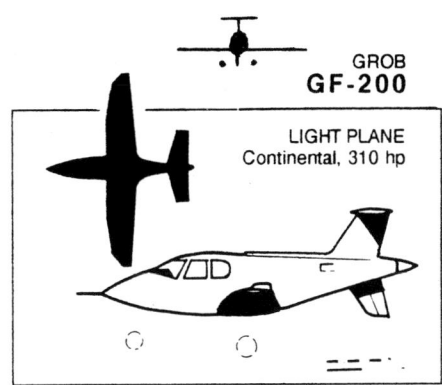

DATA	IMPERIAL		METRIC	
Span	36	ft	11	m
Wing area	134	ft^2	12.5	m^2
Aspect ratio	9.7		9.7	
Empty weight	2422	lb	1100	kg
Loaded weight	3670	lb	1700	kg
Wing loading	28	lb/ft^2	136	kg/m^2
Max speed	270	mph	432	kmh
Cruise speed	230	mph	368	kmh
Stalling speed	80	mph	129	kmh
Climb rate	1221	ft/min	366	m/min
Range	1464	mls	2356	km

This good-looking light plane hails from Italy (where they know a thing or two about *style*) and first flew in 1992.
The two seats, with side stick dual controls, are within the well glazed nose pod and the rear boom carries a 'T' tail. The Rotax engine is mounted above the single strut braced wing and drives a two or three bladed (Airplast) prop. The fuselage and integral fin are all composites, the wing may be either all metal or composites. The main wheels are on a composites 'bow spring' and the nose wheel is castoring and rubber sprung.
The Sky Arrow comes in several variants, all outwardly the same (except the Exocet, which is a float plane amphibian) - they are all powered by Rotax 912 or 914 engines. In the UK, the plastic winged 650T has been PFA approved. Three 'ultralight' models with a much lighter structure weight are pending. One on the UK Register and two being built.
Details below are for the 650T with a Rotax 912.

SKY ARROW INITIATIVE
SKY ARROW

ULTRALIGHT/LIGHT PLANE
Rotax 912/914 79/100 hp

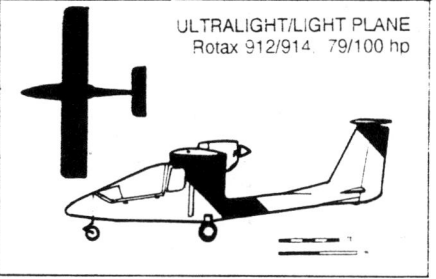

DATA	IMPERIAL		METRIC	
Span	31.5	ft	9.7	m
Wing area	144	ft^2	13.5	m^2
Aspect ratio	6.9		6.9	
Empty weight	770	lb	350	kg
Loaded weight	1450	lb	658	kg
Wing loading	10	lb/ft^2	48.3	kg/m^2
Max speed	120	mph	192	kmh
Cruise speed	104	mph	166	kmh
Stalling speed	37	mph	60	kmh
Climb rate	890	ft/min	274	m/min
Range	415	mls	664	km

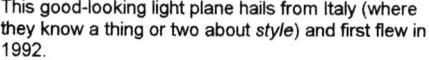

This delightful British one off from the Mike Whittaker stable is currently in *limbo* - and I, for one, hope that it is revived!

Built primarily for competition purposes, the MW8, which first flew in 1992, is powered by a Rotax 508 four stroke engine, with an extension shaft, in pusher configuration. It is a single seater with aerobatic capability and has a mid mounted strut braced wing based on the MW7. The cockpit is fully enclosed and contained in a neat wood and GRP nacelle.

The tricycle undercarriage has a steerable nose wheel and cantilever main legs carrying braked wheels.

An all moving 'stabilator' is hinged on the end of a slender tubular boom - in a similar fashion to its predecessors.

The performance of this pretty microlight was considered disappointing, in spite of its more slippery shape, when compared with its older, more rugged brothers. There are no plans to produce plans or build other examples.

WHITTAKER
MW 8

MICROLIGHT
Rotax 508, 43 hp.

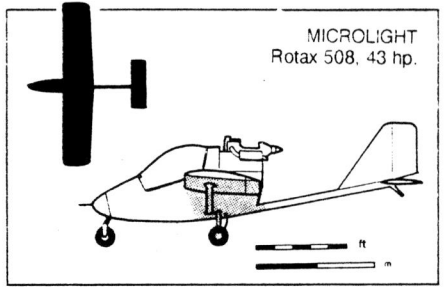

DATA	IMPERIAL	METRIC
Span	29.6 ft	9.1 m
Wing area	133 ft^2	12.5 m^2
Aspect ratio	6.6	6.6
Empty weight	405 lb	184 kg
Loaded weight	680 lb	309 kg
Wing loading	5.1 lb/ft^2	25 kg/m^2
Max speed	85 mph	136 kmh
Cruise speed	70 mph	112 kmh
Stalling speed	30 mph	48 kmh
Climb rate	700 ft/min	215 m/min
Range	300 mls	480 km

Henri Mignet is the true father of home building; his **1934 HM14 was the first genuine small plane** designed specifically for easy, cheap, amateur construction and fool-proof flying.

It had single stick control, fore and aft for mainplane incidence, and sideways for rudder control. It had no tailplane, elevator, or ailerons and the disposition of the tandem wings was supposedly proof against al aerodynamic screw ups! This, however, proved to be a fallacy when the home built Fleas took to the air, several fatal accidents caused the type to be grounded after they entered unrecoverable dives.

The fault was rectified and many flew on, in redesigned form, retaining a following to the present day.

All wood with fabric covered wings and plywood fuselage the motor was anything you could get hold of between 0.5 and 1.0 Litre - and in Mignet's book he even tells you how to carve the prop!

20 are on the UK Reg. – none flying here, but in France a few still spread their wings.

MIGNET
POU du CEIL

ULTRALIGHT
Various 20 - 30 hp.

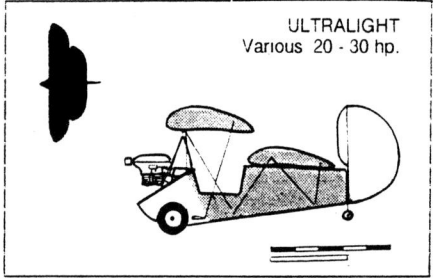

DATA	IMPERIAL	METRIC
Span	22 ft	6.7 m
Wing area	140 ft^2	13 m^2
Aspect ratio	5 Fore plane 5	
Empty weight	220 lb	100 kg
Loaded weight	450 lb	204 kg
Wing loading	3.2 lb/ft^2	15.7 kg/m^2
Max speed	70 mph	113 kmh
Cruise speed	50 mph	80 kmh
Stalling speed	30 mph	48 kmh
Climb rate	300 ft/min	92 m/min
Range	200 mls	320 km

The Falcon XP single seater canard is produced by American Aircraft of Albuquerque USA in kit or ready built form. Originally designed by Larry Newman the Falcon had a chequered production history before settling down at Albuquerque.

Currently there are several hundred of the type flying including a two seat version which will be available in the UK featuring structural and aerodynamic improvements.

The fuselage is of composite construction- Kevlar and GRP sandwich- whilst the wing is built around an aluminium 'D' section main spar which forms a smooth and strong leading edge, the ribs are alloy capped Styrofoam skinned with Tedlar.

There are two on the UK Reg. at the time of writing.

Well engineered with a simple and tough airframe the Falcon is a well mannered 'stall proof' aeroplane

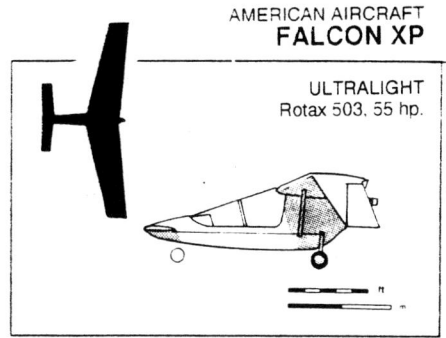

AMERICAN AIRCRAFT
FALCON XP

ULTRALIGHT
Rotax 503, 55 hp.

DATA	IMPERIAL		METRIC	
Span	36	ft	11	m
Wing area	184	ft^2	17.3	m^2
Aspect ratio	7		7	
Empty weight	550	lb	249	kg
Loaded weight	1200	lb	544	kg
Wing loading	6.5	lb/ft^2	31.7	kg/m^2
Max speed	110	mph	176	kmh
Cruise speed	85	mph	136	kmh
Stalling speed	45	mph	72	kmh
Climb rate	500	ft/min	154	m/min
Range	250	mls	400	km

Designed in America by British born Craig Catto and first flown in 1974 the Goldwing is one of the pioneering microlights. With over 1000 flying, its streamlined shape and cantilever wing, in canard configuration, are still outstanding features among the microlights.

Nice to fly, a good safety record and an excellent engine off performance allied with the canard soft stall characteristic have made the Goldwing a popular aeroplane - there are 38 on the British Register.

The wing is constructed of composites with aluminium honeycomb, foam and GRP whilst the fuselage is light alloy tube and GRP mouldings.

The main wheels are sprung and the nose wheel is steerable

Several were produced in the UK by the now defunct Eurowing in Scotland in the early eighties.(30 on 'Reg) 29 on the 'Register – only eight airworthy.

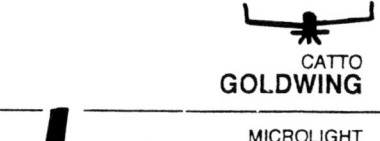

CATTO
GOLDWING

MICROLIGHT
Rotax 277 28 hp

DATA	IMPERIAL		METRIC	
Span	30	ft	9.2	m
Wing area	128	ft^2	11.9	m^2
Aspect ratio	7.8		7.8	
Empty weight	220	lb	100	kg
Loaded weight	480	lb	218	kg
Wing loading	3.75	lb/ft^2	18.3	kg/m^2
Max speed	70	mph	113	kmh
Cruise speed	60	mph	97	kmh
Stalling speed	24	mph	38	kmh
Climb rate	600	ft/min	184	m/min
Range	360	mls	579	km

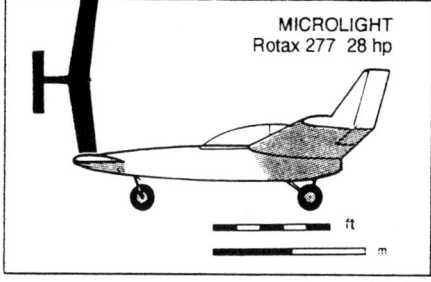

Brain child of the brothers Rutan, Dick and Burt, the Long Eze is a fast two seater straight out of Star Wars! - and the first popular all composites homebuilt.

Preceded by the look-a-like Vari Eze that first flew in 1975, the improved Long Eze is a plans only plane - all you need is a big block of expanded polystyrene, a roll of 'glass and a tin or two of epoxy resin and away you go! Construction of the sparless wing and the box like fuselage can be relatively quick but calls for a lot of expertise.

The Rutan Aircraft Factory (RAF) at Mojave, California, has become the Mecca for *avant garde* homebuilders - and from which emerged the Voyager to encircle the Globe.

Only the nose wheel is retractable on the Vari and Long Eze. An all retracting version with a 200 hp. engine, the Berkut, retains the Rutan main and fore plane. 3 and 4 seat variants are the Puffer Cozy and Dan Mahers Velocity.

PFA approved, 43 on the 'Reg, others being built.

RUTAN
LONG EZE

LIGHT PLANE
Lycoming, 100 hp.

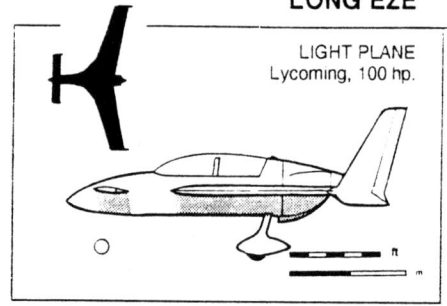

DATA	IMPERIAL		METRIC	
Span	26.3	ft	8.1	m
Wing area	94.1	ft²	8.8	m²
Aspect ratio	7.4		7.4	
Empty weight	750	lb	340	kg
Loaded weight	1325	lb	601	kg
Wing loading	14.1	lb/ft²	68.8	kg/m²
Max speed	195	mph	312	kmh
Cruise speed	160	mph	256	kmh
Stalling speed	60	mph	96	kmh
Climb rate	1500	ft/min	462	m/min
Range	1100	mls	1760	km

This tiny two seater is developed from the even smaller Quickie 1 single seater designed by Burt Rutan which first flew in 1977 powered by an 18 hp. Onan engine.

The Quickie Q2 is an all composites tandem wing tractor powered by a 75 hp. Revmaster engine (a VW relative) which, unlike the all composite Rutan range, is available in kit form. The Q1 to Q2 design hike was masterminded by Gene Sheenan and Tom Jewett in close collaboration with Rutan at RAF Mojave and appeared as the Quickie Aircraft Corporation Quickie Q2 in 1978.

Apart from the unusual arrangement of its lifting surfaces the Q2s main wheels are mounted on the fore plane wing tips and the flexibility of the wing provides the springing.

The performance is outstanding for its power - with a cruise of 170 mph. at 50 miles/gallon!

The type is PFA approved and there are 23 on the UK Register (including Q1s).

QAC
QUICKIE 2

ULTRALIGHT
Revmaster, 75 hp.

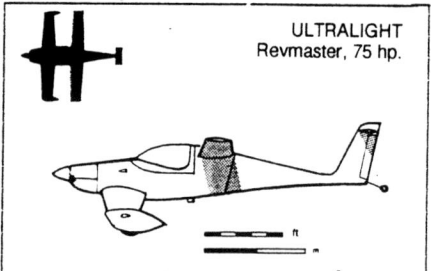

DATA	IMPERIAL		METRIC	
Span	16.6	ft	5.1	m
Wing area	67	ft²	6.3	m²
Aspect ratio (each)	8		8	
Empty weight	600	lb	272	kg
Loaded weight	1100	lb	499	kg
Wing loading	16.4	lb/ft²	80	kg/m²
Max speed	180	mph	288	kmh
Cruise speed	170	mph	272	kmh
Stalling speed	65	mph	104	kmh
Climb rate	700	ft/min	215	m/min
Range	1020	mls	1632	km

Great, great grandson of the famous Flying Flea of the 30's this 'high tech' two seater follows the aerodynamic principles of its illustrious forebear. Mignet's close-coupled tandem wings without ailerons and single stick control - rudder operated by sideways stock movement- are all here in the 1984 Balerit.

Pierre Mignet (Henri's second son) set up Avions Mignet in 1983 to design and build updated 'Fleas. (Later Mignet Aviation).

There are seven on the UK Register and over 100 have been built in France, including 24 for the French Army and several for electricity grid surveillance.

To meet the UK microlight weight limit the (British) Balerit has had to be sparsely equipped, with an open cockpit, small fuel tank (90 miles range) and no electric engine start. (The Ballerit will now benefit from the new UK 450 kg limit.)

The wings are fabric covered light alloy and the fuselage (clearly) also light alloy tubing. The wheels are well sprung trailing link type fitted with brakes - and mudguards!

MIGNET AVIATION
HM 1000 BALERIT

MICROLIGHT
Rotax 582, 64 hp.

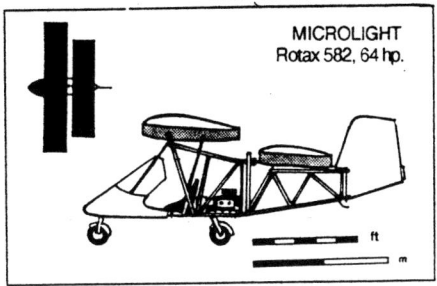

DATA	IMPERIAL		METRIC	
Span	23.7	ft	7.3	m
Wing area	186	ft²	17.5	m²
Aspect ratio	6		6	
Empty weight	451	lb	205	kg
Loaded weight	859	lb	390	kg
Wing loading	4.6	lb/ft²	22.5	kg/m²
Max speed	90	mph	144	kmh
Cruise speed	72	mph	115	kmh
Stalling speed	37	mph	59	kmh
Climb rate	500	ft/min	154	m/min
Range	90	mls	144	km

The Cozy, a Nat Puffer design, is a 'wide bodied' version of the Rutan Long Ez, with side-by-side seating and an optional third seat in the rear. The Cozy 4 is a four seat model.

Uli and Linda Wolters acquired the Cozy design rights in 1987 and market it through Cozy Europe, a German company.

The standard Rutan wing is spar-less and rib-less, all the loads being taken by the GRP skin laid over a rigid foam core. The fuselage is mainly GRP with some plywood content.

The French company Stratifies Composites Aeronautiques supplies Cozy kits and the Cozy 4 is available, plans-only in the USA.

Seven Cozys are on the UK Register and others are under construction as PFA approved.

The Cozy despite its wider body retains its sleek 'Star ship' appearance – and has the performance to prove it! - with a cruise of nearly 200 mph and an initial climb rate of 1500 fpm.

Co Z / Cozy

LIGHT PLANE
Textron Lycoming O-320, 160 hp.

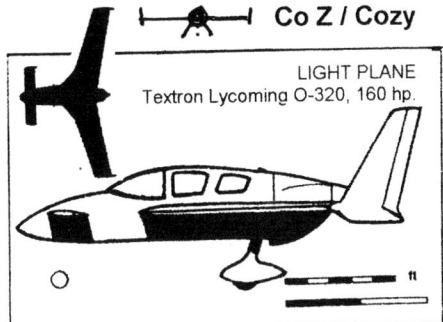

DATA	IMPERIAL		METRIC	
Span	26.3	ft	8.03	m
Wing area	94.1	sq.ft	8.8	sq.m
Aspect ratio	7.4			
Empty wt	960	lb.	435	kg.
Loaded wt	1750	lb.	794	kg.
Wing loading	18.6	lb/sq.ft	90.7	kg/sq.m
Max speed	225	mph	362	kmph
Cruising speed	187	mph	301	kmph
Stall speed	67	mph	108	kmph
Climb	1500	fpm	457	mpm
Range	1000	mls	1609	km

RENAISSANCE COMPOSITES
BERKUT

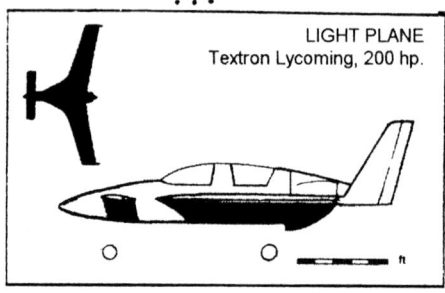

LIGHT PLANE
Textron Lycoming, 200 hp.

Based on the Rutan LongEze, the Berkut has more roomy cockpits, a retractable undercarriage and an engine of twice the power.

Dave Ronnenburg, who has built seven Longezes, masterminded the design of the super slick Berkut (name of an eagle) and it first flew in 1991.

Construction is *a la* Rutan – GRP over polystyrene foam and balsa wood, the skin taking all the loads in the spar-less wing.

The main gear legs are hydraulically operated and carry small disc braked wheels, whilst the nose leg is electrically operated independently to allow nose down parking – Longeze 'trademark'!

Renaissance Composites, having taken over from Experimental Aviation, produce the kits at their Santa Monica plant. A British built Berkut (G-REDX) won the Best Kit Built Aircraft at the 1999 PFA Rally – and is the only one on the UK Register.

A real eye-catcher, the super clean Berkut will cruise at over 200 mph on its 200 hp and keep it up for 1500 miles.

The longer nose, separate cockpit canopies and retracting undercarriage distinguish it from the Rutan Longeze.

DATA	IMPERIAL		METRIC	
Span	26.6	ft	8.13	m
Wing area	110	sq.ft	10.2	sq.m
Aspect ratio main	7.4			
Empty wt	1035	lb.	469	kg.
Loaded wt	2000	lb.	907	kg.
Wing loading	18.2	lb/sq.ft	88.8	kg/sq.m
Max speed	248	mph	399	kmph
Cruising speed	239	mph	385	kmph
Stall speed	62	mph	100	kmph
Climb	2000	fpm	610	mpm
Range	1485	mls	2389	km

EAM
EAGLE X-TS

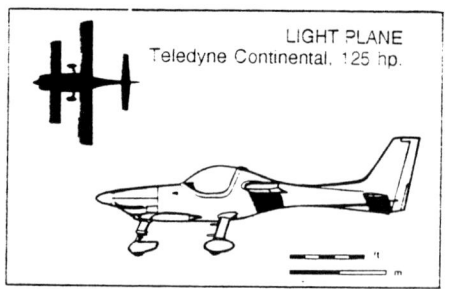

LIGHT PLANE
Teledyne Continental, 125 hp.

Originally designed and built in Australia the rakish Eagle X-TS canard (or is it a much staggered biplane? - it's got a tailplane!) is now produced in Malaysia where a big joint venture project has borne fruit in the form of a large factory and production line.

An all-composites two seater of advanced design the Eagle spans only 23 ft (7.1 m). Seating is side by side under a single piece blown canopy in a well equipped cockpit which has a central console, between the seats. A central stubby 'joy stick' protrudes from the console - rather like a gear lever - and ground steering is affected by differential brakes and a castoring nose wheel.

All canards claim to be 'stall proof' - they have, in effect, a different sort of stall. In a power-off, 'loss of lift situation', the Eagle's fore plane drops and in the subsequent dive, starts to lift again. If the stick is held back this continues in a series of nods until power is applied when recovery is immediate.

Much research flying and subsequent 'tweaking' has been carried out to bring this striking aeroplane up to JAR/VLA requirements and limited production is now under way. None yet in the UK.

DATA	IMPERIAL		METRIC	
Span	23.5	ft	7.23	m
Wing area	91.5	ft^2	8.9	m^2
Aspect ratio	10		10	
Empty weight	948	lb	430	kg
Loaded weight	1433	lb	650	kg
Wing loading	15.7	lb/ft^2	76.6	kg/m^2
Max speed	150	mph	240	kmh
Cruise speed	127	mph	203	kmh
Stalling speed	63	mph	101	kmh
Climb rate	633	ft/min	194	m/min
Range	615	mls	985	km

In production for just one year, from 1946 to '7; over 1000 Seabees were built by the company famous for its legendary P47 Thunderbolt fighter.

The prototype, RC1, first flew in 1944 as a three seater with a 175 hp Franklin engine, the developed RC3 followed as a four seater with a 215 hp Franklin.

All metal and of pleasing appearance, one is shown on the UK Register as waiting certification at Nottingham.

Republic had plans for a twin engined Seabee, a landplane version and a low powered two seat trainer – all came to nought as the company concentrated on the Thunderjet.

The Seabee has always been in need of a few more 'horses' and in 1966 United Consultants of Massachusetts produced the Twin Bee with two 180 hp Lycomings – and a fifth occupant where the central engine used to be. 24 of these conversions have been made.

Apart from those still operating, four reside in museums in Italy and New Zealand.

REPUBLIC SEABEE

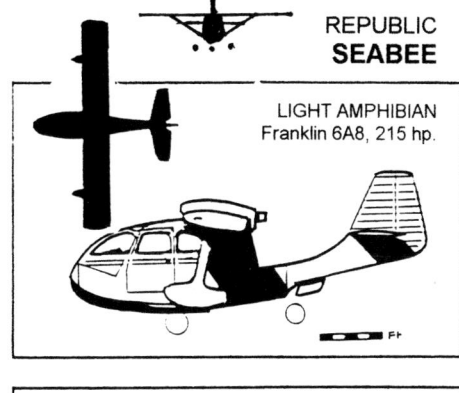

LIGHT AMPHIBIAN
Franklin 6A8, 215 hp.

DATA	IMPERIAL		METRIC	
Span	37.6	ft	11.5	m
Wing area	196	sq.ft	18.2	sq.m
Aspect ratio	7.2			
Empty wt	1950	lb.	885	kg.
Loaded wt	3000	lb.	1360	kg.
Wing loading	15.3	lb/sq.ft	74.6	kg/sq.m
Max speed	120	mph	193	kmph
Cruising speed	103	mph	166	kmph
Stall speed	60	mph	96	kmph
Climb	700	fpm	216	mpm
Range	543	mls	870	km

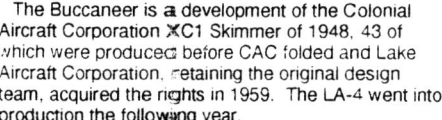

The Buccaneer is a development of the Colonial Aircraft Corporation XC1 Skimmer of 1948, 43 of which were produced before CAC folded and Lake Aircraft Corporation, retaining the original design team, acquired the rights in 1959. The LA-4 went into production the following year.

A shoulder wing amphibian with tricycle undercarriage, the LA-4 is all metal and seats four, its distinctive outline with pylon mounted pusher engine, mid fin mounted tailplane with large upturned trim tabs, and boat hull make it an identification 'pushover'.

Taken over by Consolidated Aeronautics Inc. in 1962, but retaining the Lake tag, LA-4 production continued, plus the 6 seat, 270 hp, Rengade and military Seawolf.

In the last 35 years Lake have turned out 1300 amphibians. There are 7 LA-4s on the UK Register.

LAKE LA-4 BUCCANEER

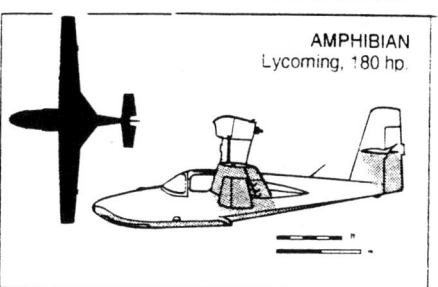

AMPHIBIAN
Lycoming, 180 hp.

DATA	IMPERIAL		METRIC	
Span	38	ft	11.6	m
Wing area	170	ft^2	15.8	m^2
Aspect ratio	8.5		8.5	
Empty weight	1575	lb	714	kg
Loaded weight	2400	lb	1089	kg
Wing loading	14.1	lb/ft^2	69	kg/m^2
Max speed	131	mph	211	kmh
Cruise speed	125	mph	201	kmh
Stalling speed	40	mph	64	kmh
Climb rate	800	ft/min	246	m/min
Range	627	mls	1010	km

A side by side two seat amphibian designed and built by Volmer Jensen of Volmer Aircraft, Burbank, California.
The Sportsman which first flew in 1958 is available as a PFA approved plans built aeroplane, many sets of which have been sold – mainly in the USA. (One is shown on the UK Register; believed un-airworthy).
The Sportsman utilises the wings of Aeronca Chiefs or Champions which are 'V' strutted, wooden spar red with metal ribs and fabric covering.
The fuselage/hull is wooden with GRP cladding over a plywood skin. The Bungee sprung undercarriage rotates upwards for water operation, and this is carried out manually. The main wheels are equipped with brakes.
The 'T' tail unit is a fabric covered welded steel structure - akin to the Aeroncas.
A Continental of 85 to 100 hp. is pylon mounted in pusher configuration above the mainplane.
Amphibians with their two environments, live a hard life and the 40 yr. old Sportsman (the first homebuilt amphibian ?) may now be 'putting its feet up'.
STOP PRESS - One is being built in Lancashire!

VOLMER SPORTSMAN

LIGHT AMPHIBIAN
Continental, 85 hp.

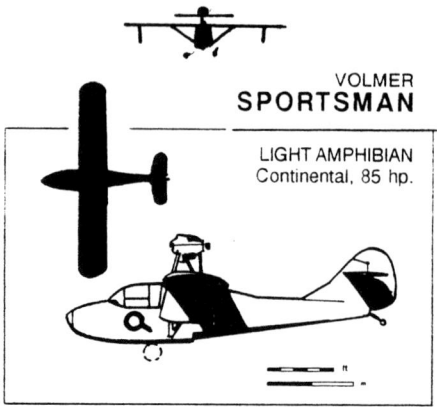

DATA	IMPERIAL		METRIC	
Span	36.5	ft	11.1	m
Wing area	175	ft²	16.3	m²
Aspect ratio	7.2		7.2	
Empty weight	1000	lb	454	kg
Loaded weight	1500	lb	680	kg
Wing loading	8.57	lb/ft²	41.8	kg/m²
Max speed	95	mph	153	kmh
Cruise speed	85	mph	137	kmh
Stalling speed	45	mph	72	kmh
Climb rate	600	ft/min	183	m/min
Range	300	mls	480	km

The innovative designer George Pereira, who works in the USA, built an 'inland waters' seaplane, the Osprey 1, which first flew in 1971 and was specifically for the home-builder. In 1973 the Osprey 2 appeared - this time an amphibian powered by a Franklin Sport engine. Construction of the tricky hull was achieved by blocking polyurethene foam over a basic wooden 'boat', then shaping it to form the keel, chine, step etc. and then 'glassing over the finished shape.
The wings, which fold, have a big wooden box spar and an auxiliary rear spar and foam/GRP tip floats.
The wheels are manually operated and, when up, are enclosed behind doors. The water rudder springs up in to the air rudder and the dual controls fitted cockpit has an upward and backward sliding hood.
Over 1000 plans have been sold and 50+ are flying.
The Osprey 2, now powered by a 150 hp. Lycoming, is small, sleek, good looking and said to be easy to build.
There are three on the UK Register + 1 being built.

PEREIRA OSPREY 2

LIGHT AMPHIBIAN
Lycoming O-320, 150 hp.

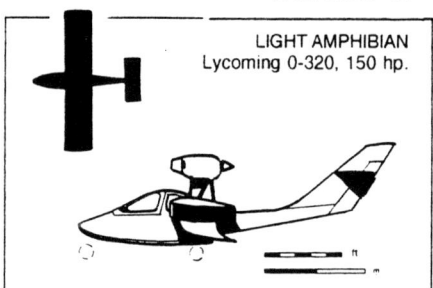

DATA	IMPERIAL		METRIC	
Span	26	ft	7.9	m
Wing area	130	ft²	12.1	m²
Aspect ratio	5.1		5.1	
Empty weight	970	lb	440	kg
Loaded weight	1560	lb	707	kg
Wing loading	12	lb/ft²	58.5	kg/m²
Max speed	130	mph	241	kmh
Cruise speed	109	mph	209	kmh
Stalling speed	60	mph	97	kmh
Climb rate	1200	ft/min	365	m/min
Range	360	mls	576	km

In 1972, leading glider builders, Schwiezer Aircraft Corporation acquired the rights of the two seat Teal 1 amphibian from its designer / constructor David Thurston (co designer of the Lake LA-4 amphibian) and transferred all jigs and tools to their plant at Elmira. NY. with Thurston engaged as Engineering Manager.

The Teal, which first flew in 1968, is an metal with some GRP topside fairings, a tractor airscrew, trouser type wing floats and main wheels that simply hinge upwards and backwards but remain, joyously, in the slipstream!

Fifteen Thurston Teal 1s were made plus the Schwiezer Teal 2 and 3 (which has more power and four seats)

In 1976 Schwiezer sold the rights to Teal Aircraft Corp. who built 38 before changing its production base to International Aeromarine in Canada - who have fitted the Teal 3 with a tricycle undercarriage.

There are only two currently on our Register.

SCHWIEZER / THURSTON
TEAL 2

LIGHT AMPHIBIAN
Lycoming, 150 hp.

DATA	IMPERIAL		METRIC	
Span	32	ft	9.8	m
Wing area	157	ft^2	14.7	m^2
Aspect ratio	6.5		6.5	
Empty weight	1435	lb	651	kg
Loaded weight	2200	lb	998	kg
Wing loading	14	lb/ft^2	68.3	kg/m^2
Max speed	120	mph	192	kmh
Cruise speed	110	mph	176	kmh
Stalling speed	52	mph	83	kmh
Climb rate	650	ft/min	200	m/min
Range	472	mls	755	km

This incredibly sleek and futuristic looking amphibian hailed from Seawind International of Ontario, but is now under the wing of Seawind SNA Inc. of Kimberton, Penn. and marketed in Europe by Tony Irwin, Seawind Europe Ltd. of Loughborough, Liecs, UK.

This all composites aeroplane is a fast four seater that has been under continual development since it first flew in 1982. Supplied in a comprehensive kit of major pre-constructed assemblies: the method of construction is similar to that of 1/72 plastic models - on a larger scale! 250 and 300 hp. Lycomings are fitted to four sub classifications, De Luxe, Standard, Club and Kit.

The cabin is exceptionally roomy, the undercarriage and flaps are hydraulically operated and the tanks provide a cruise range of 1460 miles at 55% power and169 mph.

Having natural 'star quality', the Seawind was scripted to be in the James Bond blockbuster *Goldeneye*. 20 are now flying and a 140 kits have been sold - seven on this side of the Atlantic.

SEAWIND SNA INC
SEAWIND 3000

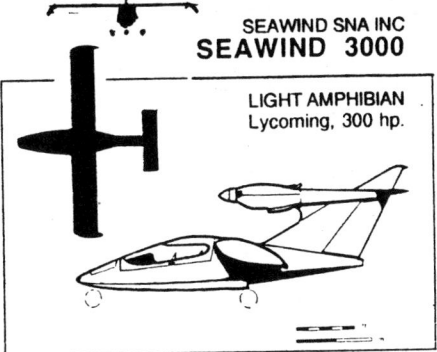

LIGHT AMPHIBIAN
Lycoming, 300 hp.

DATA	IMPERIAL		METRIC	
Span	35	ft	10.65	m
Wing area	160	ft^2	14.9	m^2
Aspect ratio	7.6		7.6	
Basic MT weight	2300	lb	1044	kg
Loaded weight	3400	lb	1542	kg
Wing loading	20	lb/ft^2	97.6	kg/m^2
Max speed	200	mph	320	kmh
Cruise speed	186	mph	300	kmh
Stalling speed	59	mph	94	kmh
Climb rate	1250	ft/min	410	m/min
Range	1460	mls	2336	km

SMAN BILLIE MARINE PETREL

This French designed and manufactured Ultralight amphibian is being produced at Auray in Brittany by S.M.A.N, a firm of boat builders.

Construction is a mixture of wood, composites, light alloys and carbon fibre with the wings all Dacron covered.

At the time of writing 30 of these pretty little aircraft have taken wing - including one under evaluation by the French Army.

The tricycle undercarriage retracts neatly into the under surface of the lower wing and the nose wheel - protruding a little at the bow - makes an effective fender!

The main wheels are fitted with differential brakes and the nose wheel castors; there are no landing flaps and ailerons on the top plane only.

Open cockpit or bubble canopy versions are available as are the two Rotax engines, the four stroke 912 giving the performance shown below.

SMAN Billie Marine market a kit version and one is on the UK Register.

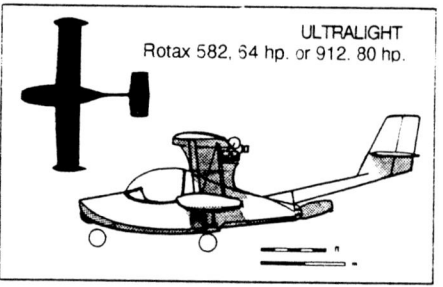

ULTRALIGHT
Rotax 582, 64 hp. or 912, 80 hp.

DATA	IMPERIAL		METRIC	
Span	27.6	ft	8.5	m
Wing area	220	ft²	20.7	m²
Aspect ratio	7		7	
Empty weight	506	lb	230	kg
Loaded weight	909	lb	450	kg
Wing loading	4.1	lb/ft²	20	kg/m²
Max speed	85	mph	136	kmh
Cruise speed	75	mph	120	kmh
Stalling speed	32	mph	50	kmh
Climb rate	650	ft/min	200	m/min
Range	250	mls	400	km

A ghost - from Small Plane Publishing's archives.

Planet Satellite

I remember the blue Planet Satellite parked at the 1948 SBAC show and how exiting it was - this was the shape of light aeroplanes to come, in the bright light of peace - we thought!

Planet Aircraft Ltd was formed in 1946 as part of Distillers Co Ltd and Maj Dundas Heenan, under whose initiative the company was formed, designed the futuristic Satellite. Heenan, who had no experience in aircraft design, came up with this highly advanced concept - a four seat pusher, with the propeller behind the tail, a retracting tricycle undercarriage and a butterfly tailplane/rudder. Not only was the configuration revolutionary but the structure itself was ground-breaking, being of all magnesium alloy. And carrying structural principles to theoretical perfection, Heenan adopted the 'lobster claw' principle of all loads being carried by the skin with little, or no, internal bracing. The wing and tail cone were pure 'lobster claw'.

The nose-wheel, cabin, wings, main 'gear and engine all attached to an 'alloy keel. During the winter of 48/49 the, now reg. G-ALOI, Satellite was moved to Blackbushe aerodrome for flight trials - having been built by Redwing Ltd at Thornton Heath. Hops up to 20 feet 'altitude' resulted in a collapsed undercarriage on one occasion and, devastatingly, a cracked central keel on another. This last named fault spelled the end of the Satellite. It was going to cost so much to repair that the project was wound up.

Strangely, a second Satellite fuselage built in 1950 and reg. G-ALXP was used in the Firth helicopter (another Heenan design) a twin engine, twin rotor design that came to nought. Presented to the College at Cranfield, it was stored for many years until broken up in the early 60's. G-ALOI was also broken up at Redhill in 1958. (Why? - such a splendid failure was a natural museum exhibit).

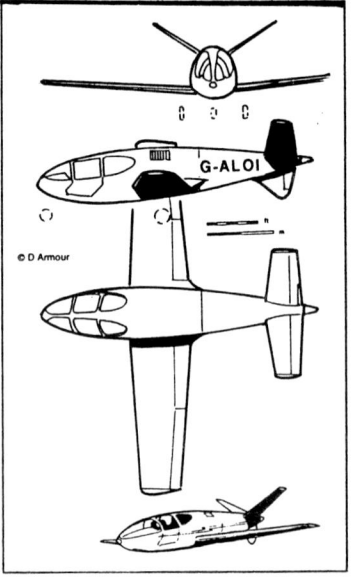

Span	32.5 ft (10 m)	Wing loading,	119 lb/ft² (93 kg)
Length	26.2 ft (8 m)	V max,	208 mph (332 kmh)
Wing Area	153 ft² (14.4	V cruise,	191 mph (305 kmh)
Aspect ratio	7.34	V min,	62 mph (99 kph)
Empty wt,	2025 lb (919 kg)	Climb,	1450 ft min (446 m/min)
Loaded wt,	2905 lb (1319 kg)	Range,	1000 mls (1600 km)

The best selling Robinson R22, which first appeared in 1975 has proved a popular two seater, particularly in the training role, with 200 on the UK Register.
The four seater R44 came onto the scene in 1991 and sports 20+ on our Register. Its power unit is the Textron Lycoming 0-540, flat six of 225 take off hp. driving a two blade rotor
Though bearing a family resemblance to its smaller sister R22, the R44 is a much bigger aircraft - about the same size as a Bell Jet Ranger!
Although a bigger machine, the R44 continues the Robinson theme of simple, light weight construction, making it fast for its power group and considerably cheaper than its contemporaries.
Produced at the Robinson Helicopter Company's plant at Torrance, California the R44 is in full production. The floatplane version is typed as the R44 Clipper.

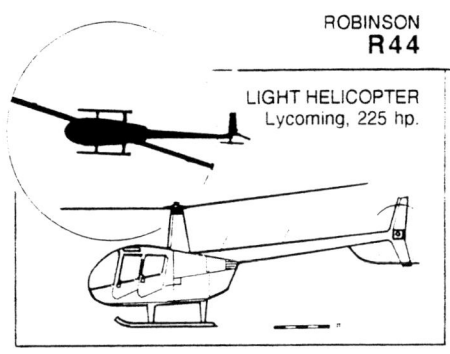

ROBINSON
R44

LIGHT HELICOPTER
Lycoming, 225 hp.

DATA	IMPERIAL		METRIC	
Rotor Dia.	33	ft	10.1	m
Length	38.2	ft	11.7	m
Empty weight	1400	lb	635	kg
Loaded weight	2400	lb	1089	kg
Disc loading	2.8	lb/ft^2	13.6	kg/m^2
Max speed	140	mph	224	kmh
Cruise speed	129	mph	206	kmh
Climb rate	1000	ft/min	308	m/min
Range	402	mls	643	km

Rotary Air Force Inc of Saskatchewan are a small team who have made a big impact on the gyroplane scene. Entering the market in 1987 with the single seat RAF 1000 they have embodied its design principles in the best selling, two seat, RAF 2000.
This neat, Subaru powered, autogyro is produced as an easy build kit (300-400 hours) which comes complete with engine, instruments and rotors, promises to be the shape of the small gyro future! Kits have been sold world wide and a dozen or more are currently being built in the UK plus 17 flying.
Unusual for the type, the 2000 has a fully enclosed cockpit with coloured upholstery and carpets, plus a two speed heater, a comprehensive panel and landing lights.
The rotor blades are composites moulded over a foam profiled dural spar, the sturdy main structure also being of dural tube. Water cooled, the Subaru engine runs on unleaded auto gas and drives a three bladed Warp Drive prop.
The design is CAA and PFA approved and Newtonair of Newton Abbot, Devon, the sole UK agents operate a demonstration and training facility at Dunkeswell Airfield.

RAF
2000

LIGHT GYROPLANE
Subaru Legacy, 130 hp.

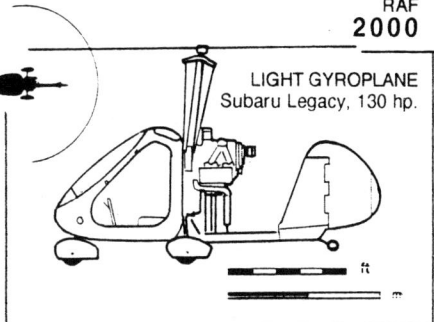

DATA	IMPERIAL		METRIC	
Rotor Dia.	30	ft	9.24	m
Length	13.6	ft	4.18	m
Empty weight	730	lb	331	kg
Loaded weight	1540	lb	700	kg
Disc loading	2.18	lb/ft^2	10.6	kg/m^2
Max speed	100	mph	160	kmh
Cruise speed	80	mph	128	kmh
Climb rate	1200	ft/min	370	m/min
Range	280	mls	448	km

The prototype Robinson R22 first flew in 1975 after two years of extensive development and went into production in 1979. Production has continued up to the present day and over 2500 of the type have been delivered.

The first 500 R22s were designated Alpha, and the subsequent models, Beta. There is a float plane version, the R22 Mariner and a law enforcement model, appropriately called R22 Police, and the High Performance R22 HP.

When fitted with a belly tank the R22 can be used for crop spraying with a 24 ft spray boom.

The R22 is a two seater with dual control and is popular as a trainer - '80% of helicopter pilots have learned on a R22'.

Very moderately priced, for a two seat helicopter, the R22s in this country are legion – 240 on the UK Register. The four seat R44 appeared in 1991

ROBINSON R22 ALPHA/BETA

Lycoming, 160 hp.

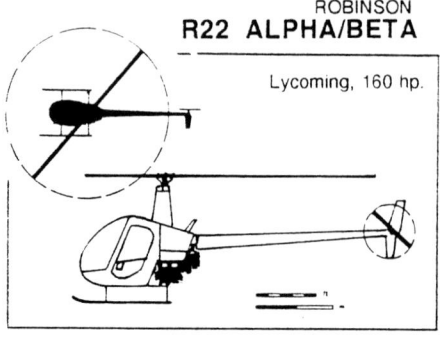

DATA	IMPERIAL		METRIC	
Rotor Dia.	25.1	ft	7.7	m
Length	28.7	ft	8.8	m
Empty weight	835	lb	379	kg
Loaded weight	1370	lb	622	kg
Disc loading	2.75	lb/ft^2	13.4	kg/m^2
Max speed	112	mph	179	kmh
Cruise speed	110	mph	176	kmh
Climb rate	1200	ft/min	370	m/min
Range	368	mls	588	km

A development of the earlier, and very similar, Enstrom F28 of 1960. The Model 280 first flew in 1973 and had a bigger cabin, swept stabiliser fins and a tail skid.

The '280 is sleek for a rotorcraft, with it's fully enclosed fuselage, monocoque tail boom, single spindle rotor drive and general lack of protuberances. (The prototype had a n open work lattice boom).

The 280s, from B, to F, are three seaters, the only four place being the 280L which first flew in 1978.

The standard power unit is a turbo charged Lycoming H10-360-E1AD of 205 hp. - or 153 kW.

Still in production at the Michigan factory, some 200 have been made to date.

The F28 and Model 280 are physically almost identical, but the fin type tail skid differentiates the '280 from the F28 which has a bent tube skid/tail rotor guard.

There are 32 F28s on the 'Reg and 47 Model 280s.

ENSTROM MODEL 280 SHARK

LIGHT HELICOPTER
Lycoming, 205 hp.

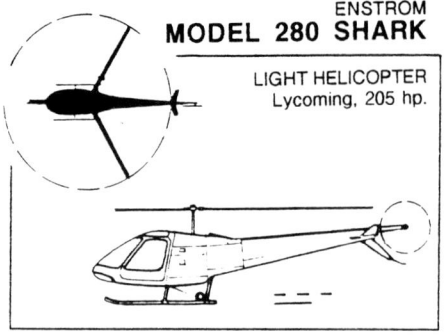

DATA	IMPERIAL		METRIC	
Rotor Dia.	32	ft	9.75	m
Length	29.3	ft	8.9	m
Empty weight	1495	lb	678	kg
Loaded weight	2200	lb	998	kg
Disc loading	2.74	lb/ft^2	13.4	kg/m^2
Max speed	117	mph	188	kmh
Cruise speed	100	mph	161	kmh
Climb rate	1300	ft/min	396	m/min
Range	237	mls	381	km

First flown as far back as 1947 the Model 360, or UH-12 was designed by the innovative rotorcraft pioneer Stanley Hiller. The Rotormatic system, which bears his name, has a pair of paddles on a boom below the main rotor which operate the cyclic pitch control.
Originally a three seater with a 178 hp. Franklin engine and enclosed cabin and engine bay, the first production models appeared with open cockpit and engine bay, and were type approved in '48. (One of these made the first coast to coast flight by a commercial helicopter in the USA).
In 1950 came the 12-A with new type rotor and a 200 hp. Franklin - these were ordered by the Army as H23-A Ravens.
The 12-B, with minor mods. were again ordered by the Army, 273 being delivered as H23-Bs.
The 12-C introduced the 'gold fish bowl' canopy, going out of production in '65 - but started up again in '73 with the reformed Hiller Aviation Co.
2000 UH-12s have been built and 5 are on the UK Reg

HILLER
UH-12

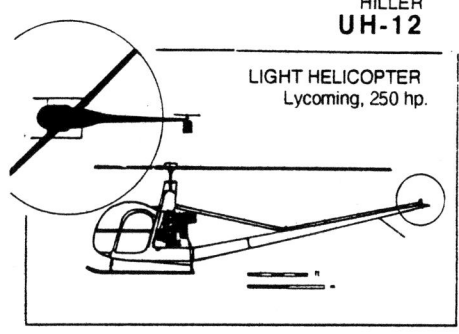

LIGHT HELICOPTER
Lycoming, 250 hp.

DATA	IMPERIAL		METRIC	
Rotor Dia.	35.4	ft	10.8	m
Length	26.6	ft	8.1	m
Empty weight	1700	lb	771	kg
Loaded weight	2750	lb	1247	kg
Disc loading	2.8	lb/ft^2	13.6	kg/m^2
Max speed	95	mph	153	kmh
Cruise speed	87	mph	140	kmh
Climb rate	1290	ft/min	393	m/min
Range	225	mls	362	km

First flown in 1956, the bug like Model 269 went into production in 1961 at the initial rate of about one hundred a year.
They are in use for both civil and military purposes and have been supplied to various foreign air forces.
The US Army employs the basic 269A - re-designated TH-55-AS Osage - as its standard helicopter trainer and has taken delivery of over 800.
The 300C variant is the model currently in production at Schweizer where it is sometimes fitted with an Allison 250-C20W turbine. The 300CQ is an extra quiet Schweizer built version.
There are 60 269s on the UK Register.

HUGHES
MODEL 269

Lycoming, 160 hp.

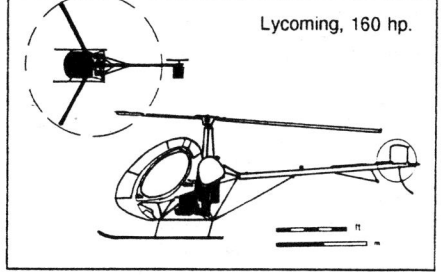

DATA	IMPERIAL		METRIC	
Rotor Dia.	25	ft	7.7	m
Length	22.2	ft	6.8	m
Empty weight	910	lb	413	kg
Loaded weight	1550	lb	703	kg
Disc loading	3.16	lb/ft^2	15.4	kg/m^2
Max speed	86	mph	137	kmh
Cruise speed	70	mph	112	kmh
Climb rate	1450	ft/min	446	m/min
Range	200	mls	320	km

The Bell 206 A first flew in 1966 and was developed from Bell's losing contender in the Army Light Observation Helicopter trials.
Probably the most successful commercial helicopter ever made, with over 6000 aircraft produced and in use all over the world – 150 are on the latest UK Register.
The attractively styled fuselage embodies in it's semi monocoque construction, aluminium sheet and honeycomb sandwich. The engine is mounted behind the rotor and above the passenger compartment.
This fast, comfortable and popular helicopter is much used by big corporations for executive travel, and oil and electricity companies for surveillance work.
The first 206A ran to a production of 660 units; in '71 came the JetRanger 2 with the 400 shp Allison, 1600 of which were made before the JetRanger 3, with 425 shp. entered the lists, and is still in production.
A military version with bigger rotor has been delivered in considerable numbers and is typed as OH-58 Kiowa.
Data for JetRanger 2.

BELL JETRANGER

LIGHT HELICOPTER
Allison, 400 shp.

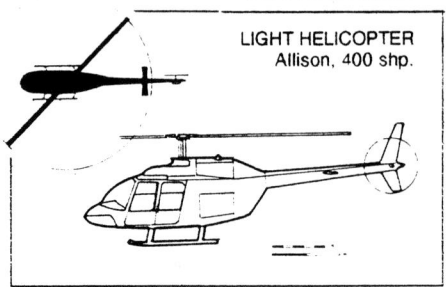

DATA	IMPERIAL		METRIC	
Rotor Dia.	33.3	ft	10.16	m
Length	31.2	ft	9.56	m
Empty weight	1455	lb	660	kg
Loaded weight	3200	lb	1451	kg
Disc loading	3.7	lb/ft^2	18	kg/m^2
Max speed	140	mph	225	kmh
Cruise speed	134	mph	216	kmh
Climb rate	1260	ft/min	384	m/min
Range	388	mls	624	km

The prototype Model 47, three seat helicopter, first flew in 1945. First production models were for the military and type named H13 Sioux.
Type designations run to fifty or more and space permits only a few to be mentioned.
The first civil version, the 47B, appeared in 1946 and was the worlds first commercial helicopter to be CAA type approved.
All the early models had 178 hp. Franklin engines and the well known Bell rotor stabilising bar, car type cabin and covered tail boom. The 'gold fish bowl' cabin came in with the '47D in 1948 and with it the open frame tail boom.
the '47E was a two seater with a 200 hp. Franklin engine, and the '47G of 1953 was similarly powered, but had three seats.
From '55, Lycoming engines supplanted the Franklins.
Built by Augusta in Italy, Kawasaki in Japan and Westland in the UK, it is the most prolific helicopter in the world - in production for over 40 years - with over 4000 built, 29 of which are on the UK Register.

BELL MODEL 47

LIGHT HELICOPTER
Lycoming, 240 hp.

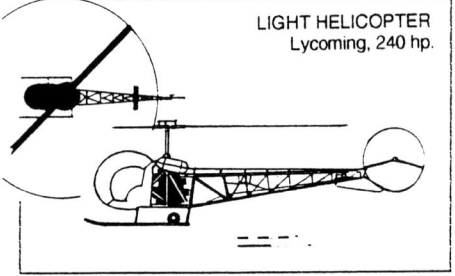

DATA	IMPERIAL		METRIC	
Rotor Dia.	37.1	ft	11.3	m
Length	31.5	ft	9.6	m
Empty weight	1650	lb	748	kg
Loaded weight	2850	lb	1293	kg
Disc loading	2.64	lb/ft^2	12.9	kg/m^2
Max speed	105	mph	169	kmh
Cruise speed	90	mph	145	kmh
Climb rate	800	ft/min	244	m/min
Range	290	mls	467	km

Developed from a range of gyro gliders - towed autogyros - by Igor Bensen and his company, Bensen Aircraft Corporation. The first motorised model, the B8-M - (M for motorised) first flew in 1957 and was powered by a two stroke Mc Culloch engine of 72 hp. Later power options include the 90 hp. Mc Culloch or a 64 hp VW engine - this model classified as B8V.
A mechanical rotor drive, enabling jump take offs may be fitted and two seats are an option. The B8M may be kit or factory built - the company now, however, is no longer in existence.
The rotor blades are of laminated wood on a steel spar and are controlled in cyclic pitch and yaw only.
The overhead control stick is replaced in many models by a 'floor' mounted stick.
Many thousands of Bensen gyrocopters and their powered brethren have been built, mainly in the USA; over 100 are on the UK Register as a PFA approved type.

BENSEN
B8 M

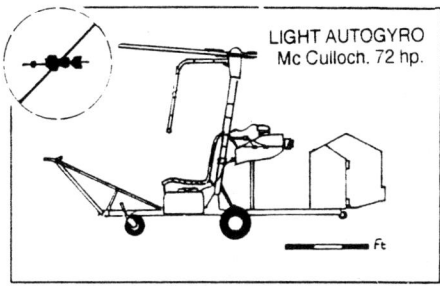

LIGHT AUTOGYRO
Mc Culloch. 72 hp.

DATA	IMPERIAL		METRIC	
Rotor Dia.	20	ft	6.16	m
Length	11.3	ft	3.5	m
Empty weight	247	lb	112	kg
Loaded weight	500	lb	227	kg
Disc loading	1.6	lb/ft²	7.8	kg/m²
Max speed	85	mph	136	kmh
Cruise speed	60	mph	96	kmh
Climb rate	1000	ft/min	308	m/min
Range	100	mls	160	km

The two seat Brantly B2 first flew in 1953; development continued for six years and production commenced in 1959.
The B2 A is an up-dated version of the original B2, with re-designed cabin and improved equipment. The B2 B has more power with a 180 hp. fuel injected Lycoming. All B2s have dual control and a unique rotor of extruded aluminium which has flapping hinges at the root and half way along the blade. The type approval was issued by the FAA in 1963. In 1989 Japan acquired build rights and, in the same year, the new Brantly Helicopter Industries was formed in Texas.
The flat four engine is mounted vertically and the clean tapered fuselage give the B2 very tidy lines, further enhanced by the minimal rotor pylon.
There are 10 B2s on the UK Register of the 400 produced.
Of very similar appearance, the Brantly B305 is a five seater.

BRANTLY
B2A

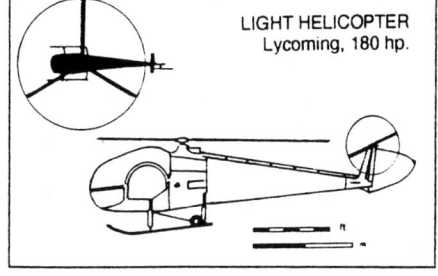

LIGHT HELICOPTER
Lycoming, 180 hp.

DATA	IMPERIAL		METRIC	
Rotor Dia.	23.9	ft	7.4	m
Length	23.9	ft	7.4	m
Empty weight	1020	lb	463	kg
Loaded weight	1670	lb	758	kg
Disc loading	3.78	lb/ft²	18.5	kg/m²
Max speed	100	mph	160	kmh
Cruise speed	92	mph	147	kmh
Climb rate	1400	ft/min	431	m/min
Range	250	mls	400	km

A very neat home-built two seat helicopter from the USA. Originally factored by Rotorcraft Aircraft Inc. up to 1990 when all the Corporation's assets were purchased by English businessman John Netherwood who was new to the field. Netherwood's company was named Rotorway International. (Rotorway *Inc.* had marketed single and two seat kit helicopters in the 70's)
The Executive 162F arose from the combination of this corporate mix - and very successful it has been to. Powered by Rotorway's own engine, a flat four cylinder unit developing 152 hp. the Executive 162 replaces the earlier '90, and can be built from a complete kit or from quick build ready assembled units.
The Executive 90 established the market for the type and it has been taken up by distributors world wide.
There are 30 Executives on the UK Register.

ROTORWAY
EXECUTIVE 162

LIGHT HELICOPTER
Rotorway, 152 hp

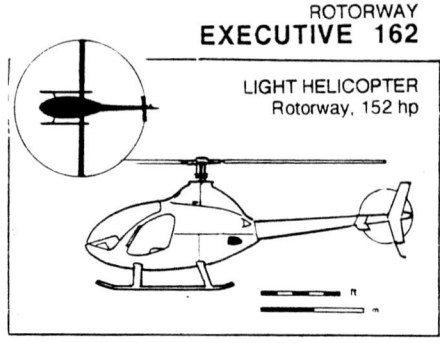

DATA	IMPERIAL		METRIC	
Rotor Dia.	25	ft	7.6	m
Length	22	ft	6.7	m
Empty weight	925	lb	420	kg
Loaded weight	1425	lb	646	kg
Disc loading	1.9	lb/ft^2	7.27	kg/m^2
Max speed	115	mph	185	kmh
Cruise speed	95	mph	153	kmh
Climb rate	1000	ft/min	305	m/min
Range	180	mls	290	km

Wing Commander K H Wallis began designing and experimenting with a small single seat autogyro in 1950, and having patented various unique features, the prototype WA 116 first flew in 1961 with a 72 hp two stroke McCulloch drone engine - having experimented earlier with a Triumph motor cycle engine.
In the following year three Beagle built WA 116s were evaluated by the British Army - but no order ensued.
In 1964 Wallis Autogyros was formed and modest production commenced. In 1969 the first two seat trainer flew and a nacelle was added to the, hitherto, exposed seating.
In 1968 the WA 116 broke the world height record for autogyros and a year later the speed record at 111 mph. The WA 116 became well known as the deadly little 'chopper' in the film *'You only Live Twice'*.
To achieve full British certification a 100 hp RR Continental was fitted in 1995 and was later re- typed as WA 117. Twenty WA 116s are on the UK Register.

WALLIS
WA 116 AGILE

ULTRALIGHT AUTOGYRO
Mc Culloch, 72 hp.

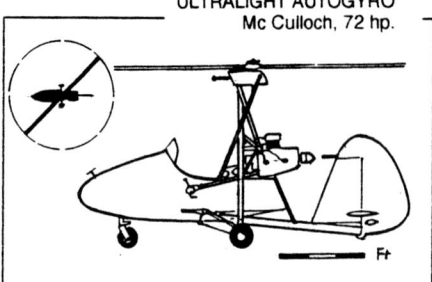

DATA	IMPERIAL		METRIC	
Rotor Dia.	20.3	ft	6.2	m
Length	11.1	ft	3.4	m
Empty weight	295	lb	134	kg
Loaded weight	550	lb	250	kg
Disc loading	1.72	lb/ft^2	8.4	kg/m^2
Max speed	80	mph	128	kmh
Cruise speed	60	mph	96	kmh
Climb rate	1000	ft/min	308	m/min
Range	100	mls	160	km

This helicopter is a civilian development of the US Army's OH-6A Cayuse that first flew in 1963 - and was to set several world records for it's class in 1966.
The first '500 flew in 1967 powered by an Allison 736 turbine of 278 shp. driving a four bladed main rotor and seating pilot and four passengers.
The '500 C of 1970 has a 400 shp. Allison and consequently flies faster and higher.
the '500 D has a five bladed rotor and a 'T' tail with small end plates and the '500 E has a more pointed nose and bigger tailplane end plates.
Military versions of the '500 have been supplied to many foreign air forces and Kawasaki of Japan and Nardi SA in Italy are licensed to build the type.
The design of the rotor head is unusual; the opposing blades, of the four, are joined by a laminated stainless steel strap that allows feathering and flapping movement and considerably simplifies the head machinery.
There are 33 of the type on the UK Register.

HUGHES
MODEL 500

LIGHT HELICOPTER
Allison, 400 shp.

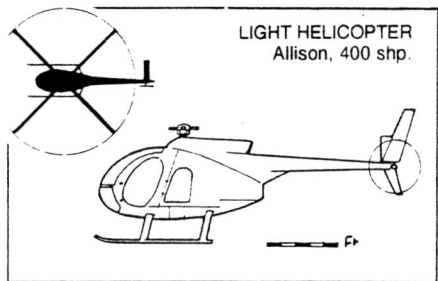

DATA	IMPERIAL		METRIC	
Rotor Dia.	26.5	ft	8.05	m
Length	23	ft	7.01	m
Empty weight	1320	lb	598	kg
Loaded weight	3000	lb	1360	kg
Disc loading	5.4	lb/ft²	26.6	kg/m²
Max speed	160	mph	258	kmh
Cruise speed	150	mph	241	kmh
Climb rate	800	ft/min	244	m/min
Range	335	mls	539	km

Lake LA-4 Buccaneer

Name	Page
60 Moth, De Haviland	12 d
3202 NORD	61 e
AA-5, Gulfstream American	109 e
AA1, Gulfstream American	104 e
Acro Advanced, Smith	50 d
Acrosport, EAA	136 e
Active, Arrow	130 d
Aero Designs Pulsar	114 d
Aero Dynamics Sparrowhawk	158 e
Aeromot Super Ximango	59 s
Aeronca C3	5 d
Aeronca Champion/ Citabria	27 d
Aeronca Model 11, Chief	18 d
Aeroprakt A22 Foxbat	43 ae
Aerosport Scamp	137 e
Aerosport Woody Pusher	152 pk
Aero Technik EV97 Eurostar	119 e
Agile, Wallis	174 pk
Airaile, Rans S 12	158 s
Aiglet Trainer, Auster	22 pk
Aircamper, Pietenpol	7 e
Airedale, A109, Beagle	35 e
Airtourer, Victa	102 pk
Akro, Stephens	46 a
Ambassadeur, DR1050, Jodel	78 d
American Aircraft Falcon XP	161 e
AMF Microlight Chevron	52 d
Andreasson BA-4	134 d
AOP 6, Auster	14 d
AOP 9, Auster	23 pk
Apache, Piper	144 pk
Argus, Fairchild	8 pk
Arrow, J2, Auster	16 pk
Arrow Active	130 d
Arrow, Spartan	124 a
ARV 2, Noble	52 e
AS-K16, Schleicher	56 d
ATL Robin	113 e
Auster AOP 6	14 d
Auster AOP 9	23 pk
Auster J1 Autocrat	15 ftp
Auster J2 Arrow	16 pk
Auster J4	14 e
Auster J5 Autocar	22 e
Auster J5F Aiglet Trainer	22 pk
Auster Mark 4,5,5D	12 d
Autocar, J5, Auster	22 e
Autocrat, J1, Auster	15 ftp
Avia Sud Mistral	140 d
Avian, Avro	124 sp
Avid Flyer, Light Aero	28 d
Avro 504	122 a
Avro Avian	124 sp
Avro Tutor	126 sp
Ax3 Cyclone	37 e
B206, Beagle	146 e
B/Trainer, Tipsy	63 e
B2 Blackburn	128 a
B2A, Brantly	173 ftp
B8M, Bensen	173 pk
BA Eagle	62 pk
BA Swallow	61 pk
BA-4, Andreasson	134 d
Baby Ace, Corben	7 s
Baby Great Lakes, Oldfield	134 d
BAC Drone	151 sp
Balerit, Mignet Aviation	163 e
Banbi, Colomban	118 e
Baron, Beech	145 pk
BD-4, Bede	27 e
BD-5, Bede	153 e
Beagle A109 Airedale	35 e
Beagle A61 Terrier	24 e
Beagle Husky	24 d
Beagle Pup	107 d
Beagle B206	146 e
Beaver, DHC	17 ph
Bebe, D9, Jodel	72 d
Bede BD-4	27 e
Bede BD-5	153 e
Beech 17 Staggerwing	129 e
Beech 180 Sundowner	102 e
Beech Bonanza	92 e
Beech C55 Baron	145 pk
Beech Musketeer	102 e
Beech Sierra 200	102 e
Beechcraft Duchess	150 ftp
Bell Jetranger	172 e
Bell Model 47	172 pk
Bellanca Citabria	27 d
Bensen B8M	173 pk
Berkut, Renaissance Comp.	164 e
Bestmann, Bucker	66 a
Beta Bird, Hovey	153 s
BGP-1, Plumb	139 s
Bird Dog, Cessna	21 e
Blackburn B2	128 a
Boeing Stearman Kaydet	131 e
Bolkow Bo 209 Monsun	120 d
Bolkow Bo208 Junior	51 e
Bonanza, Beech	92 e
Bowers Fly Baby	81 e
Brandli BX-2 Cherry	98 e
Brantly B2A	173 ftp
Bravo, FWA	109 sp
Bristol Bulldog	125 sp
Britten-Norman BN-3 Nymph	36 bn
Brugger MB2 Colibri	81 e
Buccaneer, Lake	165 e
Bucker Bestmann	66 a
Bucker Jungmann	130 e
Bulldog, Bristol	125 sp
Bushby Midget Mustang	73 pk
C3, Aeronca	5 d
Cadet, Culver	54 sp
CAP 10, Mudry	84 e
CAP 231, Mudry	91 sp
CB-1, Hatz	135 e
Cardinal, Cessna	45 pk
Carlson Sparrow	40 e

Aircraft	Page
Cassutt Special	46 e
Catto Goldwing	161 pk
Cavalier, K & S	110 e
Cessna Model 120/140	19 d
Cessna 150/152	34 e
Cessna 170	17 s
Cessna 172 Skyhawk	33 e
Cessna 177 Cardinal	45 e
Cessna 182 Skylane	34 ce
Cessna 195	18 s
Cessna Bird Dog	21 e
Cessna Model 206	35 ce
Cessna Model 210 Centurion	45 ce
Cessna Model 310	145 e
Cessna Model 337 Skymaster	152 e
Cessna 421 Golden Eagle	147 ftp
CFM Shadow Streak	157 d
CGS Hawk Arrow	156 e
CH701, Zenair	39 e
Challenger, Quad City	157 e
Champion, Aeronca	27 d
Chaparall, M20, Mooney	93 d
Charger, Marquart	135 s
Cherokee, PA28, Piper	103 d
Cherokee Six PA 32, Piper	104 d
Cherry, BX-2, Brandli	98 e
Chevron, AMF Microlight	52 d
Chichester-Miles Leopard	155 c
Chief, Model 11, Aeronca	18 d
Chilton DW-1 Monoplane	64 pk
Chipmunk, De Haviland	70 d
Chrislea Super Ace	32 e
Christen Eagle	138 e
Citabria, Bellanca	27 d
Civilian Coupe	5 sp
Clutton FRED	26 e
Cmelak, LET	82 sp
Colibri, MB2, Brugger	81 e
Colomban Banbi	118 e
Colomban Cri Cri	149 e
Comanche, PA24, Piper	94 e
Commander, Rockwell	95 e
Comper Swift	6 pk
Condor, Druine-Rollason	80 e
Condor, Rollason	54
Corben Baby Ace	7 s
Corby Starlet	86 s
Cornell, Fairchild	66 s
Cougar, Gulfstream American	149 e
Coupe, Civilian	5 sp
Coyote, S6, RANS	40 e
CoZ / Cozy	163 e
Cranfield A1-200 Eagle	88 a
Cri Cri, Colomban	149 e
Culver Cadet	54 sp
Currie Wot	132 e
Cyclone AX3	37 e
Cygnet, Hapi	47 m
Cygnet, General Aircraft	100 a
Cygnet Hawker	123 a
D112, Club, Jodel	75 d
D120, Jodel	85 s
D9, Jodel	72 e
D140, Jodel	77 e
D18, Jodel	89 e
DA 2, Davis	106 pk
Dart Kitten	65 a
Davis DA 2	106 pk
De Haviland 60 Moth	123 d
De Haviland Dragon	142 d
De Haviland Fox Moth	128 s
De Haviland Hornet Moth	131 d
De Haviland Humming Bird	61 a
De Haviland Leopard Moth	8 ftp
De Haviland Tiger Moth	127 d
De Haviland '71 Tiger Moth	62 sp
De Haviland Moth Minor	67 s
De Haviland Chipmunk	70 d
De H Canada Beaver	17 ph
Denney Kitfox	29 sp
Dessouter Monoplane	6 sp
Diamond Katana	118 e
Dragon, De Haviland	142 d
Drone, BAC	151 sp
Druine- Rollason Condor	80 e
Druine Turbi	72 s
Druine Turbulent	71 d
Duchess, Beechcraft	150 ftp
Dyn Aero MCR 01	117 d
EAA Acrosport	136 e
Eagle A1-200, Cranfield	88 a
Eagle, BA	62 pk
Eagle XTS, EAM	164 d
Eagle, Christen	138 e
EAM Eagle XTS	164 d
Echo, Technam	41 e
Eippper Quicksilver	154 e
Elster, Putzer	33 a
Emeraude, Piel	76 e
Enstrom Shark	170 pk
Ercoupe	100 e
Europa Aviation Europa	59 e
Europa Aviation Europa Tri-gear	119 s
Europa Tri Gear,	119 s
Eurostar, Aero Technik	119 e
Evans VP-1	84 e
Evans VP-2	87 s
Executive, Rotorway	174 pk
Extra 300	50 e
Fairchild F24 Argus	8 pk
Fairchild Cornell	66 s
Fairey Junior	69 a
Falco, Sequoia/Frati	94 e
Falcon XP, American Aircraft	161 e
Falcon, Miles	65 mc
Firefly, T67, Slingsby	116 e
Fisher Super Koala	29 ama
Flaglor Sky Scooter	26 bs
Flex Wings	120 ma
Flitzer, Staaken	141 s

Aircraft	Page
FLS Aerospace Sprint	114 e
FLS Aerospace Optica	154 e
Fly Baby, Bowers	81 e
Fokker S11 Instructor	71 sp
Fokker Dr1 Tri-plane	121 e
Foster Wikner Wicko	9 sp
Fournier RF-4, RF-5	56 e
Fournier RF 47	117 s
Fox Moth, De Haviland	128 s
Foxbat, Aeroprakt	43 ae
FRED, Clutton	26 e
Fuji FA200 Subaru	105 d
Fury, Isaacs	133 e
FW 190, WAR	57 e
FWA AS 202 Bravo	109 sp
G109, Grob	89 e
G115, Grob	116 e
GA7, Gulfstream American	149 e
Gardan GY80 Horizon	95 d
Gardan Minicab	73 pk
Gemini, Miles	143 mc
General Aircraft Cygnet	100 a
General Aircraft Monospar	142 sp
Glasair, Stoddart-Hamilton	99 pk
Glastar, Stoddard-Hamilton	43 e
Globe Swift	55 sp
Golden Eagle, Cessna	147 ftp
Goldwing, Catto	161 pk
GP-4, Pereira	98 gp
Grinvalds Orion	155 s
Grob G109	89 e
Grob G115	116 e
Grob GF200	159 s
Gulfstream American AA-5	109 e
Gulfstream American AA1	104 e
Gulfstream American Cougar	149 e
Hapi Cygnet	47 m
Harvard, North American	54 e
Hatz CB-1	135 e
Hawk Arrow, CGS	156 e
Hawker Cygnet	123 a
Hawker Tomtit	126 a
Heintz/Zenair CH601 Zodiac	115 d
Hiller UH-12	171 pk
Hiperbipe, Sorrell	137 e
Horizon, GY80, Gardan	95 d
Hornet Moth, De Haviland	131 d
Hovey Beta Bird	153 s
Hunting-Percival Provost	74 a
HR100, Robin	96 e
HR200, Robin	110 d
Hughes Model 269	171 pk
Hughes Model 500	175 pk
Humming Bird, De Haviland	61 a
Husky, Beagle	24 d
Ikarus Comco C42	44 i
Instructor S11, Fokker	71 sp
Isaacs Fury	133 e
Isaacs Spitfire	88 pk
J2 Arrow, Auster	16 pk
J3 Cub, Piper	10 d
J4 Cub, Piper	11 a
J4 Auster	14 d
Jabiru	39 e
Jetranger, Bell	172 pk
Jodel D9 Bebe	72 d
Jodel D18	89 e
Jodel D112 Club	75 d
Jodel D120	85 s
Jodel D140 Mousquetaire	77 e
Jodel DR1050 Ambassadeur	78 d
Jungmann, Bucker	130 e
Junior, Bo208, Bolkow	51 e
Junior, Fairey	69 a
Jurca Tempette	77 d
Jutca Sirrocco	62 e
K & S Cavalier	110 e
Katana, Diamond	118 e
Kaydet, Boeing Stearman	131 e
KIS Tri - R	115 d
Kitfox, Denney	29 sp
Kitten, Dart	65 a
Kittiwake, Mitchell-Proctor	108 pk
Kolb Twinstar	156 d
KR-2, Rand Robinson	57 e
Lake LA-4 Buccaneer	165 e
Lambada, Urban	53 u
Lancair, Neico	97 e
Leopard, CMC	155 c
Leopard Moth, De Haviland	8 ftp
LET Cmelak	82 sp
LET 200, Morava	144 s
Letov Sluka	42 e
Light Aero Avid Flyer	28 d
Lohele Mustang	58 e
Long Eze, Rutan	162 d
Lunar Rocket, M5, Maule	25 d
Luscombe Silvaire	10 d
Luton Major	13 e
Luton Minor	9 e
Magister, Miles	68 sp
Mainair Blade	120 ma
Major, Luton	13 e
Malibu P-46, Piper	97 ftp
Marquart Charger	135 s
Martlet, Southern	125 mc
Maule M5 Lunar Rocket	25 d
MBA Tiger Cub	138 d
MCR 01, Dyn Aero	117 d
Menestrel, HN700, Nicollier	90 e
Messenger, Miles	69 e
Mew Gull, Percival	63 a
Midget Mustang, Bushby	73 pk
Mignet Pou du Ceil	160 a
Mignet Aviation HM1000 Balerit	163 e
Miles Falcon	65 mc
Miles M65 Gemini	143 mc
Miles Magister	68 sp
Miles Messenger	69 e
Miles Monarch	64 s

Miles Student	151 mc
Minicab, Gardan	73 pk
Minimax, TEAM	49 d
Minor, Luton	9 e
Mistral, Avia Sud	140 d
Mitchell-Proctor Kittiwake	108 pk
Model 11 Chief, Aeronca	18 d
Model 47, Bell	172 pk
Model 120/140, Cessna	19 d
Model 150/152. Cessna	34 e
Model 170, Cessna	17 s
Model 177, Cessna	45 e
Model 182 Skylane, Cessna	34 e
Model 195, Cessna	18 s
Model 206, Cessna	35 ce
Model 210, Cessna	45 ce
Model 269, Hughes	171 pk
Model 310, Cessna	145 e
Model 337, Cessna	152 e
Model 500, Hughes	175 pk
Monarch, Miles	64 s
Monnett Moni	60 s
Monnett Sonerai	47 d
Monoplane, Dessouter	6 sp
Monoplane, DW-1, Chilton	64 pk
Monoplane, JT-1, Taylor	78 e
Monospar, General Aircraft	142 sp
Monsun, Bo209, Bolkow	120 d
Mooney M20 Chaparall	93 d
Morava LET 200	144 s
Moth Minor, DH	67 s
Motor Tutor, Slingsby	19 d
Mousquetaire D140, Jodel	77 e
Mudry CAP 10	84 e
Mudry CAP 231	91 sp
Murphy Rebel	30 d
Murphy Renegade Spirit	139 e
Musketeer, Beech	102 e
Mustang, Lohele	58 e
MW 5, Whittaker	36 e
MW 6, Whittaker	38 e
MW 7, Whittaker	30 e
MW-8, Whittaker	160 e
Navajo, Piper	147 e
Neico Lancair	97 e
Nicollier HN700 Menestrel	90 e
Nieuport Scout	121 e
Nipper, Tipsy	51 e
Noble ARV2	52 e
Noble-Hardman Snowbird	37 e
NORD NC 858	15 d
NORD 3202	76 a
North American Harvard	54 e
North American Texan	54 e
Nymph BN-3, Britten-Norman	36 bn
Oldfield Baby Great Lakes	134 d
Optica, FLS Aerospace	154 e
Orion, Grinvalds	155 s
Osprey, Pereira	166 s
P2, Pilatus	55 s
Pacer, PA20, Piper	21 e
Partenavia P68 Victor	148 e
Pawnee Piper	79 sp
Pazmany PL-4A	86 e
Pelican, Ultravia	38 e
Percival Mew Gull	63 a
Percival Prentice	74 a
Percival Proctor	68 d
Percival Q6	143 sp
Pereira GP-4	98 gp
Pereira Osprey	166 s
Petrel, SMAN	168 d
Phillips Speedtwin	150 s
Piel Emeraude	76 e
Pietenpol Aircamper	7 e
Pilatus P2	55 s
Pilot Sprite, Practavia	111 e
Piper J3 Cub	10 d
Piper J4 Cub	11 a
Piper PA 12 Super Cruiser	16 e
Piper PA15 Vagabond	20 d
Piper PA18 Super Cub	20 e
Piper PA20 Pacer	21 e
Piper PA22 Tri Pacer	32 d
Piper PA23 Apache	144 pk
Piper PA24 Comanche	94 e
Piper PA28 Cherokee	103 e
Piper PA30 Twin Comanche	146 e
Piper PA31 Navajo	147 e
Piper PA 32 Cherokee Six	104 d
Piper PA34 Seneca	148 e
Piper PA38 Tomahawk	111 e
Piper P-46 Malibu	97 ftp
Piper Pawnee	79 sp
Pitts S1 Special	132 d
PL-4A, Pazmany	86 e
Playboy, Stitts	75 a
Plumb BGP-1	139 s
Plus C, Taylorcraft	12 d
Plus D Taylorcraft	11 e
Pou du Ceil, Mignet	160 a
Practavia Pilot Sprite	111 e
Prentice, Percival	74 a
Proctor, Percival	68 d
Provost, Hunting-Percival	74 a
Pulsar, Aero Designs	114 d
Pup, Beagle	107 d
Putzer Elster	33 a
PZL Wilga	25 d
Q6, Percival	143 sp
QAC Quickie	162 e
Quad City Challenger	157 e
Quickie Q2, QAC	162 e
Quicksilver, Eipper	154 e
R22, Robinson	170 d
R44, Robinson	169 s
R 90, Ruschmeyer	99 e
R 2160, Robin	112 d
RAF 2000	169 n
Rallye, SOCATA	101 d

Aircraft	Code
Rand Robinson KR-2	57 e
Ranger, Sherwood	140 tcd
RANS S10 Sakota	48 e
RANS S6 Coyote	40 e
RANS S12 Airaile	158 s
Rebel, Murphy	30 d
Recruit PT-22, Ryan	67 e
Redwing, Robinson	127 a
Regent, DR400, Robin	106 e
Renaissance Comp. Berkut	164 e
Renegade Spirit, Murphy	139 e
Republic Seabee	165 e
RF 4 and RF5, Fournier	56 e
RF 47, Fournier	117 s
Robin ATL	113 e
Robin DR400 Regent	106 e
Robin HR100	96 e
Robin HR200	110 d
Robin R2160	112 d
Robinson R22	170 d
Robinson R44	169 s
Robinson Redwing	127 a
Rockwell Commander 112	95 e
Rollason Condor	80 e
Rotorway Executive 162	174 pk
Ruschmeyer R90	99 e
Rutan Long Eze	162 d
Rutan Vari Eze	162 d
RV-4 VANS	90 e
RV-6, VANS	87 e
Ryan PT-22 Recruit	67 e
S1 Special, Pitts	132 d
S 205, SIAI-Marchetti	105 e
S903, SIPA	70 e
Sakota, S10, RANS	48 e
Scamp, Aerosport	137 e
Schleicher AS-K16	56 d
Schwiezer Teal	167 e
Scout, Nieuport	121 e
SE 5 replica	122 d
Seabee, Republic	165 e
Seawind 3000	167 sw
Seneca, Piper	148 e
Sequoia/Frati Falco	94 e
Shadow Streak, CFM	157 d
Shark, Enstrom	170 pk
Sherwood Ranger	140 tcd
Shield Xyla	85 d
SIAI Marchetti S205	105 e
Sidewinder, Smyth	108 ib
Sierra 200, Beech	102 e
Silvaire, Luscombe	10 d
SIPA S 903	70 e
Sirrocco, Jurca	62 e
Sky Arrow	159 d
Skybolt, Steen	136 e
Sky Scooter, Flaglor	26 bs
Skyhawk, 172, Cessna	33 ce
Skylane, 182, Cessna	34 d
Skymaster, Cessna	152 e
Skystar Vixen	42 s
Slingsby Motor Tutor	19 d
Slingsby T61 Venture	60 d
Slingsby T67 Firefly	116 e
Sluka, Letov	42 e
SMAN Petrel	168 d
Smith Acro Advanced	50 d
Smyth Sidewinder	108 ib
Snowbird, Noble-Hardman	37 e
SOCATA Rallye	101 d
SOCATA Tobago	113 e
Sonerai, Monnet	47 d
Sorrell SN-7 Hiperbipe	137 e
Southern Martlet	125 mc
Sparrow, Carlson	40 e
Sparrowhawk, Aero Dynamics	158 e
Spartan Arrow	124 a
Special, Cassutt	46 e
Speedtwin, Phillips	150 s
Spezio Tuholer	80 d
Spitfire, Isaacs	88 pk
Sportavia RF-4,RF-5	56 e
Sportsman, Volmer	166 s
Sprint, FLS Aerospace	114 e
Staggerwing, Beech	102 e
Staaken Flitzer	141 s
Staggerwing, Beech	129 e
Stampe SV-4	129 e
Starduster, Stolp	133 e
Starlet, Corby	86 s
Steen Skybolt	136 e
Stephens Akro	46 a
Stitts Playboy	75 a
Stoddard-Hamilton Glastar	43 e
Stoddart- Hamilton Glasair	99 pk
Stolp Starduster	133 e
Storey TSR 3 Wonderplane	83 dn
Student, Miles	151 mc
SU 26, Sukhoi	49 sp
Subaru, FA200, Fuji	105 d
Sukhoi SU26	49 sp
Sundowner, Beech	102 e
Super Cruiser, PA12, Piper	16 e
Super Ace, Chrislea	32 e
Super Cub, PA18, Piper	20 e
Super Koala, Fisher	29 ama
Super Ximango. Aeromot	59 s
SV-4 Stampe	129 e
Swallow, BA	61 pk
Swift, Comper	6 pk
Swift, Globe	55 sp
T18, Thorp	82 d
T40, Turner	79 dm
T211, Thorp	101 e
Tailwind, Wittman	23 sp
Taylor JT-1 Monoplane	78 e
Taylor Titch	83 tt
Taylorcraft Plus C	12 d
Taylorcraft Plus D	11 e
Teal, Schwiezer	167 e

Teal, Thurston	167 e	YAK 52, Yakolev	96 s
TEAM Minimax	49 d	YAK 55, Yakolev	48 ftp
Technam Echo	41 e	YAK18, Yakolev	92 e
Tempette, Jurca	77 d	YAK 18T, Yakolev	93 d
Terrier, A61, Beagle	24 e	Yakolev YAK 18	92 e
Texan, North American	54 e	Yakolev YAK 18T	93 d
Thorp T18	82 d	Yakolev YAK 52	96 s
Thorp T211	101 e	Yakolev YAK 55	48 d
Thruster, TNT	28 e	Yankee, Gulfstream American	104 e
Thurston Teal	167 e	Zenair CH701 STOL	39 e
Tiger, Gulfstream-American	109 e	Zlin Z242	107 e
Tiger Cub, MBA	138 d	Zlin Z526 Trener	58 e
Tiger Moth, De Haviland	127 d	Zodiac, CH601, Heintz/Zenair	115 d
Tiger Moth DH71	62 sp		
Tipsy B/Trainer	63 e		
Tipsy Nipper	51 d		
Titch, Taylor	83 tt		
TNT, Thruster	28 e		
Tobago, SOCATA	113 e		
Tomahawk, PA38, Piper	111 e		
Tomtit, Hawker	126 a		
Trener, Z526, Zlin	58 e		
Tri - R KIS	115 d		
Tri Pacer, PA22, Piper	32 d		
Tri-plane Dr1, Fokker	121 e		
Tuholer, Spezio	80 d		
Turbi, Druine	72 s		
Turbulent, Druine	71 d		
Turner T40	79 dm		
Tutor, Avro	126 sp		
Twin Comanche, Piper	146 e		
Twinstar, Kolb	156 d		
UH-12, Hiller	171 pk		
Ultravia Pelican	38 e		
Urban Lambada	53 u		
Vagabond,PA15, Piper	20 d		
VANS RV-4	90 e		
VANS RV-6	87 e		
Vari Eze, Rutan	162 e		
Venture, T61, Slingsby	60 d		
Victa Airtourer	102 pk		
Victor P68, Partenavia	148 e		
Vixen, Skystar	42 s		
Volmer Sportsman	166 s		
VP-1, Evans	84 e		
VP-2, Evans	87 s		
Wallis WA116 Agile	174 pk		
WAR FW190	57 e		
Wicko, Foster Wikner	9 sp		
Whitaker MW-8	160 e		
Whittaker MW 5	36 e		
Whittaker MW 6	38 e		
Whittaker MW 7	30 e		
Wilga, PZL	25 d		
Wittman Tailwind	23 sp		
Wonderplane TSR3, Storey	83 dn		
Woody Pusher, Aerosport	152 pk		
Wot, Currie	132 e		
X'Air	44 e		
Xyla, Shield	85 d		